H.Pe
9.95

D1533284

HOMEPLANNERS

ULTIMATE

HOME PLAN REFERENCE

DISCARD
Helen Hall Library
100 West Walker
League City, TX 77573-3899

COUNTRY, TRADITIONAL, SOUTHWESTERN, MEDITERRANEAN, AND **MORE**

OCT   2004

HOMEPLANNERS
ULTIMATE
HOME PLAN REFERENCE

Published by Home Planners, LLC
Wholly owned by Hanley-Wood, LLC

President, Jayne Fenton
Chief Financial Officer, Joe Carroll
Vice President, Publishing, Jennifer Pearce
Vice President, General Manager, Marc Wheeler
Executive Editor, Linda Bellamy
National Sales Manager, Book Division, Julie Marshall
Managing Editor, Jason D. Vaughan
Special Projects Editor, Kristin Schneidler
Editor, Nate Ewell
Associate Editor, Kathryn R. Sears
Lead Plans Associate, Morenci C. Clark
Plans Associates, Jill M. Hall, Elizabeth Landry, Nick Nieskes
Proofreaders/Copywriters, Douglas Jenness, Sarah Lyons
Technical Specialist, Jay C. Walsh
Lead Data Coordinator, Fran Altemose
Data Coordinators, Misty Boler, Melissa Siewert
Production Director, Sara Lisa
Production Manager, Brenda McClary

Big Designs, Inc.
President, Creative Director, Anthony D'Elia
Vice President, Business Manager, Megan D'Elia
Vice President, Design Director, Chris Bonavita
Editorial Director, John Roach
Assistant Editor, Tricia Starkey
Director of Design and Production, Stephen Reinfurt
Group Art Director, Kevin Limongelli
Photo Editor, Christine DiVuolo
Managing Art Director, Jessica Hagenbuch
Graphic Designer, Mary Ellen Mulshine
Graphic Designer, Lindsey O'Neill-Myers
Graphic Designer, Jacque Young
Assistant Photo Editor, Brian Wilson
Project Director, David Barbella
Assistant Production Manager, Rich Fuentes

Photo Credits
Front Cover and Title Page: HPT9600261 on page 198. Photo courtesy of Stephen Fuller, Inc.
Facing Page Top: HPT9600012 on page 16. Photo by David Papazian.
Facing Page Center: HPT9600001 on page 5. Photo by Russell Kingman.
Facing Page Bottom: HPT9600008 on page 12. Photo by Mark England.
Back Cover: HPT9600006 on page 10. Photo by Bob Greenspan.

Hanley Wood HomePlanners Corporate Office
3275 W. Ina Road, Suite 220
Tucson, Arizona 85741

Distribution Center
29333 Lorie Lane
Wixom, Michigan 48393

© 2004

10 9 8 7 6 5 4 3 2 1

All floor plans and elevations copyright by the individual designers and may not be reproduced by any means without permission. All text, designs, and illustrative material copyright ©2004 by Home Planners, LLC, wholly owned by Hanley-Wood, LLC. All rights reserved. No part of this publication may be reproduced in any form or by any means — electronic, mechanical, photomechanical, recorded, or otherwise — without the prior written permission of the publisher.

Printed in the United States of America

Library of Congress Catalog Control Number: 2003113855

ISBN #: 1-931131-23-6

HOMEPLANNERS
ULTIMATE
HOME PLAN REFERENCE

16

5

12

Table of Contents

©1991 DONALD A. GARDNER ARCHITECTS, INC. PHOTOGRAPHY COURTESY OF DONALD A. GARDNER ARCHITECTS, INC. THIS HOME, AS SHOWN IN THE PHOTOGRAPH, MAY DIFFER FROM THE ACTUAL BLUEPRINTS. FOR MORE DETAILED INFORMATION, PLEASE CHECK THE FLOOR PLANS CAREFULLY.

Living the Dream

Chances are you've purchased this home plan collection with a very specific dream in mind—to pick a design that's perfect for you and your family and ultimately build your own home. But with more than 500 plans, how do you even begin narrowing down your search to find the one? Because your tastes and needs are individual, what you envision as your dream home likely differs from what your friends, neighbors, or coworkers would envision as their dream homes. That's why we've put together this comprehensive collection of homes—to give you one of the largest selections of stock home plans on the market today in one location. The greater the selection from which to choose, the greater the chance you'll find the home that's just right for you!

As you browse the plans throughout this book, you'll notice that the homes are conveniently divided up by square feet. An assortment of styles—such as country, traditional, and European—is included in each square footage range, making for a broad selection that'll appeal to homeowners from coast to coast. If you discover that you'd like to be able to search for homes using criteria in addition to square feet, log on to **www.eplans.com** (which includes 10,000+ designs) and search by home style or number of bedrooms, baths, or floors. This will help you narrow down your search.

When you're ready to order, turn to page 457 for all the information you'll need to set your plans in motion. Or buy your blueprints directly online at **www.eplans.com**. Either way, you can place your order 24 hours a day, seven days a week. Purchasing plans is your first step in making your dreams come true.

PHOTO BY RUSSELL KINGMAN

THIS HOME, AS SHOWN IN THE PHOTOGRAPH, MAY DIFFER FROM THE ACTUAL BLUEPRINTS. FOR MORE DETAILED INFORMATION, PLEASE CHECK THE FLOOR PLANS CAREFULLY.

plan
HPT9600001

STYLE: MISSION
SQUARE FOOTAGE: 3,424
BONUS SPACE: 507 SQ. FT.
BEDROOMS: 5
BATHROOMS: 4
WIDTH: 82' - 4"
DEPTH: 83' - 8"
FOUNDATION: SLAB

SEARCH ONLINE @ EPLANS.COM

This lovely five-bedroom home exudes the beauty and warmth of a Mediterranean villa. The foyer views explode in all directions with the dominant use of octagonal shapes throughout. Double doors lead to the master wing, which abounds with niches. The sitting area of the master bedroom has a commanding view of the rear gardens. A bedroom just off the master suite is perfect for a guest room or office. The formal living and dining rooms share expansive glass walls and marble or tile pathways. The mitered glass wall of the breakfast nook can be viewed from the huge island kitchen. Two secondary bedrooms share the convenience of a Pullman-style bath. An additional rear bedroom completes this design.

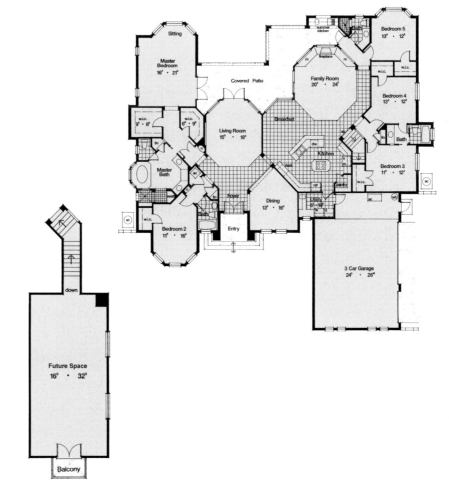

© HOME DESIGN SERVICES, INC.

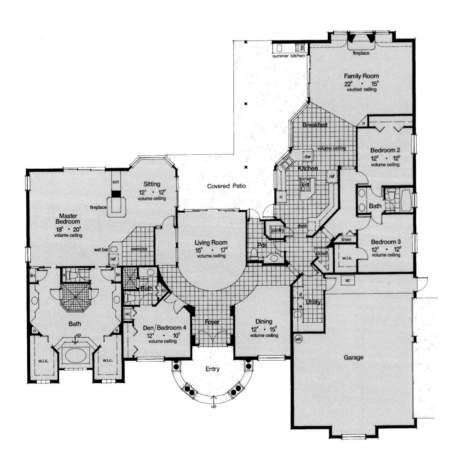

plan
HPT9600002

STYLE: MEDITERRANEAN
SQUARE FOOTAGE: 3,556
BEDROOMS: 4
BATHROOMS: 3½
WIDTH: 85' - 0"
DEPTH: 85' - 0"
FOUNDATION: SLAB

SEARCH ONLINE @ EPLANS.COM

A beautiful curved portico provides a majestic entrance to this one-story home. To the left of the foyer is a den/bedroom with a private bath, ideal for use as a guest suite. The exquisite master suite features a see-through fireplace and an exercise area with a wet bar. The family wing is geared for casual living with a powder room/patio bath, a huge island kitchen with a walk-in pantry, a glass-walled breakfast nook, and a grand family room with a fireplace and media wall. Two family bedrooms share a private bath.

ORDER BLUEPRINTS 24 HOURS, 7 DAYS A WEEK, AT 1-800-521-6797

© HOME DESIGN SERVICES, INC.

plan#
HPT9600003

STYLE: MEDITERRANEAN
FIRST FLOOR: 3,236 SQ. FT.
SECOND FLOOR: 494 SQ. FT.
TOTAL: 3,730 SQ. FT.
BEDROOMS: 4
BATHROOMS: 3½
WIDTH: 80' - 0"
DEPTH: 89' - 10"
FOUNDATION: SLAB

SEARCH ONLINE @ EPLANS.COM

If you want to build a home light years ahead of most other designs, nontraditional, yet addresses every need for your family, this showcase home is for you. From the moment you walk into this home, you are confronted with wonderful interior architecture that reflects modern, yet refined taste. The exterior says contemporary; the interior creates special excitement. Note the special rounded corners found throughout the home and the many amenities. The master suite is especially appealing with a fireplace and grand bath. Upstairs are a library/sitting room and a very private den or guest bedroom.

SECOND FLOOR

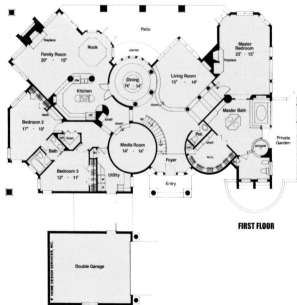

FIRST FLOOR

Fieldstone, stucco, and brick give this cottage harmony in variety. The foyer opens to a private study with bay windows and fireplace. The formal dining room is just down the hall and opens through column accents to the living room. The kitchen serves both the formal and casual spaces. The family room is as cozy with a fireplace and rear-window display. The master suite is really a work of luxury and features His and Hers walk-in closet entrances, vanities, and compartmented toilet. The second level houses three additional bedrooms, two full baths, and bonus space.

plan#
HPT9600004

STYLE: EUROPEAN COTTAGE
FIRST FLOOR: 2,144 SQ. FT.
SECOND FLOOR: 920 SQ. FT.
TOTAL: 3,064 SQ. FT.
BONUS SPACE: 212 SQ. FT.
BEDROOMS: 4
BATHROOMS: 3½
WIDTH: 59' - 0"
DEPTH: 79' - 3"
FOUNDATION: CRAWLSPACE, SLAB

SEARCH ONLINE @ EPLANS.COM

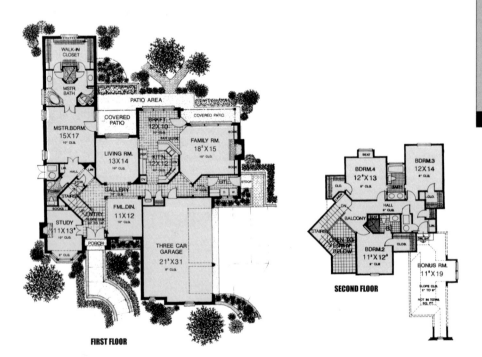

FIRST FLOOR

SECOND FLOOR

plan#
HPT9600005

STYLE: EUROPEAN COTTAGE
SQUARE FOOTAGE: 2,778
BEDROOMS: 4
BATHROOMS: 3½
WIDTH: 74' - 0"
DEPTH: 74' - 1"
FOUNDATION: SLAB

SEARCH ONLINE @ EPLANS.COM

Welcome to a modern home with an outdoor rustic flair! A flagstone facade, a sloping dormer window, an oval window, fanlights above the front door, and sidelights flanking it lend this home distinctive charm and character. The sprawling floor plan begins with an entry with wood-plank flooring, which leads through the gallery into a spacious kitchen. With plenty of counter space, the kitchen can easily serve the dining room, which also has wood flooring. The master bedroom resides on the right side of the plan and is graced with a vaulted ceiling, luxurious full bath, and a large walk-in closet. Bedrooms 2, 3, and 4 are on the left side of the plan; each contains its own walk-in closet.

PHOTO BY BOB GREENSPAN
THIS HOME, AS SHOWN IN THE PHOTOGRAPH, MAY DIFFER FROM THE ACTUAL BLUEPRINTS. FOR MORE DETAILED INFORMATION, PLEASE CHECK THE FLOOR PLANS CAREFULLY.

Multipane glass windows, French doors, and an arched pediment with columns create a spectacular exterior with this blue-ribbon European design. A two-story foyer opens to formal areas and, through French doors, to a secluded den with built-in cabinetry and a coat closet. The gourmet kitchen enjoys a morning nook. Second-floor sleeping quarters include a master bedroom with a tile-rimmed spa tub, a double-basin vanity and a walk-in closet. This plan offers the option of replacing the family room's vaulted ceiling with a fifth bedroom above.

plan #

HPT9600006

STYLE: TRADITIONAL
FIRST FLOOR: 1,470 SQ. FT.
SECOND FLOOR: 1,269 SQ. FT.
TOTAL: 2,739 SQ. FT.
BEDROOMS: 4
BATHROOMS: 2½
WIDTH: 70' - 0"
DEPTH: 47' - 0"
FOUNDATION: CRAWLSPACE

SEARCH ONLINE @ EPLANS.COM

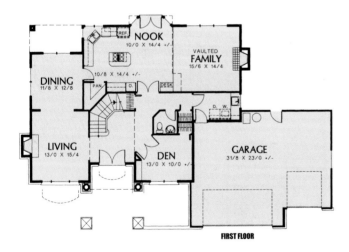

FIRST FLOOR

SECOND FLOOR

ORDER BLUEPRINTS 24 HOURS, 7 DAYS A WEEK, AT 1-800-521-6797

plan
HPT9600007

STYLE: TRANSITIONAL
FIRST FLOOR: 1,923 SQ. FT.
SECOND FLOOR: 1,710 SQ. FT.
TOTAL: 3,633 SQ. FT.
BEDROOMS: 4
BATHROOMS: 2½
WIDTH: 66' - 0"
DEPTH: 60' - 0"
FOUNDATION: CRAWLSPACE

SEARCH ONLINE @ EPLANS.COM

This uniquely designed home is dazzled in Mediterranean influences and eye-catching luxury. A grand arching entrance welcomes you inside to a spacious foyer that introduces a curved staircase and flanking living and dining rooms on either side. Casual areas of the home are clustered to the rear left of the plan and include a kitchen, nook, and family room warmed by a fireplace. The professional study is a quiet retreat. The three-car garage offers spacious storage. Upstairs, the master bedroom enjoys a private bath and roomy walk-in closet. Three additional bedrooms share a hall bath and open playroom.

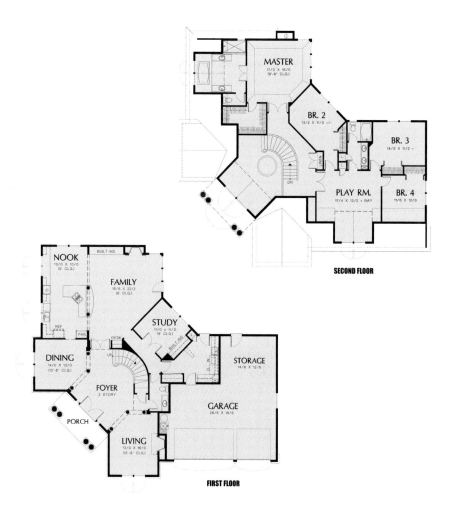

SECOND FLOOR

FIRST FLOOR

PHOTO BY MARK ENGLUND

THIS HOME, AS SHOWN IN THE PHOTOGRAPH, MAY DIFFER FROM THE ACTUAL BLUEPRINTS.

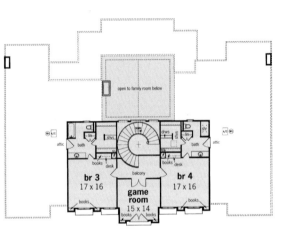

SECOND FLOOR

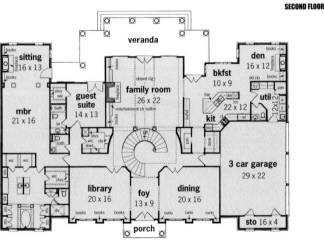

FIRST FLOOR

plan
HPT9600008

STYLE: LUXURY
FIRST FLOOR: 4,208 SQ. FT.
SECOND FLOOR: 1,352 SQ. FT.
TOTAL: 5,560 SQ. FT.
BEDROOMS: 4
BATHROOMS: 4½ + ½
WIDTH: 94' - 0"
DEPTH: 68' - 0"
FOUNDATION: CRAWLSPACE, SLAB

SEARCH ONLINE @ EPLANS.COM

Two-story pilasters create a sense of the Old South on the facade of this modern home updating of the classic Adam style. The foyer opens through an archway, announcing the breathtaking circular staircase. The formal dining room is situated on the right, and the private library is found to the left. The grand family room is crowned with a sloped ceiling. The angled, galley kitchen adjoins the breakfast nook; the butler's pantry facilitates service to the dining room. The master suite finds privacy on the left with an elegant sitting area defined with pillars. Two bedroom suites, each with walk-in closets, share the second floor with the game room.

ORDER BLUEPRINTS 24 HOURS, 7 DAYS A WEEK, AT 1-800-521-6797

plan
HPT9600009

STYLE: CHARLESTON
FIRST FLOOR: 1,901 SQ. FT.
SECOND FLOOR: 1,874 SQ. FT.
TOTAL: 3,775 SQ. FT.
BEDROOMS: 4
BATHROOMS: 3½
WIDTH: 50' - 0"
DEPTH: 70' - 0"
FOUNDATION: PIER

SEARCH ONLINE @ EPLANS.COM

This elegant Charleston townhouse is enhanced by Southern grace and three levels of charming livability. Covered porches offer outdoor living space at every level. The first floor offers a living room warmed by a fireplace, an island kitchen serving a bayed nook, and a formal dining room. A first-floor guest bedroom is located at the front of the plan, along with a laundry and powder room. The second level offers a sumptuous master suite boasting a private balcony, a master bath, and an enormous walk-in closet. Two other bedrooms sharing a Jack-and-Jill bath are also on this level. The basement level includes a three-car garage and game room warmed by a fireplace.

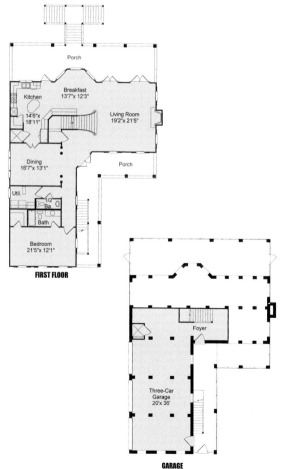

FIRST FLOOR

Porch
Kitchen 14'6"x 18'11"
Breakfast 13'7"x 12'3"
Living Room 19'2"x 21'5"
Dining 16'7"x 13'1"
Porch
Util.
1/2 Ba
Bath
Bedroom 21'5"x 12'1"

GARAGE

Foyer
Three-Car Garage 20'x 36'

SECOND FLOOR

Deck 21'x 12'
Master Bath
WIC
Master Bedroom 19'1"x 21'5"
12'3"x 19'5"
Porch
Bedroom 16'7"x 12'1"
WIC
Bath
WIC
Bedroom 18'1"x 12'1"

SECOND FLOOR

plan

HPT9600010

STYLE: TRADITIONAL
FIRST FLOOR: 1,803 SQ. FT.
SECOND FLOOR: 548 SQ. FT.
TOTAL: 2,351 SQ. FT.
BONUS SPACE: 277 SQ. FT.
BEDROOMS: 4
BATHROOMS: 3
WIDTH: 55' - 0"
DEPTH: 48' - 0"
FOUNDATION: CRAWLSPACE, SLAB, BASEMENT

SEARCH ONLINE @ EPLANS.COM

This Early American home will delight with brick and siding, a flower-box window, and lots of natural light. The two-story foyer leads to the vaulted great room, perfect for entertaining with a fireplace and serving bar from the island kitchen. The bayed breakfast nook is a lovely morning treat. A first-floor bedroom would make a fine guest room or study. The entire left side of the home is devoted to the master suite, stunning with a vaulted sitting room and pampering bath, brightened by a radius window. Two upstairs bedrooms share bonus space and a full bath.

FIRST FLOOR

ORDER BLUEPRINTS 24 HOURS, 7 DAYS A WEEK, AT 1-800-521-6797

plan #

HPT9600011

STYLE: TRADITIONAL

FIRST FLOOR: 2,292 SQ. FT.

SECOND FLOOR: 1,028 SQ. FT.

TOTAL: 3,320 SQ. FT.

BEDROOMS: 5

BATHROOMS: 3½ + ½

WIDTH: 68' - 0"

DEPTH: 56' - 6"

FOUNDATION: BASEMENT

SEARCH ONLINE @ EPLANS.COM

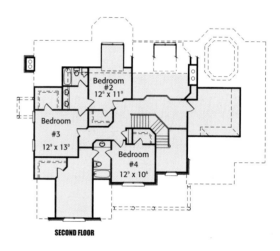

SECOND FLOOR

This majestic brick home fits new traditional neighborhoods perfectly, with an inviting front porch and a side-loading garage. Formal and flex rooms accommodate modern lifestyles and allow space for surfing online or even a home office. The foyer opens to the dining room and a study—or make it a guest bedroom. The gourmet kitchen boasts an island counter and opens to an old-fashioned keeping room, which features a fireplace. The breakfast room offers a bay window to let the sunlight in and opens to an expansive deck. The master suite sports a tray ceiling and a bath that provides more than just a touch of luxury. Upstairs, two family bedrooms share a full bath; a guest bedroom features a private bath.

FIRST FLOOR

DAVID PAPAZIAN

THIS HOME, AS SHOWN IN THE PHOTOGRAPH, MAY DIFFER FROM THE ACTUAL BLUEPRINTS. FOR MORE DETAILED INFORMATION, PLEASE CHECK THE FLOOR PLANS CAREFULLY.

plan
HPT9600012

STYLE: CRAFTSMAN

FIRST FLOOR: 2,597 SQ. FT.

SECOND FLOOR: 2,171 SQ. FT.

TOTAL: 4,768 SQ. FT.

BEDROOMS: 4

BATHROOMS: 4½

WIDTH: 76' - 6"

DEPTH: 68' - 6"

FOUNDATION: CRAWLSPACE

SEARCH ONLINE @ EPLANS.COM

This splendid Craftsman home will look good in any neighborhood. Inside, the foyer offers a beautiful wooden bench to the right, flanked by built-in curio cabinets. On the left, double French doors lead to a cozy study. The formal dining room is complete with beamed ceilings, a built-in hutch, and cabinets. The large L-shaped kitchen includes a work island/snack bar, plenty of storage, and an adjacent sunny nook. The two-story great room surely lives up to its name, with a massive stone fireplace and a two-story wall of windows. Upstairs, two family bedrooms share a full bath, and the guest suite features its own bath. The lavish master bedroom suite pampers the homeowner with two walk-in closets, a fireplace, and a private deck.

SECOND FLOOR

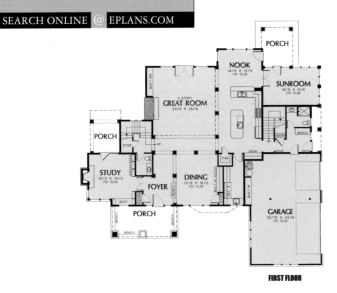

FIRST FLOOR

ORDER BLUEPRINTS 24 HOURS, 7 DAYS A WEEK, AT 1-800-521-6797

© 2002 Donald A. Gardner, Inc.

plan#
HPT9600013

STYLE: STICK VICTORIAN

FIRST FLOOR: 1,687 SQ. FT.

SECOND FLOOR: 807 SQ. FT.

TOTAL: 2,494 SQ. FT.

BEDROOMS: 4

BATHROOMS: 2½

WIDTH: 52' - 8"

DEPTH: 67' - 0"

SEARCH ONLINE @ EPLANS.COM

This glorious farmhouse was designed with the best of family living in mind. The beautiful wrap-around porch is accented with stone and columns, and varying window detail adds a custom look to the facade. Inside, a soaring two-story foyer opens to a gallery hall that opens to the great room through columns. A fireplace, built-ins, and rear-porch access make this room perfect for entertaining or just hanging out. The swanky master suite takes up the entire left wing of the plan with its enormous private bath and double closets. To the right of the plan, the spacious kitchen is book-ended by a formal dining room at the front and a cozy breakfast nook to the rear. A utility room opens to the garage. Upstairs, three bedrooms share a bath as well as attic storage. A balcony looks down into the foyer and great room.

SECOND FLOOR

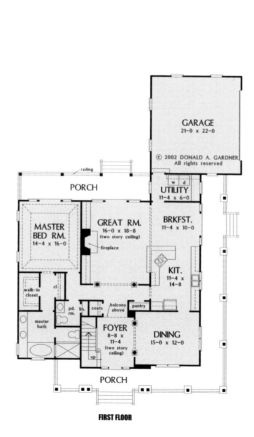

FIRST FLOOR

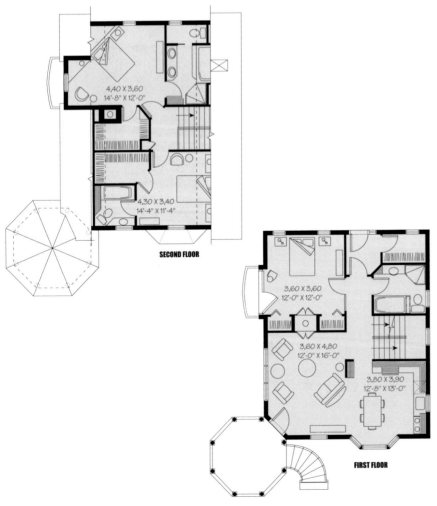

SECOND FLOOR

4,40 X 3,60
14'-8" X 12'-0"

4,30 X 3,40
14'-4" X 11'-4"

FIRST FLOOR

3,60 x 3,60
12'-0" X 12'-0"

3,60 X 4,80
12'-0" X 16'-0"

3,80 X 3,90
12'-8" X 13'-0"

plan #
HPT9600014

STYLE: VICTORIAN
FIRST FLOOR: 840 SQ. FT.
SECOND FLOOR: 757 SQ. FT.
TOTAL: 1,597 SQ. FT.
BEDROOMS: 3
BATHROOMS: 3
WIDTH: 26' - 0"
DEPTH: 32' - 0"
FOUNDATION: BASEMENT

SEARCH ONLINE @ EPLANS.COM

The amazing turret/gazebo porch on this classy home has an authentic Victorian flavor. Exceptional details accent this classic view. The bedroom on the first level offers a protruding balcony, which adds appeal both inside and outside. The entrance leads to the living room, located just left of the dining area and L-shaped kitchen. The master suite features a walk-in closet and a private bath with dual sinks. Two more family bedrooms are located on the second level.

plan
HPT9600015

STYLE: FOLK VICTORIAN
FIRST FLOOR: 960 SQ. FT.
SECOND FLOOR: 841 SQ. FT.
TOTAL: 1,801 SQ. FT.
BEDROOMS: 3
BATHROOMS: 1½
WIDTH: 36' - 0"
DEPTH: 30' - 0"
FOUNDATION: BASEMENT

SEARCH ONLINE @ EPLANS.COM

This romantic cottage design is ideal for any countryside setting. Lively Victorian details enhance the exterior. A wrapping porch with a gazebo-style sitting area encourages refreshing outdoor relaxation; interior spaces are open to each other. The kitchen with a snack bar is open to both the dining area and the living room. A powder bath with laundry facilities completes the first floor. The second floor offers space for three family bedrooms with walk-in closets and a pampering whirlpool bath.

SECOND FLOOR

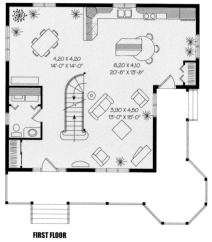

FIRST FLOOR

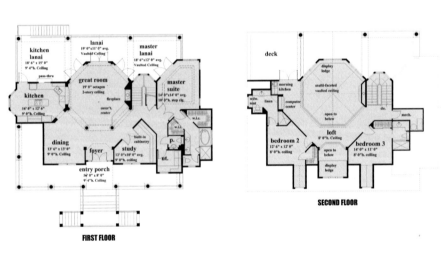

FIRST FLOOR

SECOND FLOOR

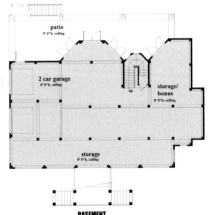

BASEMENT

plan#
HPT9600016

STYLE: TIDEWATER

FIRST FLOOR: 1,855 SQ. FT.

SECOND FLOOR: 901 SQ. FT.

TOTAL: 2,756 SQ. FT.

BEDROOMS: 3

BATHROOMS: 3½

WIDTH: 66' - 0"

DEPTH: 50' - 0"

FOUNDATION: BASEMENT

SEARCH ONLINE @ EPLANS.COM

This Southern tidewater cottage is the perfect vacation hideaway. An octagonal great room with a multifaceted vaulted ceiling illuminates the interior. The island kitchen is brightened by a bumped-out window and a pass-through to the lanai. Two walk-in closets and a whirlpool bath await to indulge the homeowner in the master suite. A set of double doors opens to the vaulted master lanai for quiet comfort. The U-shaped staircase leads to a loft, which overlooks the great room and the foyer. Two additional family bedrooms offer private baths. A computer center and a morning kitchen complete the upper level.

plan#
HPT9600017

STYLE: LAKEFRONT

FIRST FLOOR: 1,212 SQ. FT.

SECOND FLOOR: 620 SQ. FT.

TOTAL: 1,832 SQ. FT.

BEDROOMS: 3

BATHROOMS: 2

WIDTH: 38' - 0"

DEPTH: 40' - 0"

FOUNDATION: BASEMENT

SEARCH ONLINE @ EPLANS.COM

This comfortable vacation design provides two levels of relaxing family space. The main level offers a spacious wrapping front porch and an abundance of windows, filling interior spaces with the summer sunshine. A two-sided fireplace warms the living room/dining room combination and a master bedroom that features a roomy walk-in closet. Nearby, the hall bath offers a relaxing whirlpool tub. The kitchen is open and features an island snack bar and pantry storage. A cozy sunroom accesses the wrapping deck. Upstairs, two additional bedrooms feature ample closet space and share a second-floor bath.

SECOND FLOOR

FIRST FLOOR

©1991 DONALD A. GARDNER ARCHITECTS, INC. PHOTOGRAPHY COURTESY OF DONALD A. GARDNER ARCHITECTS, INC. THIS HOME, AS SHOWN IN THE PHOTOGRAPH, MAY DIFFER FROM THE ACTUAL BLUEPRINTS. FOR MORE DETAILED INFORMATION, PLEASE CHECK THE FLOOR PLANS CAREFULLY.

The welcoming charm of this country farmhouse is expressed by its many windows and its covered wraparound porch. A two-story foyer is enhanced by a Palladian window in a clerestory dormer above to let in natural lighting. The first-floor master suite allows privacy and accessibility. The master bath includes a whirlpool tub, separate shower, double-bowl vanity, and walk-in closet. The first floor features nine-foot ceilings throughout with the exception of the kitchen area, which sports an eight-foot ceiling. The second floor contains two additional bedrooms, a full bath, and plenty of storage space. The bonus room provides room to grow.

plan #
HPT9600018

STYLE: SOUTHERN COLONIAL
FIRST FLOOR: 1,356 SQ. FT.
SECOND FLOOR: 542 SQ. FT.
TOTAL: 1,898 SQ. FT.
BONUS SPACE: 393 SQ. FT.
BEDROOMS: 3
BATHROOMS: 2½
WIDTH: 59' - 0"
DEPTH: 64' - 0"

SEARCH ONLINE @ EPLANS.COM

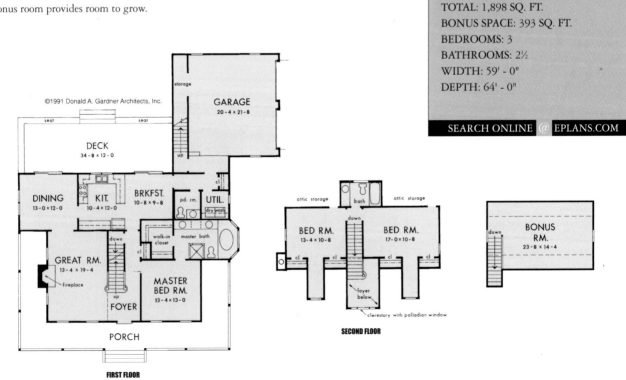

©1991 Donald A. Gardner Architects, Inc.

FIRST FLOOR

SECOND FLOOR

THIS HOME, AS SHOWN IN THE PHOTOGRAPH, MAY DIFFER FROM THE ACTUAL BLUEPRINTS. FOR MORE DETAILED INFORMATION, PLEASE CHECK THE FLOOR PLANS CAREFULLY.

CHRIS A. LITTLE FROM ATLANTA, CHATHAM HOME PLANNING, INC.

plan #

HPT9600019

STYLE: SOUTHERN COLONIAL
FIRST FLOOR: 2,390 SQ. FT.
SECOND FLOOR: 1,200 SQ. FT.
TOTAL: 3,590 SQ. FT.
BEDROOMS: 4
BATHROOMS: 3
WIDTH: 61' - 0"
DEPTH: 64' - 4"
FOUNDATION: WORKING

SEARCH ONLINE @ EPLANS.COM

This luxurious waterfront design sings of Southern island influences. A front covered porch opens to a foyer, flanked by a study and dining room. The living room, warmed by a fireplace and safe from off-season ocean breezes, overlooks the rear covered porch. The island kitchen extends into a breakfast room. Beyond the covered porch, the wood deck is also accessed privately from the master suite. This suite includes a private whirlpool bath and huge walk-in closet. A guest suite is located on the first floor, and two additional bedrooms and a multi-media room are located on the second level.

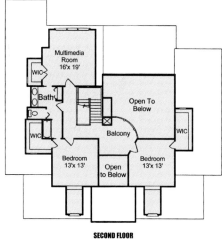

SECOND FLOOR

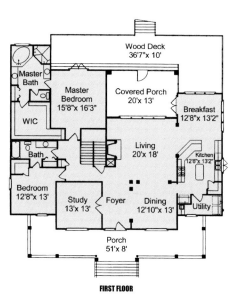

FIRST FLOOR

Dormers and columns decorate the exterior of this three-bedroom country home. Inside, the foyer has immediate access to one family bedroom and the formal dining area. Ahead is the great room with a warming fireplace and ribbon of windows for natural lighting. The master suite is set to the back of the plan and has a lavish bath with a garden tub, separate shower, and two vanities.

plan #

HPT9600020

STYLE: SOUTHERN COLONIAL
SQUARE FOOTAGE: 1,688
BEDROOMS: 3
BATHROOMS: 2
WIDTH: 70' - 1"
DEPTH: 48' - 0"
FOUNDATION: CRAWLSPACE, SLAB, BASEMENT

SEARCH ONLINE @ EPLANS.COM

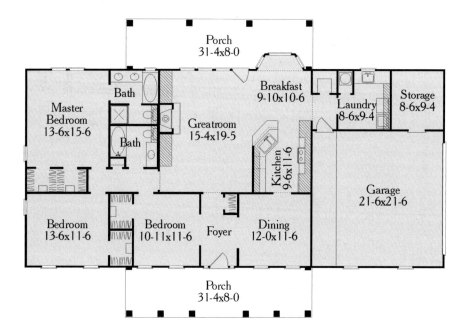

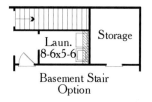

plan#
HPT9600021

STYLE: COUNTRY COTTAGE

FIRST FLOOR: 576 SQ. FT.

SECOND FLOOR: 489 SQ. FT.

TOTAL: 1,065 SQ. FT.

BEDROOMS: 2

BATHROOMS: 1½

WIDTH: 24' - 0"

DEPTH: 31' - 0"

FOUNDATION: CRAWLSPACE

SEARCH ONLINE @ EPLANS.COM

The steep rooflines on this home offer a sophisti-cated look that draws attention. Three dormers flood the home with light. The covered porch adds detailing to the posts. The entry leads to the two-story living room complete with a fireplace. The dining room is quite spacious and contains convenient access to the kitchen where a pantry room and plenty of counter space make cooking a treat in this home. The stairs to the second floor wrap around the fireplace and take the home-owners to the master bedroom and loft area.

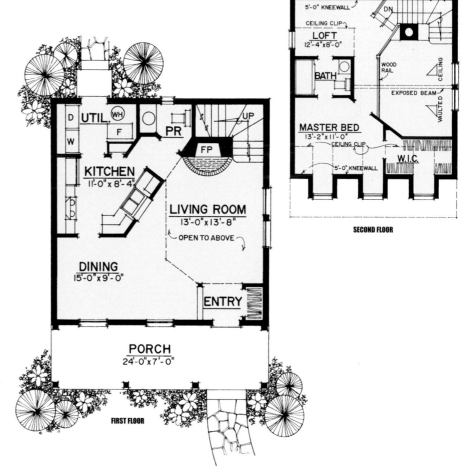

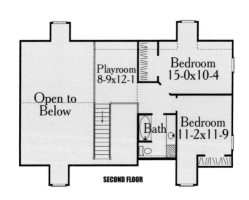

SECOND FLOOR

ptan#
HPT9600022

STYLE: COLONIAL REVIVAL
FIRST FLOOR: 1,501 SQ. FT.
SECOND FLOOR: 631 SQ. FT.
TOTAL: 2,132 SQ. FT.
BEDROOMS: 3
BATHROOMS: 2½
WIDTH: 76' - 0"
DEPTH: 48' - 4"
FOUNDATION: SLAB, BASEMENT, CRAWLSPACE

SEARCH ONLINE @ EPLANS.COM

This home reveals its rustic charm with a metal roof, dormers, and exposed-column rafters. The full-length porch is an invitation to comfortable living inside. The great room shares a fireplace with the spacious dining room that has rear-porch access. The kitchen is this home's focus, with plenty of counter and cabinet space, a window sink, and an open layout. The first-floor master suite features two walk-in closets and a grand bath. Two family bedrooms and a playroom reside on the second floor.

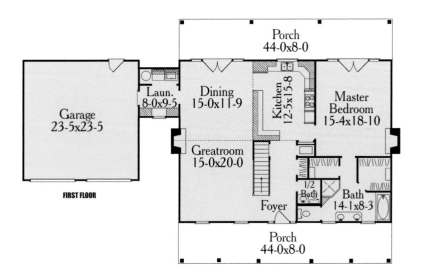

FIRST FLOOR

plan
HPT9600023

STYLE: GREEK REVIVAL
FIRST FLOOR: 2,891 SQ. FT.
SECOND FLOOR: 1,336 SQ. FT.
TOTAL: 4,227 SQ. FT.
BONUS SPACE: 380 SQ. FT.
BEDROOMS: 4
BATHROOMS: 3½ + ½
WIDTH: 90' - 8"
DEPTH: 56' - 4"
FOUNDATION: CRAWLSPACE,
BASEMENT

SEARCH ONLINE @ EPLANS.COM

This Southern coastal cottage radiates charm and elegance. Step inside from the covered porch and discover a floor plan with practicality and architectural interest. The foyer has a raised ceiling and is partially open to above. The library and great room offer fireplaces and built-in shelves; the great room also provides rear porch access. The kitchen, featuring an island with a separate sink, is adjacent to the breakfast room and a study with a built-in desk. On the far right, the master bedroom will amaze, with a sumptuous bath and enormous walk-in closet. Three upstairs bedrooms share a loft and recreation room. Convenient storage opportunities make organization easy.

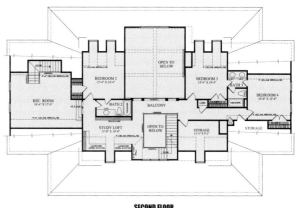

SECOND FLOOR

FIRST FLOOR

PHOTO COURTESY OF WILLIAM E. POOLE DESINGS INC., COURTESY OF THE ISLANDS OF BEAUFORT, BEAUFORT, SC THIS HOME, AS SHOWN IN THE PHOTOGRAPH, MAY DIFFER FROM THE ACTUAL BLUEPRINTS. FOR MORE DETAILED INFORMATION, PLEASE CHECK THE FLOOR PLANS CAREFULLY

OPTIONAL LAYOUT

plan #
HPT9600024

STYLE: COLONIAL REVIVAL
SQUARE FOOTAGE: 2,151
BONUS SPACE: 814 SQ. FT.
BEDROOMS: 3
BATHROOMS: 2
WIDTH: 61' - 0"
DEPTH: 55' - 8"
FOUNDATION: CRAWLSPACE,
BASEMENT

SEARCH ONLINE @ EPLANS.COM

Country flavor is well established on this fine three-bed-room home. The covered front porch welcomes friends and family alike to the foyer, where the formal dining room opens off to the left. The vaulted ceiling in the great room enhances the warmth of the fireplace and wall of windows. An efficient kitchen works well with the bayed breakfast area. The secluded master suite offers a walk-in closet and a lavish bath; on the other side of the home, two family bedrooms share a full bath. Upstairs, an optional fourth bedroom is available for guests or in-laws and provides access to a large recreation room.

PHOTO COURTESY OF: WILLIAM E. POOLE DESIGNS, INC. - ISLANDS OF BEAUFORT, SC. THIS HOME, AS SHOWN IN THE PHOTOGRAPH, MAY DIFFER FROM THE ACTUAL BLUEPRINTS. FOR MORE DETAILED INFORMATION, PLEASE CHECK THE FLOOR PLANS CAREFULLY.

plan
HPT9600025

STYLE: COLONIAL REVIVAL
FIRST FLOOR: 1,704 SQ. FT.
SECOND FLOOR: 734 SQ. FT.
TOTAL: 2,438 SQ. FT.
BONUS SPACE: 479 SQ. FT.
BEDROOMS: 3
BATHROOMS: 3½
WIDTH: 50' - 0"
DEPTH: 82' - 6"
FOUNDATION: CRAWLSPACE

SEARCH ONLINE @ EPLANS.COM

Elegant country—that's one way to describe this attractive three-bedroom home. Inside, comfort is clearly the theme, with the formal dining room flowing into the U-shaped kitchen and casual dining taking place in the sunny breakfast area. The spacious, vaulted great room offers a fireplace and built-ins. The first-floor master suite is complete with a walk-in closet, a whirlpool tub and a separate shower. Upstairs, the sleeping quarters include two family bedrooms with private baths and walk-in closets.

FIRST FLOOR

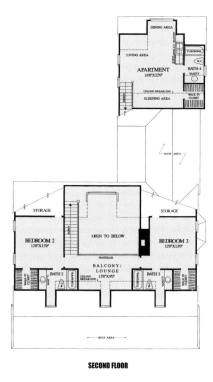

SECOND FLOOR

SECOND FLOOR

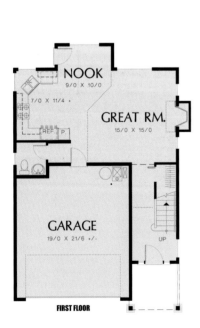

FIRST FLOOR

plan⊕#
HPT9600026

STYLE: CRAFTSMAN
FIRST FLOOR: 636 SQ. FT.
SECOND FLOOR: 830 SQ. FT.
TOTAL: 1,466 SQ. FT.
BEDROOMS: 3
BATHROOMS: 2½
WIDTH: 28' - 0"
DEPTH: 43' - 6"
FOUNDATION: CRAWLSPACE

SEARCH ONLINE @ EPLANS.COM

Traditional and Craftsman elements shape the exterior of this lovely family home. The two-story foyer leads down the hall to a great room with a warming fireplace. The U-shaped kitchen includes a window sink and is open to the breakfast nook. A powder room is located near the garage. Upstairs, the master suite provides a private bath and walk-in closet. The two family bedrooms share a full hall bath, across from the second-floor laundry room. Linen closets are available in the hall and inside the full hall bath.

plan#
HPT9600027

STYLE: TRADITIONAL
SQUARE FOOTAGE: 1,759
BEDROOMS: 3
BATHROOMS: 2
WIDTH: 82' - 10"
DEPTH: 47' - 5"
FOUNDATION: BASEMENT

SEARCH ONLINE @ EPLANS.COM

With its brick facade and gables, this home brings great curb appeal to any neighborhood. This one-story home features a great room with a cozy fireplace, a laundry room tucked away from the spacious kitchen, and a breakfast area accessing the screened porch. Completing this design are two family bedrooms and an elegant master bedroom suite featuring an ample walk-in closet. A dressing area in the master bathroom is shared by a dual vanity and a step-up tub.

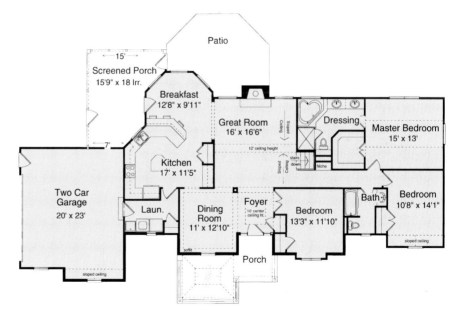

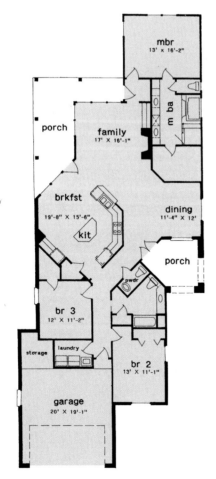

plan #
HPT9600028

STYLE: EUROPEAN COTTAGE
SQUARE FOOTAGE: 2,007
BEDROOMS: 3
BATHROOMS: 2½
WIDTH: 40' - 0"
DEPTH: 94' - 10"
FOUNDATION: SLAB

SEARCH ONLINE @ EPLANS.COM

An ornate stucco facade with brick highlights refines this charming French cottage. The double-door entrance sits to the side—perfect for a courtyard welcome. The dining and family rooms utilize an open layout for easy traffic flow. The circular kitchen space features an island and complementary breakfast bay. Bedrooms 2 and 3 share a hall bath. The master suite, apart from the main living areas, enjoys privacy and a full bath with a spacious walk-in closet. The rear porch encourages outdoor relaxation.

ORDER BLUEPRINTS 24 HOURS, 7 DAYS A WEEK, AT 1-800-521-6797

plan
HPT9600029

STYLE: COUNTRY COTTAGE

FIRST FLOOR: 672 SQ. FT.

SECOND FLOOR: 401 SQ. FT.

TOTAL: 1,073 SQ. FT.

BEDROOMS: 3

BATHROOMS: 1½

WIDTH: 24' - 0"

DEPTH: 36' - 0"

FOUNDATION: CRAWLSPACE, BASEMENT

SEARCH ONLINE @ EPLANS.COM

This chalet plan is enhanced by a steep gable roof, scalloped fascia boards, and fieldstone chimney detail. The front-facing deck and covered balcony add to outdoor living spaces. The fireplace is the main focus in the living room. The bedroom on the first floor enjoys access to a full hall bath. A storage/mudroom at the back of the plan is perfect for keeping skis and boots. Two additional bedrooms and a half-bath occupy the second floor. The master bedroom provides a walk-in closet. Three storage areas are also found on the second floor.

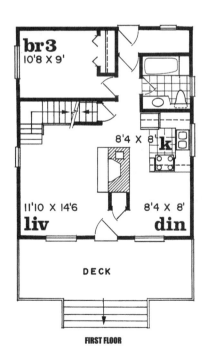

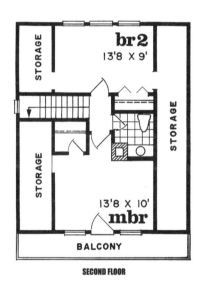

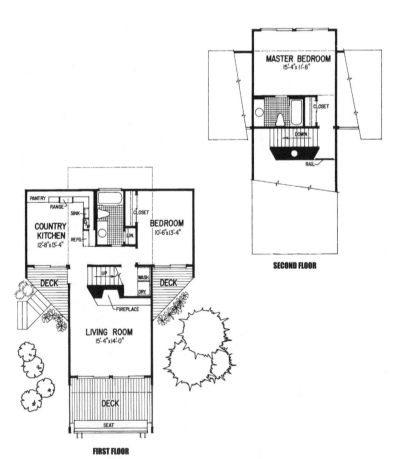

MASTER BEDROOM
15'-4"x11'-8"

CLOSET

DOWN

RAIL

SECOND FLOOR

PANTRY

RANGE   SINK

COUNTRY
KITCHEN
12'-8"x13'-4"   REFG.

CLOSET

BEDROOM
10'-6"x13'-4"

LIN.

DECK   UP   WASH.   DECK
DRY.

FIREPLACE

LIVING ROOM
15'-4"x14'-0"

DECK

SEAT

FIRST FLOOR

WIDTH 48' 0" DEPTH 32' 0"

plan #
HPT9600030

STYLE: NW CONTEMPORARY
FIRST FLOOR: 768 SQ. FT.
SECOND FLOOR: 288 SQ. FT.
TOTAL: 1,056 SQ. FT.
BEDROOMS: 2
BATHROOMS: 2
WIDTH: 32' - 0"
DEPTH: 48' - 0"
FOUNDATION: CRAWLSPACE

SEARCH ONLINE @ EPLANS.COM

This unusual contemporary design is not just another pretty face. The floor plan is amazingly simple and accommodating for casual living. Three decks—one at the kitchen, one at the secondary bedroom, and one large one at the living room—provide plenty of outdoor living space. The main deck has a built-in bench seat at its outer edge. The interior consists of a large living area warmed by a fireplace, and an L-shaped kitchen with pantry and two bedrooms with baths. The master bedroom sits on the second floor and has sliding glass doors to the outdoors.

ORDER BLUEPRINTS 24 HOURS, 7 DAYS A WEEK, AT 1-800-521-6797

plan # HPT9600031

STYLE: CHALET

FIRST FLOOR: 725 SQ. FT.

SECOND FLOOR: 561 SQ. FT.

TOTAL: 1,286 SQ. FT.

BEDROOMS: 3

BATHROOMS: 2

WIDTH: 25' - 0"

DEPTH: 36' - 6"

FOUNDATION: CRAWLSPACE

SEARCH ONLINE @ EPLANS.COM

FIRST FLOOR

SECOND FLOOR

plan # HPT9600032

STYLE: VACATION

FIRST FLOOR: 1,042 SQ. FT.

SECOND FLOOR: 456 SQ. FT.

TOTAL: 1,498 SQ. FT.

BEDROOMS: 3

BATHROOMS: 2

WIDTH: 36' - 0"

DEPTH: 35' - 8"

FOUNDATION: CRAWLSPACE, BASEMENT

SEARCH ONLINE @ EPLANS.COM

FIRST FLOOR

SECOND FLOOR

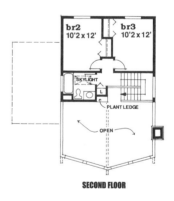

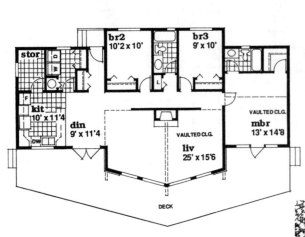

stor

br2
10'2 x 10'

br3
9' x 10'

VAULTED CLG.

kit
10' x 11'4

din
9' x 11'4

VAULTED CLG.

mbr
13' x 14'8

liv
25' x 15'6

DECK

plan #
HPT9600033

STYLE: NW CONTEMPORARY

SQUARE FOOTAGE: 1,495

BEDROOMS: 3

BATHROOMS: 2

WIDTH: 58' - 6"

DEPTH: 33' - 0"

FOUNDATION: CRAWLSPACE

SEARCH ONLINE @ EPLANS.COM

plan #
HPT9600034

STYLE: VACATION

SQUARE FOOTAGE: 680

BONUS SPACE: 419 SQ. FT.

BEDROOMS: 1

BATHROOMS: 1

WIDTH: 26' - 6"

DEPTH: 28' - 0"

FOUNDATION: CRAWLSPACE

SEARCH ONLINE @ EPLANS.COM

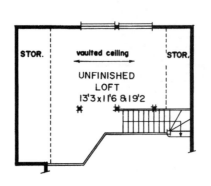

STOR.

vaulted ceiling

STOR.

UNFINISHED
LOFT
13'3 x 11'6 & 19'2

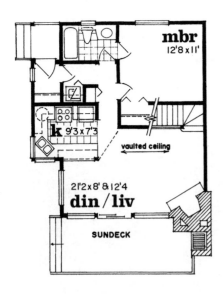

mbr
12'8 x 11'

k 9'3 x 7'3

vaulted ceiling

21'2 x 8' & 12'4

din / liv

SUNDECK

ORDER BLUEPRINTS 24 HOURS, 7 DAYS A WEEK, AT 1-800-521-6797

plan #
HPT9600035

STYLE: NW CONTEMPORARY
SQUARE FOOTAGE: 1,405
BEDROOMS: 3
BATHROOMS: 2
WIDTH: 62' - 0"
DEPTH: 29' - 0"
FOUNDATION: CRAWLSPACE,
BASEMENT

SEARCH ONLINE @ EPLANS.COM

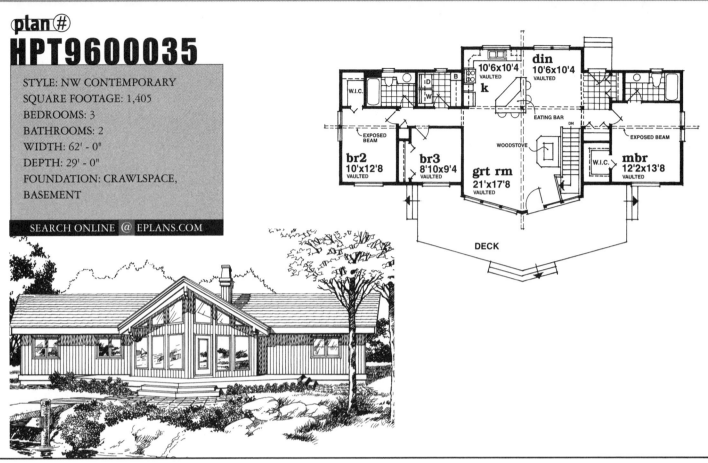

plan #
HPT9600036

STYLE: VACATION
FIRST FLOOR: 616 SQ. FT.
SECOND FLOOR: 300 SQ. FT.
TOTAL: 916 SQ. FT.
BEDROOMS: 2
BATHROOMS: 1
WIDTH: 22' - 0"
DEPTH: 28' - 0"
FOUNDATION: CRAWLSPACE

SEARCH ONLINE @ EPLANS.COM

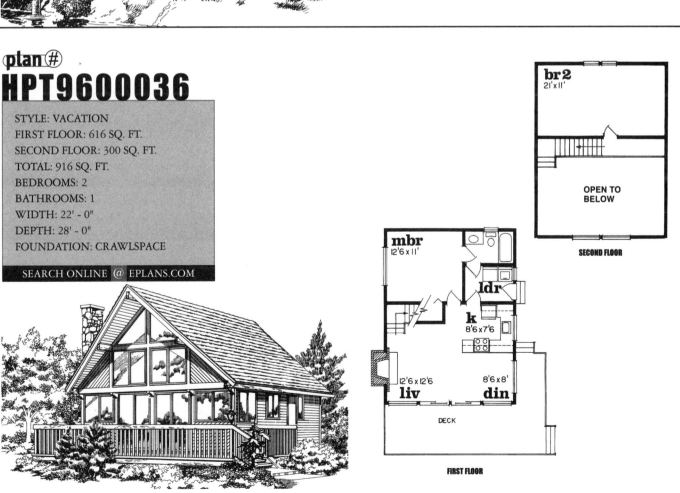

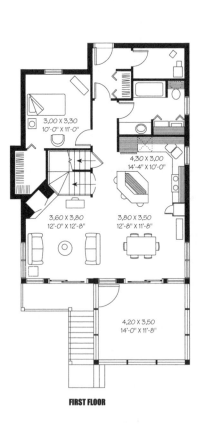

FIRST FLOOR

3,00 X 3,30
10'-0" X 11'-0"

4,30 X 3,00
14'-4" X 10'-0"

3,60 X 3,80
12'-0" X 12'-8"

3,80 X 3,50
12'-8" X 11'-8"

4,20 X 3,50
14'-0" X 11'-8"

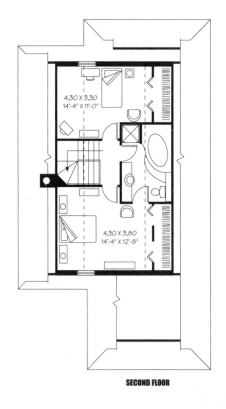

SECOND FLOOR

4,30 X 3,30
14'-4" X 11'-0"

4,30 X 3,80
14'-4" X 12'-8"

plan
HPT9600037

STYLE: VACATION
FIRST FLOOR: 895 SQ. FT.
SECOND FLOOR: 576 SQ. FT.
TOTAL: 1,471 SQ. FT.
BEDROOMS: 3
BATHROOMS: 2
WIDTH: 26' - 0"
DEPTH: 36' - 0"
FOUNDATION: BASEMENT,

SEARCH ONLINE @ EPLANS.COM

Here's a favorite waterfront home with plenty of space to kick back and relax. A lovely sunroom opens from the dining room and allows great views. An angled hearth warms the living and dining areas. Three lovely windows brighten the dining space, which leads out to a stunning sunporch. The gourmet kitchen has an island counter with a snack bar. The first-floor master bedroom enjoys a walk-in closet and a nearby bath. Upstairs, a spacious bath with a whirlpool tub is thoughtfully placed between two bedrooms. A daylight basement allows a lower-level portico.

plan#
HPT9600038

STYLE: VACATION
FIRST FLOOR: 895 SQ. FT.
SECOND FLOOR: 576 SQ. FT.
TOTAL: 1,471 SQ. FT.
BEDROOMS: 3
BATHROOMS: 2
WIDTH: 26' - 0"
DEPTH: 36' - 0"
FOUNDATION: BASEMENT

SEARCH ONLINE @ EPLANS.COM

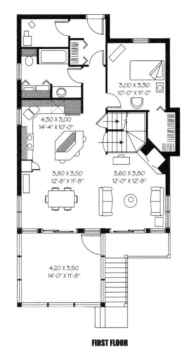

FIRST FLOOR

SECOND FLOOR

plan#
HPT9600039

STYLE: VACATION
FIRST FLOOR: 1,024 SQ. FT.
SECOND FLOOR: 456 SQ. FT.
TOTAL: 1,480 SQ. FT.
BEDROOMS: 2
BATHROOMS: 2
WIDTH: 32' - 0"
DEPTH: 40' - 0"
FOUNDATION: BASEMENT

SEARCH ONLINE @ EPLANS.COM

FIRST FLOOR

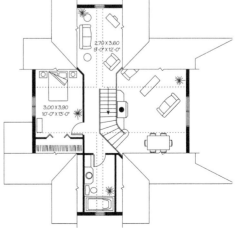

SECOND FLOOR

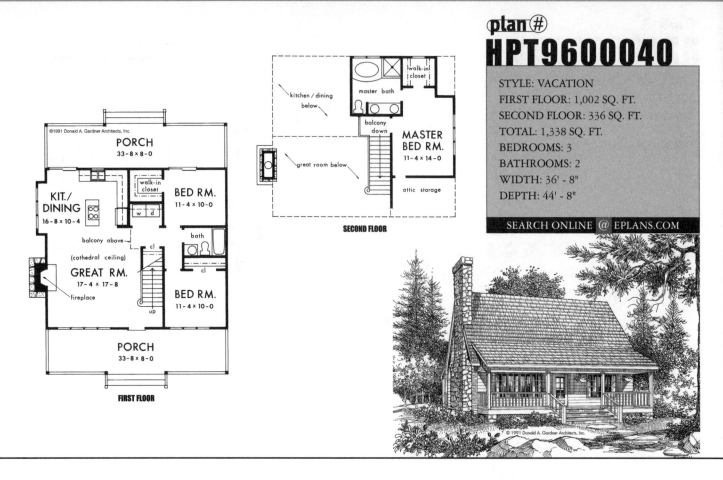

plan#
HPT9600040

STYLE: VACATION
FIRST FLOOR: 1,002 SQ. FT.
SECOND FLOOR: 336 SQ. FT.
TOTAL: 1,338 SQ. FT.
BEDROOMS: 3
BATHROOMS: 2
WIDTH: 36' - 8"
DEPTH: 44' - 8"

SEARCH ONLINE @ EPLANS.COM

plan#
HPT9600041

STYLE: RANCH
SQUARE FOOTAGE: 1,408
BEDROOMS: 3
BATHROOMS: 2
WIDTH: 70' - 0"
DEPTH: 34' - 0"
FOUNDATION: BASEMENT, CRAWLSPACE

SEARCH ONLINE @ EPLANS.COM

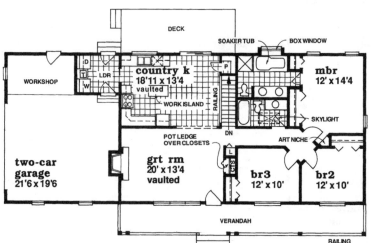

plan# HPT9600042

STYLE: COUNTRY COTTAGE
FIRST FLOOR: 843 SQ. FT.
SECOND FLOOR: 340 SQ. FT.
TOTAL: 1,183 SQ. FT.
BONUS SPACE: 217 SQ. FT.
BEDROOMS: 3
BATHROOMS: 1
WIDTH: 32' - 4"
DEPTH: 44' - 1"
FOUNDATION: CRAWLSPACE

SEARCH ONLINE @ EPLANS.COM

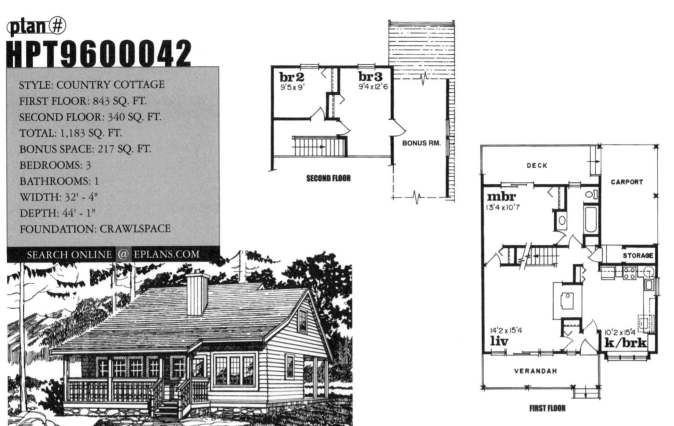

plan# HPT9600043

STYLE: FARMHOUSE
FIRST FLOOR: 1,036 SQ. FT.
SECOND FLOOR: 273 SQ. FT.
TOTAL: 1,309 SQ. FT.
BEDROOMS: 2
BATHROOMS: 2
WIDTH: 39' - 0"
DEPTH: 38' - 0"
FOUNDATION: CRAWLSPACE

SEARCH ONLINE @ EPLANS.COM

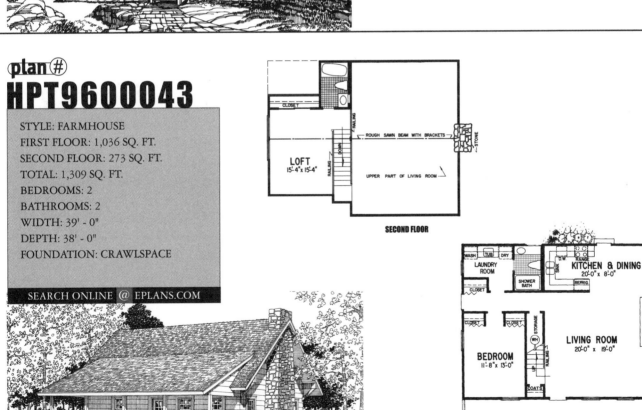

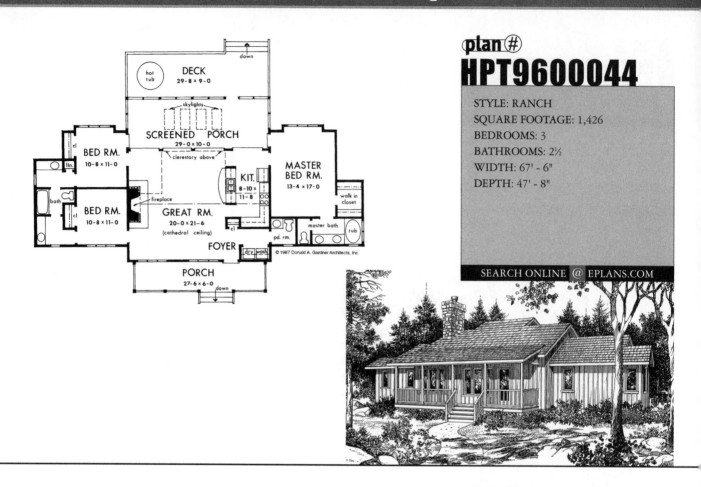

DECK
29-8 × 9-0

hot tub

down

skylights

BED RM.
10-8 × 11-0

cl

lin.

SCREENED PORCH
29-0 × 10-0

clerestory above

KIT.
8-10 ×
11-8

MASTER
BED RM.
13-4 × 17-0

walk in
closet

bath

cl

BED RM.
10-8 × 11-0

fireplace

GREAT RM.
20-0 × 21-6
(cathedral ceiling)

cl

pd. rm.

master bath

tub

dry wash

FOYER

© 1987 Donald A. Gardner Architects, Inc.

PORCH
27-6 × 6-0

down

plan #

HPT9600044

STYLE: RANCH
SQUARE FOOTAGE: 1,426
BEDROOMS: 3
BATHROOMS: 2½
WIDTH: 67' - 6"
DEPTH: 47' - 8"

SEARCH ONLINE @ EPLANS.COM

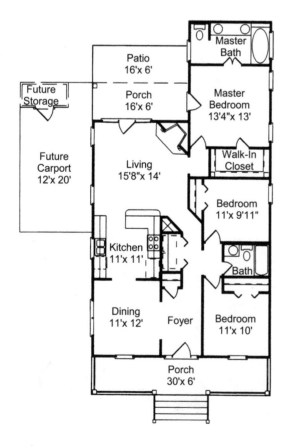

Patio
16'x 6'

Master
Bath

Future
Storage

Porch
16'x 6'

Master
Bedroom
13'4"x 13'

Future
Carport
12'x 20'

Living
15'8"x 14'

Walk-In
Closet

Bedroom
11'x 9'11"

Kitchen
11'x 11'

Bath

Dining
11'x 12'

Foyer

Bedroom
11'x 10'

Porch
30'x 6'

plan #

HPT9600045

STYLE: FARMHOUSE
SQUARE FOOTAGE: 1,363
BEDROOMS: 3
BATHROOMS: 2
WIDTH: 30' - 0"
DEPTH: 60' - 0"
FOUNDATION: SLAB

SEARCH ONLINE @ EPLANS.COM

ORDER BLUEPRINTS 24 HOURS, 7 DAYS A WEEK, AT 1-800-521-6797

plan #
HPT9600046

STYLE: VACATION
SQUARE FOOTAGE: 1,404
BONUS SPACE: 256 SQ. FT.
BEDROOMS: 2
BATHROOMS: 2
WIDTH: 54' - 7"
DEPTH: 46' - 6"
FOUNDATION: CRAWLSPACE

SEARCH ONLINE @ EPLANS.COM

OPTIONAL LAYOUT

LOFT
256 FEET

CARPORT

BEDRM 2
12-0 X 11-0

BATH 2

MASTER BEDRM
12-0 X 14-6

MASTER BATH

SCREENED
PORCH
11-0 X 11-0

PANTRY

KITCHEN
10-0 14-8

DINING RM
10-6 X 14-0

GREAT RM
20-0 X 17-6
VAULTED TO 16' CLG

FP

COVERED PORCH
38-0 X 7-0

plan #
HPT9600047

STYLE: COUNTRY COTTAGE
SQUARE FOOTAGE: 484
BONUS SPACE: 220 SQ. FT.
BEDROOMS: 1
BATHROOMS: 1
WIDTH: 22' - 0"
DEPTH: 30' - 0"
FOUNDATION: BASEMENT

SEARCH ONLINE @ EPLANS.COM

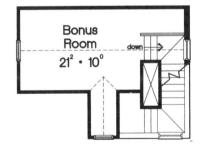

Bonus
Room
21² · 10⁰

down

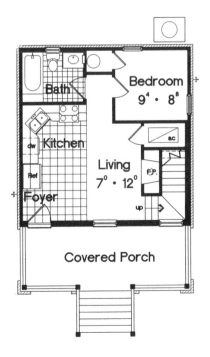

Bath

Bedroom
9⁴ · 8⁸

Kitchen

ac

Living
7⁰ · 12⁰

FP.

Foyer

up

Covered Porch

ALTERNATE EXTERIOR

ALTERNATE EXTERIOR

plan #
HPT9600048

STYLE: TRADITIONAL
SQUARE FOOTAGE: 1,317
BEDROOMS: 3
BATHROOMS: 2
WIDTH: 45' - 0"
DEPTH: 52' - 4"
FOUNDATION: SLAB

SEARCH ONLINE @ EPLANS.COM

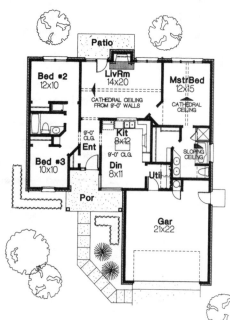

This unique little house has many attractive features. The living room has a cathedral ceiling with a wood burning fireplace. The kitchen/dinette has a nice island and adjoining utility room. The master bedroom also features a cathedral ceiling and is enhanced by a spacious walk-in closet and a private bath with a compartmented shower and tub. Two additional bedrooms and a bath make up the opposite side of the home. This plan has three exteriors to choose from.

ORDER BLUEPRINTS 24 HOURS, 7 DAYS A WEEK, AT 1-800-521-6797

plan
HPT9600049

STYLE: TRADITIONAL
SQUARE FOOTAGE: 1,232
BEDROOMS: 3
BATHROOMS: 2
WIDTH: 46' - 0"
DEPTH: 44' - 4"
FOUNDATION: BASEMENT, SLAB, CRAWLSPACE

SEARCH ONLINE @ EPLANS.COM

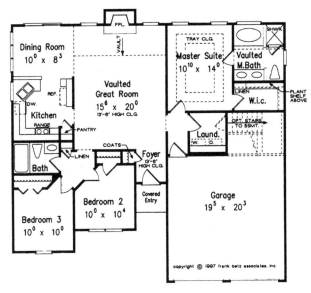

plan
HPT9600050

STYLE: TRADITIONAL
SQUARE FOOTAGE: 1,477
BONUS SPACE: 283 SQ. FT.
BEDROOMS: 3
BATHROOMS: 2
WIDTH: 51' - 0"
DEPTH: 51' - 4"
FOUNDATION: CRAWLSPACE, BASEMENT

SEARCH ONLINE @ EPLANS.COM

OPTIONAL LAYOUT

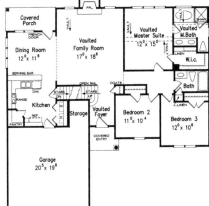

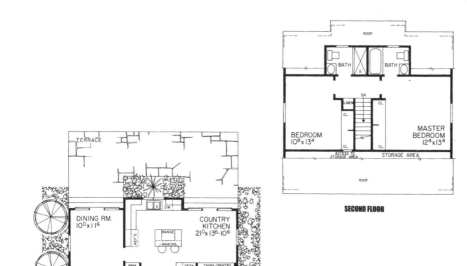

FIRST FLOOR

SECOND FLOOR

plan #
HPT9600051

STYLE: CAPE COD
FIRST FLOOR: 919 SQ. FT.
SECOND FLOOR: 535 SQ. FT.
TOTAL: 1,454 SQ. FT.
BEDROOMS: 2
BATHROOMS: 2½
WIDTH: 34' - 4"
DEPTH: 30' - 0"
FOUNDATION: BASEMENT

SEARCH ONLINE @ EPLANS.COM

Compact enough for even the smallest lot, this cozy design provides comfortable living space for a small family. At the heart of the plan is a spacious country kitchen. It features a cooking island/snack bar and a dining area that opens to a house-wide rear terrace. The nearby dining room also opens to the terrace. At the front of the plan is the living room, warmed by a fireplace. Across the centered foyer is a cozy study. Two second-floor bedrooms are serviced by two baths. Note the first-floor powder room and storage closet located next to the side entrance.

plan #
HPT9600052

STYLE: TRADITIONAL

SQUARE FOOTAGE: 1,392

BEDROOMS: 3

BATHROOMS: 2

WIDTH: 42' - 0"

DEPTH: 54' - 0"

SEARCH ONLINE @ EPLANS.COM

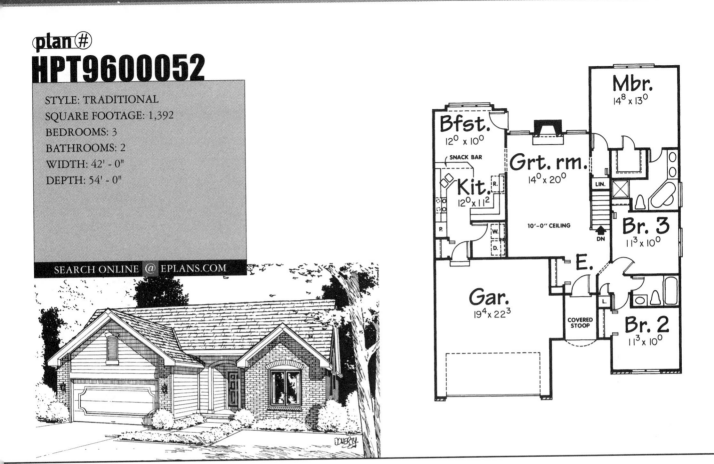

plan #
HPT9600053

STYLE: TRADITIONAL

SQUARE FOOTAGE: 1,170

BEDROOMS: 3

BATHROOMS: 2

WIDTH: 51' - 10"

DEPTH: 53' - 6"

FOUNDATION: CRAWLSPACE, SLAB

SEARCH ONLINE @ EPLANS.COM

plan# HPT9600054

STYLE: TRADITIONAL

SQUARE FOOTAGE: 993

BEDROOMS: 3

BATHROOMS: 2

WIDTH: 57' - 0"

DEPTH: 30' - 0"

FOUNDATION: CRAWLSPACE, SLAB, BASEMENT

SEARCH ONLINE @ EPLANS.COM

plan# HPT9600055

STYLE: TRADITIONAL

SQUARE FOOTAGE: 1,467

BEDROOMS: 3

BATHROOMS: 2

WIDTH: 49' - 0"

DEPTH: 43' - 0"

FOUNDATION: CRAWLSPACE, BASEMENT

SEARCH ONLINE @ EPLANS.COM

plan # HPT9600056

STYLE: TRADITIONAL

SQUARE FOOTAGE: 1,425

BEDROOMS: 3

BATHROOMS: 2

WIDTH: 40' - 0"

DEPTH: 53' - 0"

FOUNDATION: CRAWLSPACE, BASEMENT

SEARCH ONLINE @ EPLANS.COM

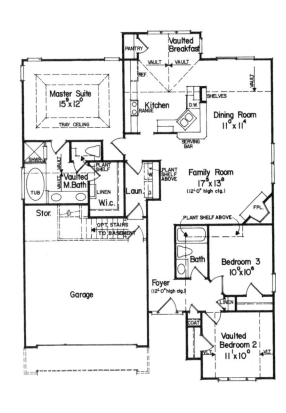

plan # HPT9600057

STYLE: TRADITIONAL

SQUARE FOOTAGE: 1,235

BEDROOMS: 3

BATHROOMS: 2

WIDTH: 47' - 0"

DEPTH: 43' - 6"

FOUNDATION: CRAWLSPACE, BASEMENT

SEARCH ONLINE @ EPLANS.COM

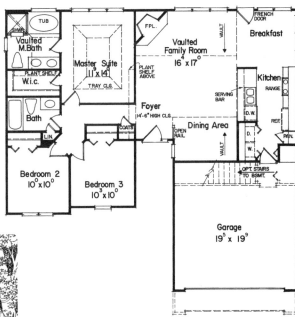

© 1999 Donald A. Gardner, Inc.

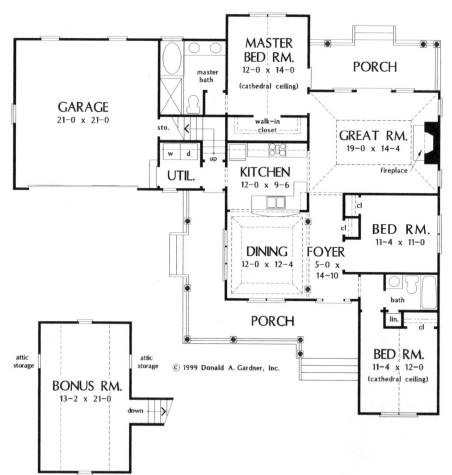

© 1999 Donald A. Gardner, Inc.

plan
HPT9600058

STYLE: COUNTRY
SQUARE FOOTAGE: 1,469
BONUS SPACE: 383 SQ. FT.
BEDROOMS: 3
BATHROOMS: 2
WIDTH: 63' - 4"
DEPTH: 57' - 0"

SEARCH ONLINE @ EPLANS.COM

Striking gables, arched windows, and a wrapping front porch grace the facade of this modest three-bedroom home. The dining room, kitchen, and great room cleverly separate the master suite from the two family bedrooms. Tray ceilings in the dining room and great room add volume and interest; the master bedroom and front family room are expanded by cathedral ceilings. The master suite features rear-porch access, a walk-in closet, and a private bath with a separate tub and shower. A bonus room over the garage offers space for storage or future expansion.

ORDER BLUEPRINTS 24 HOURS, 7 DAYS A WEEK, AT 1-800-521-6797

plan # HPT9600059

STYLE: COUNTRY

SQUARE FOOTAGE: 1,422

BEDROOMS: 3

BATHROOMS: 2

WIDTH: 45' - 6"

DEPTH: 57' - 8"

SEARCH ONLINE @ EPLANS.COM

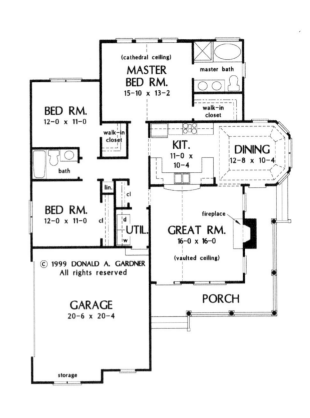

© 1999 Donald A. Gardner, Inc.

plan # HPT9600060

STYLE: COUNTRY COTTAGE

SQUARE FOOTAGE: 1,476

BONUS SPACE: 340 SQ. FT.

BEDROOMS: 3

BATHROOMS: 2

WIDTH: 63' - 4"

DEPTH: 46' - 10"

SEARCH ONLINE @ EPLANS.COM

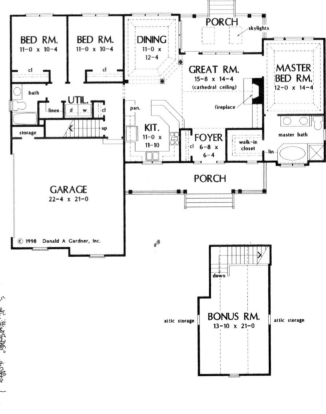

© 1998 Donald A Gardner, Inc.

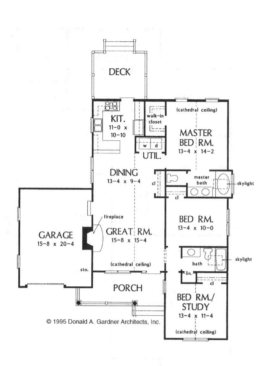

DECK

KIT.
11-0 x
10-10

walk-in
closet

(cathedral ceiling)

MASTER
BED RM.
13-4 x 14-2

w | d

UTIL.

DINING
13-4 x 9-4

cl

master
bath

skylight

fireplace

GARAGE
15-8 x 20-4

GREAT RM.
15-8 x 15-4

BED RM.
13-4 x 10-0

sto.

(cathedral ceiling)

bath

skylight

cl

PORCH

lin.

cl

BED RM./
STUDY
13-4 x 11-4

© 1995 Donald A. Gardner Architects, Inc.

(cathedral ceiling)

ptan#
HPT9600061

STYLE: FARMHOUSE
SQUARE FOOTAGE: 1,302
BEDROOMS: 3
BATHROOMS: 2
WIDTH: 47' - 0"
DEPTH: 50' - 4"

SEARCH ONLINE @ EPLANS.COM

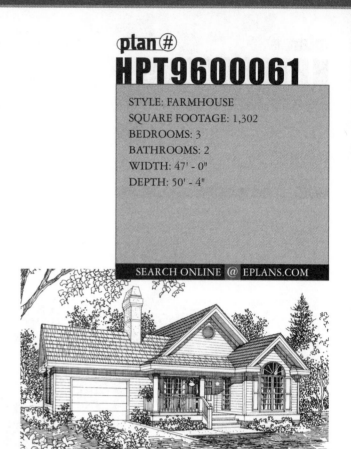

© 1995 Donald A. Gardner Architects, Inc.

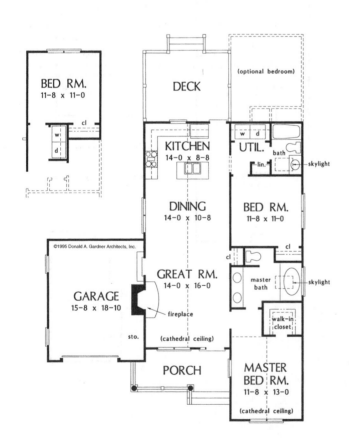

BED RM.
11-8 x 11-0

cl

w
d

DECK

(optional bedroom)

KITCHEN
14-0 x 8-8

w | d

UTIL.

bath

lin.

skylight

©1995 Donald A. Gardner Architects, Inc.

DINING
14-0 x 10-8

BED RM.
11-8 x 11-0

cl

GARAGE
15-8 x 18-10

GREAT RM.
14-0 x 16-0

master
bath

skylight

cl

fireplace

sto.

(cathedral ceiling)

walk-in
closet

PORCH

MASTER
BED RM.
11-8 x 13-0

(cathedral ceiling)

ptan#
HPT9600062

STYLE: FARMHOUSE
SQUARE FOOTAGE: 1,109
BONUS SPACE: 169 SQ. FT.
BEDROOMS: 2
BATHROOMS: 2
WIDTH: 42' - 8"
DEPTH: 47' - 4"

SEARCH ONLINE @ EPLANS.COM

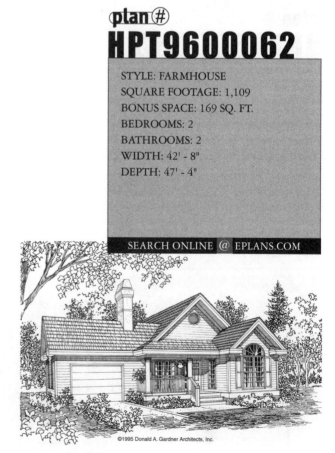

©1995 Donald A. Gardner Architects, Inc.

plan
HPT9600063

STYLE: TRADITIONAL
SQUARE FOOTAGE: 1,498
BEDROOMS: 3
BATHROOMS: 2
WIDTH: 59' - 8"
DEPTH: 46' - 8"

SEARCH ONLINE @ EPLANS.COM

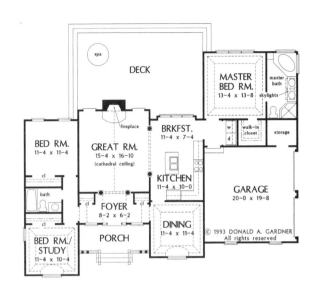

© 1993 DONALD A. GARDNER
All rights reserved

© 1993 Donald A. Gardner Architects, Inc.

plan
HPT9600064

STYLE: COUNTRY
SQUARE FOOTAGE: 1,425
BONUS SPACE: 424 SQ. FT.
BEDROOMS: 3
BATHROOMS: 2
WIDTH: 61' - 0"
DEPTH: 51' - 8"

SEARCH ONLINE @ EPLANS.COM

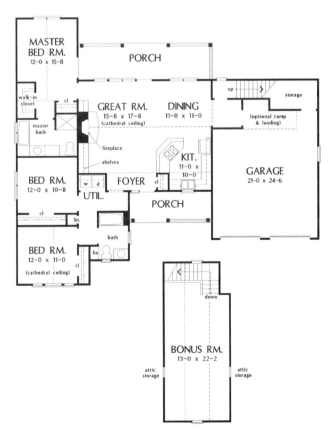

©1999 Donald A. Gardner, Inc.

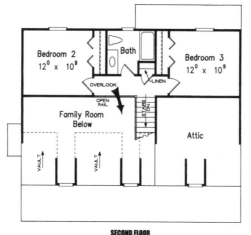

SECOND FLOOR

FIRST FLOOR

plan
HPT9600065

STYLE: SOUTHERN COLONIAL
FIRST FLOOR: 1,061 SQ. FT.
SECOND FLOOR: 430 SQ. FT.
TOTAL: 1,491 SQ. FT.
BEDROOMS: 3
BATHROOMS: 2½
WIDTH: 40' - 4"
DEPTH: 36' - 0"
FOUNDATION: BASEMENT

SEARCH ONLINE @ EPLANS.COM

This sporty hideaway retreat is great for being in the wilderness. Adorned with dormers and a covered front porch, this two-story home warms family and guests with a vaulted family room. This room features a cozy fireplace and radius windows to each side. The kitchen enjoys a serving bar and a pantry. The master bedroom boasts a tray ceiling, a walk-in closet, and a sumptuous private bath. The second floor holds two family bedrooms sharing a full bath—note the open rail overlooking the family room below.

plan#
HPT9600066

STYLE: TRADITIONAL
SQUARE FOOTAGE: 1,360
BEDROOMS: 3
BATHROOMS: 2
WIDTH: 68' - 0"
DEPTH: 30' - 0"
FOUNDATION: CRAWLSPACE, SLAB, BASEMENT

SEARCH ONLINE @ EPLANS.COM

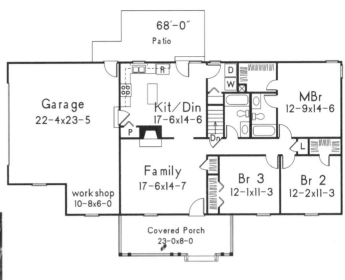

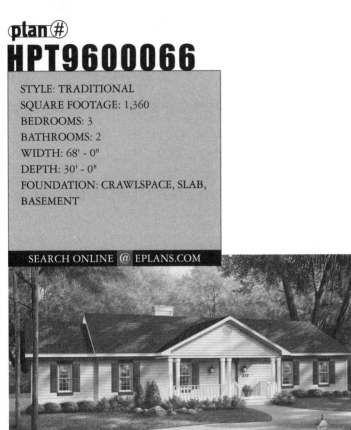

plan#
HPT9600067

STYLE: TRADITIONAL
SQUARE FOOTAGE: 1,140
BEDROOMS: 3
BATHROOMS: 2
WIDTH: 44' - 0"
DEPTH: 27' - 0"
FOUNDATION: BASEMENT

SEARCH ONLINE @ EPLANS.COM

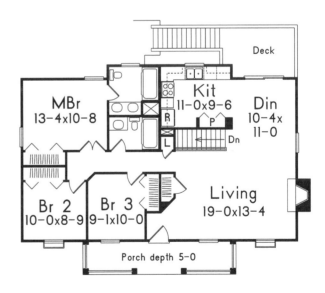

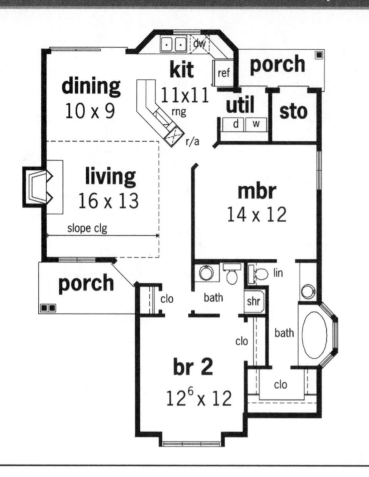

dining 10 x 9

kit 11x11

ref

porch

rng

r/a

util

d w

sto

living 16 x 13

mbr 14 x 12

slope clg

porch

clo

bath

lin

shr

clo

bath

br 2 12⁶ x 12

clo

clo

plan #

HPT9600068

STYLE: COUNTRY COTTAGE
SQUARE FOOTAGE: 984
BEDROOMS: 2
BATHROOMS: 2
WIDTH: 33' - 9"
DEPTH: 43' - 0"
FOUNDATION: CRAWLSPACE, SLAB

SEARCH ONLINE @ EPLANS.COM

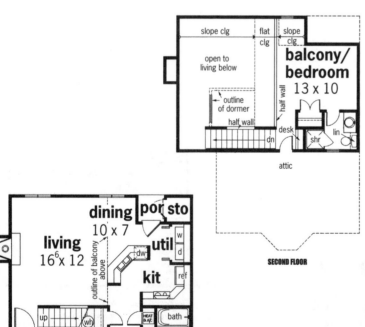

slope clg

flat clg

slope clg

open to living below

balcony/ bedroom 13 x 10

outline of dormer

desk

half wall

half wall

dn

shr

lin

attic

SECOND FLOOR

dining 10 x 7

por

sto

living 16⁶ x 12

util

w
d

dw

outline of balcony above

kit

ref

up

wh

HEAT B&C

bath

lin

por

mbr 15 x 12

wic

sitting

FIRST FLOOR

plan #

HPT9600069

STYLE: COUNTRY COTTAGE
FIRST FLOOR: 814 SQ. FT.
SECOND FLOOR: 267 SQ. FT.
TOTAL: 1,081 SQ. FT.
BEDROOMS: 2
BATHROOMS: 2
WIDTH: 28' - 0"
DEPTH: 34' - 6"
FOUNDATION: BASEMENT, CRAWLSPACE, SLAB

SEARCH ONLINE @ EPLANS.COM

plan
HPT9600070

STYLE: TUDOR
FIRST FLOOR: 665 SQ. FT.
SECOND FLOOR: 395 SQ. FT.
TOTAL: 1,060 SQ. FT.
BEDROOMS: 1
BATHROOMS: 1
WIDTH: 34' - 3"
DEPTH: 32' - 5"
FOUNDATION: SLAB

SEARCH ONLINE @ EPLANS.COM

With woodsy charm and cozy livability, this cottage plan offers comfortable living space in a smaller footprint. The exterior is geared for outdoor fun, with two flagstone patios connected by a two-way fireplace and graced by a built-in barbecue. French doors on two sides lead into the large playroom, which features a kitchen area, washer and dryer space, and a bath with corner sink and shower. Take the L-shaped stairway to the bunk room upstairs, where there is space for sleeping and relaxing.

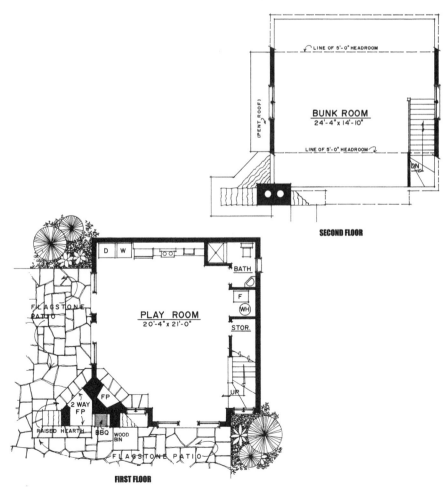

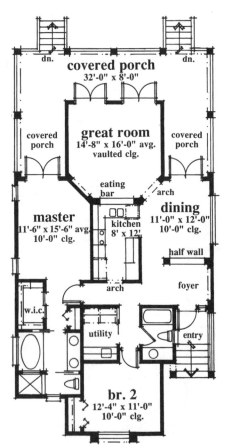

REAR EXTERIOR

plan#
HPT9600071

STYLE: TIDEWATER
SQUARE FOOTAGE: 1,288
BEDROOMS: 2
BATHROOMS: 2
WIDTH: 32' - 4"
DEPTH: 60' - 0"
FOUNDATION: CRAWLSPACE

SEARCH ONLINE @ EPLANS.COM

Welcome home to casual, unstuffy living with this comfortable tidewater design. The heart of this home is the great room, where a put-your-feet-up atmosphere prevails, and the dusky hues of sunset can mingle with the sounds of ocean breakers. An efficiently designed kitchen opens to a dining room that accesses the rear porch. French doors open the master suite to a private area of the covered porch, where sunlight and sea breezes mingle with a spirit of bon vivant.

plan #
HPT9600072

STYLE: TRADITIONAL
SQUARE FOOTAGE: 1,339
BEDROOMS: 3
BATHROOMS: 2
WIDTH: 50' - 0"
DEPTH: 46' - 0"

SEARCH ONLINE @ EPLANS.COM

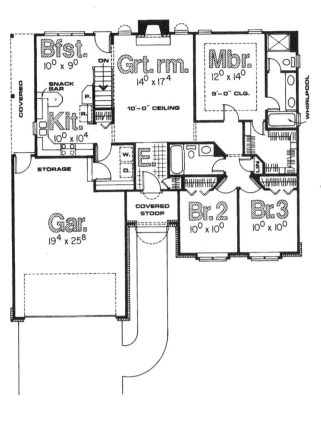

plan #
HPT9600073

STYLE: TRANSITIONAL
SQUARE FOOTAGE: 1,478
BEDROOMS: 2
BATHROOMS: 2
WIDTH: 42' - 0"
DEPTH: 55' - 8"

SEARCH ONLINE @ EPLANS.COM

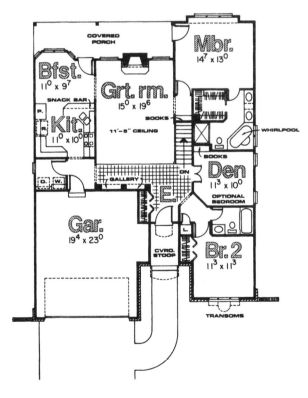

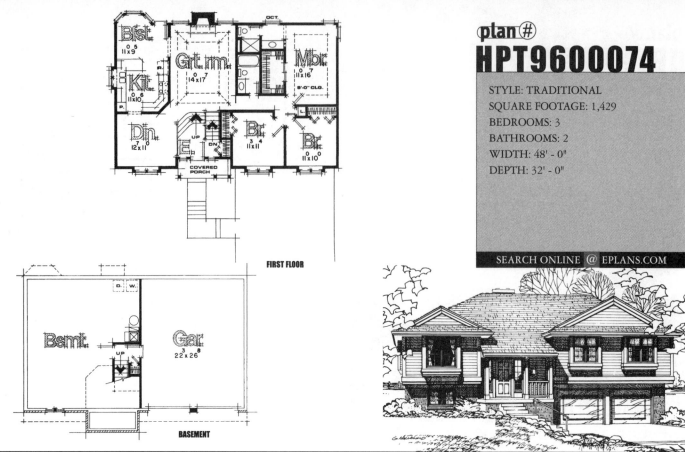

FIRST FLOOR

BASEMENT

plan#
HPT9600074

STYLE: TRADITIONAL
SQUARE FOOTAGE: 1,429
BEDROOMS: 3
BATHROOMS: 2
WIDTH: 48' - 0"
DEPTH: 32' - 0"

SEARCH ONLINE @ EPLANS.COM

FIRST FLOOR

BASEMENT

plan#
HPT9600075

STYLE: TRADITIONAL
SQUARE FOOTAGE: 1,209
BEDROOMS: 3
BATHROOMS: 2
WIDTH: 42' - 0"
DEPTH: 31' - 0"
FOUNDATION: BASEMENT

SEARCH ONLINE @ EPLANS.COM

plan
HPT9600076

STYLE: TRADITIONAL

SQUARE FOOTAGE: 1,480

BEDROOMS: 3

BATHROOMS: 2

WIDTH: 51' - 6"

DEPTH: 31' - 0"

FOUNDATION: BASEMENT

SEARCH ONLINE @ EPLANS.COM

This lovely brick-and-siding home will be a welcome addition to any neighborhood. The illusion of two stories elevates this traditional home, with the garage and unfinished basement/storage area below and a well-planned layout above. A vaulted family room invites family and friends to delight in an extended-hearth fireplace. To the left, a gourmet country kitchen has a convenient serving bar to the sunny breakfast nook. Two bedroom share a hall bath; on the far right, the master suite is secluded for privacy, with a pampering vaulted bath and plenty of natural light.

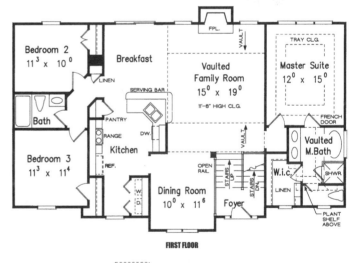

FIRST FLOOR

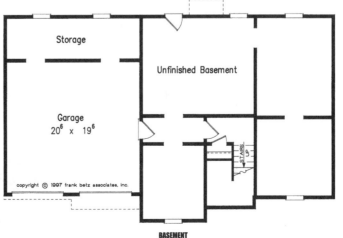

BASEMENT

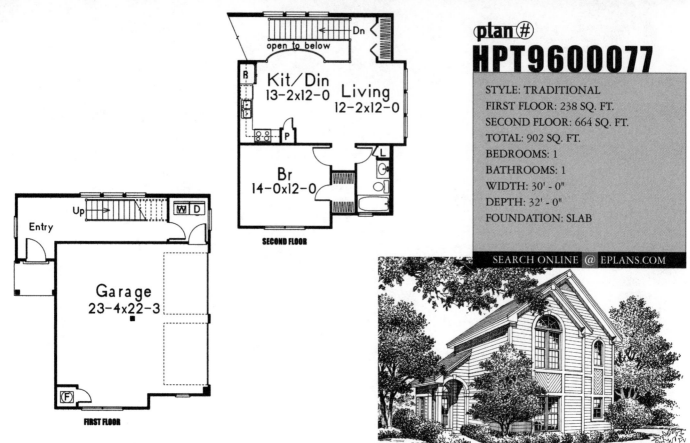

plan#

HPT9600077

STYLE: TRADITIONAL

FIRST FLOOR: 238 SQ. FT.

SECOND FLOOR: 664 SQ. FT.

TOTAL: 902 SQ. FT.

BEDROOMS: 1

BATHROOMS: 1

WIDTH: 30' - 0"

DEPTH: 32' - 0"

FOUNDATION: SLAB

SEARCH ONLINE @ EPLANS.COM

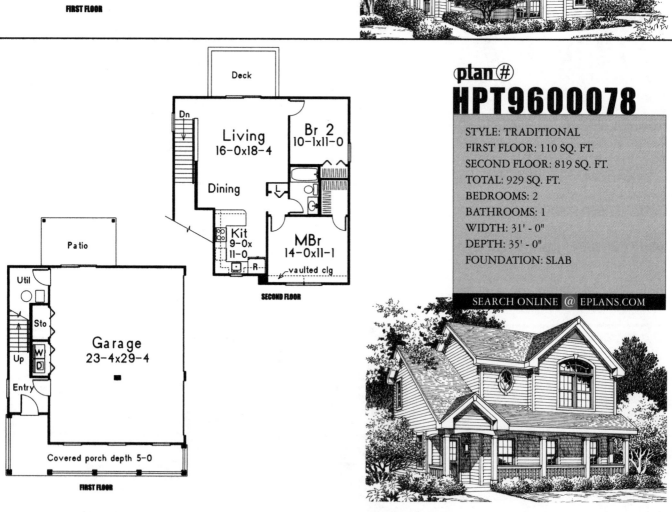

plan#

HPT9600078

STYLE: TRADITIONAL

FIRST FLOOR: 110 SQ. FT.

SECOND FLOOR: 819 SQ. FT.

TOTAL: 929 SQ. FT.

BEDROOMS: 2

BATHROOMS: 1

WIDTH: 31' - 0"

DEPTH: 35' - 0"

FOUNDATION: SLAB

SEARCH ONLINE @ EPLANS.COM

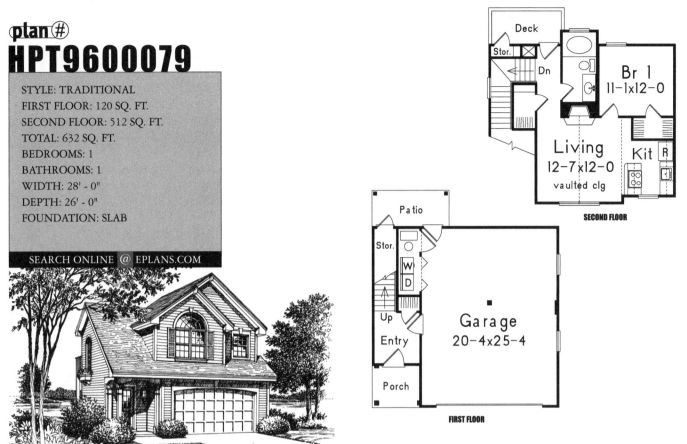

plan #
HPT9600079

STYLE: TRADITIONAL
FIRST FLOOR: 120 SQ. FT.
SECOND FLOOR: 512 SQ. FT.
TOTAL: 632 SQ. FT.
BEDROOMS: 1
BATHROOMS: 1
WIDTH: 28' - 0"
DEPTH: 26' - 0"
FOUNDATION: SLAB

SEARCH ONLINE @ EPLANS.COM

Deck
Stor.
Dn
Br 1
11-1x12-0
Living
12-7x12-0
vaulted clg
Kit
R

SECOND FLOOR

Patio
Stor.
W D
Up
Entry
Porch
Garage
20-4x25-4

FIRST FLOOR

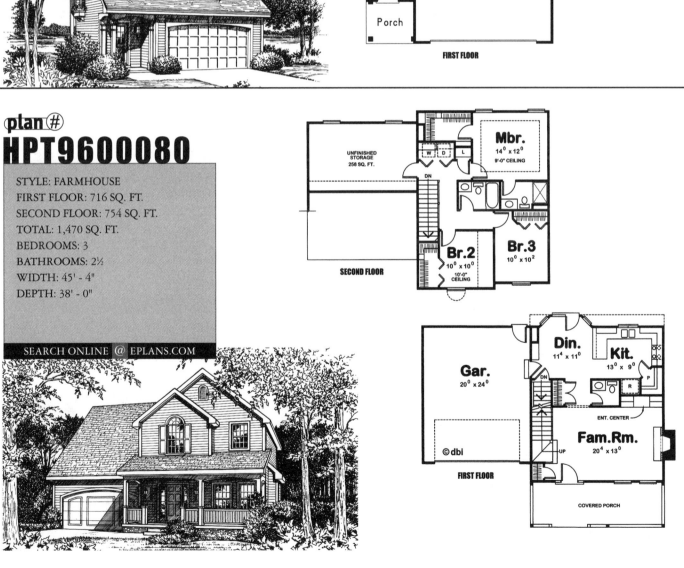

plan #
HPT9600080

STYLE: FARMHOUSE
FIRST FLOOR: 716 SQ. FT.
SECOND FLOOR: 754 SQ. FT.
TOTAL: 1,470 SQ. FT.
BEDROOMS: 3
BATHROOMS: 2½
WIDTH: 45' - 4"
DEPTH: 38' - 0"

SEARCH ONLINE @ EPLANS.COM

UNFINISHED STORAGE
258 SQ. FT.
DN
Mbr.
14⁰ x 12⁰
9'-0" CEILING
W D L
Br.2
10⁰ x 10⁰
10'-0" CEILING
Br.3
10⁰ x 10²

SECOND FLOOR

Gar.
20⁰ x 24⁰
© dbi
Din.
11⁴ x 11⁰
Kit.
13⁰ x 9⁰
P
R
ENT. CENTER
DN
UP
Fam.Rm.
20⁴ x 13⁰

FIRST FLOOR

COVERED PORCH

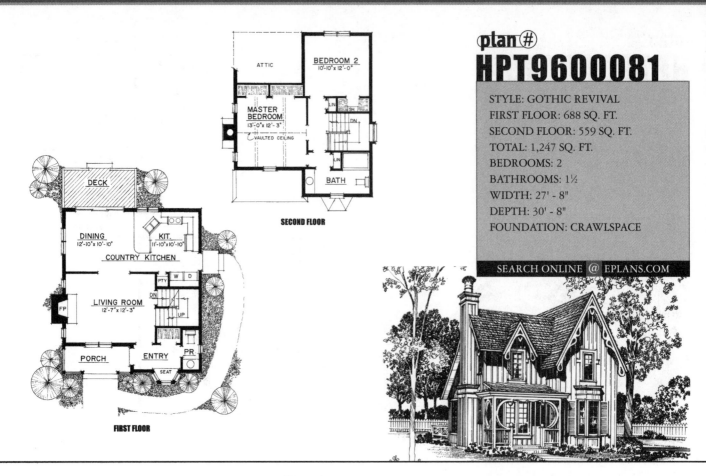

SECOND FLOOR

BEDROOM 2
10'-10" x 12'-0"

ATTIC

MASTER
BEDROOM
13'-0" x 12'-3"
VAULTED CEILING

LIN

SH

DN

LIN

BATH

DECK

DINING
12'-10" x 10'-10"

KIT.
11'-10" x 10'-10"

COUNTRY KITCHEN

W   D

PTY

LIVING ROOM
12'-7" x 12'-3"

DN

FP

UP

PORCH

ENTRY

PR

SEAT

FIRST FLOOR

plan
HPT9600081

STYLE: GOTHIC REVIVAL
FIRST FLOOR: 688 SQ. FT.
SECOND FLOOR: 559 SQ. FT.
TOTAL: 1,247 SQ. FT.
BEDROOMS: 2
BATHROOMS: 1½
WIDTH: 27' - 8"
DEPTH: 30' - 8"
FOUNDATION: CRAWLSPACE

SEARCH ONLINE @ EPLANS.COM

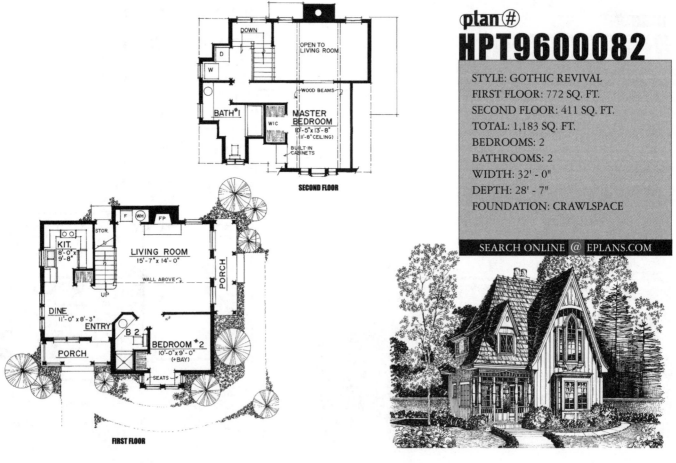

SECOND FLOOR

DOWN

OPEN TO
LIVING ROOM

D

W

WOOD BEAMS

BATH #1

MASTER
BEDROOM
10'-5" x 13'-8"
(11'-8" CEILING)

WIC

BUILT-IN
CABINETS

KIT.
8'-0" x 9'-8"

STOR.

F   WH   FP

LIVING ROOM
15'-7" x 14'-0"

PORCH

WALL ABOVE

UP

DINE
11'-0" x 8'-3"

ENTRY

B 2

BEDROOM #2
10'-0" x 9'-0"
(+BAY)

PORCH

SEATS

FIRST FLOOR

plan
HPT9600082

STYLE: GOTHIC REVIVAL
FIRST FLOOR: 772 SQ. FT.
SECOND FLOOR: 411 SQ. FT.
TOTAL: 1,183 SQ. FT.
BEDROOMS: 2
BATHROOMS: 2
WIDTH: 32' - 0"
DEPTH: 28' - 7"
FOUNDATION: CRAWLSPACE

SEARCH ONLINE @ EPLANS.COM

plan
HPT9600083

STYLE: FOLK VICTORIAN

FIRST FLOOR: 593 SQ. FT.

SECOND FLOOR: 383 SQ. FT.

TOTAL: 976 SQ. FT.

BEDROOMS: 2

BATHROOMS: 2

WIDTH: 22' - 8"

DEPTH: 26' - 8"

FOUNDATION: BASEMENT

SEARCH ONLINE @ EPLANS.COM

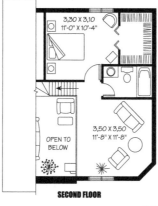

SECOND FLOOR

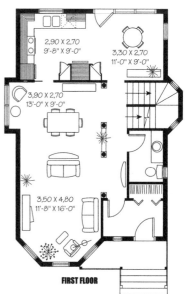

FIRST FLOOR

plan
HPT9600084

STYLE: VICTORIAN

FIRST FLOOR: 759 SQ. FT.

SECOND FLOOR: 735 SQ. FT.

TOTAL: 1,494 SQ. FT.

BEDROOMS: 3

BATHROOMS: 1½

WIDTH: 22' - 0"

DEPTH: 36' - 0"

FOUNDATION: BASEMENT

SEARCH ONLINE @ EPLANS.COM

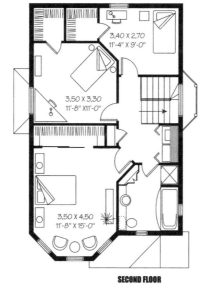

SECOND FLOOR

FIRST FLOOR

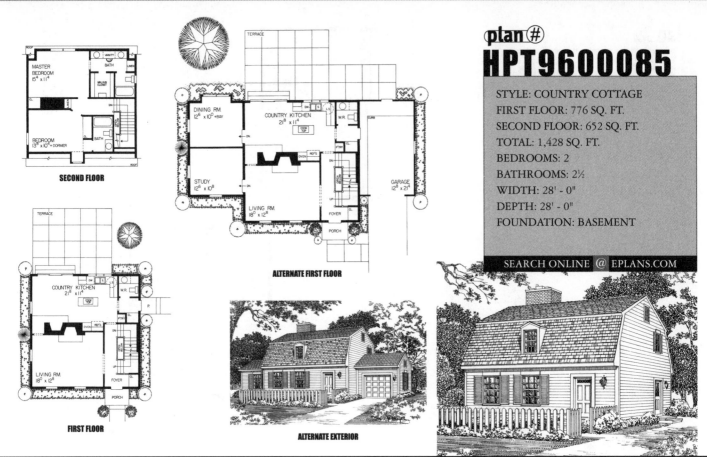

SECOND FLOOR

ALTERNATE FIRST FLOOR

FIRST FLOOR

ALTERNATE EXTERIOR

plan #
HPT9600085

STYLE: COUNTRY COTTAGE
FIRST FLOOR: 776 SQ. FT.
SECOND FLOOR: 652 SQ. FT.
TOTAL: 1,428 SQ. FT.
BEDROOMS: 2
BATHROOMS: 2½
WIDTH: 28' - 0"
DEPTH: 28' - 0"
FOUNDATION: BASEMENT

SEARCH ONLINE @ EPLANS.COM

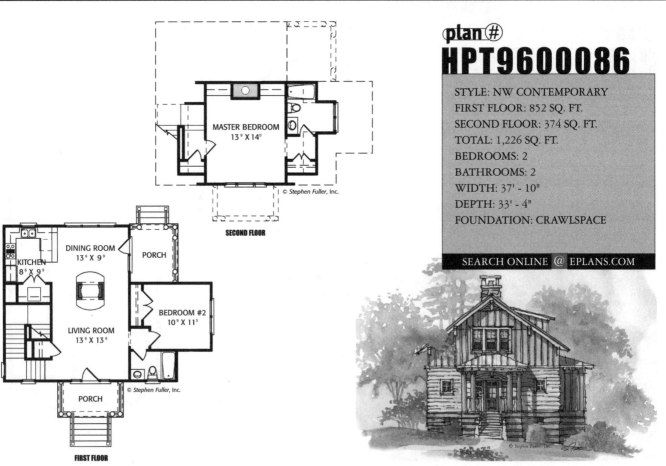

SECOND FLOOR

© Stephen Fuller, Inc.

FIRST FLOOR

© Stephen Fuller, Inc.

plan #
HPT9600086

STYLE: NW CONTEMPORARY
FIRST FLOOR: 852 SQ. FT.
SECOND FLOOR: 374 SQ. FT.
TOTAL: 1,226 SQ. FT.
BEDROOMS: 2
BATHROOMS: 2
WIDTH: 37' - 10"
DEPTH: 33' - 4"
FOUNDATION: CRAWLSPACE

SEARCH ONLINE @ EPLANS.COM

© 2001 Donald A. Gardner, Inc.

plan #

HPT9600087

STYLE: TRADITIONAL
SQUARE FOOTAGE: 1,929
BEDROOMS: 3
BATHROOMS: 2
WIDTH: 46' - 11"
DEPTH: 71' - 11"

SEARCH ONLINE @ EPLANS.COM

This traditional design features a hipped roof, multiple gables, and brick accents. Sidelights expand the front entrance and allow an abundance of natural light. The top of the front Palladian-style window visually reinforces the window above the door. Topped with a vaulted ceiling, the dining room displays a Palladian-style window that leads eyes up to the ceiling. The kitchen includes a counter that acts as a partition, separating the kitchen from the great room. The great room displays a striking fireplace, built-in shelves, and French doors that access the porch. The master suite exhibits a vaulted ceiling in the bedroom and an exquisitely designed bath with dual sinks, a large shower, and garden tub.

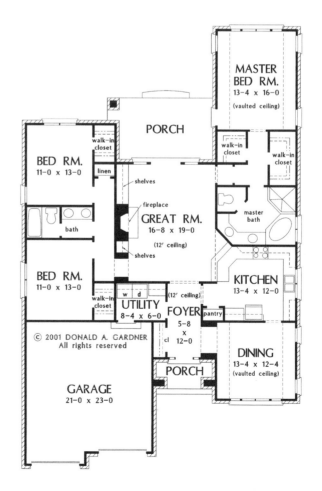

© 2001 DONALD A. GARDNER
All rights reserved

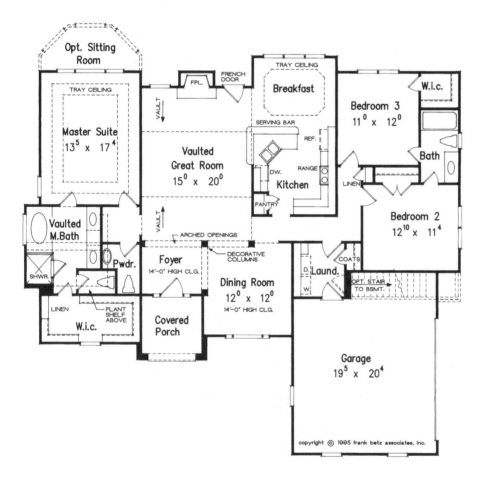

copyright © 1995 frank betz associates, inc.

plan #
HPT9600088

STYLE: TRADITIONAL
SQUARE FOOTAGE: 1,832
BONUS SPACE: 68 SQ. FT.
BEDROOMS: 3
BATHROOMS: 2½
WIDTH: 59' - 6"
DEPTH: 52' - 6"
FOUNDATION: BASEMENT,
CRAWLSPACE

SEARCH ONLINE @ EPLANS.COM

This compact one-story has plenty of living in it. The master suite features an optional sun-washed sitting area with views to the rear of the home. A vaulted great room with fireplace conveniently accesses the kitchen via a serving bar. Meals can also be taken in the cozy breakfast area. For formal occasions the dining room creates opulence with its decorative columns. Two family bedrooms flank the right of the home with a shared bath, linen storage, and easy access to laundry facilities.

plan
HPT9600089

STYLE: TRADITIONAL

FIRST FLOOR: 1,335 SQ. FT.

SECOND FLOOR: 515 SQ. FT.

TOTAL: 1,850 SQ. FT.

BONUS SPACE: 368 SQ. FT.

BEDROOMS: 3

BATHROOMS: 2½

WIDTH: 44' - 0"

DEPTH: 57' - 4"

FOUNDATION: CRAWLSPACE, BASEMENT

SEARCH ONLINE @ EPLANS.COM

This European design boasts a layout perfect for a narrow lot. A covered front porch welcomes you inside to a two-story foyer that leads to the vaulted great room. The kitchen with a pantry and serving bar easily serves the dining and breakfast rooms. The first-floor master suite is topped by a tray ceiling and includes a private bath with a walk-in closet. A laundry room leading to the two-car garage completes the first floor. Upstairs, two additional bedrooms are separated by a bridge overlook and share a hall bath. The optional bonus room is great for a home office, storage room, or guest suite.

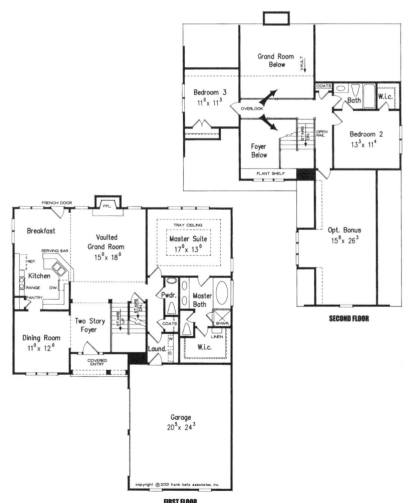

© 2000 Donald A. Gardner, Inc.

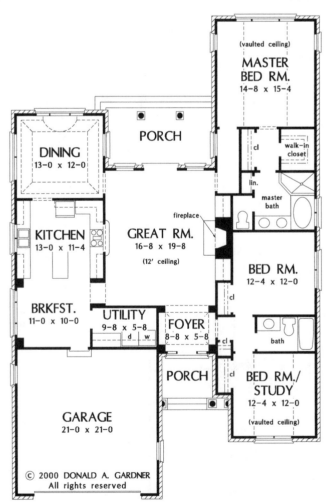

MASTER BED RM.
14-8 x 15-4
(vaulted ceiling)

PORCH

DINING
13-0 x 12-0

KITCHEN
13-0 x 11-4

GREAT RM.
16-8 x 19-8
(12' ceiling)

fireplace

walk-in closet

cl

lin.

master bath

BRKFST.
11-0 x 10-0

UTILITY
9-8 x 5-8
d w

FOYER
8-8 x 5-8

BED RM.
12-4 x 12-0

cl

bath

cl

PORCH

GARAGE
21-0 x 21-0

BED RM./ STUDY
12-4 x 12-0
(vaulted ceiling)

cl

© 2000 DONALD A. GARDNER
All rights reserved

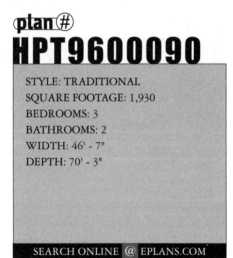

plan
HPT9600090

STYLE: TRADITIONAL
SQUARE FOOTAGE: 1,930
BEDROOMS: 3
BATHROOMS: 2
WIDTH: 46' - 7"
DEPTH: 70' - 3"

SEARCH ONLINE @ EPLANS.COM

Economical and builder-friendly, this graceful home incorporates a lot of space and amenities into its footage. Elegant tray ceilings accent the foyer and the dining room, and vaulted ceilings crown the study/bedroom and master bedroom. Adorning the great room is the fireplace embraced by built-ins, and across from the fireplace is the kitchen's handy pass-through. The spacious kitchen contains a convenient island counter and ample cabinets. The master bath is equipped with a garden tub, double vanity, shower, and compartmented toilet. Note the spacious utility room.

ORDER BLUEPRINTS 24 HOURS, 7 DAYS A WEEK, AT 1-800-521-6797

plan # HPT9600091

STYLE: FRENCH ECLECTIC

SQUARE FOOTAGE: 1,834

BEDROOMS: 3

BATHROOMS: 2

WIDTH: 55' - 0"

DEPTH: 60' - 4"

FOUNDATION: SLAB

SEARCH ONLINE @ EPLANS.COM

Corner quoins, French shutters, and rounded windows provide an Old World feel to this modern cottage design. A stunning brick facade hints at the exquisite beauty of the interior spaces. The great room is warmed by a fireplace and accesses the rear porch. The casual kitchen/dinette area provides pantry space. The master suite offers a private bath and enormous walk-in closet. Two family bedrooms on the opposite side of the home share a full hall bath and linen storage. A double garage and laundry room are located nearby.

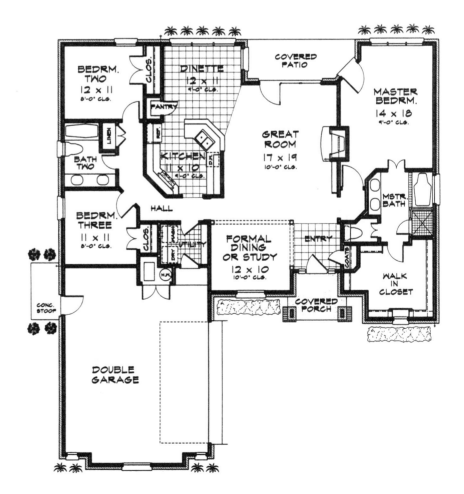

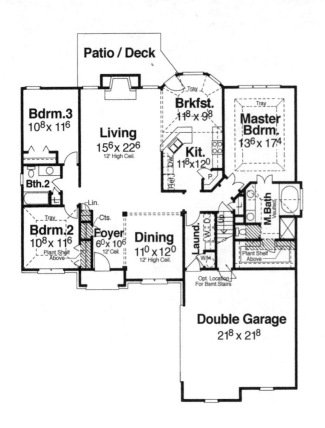

plan #
HPT9600092

STYLE: TRADITIONAL
SQUARE FOOTAGE: 1,869
BONUS SPACE: 336 SQ. FT.
BEDROOMS: 3
BATHROOMS: 2
WIDTH: 54' - 0"
DEPTH: 60' - 6"
FOUNDATION: BASEMENT,
CRAWLSPACE, SLAB

SEARCH ONLINE @ EPLANS.COM

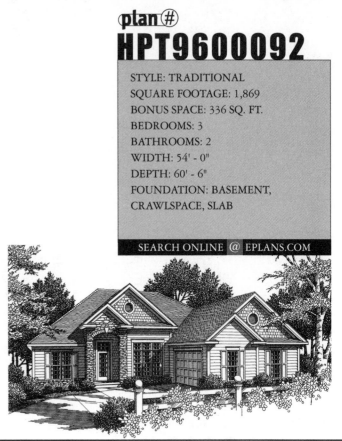

plan #
HPT9600093

STYLE: TRANSITIONAL
SQUARE FOOTAGE: 1,593
BEDROOMS: 3
BATHROOMS: 2
WIDTH: 60' - 0"
DEPTH: 48' - 10"

SEARCH ONLINE @ EPLANS.COM

plan # HPT9600094

STYLE: TRADITIONAL
SQUARE FOOTAGE: 1,966
BEDROOMS: 3
BATHROOMS: 2
WIDTH: 54' - 11"
DEPTH: 65' - 9"

SEARCH ONLINE @ EPLANS.COM

© 2000 Donald A. Gardner, Inc.

plan # HPT9600095

STYLE: TRADITIONAL
SQUARE FOOTAGE: 1,977
BONUS SPACE: 430 SQ. FT.
BEDROOMS: 3
BATHROOMS: 2
WIDTH: 69' - 8"
DEPTH: 59' - 6"

SEARCH ONLINE @ EPLANS.COM

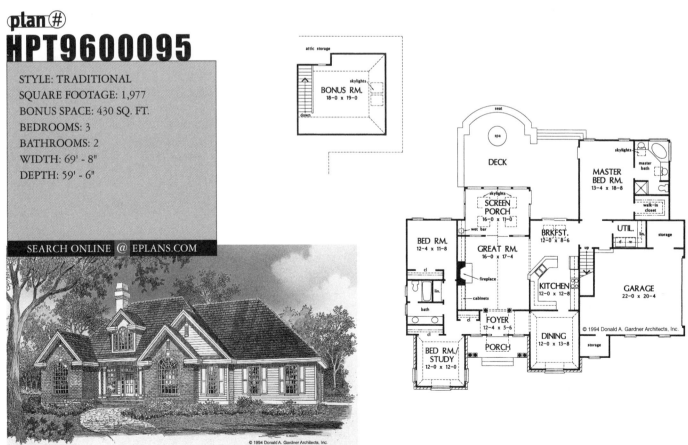

© 1994 Donald A. Gardner Architects, Inc.

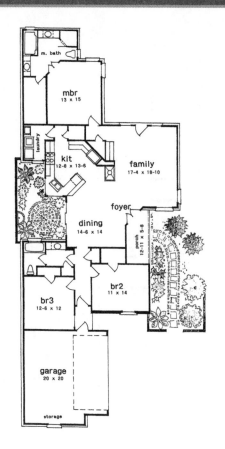

plan #

HPT9600096

STYLE: EUROPEAN COTTAGE
SQUARE FOOTAGE: 1,823
BEDROOMS: 3
BATHROOMS: 2
WIDTH: 38' - 10"
DEPTH: 94' - 10"
FOUNDATION: SLAB

SEARCH ONLINE @ EPLANS.COM

plan #

HPT9600097

STYLE: TIDEWATER
FIRST FLOOR: 1,342 SQ. FT.
SECOND FLOOR: 511 SQ. FT.
TOTAL: 1,853 SQ. FT.
BEDROOMS: 3
BATHROOMS: 2
WIDTH: 44' - 0"
DEPTH: 40' - 0"
FOUNDATION: BASEMENT

SEARCH ONLINE @ EPLANS.COM

plan #
HPT9600098

STYLE: COUNTRY COTTAGE
FIRST FLOOR: 1,050 SQ. FT.
SECOND FLOOR: 458 SQ. FT.
TOTAL: 1,508 SQ. FT.
BEDROOMS: 3
BATHROOMS: 2½
WIDTH: 35' - 6"
DEPTH: 39' - 9"
FOUNDATION: PIER

SEARCH ONLINE @ EPLANS.COM

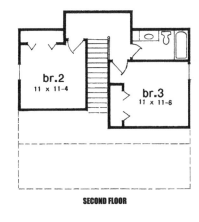

SECOND FLOOR

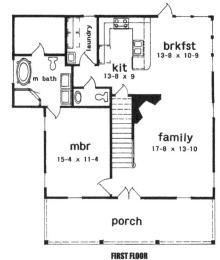

FIRST FLOOR

plan #
HPT9600099

STYLE: FRENCH COLONIAL
SQUARE FOOTAGE: 1,800
BEDROOMS: 3
BATHROOMS: 2
WIDTH: 66' - 0"
DEPTH: 60' - 0"
FOUNDATION: CRAWLSPACE, SLAB

SEARCH ONLINE @ EPLANS.COM

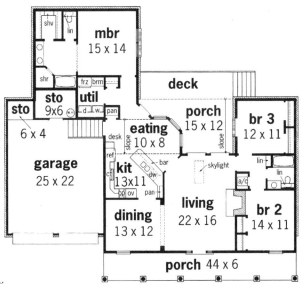

DECK

GREAT RM.
17-0 x 18-0

fireplace

shelves

BRKFST.
11-0 x 8-0

KIT.
11-0 x 10-0

MASTER
BED RM.
13-8 x 15-0

walk-in closet

lin.

master bath

UTIL.
5-8 x 6-4
d w

BED RM./
STUDY
11-0 x 12-0

bath

FOYER
5-8 x 14-4

DINING
11-0 x 13-0

GARAGE
21-0 x 21-0

BED RM.
11-0 x 12-0

PORCH

cl

cl

cl

cl

© 2000 DONALD A. GARDNER
All rights reserved

plan#
HPT9600100

STYLE: MEDITERRANEAN
SQUARE FOOTAGE: 1,707
BEDROOMS: 3
BATHROOMS: 2
WIDTH: 56' - 6"
DEPTH: 45' - 8"

SEARCH ONLINE @ EPLANS.COM

© 2000 Donald A. Gardner, Inc.

plan#
HPT9600101

STYLE: MEDITERRANEAN
SQUARE FOOTAGE: 1,834
BEDROOMS: 4
BATHROOMS: 2
WIDTH: 40' - 0"
DEPTH: 60' - 0"
FOUNDATION: SLAB

SEARCH ONLINE @ EPLANS.COM

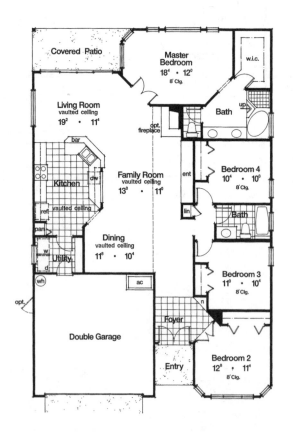

Covered Patio

Master
Bedroom
18⁴ • 12⁰
8'Clg.

w.i.c.

Living Room
vaulted ceiling
19² • 11⁴

bar

Bath

up

opt.
fireplace

Kitchen

dw

vaulted ceiling

refr

Family Room
vaulted ceiling
13⁰ • 11⁰

ent

Bedroom 4
10⁴ • 10⁰
8'Clg.

lin.

pan.

Bath

Dining
vaulted ceiling
11⁶ • 10⁴

w
d

Utility

Bedroom 3
11⁰ • 10⁴
8'Clg.

wh

ac

opt.

Double Garage

Foyer

Entry

Bedroom 2
12⁸ • 11⁴
8'Clg.

ORDER BLUEPRINTS 24 HOURS, 7 DAYS A WEEK, AT 1-800-521-6797

plan#
HPT9600102

STYLE: NW CONTEMPORARY
FIRST FLOOR: 1,375 SQ. FT.
SECOND FLOOR: 284 SQ. FT.
TOTAL: 1,659 SQ. FT.
BEDROOMS: 3
BATHROOMS: 2
WIDTH: 58' - 0"
DEPTH: 32' - 0"
FOUNDATION: CRAWLSPACE,
BASEMENT

SEARCH ONLINE @ EPLANS.COM

An expansive window wall across the great room of this home adds a spectacular view and accentuates the high ceiling. The open kitchen shares an eating bar with the dining room and features a convenient "U" shape. Sliding glass doors in the dining room lead to the deck. Two family bedrooms sit to the back of the plan and share the use of a full bath. The master suite provides a walk-in closet and private bath. The loft on the upper level adds living or sleeping space.

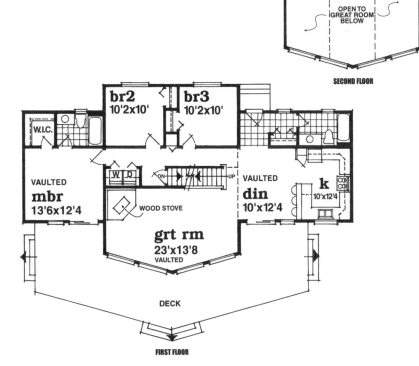

plan#

HPT9600103

STYLE: COLONIAL REVIVAL
SQUARE FOOTAGE: 1,600
BEDROOMS: 3
BATHROOMS: 2
WIDTH: 75' - 0"
DEPTH: 37' - 0"
FOUNDATION: BASEMENT,
CRAWLSPACE, SLAB

SEARCH ONLINE @ EPLANS.COM

plan#

HPT9600104

STYLE: COLONIAL REVIVAL
SQUARE FOOTAGE: 1,864
BONUS SPACE: 420 SQ. FT.
BEDROOMS: 3
BATHROOMS: 2½
WIDTH: 71' - 0"
DEPTH: 56' - 4"

SEARCH ONLINE @ EPLANS.COM

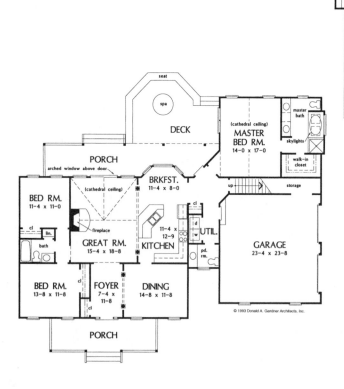

© 1993 Donald A. Gardner Architects, Inc.

ORDER BLUEPRINTS 24 HOURS, 7 DAYS A WEEK, AT 1-800-521-6797

plan
HPT9600105

STYLE: TRADITIONAL
SQUARE FOOTAGE: 1,791
BEDROOMS: 4
BATHROOMS: 2
WIDTH: 67' - 4"
DEPTH: 48' - 0"
FOUNDATION: BASEMENT

SEARCH ONLINE @ EPLANS.COM

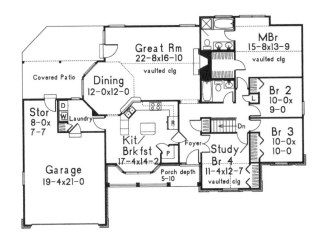

plan
HPT9600106

STYLE: COUNTRY COTTAGE
SQUARE FOOTAGE: 1,903
BEDROOMS: 4
BATHROOMS: 2
WIDTH: 65' - 8"
DEPTH: 55' - 7"

SEARCH ONLINE @ EPLANS.COM

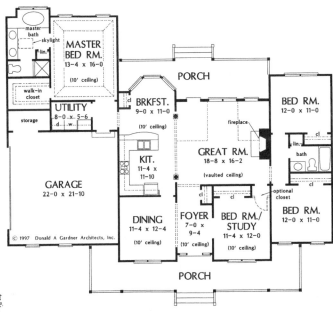

plan #
HPT9600107

STYLE: COLONIAL REVIVAL
SQUARE FOOTAGE: 1,989
BONUS SPACE: 274 SQ. FT.
BEDROOMS: 3
BATHROOMS: 2
WIDTH: 81' - 0"
DEPTH: 50' - 0"
FOUNDATION: CRAWLSPACE

SEARCH ONLINE @ EPLANS.COM

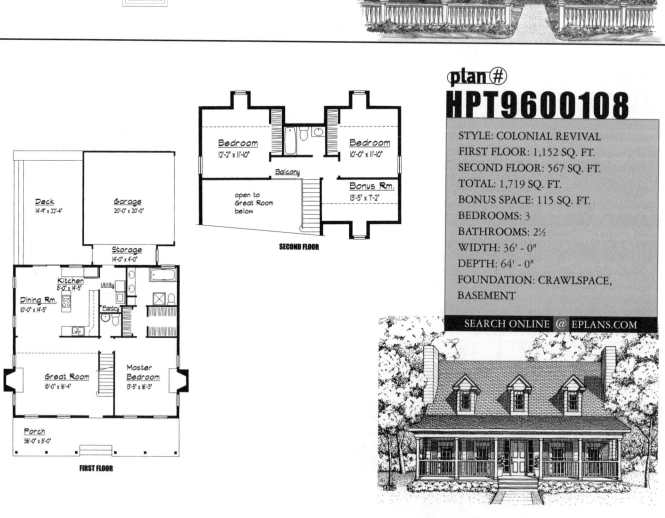

plan #
HPT9600108

STYLE: COLONIAL REVIVAL
FIRST FLOOR: 1,152 SQ. FT.
SECOND FLOOR: 567 SQ. FT.
TOTAL: 1,719 SQ. FT.
BONUS SPACE: 115 SQ. FT.
BEDROOMS: 3
BATHROOMS: 2½
WIDTH: 36' - 0"
DEPTH: 64' - 0"
FOUNDATION: CRAWLSPACE, BASEMENT

SEARCH ONLINE @ EPLANS.COM

plan
HPT9600109

STYLE: SOUTHERN COLONIAL

SQUARE FOOTAGE: 1,692

BONUS SPACE: 358 SQ. FT.

BEDROOMS: 3

BATHROOMS: 2

WIDTH: 54' - 0"

DEPTH: 56' - 6"

FOUNDATION: CRAWLSPACE, BASEMENT

SEARCH ONLINE @ EPLANS.COM

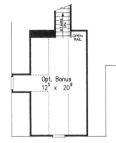

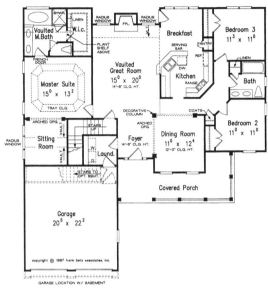

plan
HPT9600110

STYLE: COLONIAL REVIVAL

SQUARE FOOTAGE: 1,899

BONUS SPACE: 315 SQ. FT.

BEDROOMS: 3

BATHROOMS: 2

WIDTH: 58' - 8"

DEPTH: 66' - 10"

SEARCH ONLINE @ EPLANS.COM

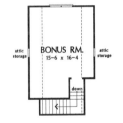

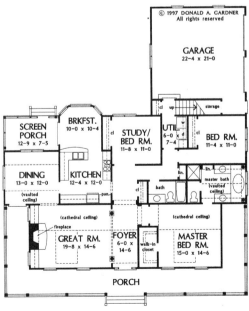

© 1997 Donald A. Gardner Architects, Inc.

© 1999 DONALD A. GARDNER
All rights reserved

plan # HPT9600111

STYLE: COUNTRY
SQUARE FOOTAGE: 1,882
BONUS SPACE: 363 SQ. FT.
BEDROOMS: 3
BATHROOMS: 2½
WIDTH: 61' - 4"
DEPTH: 55' - 0"

SEARCH ONLINE @ EPLANS.COM

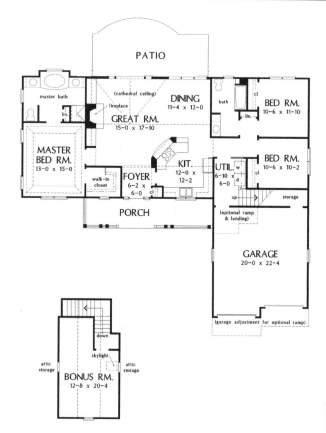

plan # HPT9600112

STYLE: TRADITIONAL
SQUARE FOOTAGE: 1,601
BONUS SPACE: 237 SQ. FT.
BEDROOMS: 3
BATHROOMS: 2
WIDTH: 61' - 4"
DEPTH: 50' - 6"

SEARCH ONLINE @ EPLANS.COM

ORDER BLUEPRINTS 24 HOURS, 7 DAYS A WEEK, AT 1-800-521-6797

plan #
HPT9600113

STYLE: STICK VICTORIAN
SQUARE FOOTAGE: 1,762
BONUS SPACE: 316 SQ. FT.
BEDROOMS: 3
BATHROOMS: 2
WIDTH: 56' - 8"
DEPTH: 59' - 0"

SEARCH ONLINE @ EPLANS.COM

© 1998 Donald A Gardner, Inc.

© 1998 Donald A. Gardner, Inc.

plan #
HPT9600114

STYLE: TRADITIONAL
SQUARE FOOTAGE: 1,671
BONUS SPACE: 348 SQ. FT.
BEDROOMS: 3
BATHROOMS: 2
WIDTH: 50' - 8"
DEPTH: 52' - 4"

SEARCH ONLINE @ EPLANS.COM

© 1999 DAG
All rights reserved

© 1999 Donald A. Gardner, Inc.

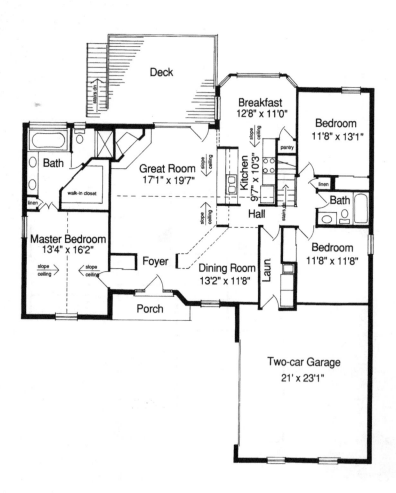

plan #
HPT9600115

STYLE: TRADITIONAL
SQUARE FOOTAGE: 1,756
BEDROOMS: 3
BATHROOMS: 2
WIDTH: 57' - 0"
DEPTH: 58' - 8"
FOUNDATION: BASEMENT

SEARCH ONLINE @ EPLANS.COM

A brick exterior and circle-top windows give this home a rich, solid look. The formal dining room is visually open to the great room, creating a combination of rooms that feel and look extra large and spacious. Located a few steps away is the well-equipped kitchen featuring a counter/bar that serves the great room. The breakfast bay is surrounded by windows and enables the family to enjoy the outdoors in any weather. Access to the deck through the great room easily expands the entertainment area to the rear yard. The master suite, with its sloped ceiling and ultralavish bath, offers the size and luxurious amenities found in today's fashionable homes.

plan # HPT9600116

STYLE: STICK VICTORIAN
SQUARE FOOTAGE: 1,792
BONUS SPACE: 338 SQ. FT.
BEDROOMS: 3
BATHROOMS: 3
WIDTH: 66' - 4"
DEPTH: 62' - 4"

SEARCH ONLINE @ EPLANS.COM

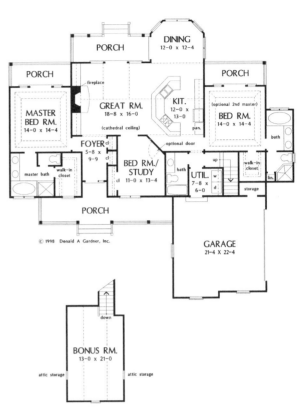

© 1998 Donald A Gardner, Inc.

© 1998 Donald A Gardner, Inc.

plan # HPT9600117

STYLE: TRADITIONAL
SQUARE FOOTAGE: 1,842
BONUS SPACE: 386 SQ. FT.
BEDROOMS: 3
BATHROOMS: 2
WIDTH: 54' - 0"
DEPTH: 63' - 0"

SEARCH ONLINE @ EPLANS.COM

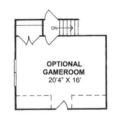

OPTIONAL GAMEROOM
20'4" X 16'

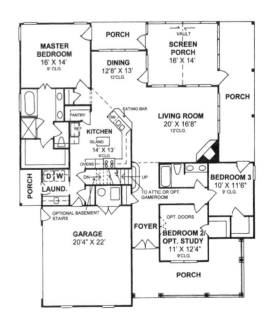

plan#

HPT9600118

STYLE: TRADITIONAL

SQUARE FOOTAGE: 1,537

BEDROOMS: 3

BATHROOMS: 2

WIDTH: 52' - 0"

DEPTH: 50' - 0"

FOUNDATION: BASEMENT

SEARCH ONLINE @ EPLANS.COM

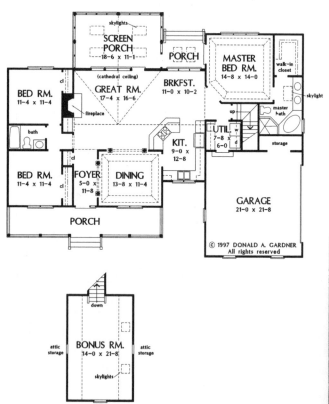

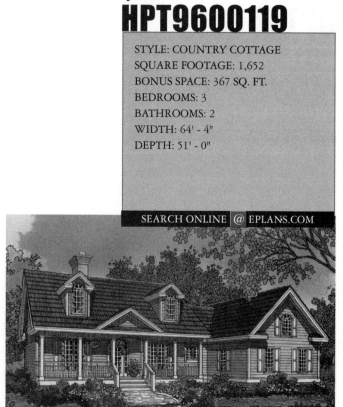

plan#

HPT9600119

STYLE: COUNTRY COTTAGE

SQUARE FOOTAGE: 1,652

BONUS SPACE: 367 SQ. FT.

BEDROOMS: 3

BATHROOMS: 2

WIDTH: 64' - 4"

DEPTH: 51' - 0"

SEARCH ONLINE @ EPLANS.COM

ORDER BLUEPRINTS 24 HOURS, 7 DAYS A WEEK, AT 1-800-521-6797

plan
HPT9600120

STYLE: SOUTHERN COLONIAL
FIRST FLOOR: 1,100 SQ. FT.
SECOND FLOOR: 584 SQ. FT.
TOTAL: 1,684 SQ. FT.
BEDROOMS: 3
BATHROOMS: 2
WIDTH: 36' - 8"
DEPTH: 45' - 0"

SEARCH ONLINE @ EPLANS.COM

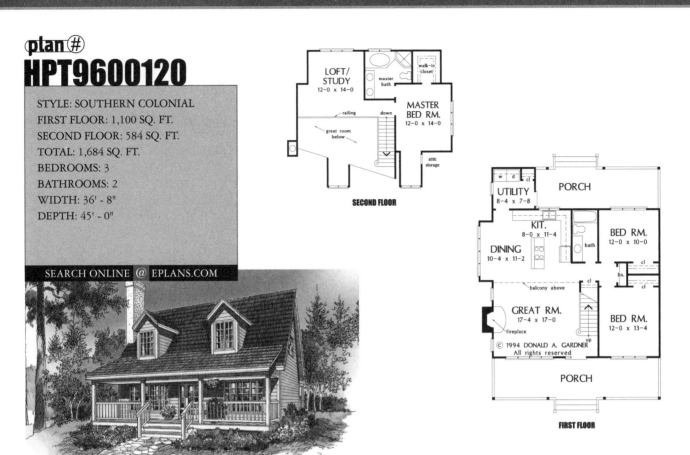

plan
HPT9600121

STYLE: NW CONTEMPORARY
SQUARE FOOTAGE: 1,680
BEDROOMS: 3
BATHROOMS: 2
WIDTH: 62' - 8"
DEPTH: 59' - 10"

SEARCH ONLINE @ EPLANS.COM

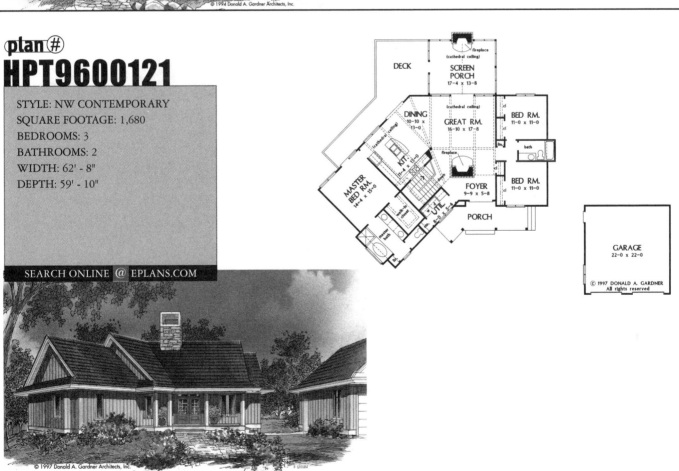

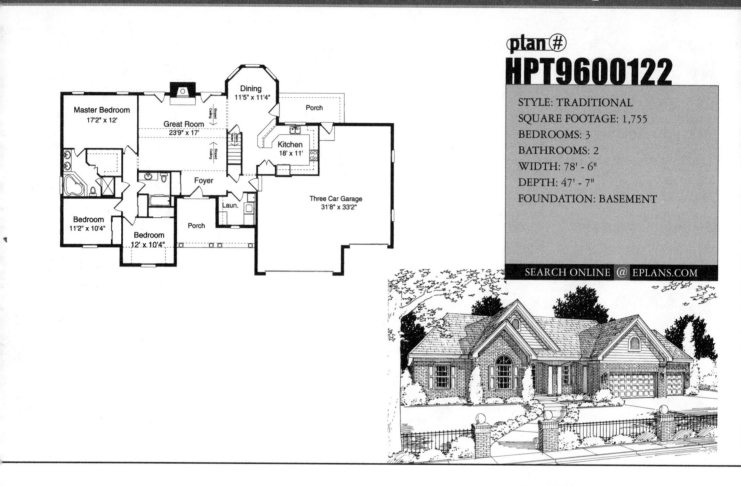

plan
HPT9600122

STYLE: TRADITIONAL
SQUARE FOOTAGE: 1,755
BEDROOMS: 3
BATHROOMS: 2
WIDTH: 78' - 6"
DEPTH: 47' - 7"
FOUNDATION: BASEMENT

SEARCH ONLINE @ EPLANS.COM

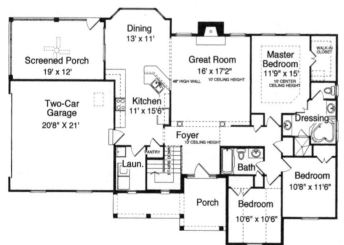

plan
HPT9600123

STYLE: COUNTRY
SQUARE FOOTAGE: 1,611
BEDROOMS: 3
BATHROOMS: 2
WIDTH: 66' - 4"
DEPTH: 43' - 10"
FOUNDATION: BASEMENT

SEARCH ONLINE @ EPLANS.COM

ORDER BLUEPRINTS 24 HOURS, 7 DAYS A WEEK, AT 1-800-521-6797

plan
HPT9600124

STYLE: TRADITIONAL

SQUARE FOOTAGE: 1,606

BEDROOMS: 3

BATHROOMS: 2

WIDTH: 62' - 11"

DEPTH: 52' - 0"

FOUNDATION: BASEMENT, CRAWLSPACE, SLAB

SEARCH ONLINE @ EPLANS.COM

This ranch home enjoys a large covered front porch and a covered porch/patio in the rear, ready for the weekend barbecue. The great room sets the stage with a fireplace flanked by windows. The breakfast nook is illuminated by natural lighting via two skylights. The adjoining kitchen is generous with its allowance of counter space. A split-bedroom plan places the master suite on the far right for privacy, with two family bedrooms sharing a full bath on the far left.

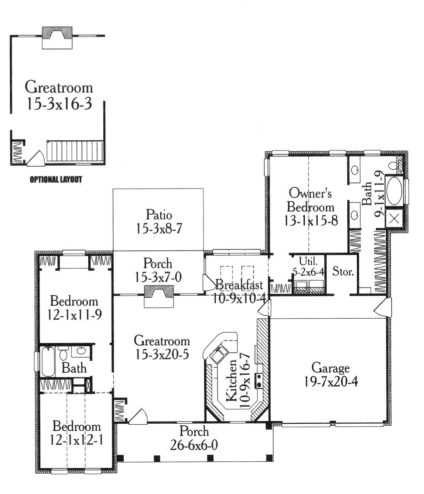

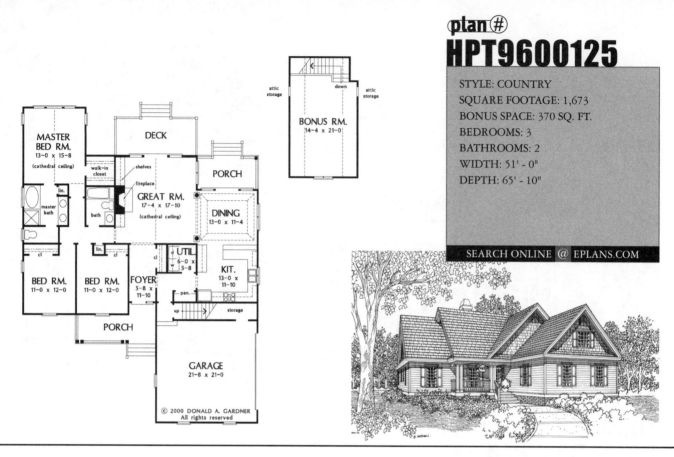

plan#

HPT9600125

STYLE: COUNTRY
SQUARE FOOTAGE: 1,673
BONUS SPACE: 370 SQ. FT.
BEDROOMS: 3
BATHROOMS: 2
WIDTH: 51' - 0"
DEPTH: 65' - 10"

SEARCH ONLINE @ EPLANS.COM

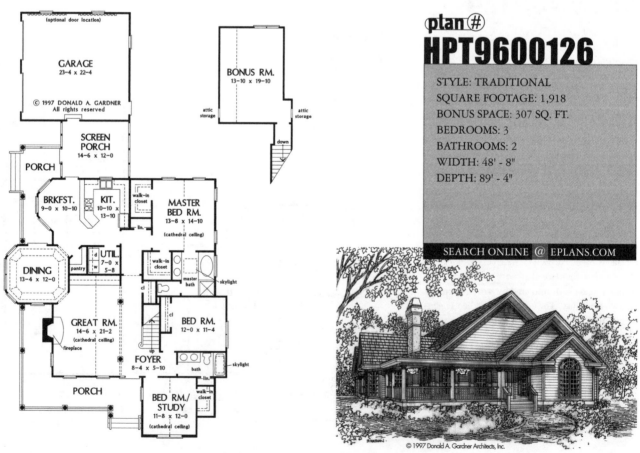

plan#

HPT9600126

STYLE: TRADITIONAL
SQUARE FOOTAGE: 1,918
BONUS SPACE: 307 SQ. FT.
BEDROOMS: 3
BATHROOMS: 2
WIDTH: 48' - 8"
DEPTH: 89' - 4"

SEARCH ONLINE @ EPLANS.COM

ORDER BLUEPRINTS 24 HOURS, 7 DAYS A WEEK, AT 1-800-521-6797

plan # HPT9600127

STYLE: TRADITIONAL
SQUARE FOOTAGE: 1,821
BONUS SPACE: 409 SQ. FT.
BEDROOMS: 3
BATHROOMS: 2
WIDTH: 54' - 4"
DEPTH: 61' - 6"

SEARCH ONLINE @ EPLANS.COM

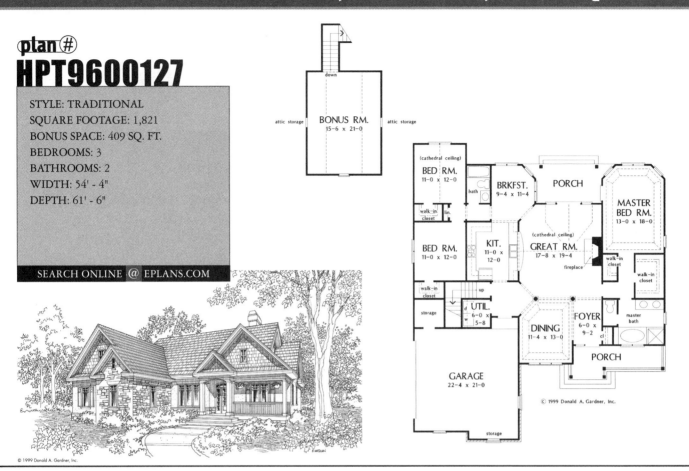

© 1999 Donald A. Gardner, Inc.

plan # HPT9600128

STYLE: COUNTRY COTTAGE
MAIN LEVEL: 1,230 SQ. FT.
LOWER LEVEL: 769 SQ. FT.
TOTAL: 1,999 SQ. FT.
BEDROOMS: 3
BATHROOMS: 2½
WIDTH: 40' - 0"
DEPTH: 52' - 6"
FOUNDATION: BASEMENT

SEARCH ONLINE @ EPLANS.COM

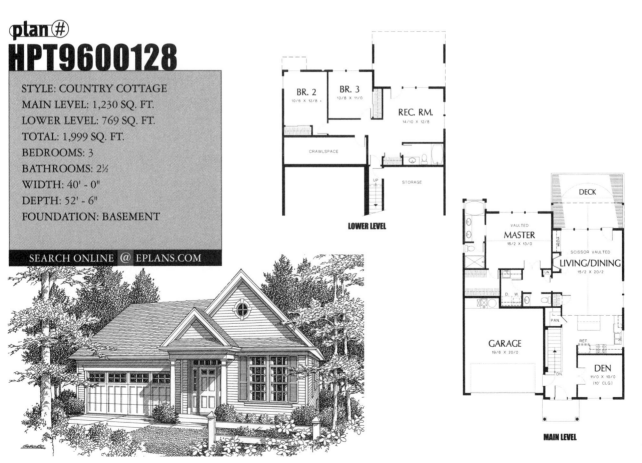

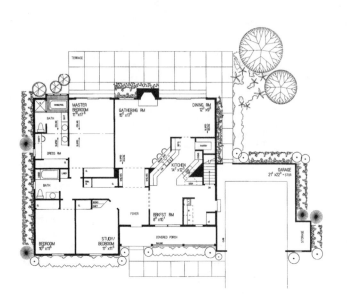

plan#
HPT9600129

STYLE: TRADITIONAL
SQUARE FOOTAGE: 1,830
BEDROOMS: 3
BATHROOMS: 2
WIDTH: 75' - 0"
DEPTH: 43' - 5"
FOUNDATION: BASEMENT

SEARCH ONLINE @ EPLANS.COM

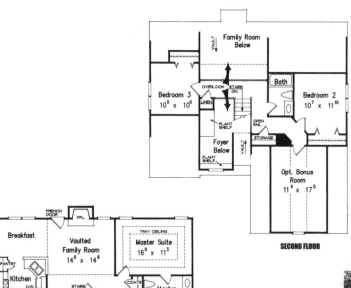

plan#
HPT9600130

STYLE: COUNTRY COTTAGE
FIRST FLOOR: 1,067 SQ. FT.
SECOND FLOOR: 464 SQ. FT.
TOTAL: 1,531 SQ. FT.
BONUS SPACE: 207 SQ. FT.
BEDROOMS: 3
BATHROOMS: 2½
WIDTH: 41' - 0"
DEPTH: 44' - 4"
FOUNDATION: CRAWLSPACE,
BASEMENT, SLAB

SEARCH ONLINE @ EPLANS.COM

plan
HPT9600131

STYLE: COUNTRY COTTAGE
FIRST FLOOR: 1,219 SQ. FT.
SECOND FLOOR: 450 SQ. FT.
TOTAL: 1,669 SQ. FT.
BONUS SPACE: 406 SQ. FT.
BEDROOMS: 3
BATHROOMS: 2½
WIDTH: 50' - 4"
DEPTH: 49' - 2"

SEARCH ONLINE @ EPLANS.COM

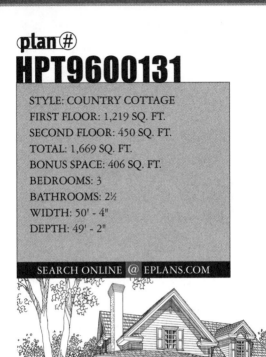

© 1997 Donald A Gardner Architects, Inc.

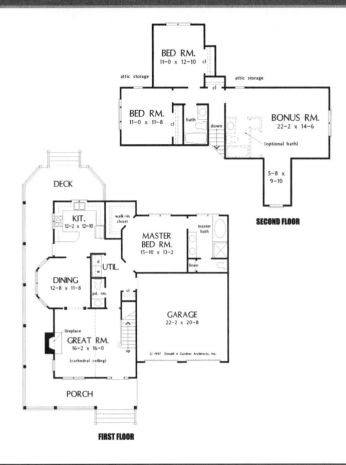

SECOND FLOOR

FIRST FLOOR

plan
HPT9600132

STYLE: TRADITIONAL
SQUARE FOOTAGE: 1,501
BEDROOMS: 3
BATHROOMS: 2
WIDTH: 48' - 0"
DEPTH: 57' - 4"
FOUNDATION: CRAWLSPACE, SLAB, BASEMENT

SEARCH ONLINE @ EPLANS.COM

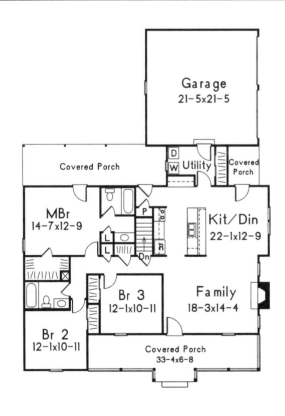

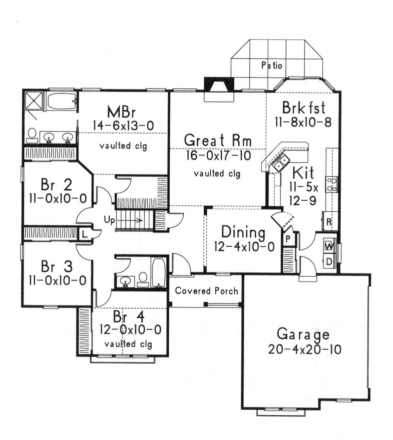

plan #
HPT9600133

STYLE: TRADITIONAL
SQUARE FOOTAGE: 1,761
BEDROOMS: 4
BATHROOMS: 2
WIDTH: 57' - 0"
DEPTH: 52' - 2"
FOUNDATION: BASEMENT

SEARCH ONLINE @ EPLANS.COM

Residing peacefully in a serene mountain setting, this small family home brings quaint style to an efficient floor plan. The covered porch leads inside to formal vistas from the dining and great rooms. Warmed by a cozy fireplace, the vaulted great room connects to the kitchen/breakfast area, opening onto a rear patio. The master bedroom is vaulted and includes a walk-in closet and private bath. Three additional family bedrooms share a full hall bath. A two-car garage completes this charming plan.

plan
HPT9600134

STYLE: TRADITIONAL
SQUARE FOOTAGE: 1,721
BEDROOMS: 3
BATHROOMS: 2
WIDTH: 83' - 0"
DEPTH: 42' - 0"
FOUNDATION: BASEMENT

SEARCH ONLINE @ EPLANS.COM

This home offers a beautifully textured facade. Keystones and lintels highlight the beauty of the windows. The vaulted great room and dining room are immersed in light from the atrium window wall. The breakfast room opens to the covered porch in the backyard. The bedrooms share the right side of the plan, each with a large window of its own.

plan#
HPT9600135

STYLE: TRADITIONAL
FIRST FLOOR: 1,074 SQ. FT.
SECOND FLOOR: 901 SQ. FT.
TOTAL: 1,975 SQ. FT.
BEDROOMS: 3
BATHROOMS: 2½
WIDTH: 50' - 0"
DEPTH: 39' - 0"
FOUNDATION: CRAWLSPACE

SEARCH ONLINE @ EPLANS.COM

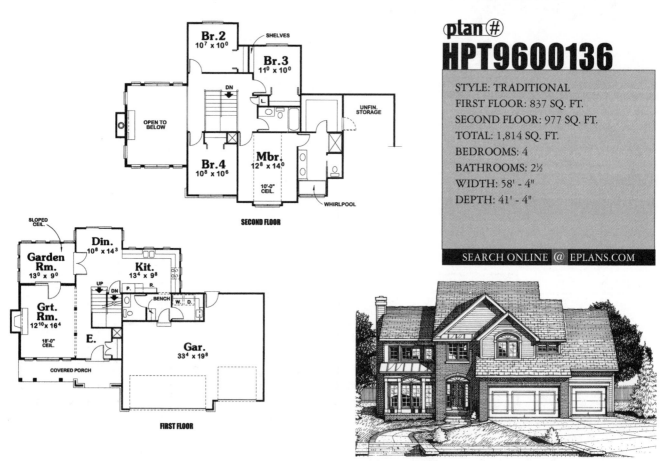

plan#
HPT9600136

STYLE: TRADITIONAL
FIRST FLOOR: 837 SQ. FT.
SECOND FLOOR: 977 SQ. FT.
TOTAL: 1,814 SQ. FT.
BEDROOMS: 4
BATHROOMS: 2½
WIDTH: 58' - 4"
DEPTH: 41' - 4"

SEARCH ONLINE @ EPLANS.COM

plan # HPT9600137

STYLE: SEASIDE
FIRST FLOOR: 871 SQ. FT.
SECOND FLOOR: 1,047 SQ. FT.
TOTAL: 1,918 SQ. FT.
BEDROOMS: 3
BATHROOMS: 2½
WIDTH: 32' - 0"
DEPTH: 47' - 0"
FOUNDATION: CRAWLSPACE

SEARCH ONLINE @ EPLANS.COM

plan # HPT9600138

STYLE: GREEK REVIVAL
FIRST FLOOR: 1,044 SQ. FT.
SECOND FLOOR: 719 SQ. FT.
TOTAL: 1,763 SQ. FT.
BONUS SPACE: 206 SQ. FT.
BEDROOMS: 3
BATHROOMS: 2½
WIDTH: 45' - 0"
DEPTH: 63' - 2"

SEARCH ONLINE @ EPLANS.COM

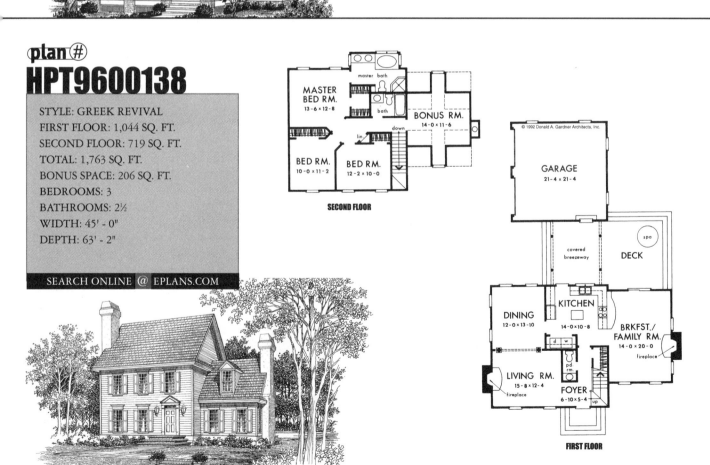

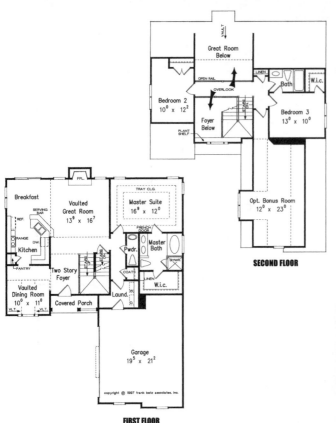

SECOND FLOOR

FIRST FLOOR

copyright © 1997 frank betz associates, inc.

plan#
HPT9600139

STYLE: TRADITIONAL
FIRST FLOOR: 1,179 SQ. FT.
SECOND FLOOR: 460 SQ. FT.
TOTAL: 1,639 SQ. FT.
BONUS SPACE: 338 SQ. FT.
BEDROOMS: 3
BATHROOMS: 2½
WIDTH: 41' - 6"
DEPTH: 54' - 4"
FOUNDATION: CRAWLSPACE,
BASEMENT, SLAB

SEARCH ONLINE @ EPLANS.COM

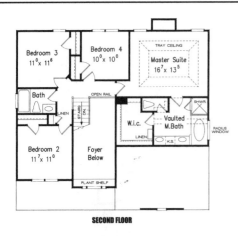

SECOND FLOOR

OPTIONAL LAYOUT

FIRST FLOOR

copyright © 2002 frank betz associates, inc.

plan#
HPT9600140

STYLE: TRADITIONAL
FIRST FLOOR: 947 SQ. FT.
SECOND FLOOR: 981 SQ. FT.
TOTAL: 1,928 SQ. FT.
BEDROOMS: 4
BATHROOMS: 2½
WIDTH: 41' - 0"
DEPTH: 39' - 4"
FOUNDATION: CRAWLSPACE,
BASEMENT

SEARCH ONLINE @ EPLANS.COM

ORDER BLUEPRINTS 24 HOURS, 7 DAYS A WEEK, AT 1-800-521-6797

plan # HPT9600141

STYLE: SOUTHERN COLONIAL
FIRST FLOOR: 1,071 SQ. FT.
SECOND FLOOR: 924 SQ. FT.
TOTAL: 1,995 SQ. FT.
BONUS SPACE: 280 SQ. FT.
BEDROOMS: 3
BATHROOMS: 2½
WIDTH: 55' - 10"
DEPTH: 38' - 6"
FOUNDATION: CRAWLSPACE, BASEMENT

SEARCH ONLINE @ EPLANS.COM

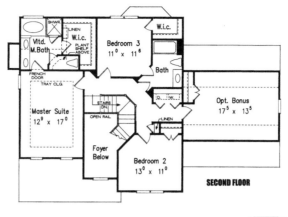

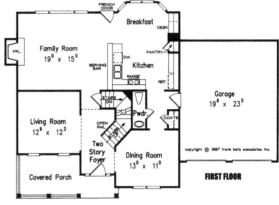

plan # HPT9600142

DESIGN: HPT9600142
STYLE: COUNTRY
FIRST FLOOR: 1,412 SQ. FT.
SECOND FLOOR: 506 SQ. FT.
TOTAL: 1,918 SQ. FT.
BONUS SPACE: 320 SQ. FT.
BEDROOMS: 3
BATHROOMS: 2½
WIDTH: 49' - 8"
DEPTH: 52' - 0"

SEARCH ONLINE @ EPLANS.COM

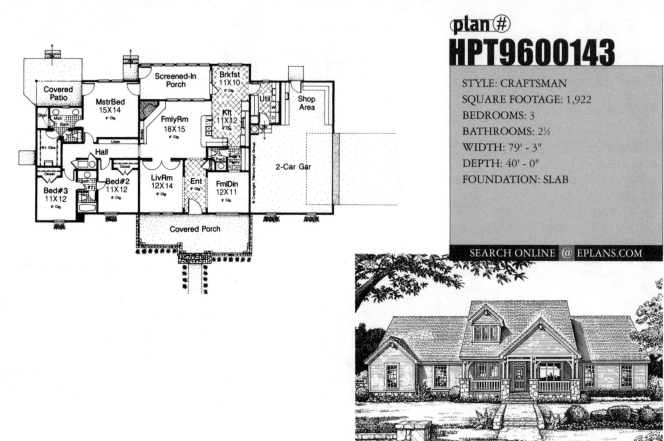

plan #
HPT9600143

STYLE: CRAFTSMAN
SQUARE FOOTAGE: 1,922
BEDROOMS: 3
BATHROOMS: 2½
WIDTH: 79' - 3"
DEPTH: 40' - 0"
FOUNDATION: SLAB

SEARCH ONLINE @ EPLANS.COM

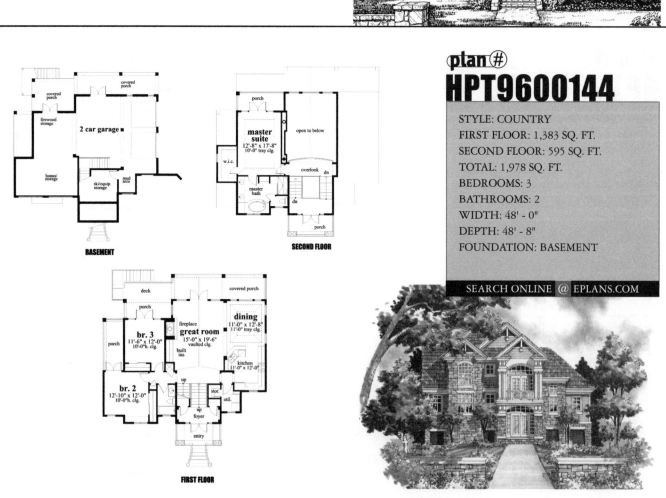

plan #
HPT9600144

STYLE: COUNTRY
FIRST FLOOR: 1,383 SQ. FT.
SECOND FLOOR: 595 SQ. FT.
TOTAL: 1,978 SQ. FT.
BEDROOMS: 3
BATHROOMS: 2
WIDTH: 48' - 0"
DEPTH: 48' - 8"
FOUNDATION: BASEMENT

SEARCH ONLINE @ EPLANS.COM

© 1998 Donald A. Gardner, Inc.

B. NATHAN

plan
HPT9600145

STYLE: TRANSITIONAL

FIRST FLOOR: 1,701 SQ. FT.

SECOND FLOOR: 534 SQ. FT.

TOTAL: 2,235 SQ. FT.

BONUS SPACE: 274 SQ. FT.

BEDROOMS: 3

BATHROOMS: 2½

WIDTH: 65' - 11"

DEPTH: 43' - 5"

SEARCH ONLINE @ EPLANS.COM

Columns, gables, multipane windows, and a stone-and-stucco exterior give this home its handsome appearance. The interior amenities are just as impressive. The formal rooms are to the right and left of the foyer with a powder room and coat closet down the hall. The family room, with a cathedral ceiling, fireplace, built-ins, and access to the rear patio, is open to the breakfast room through a pair of decorative columns. On the opposite side of the plan, the master suite offers two walk-in closets and a compartmented bath. Two family bedrooms on the second floor share a bath and a loft that overlooks the family room.

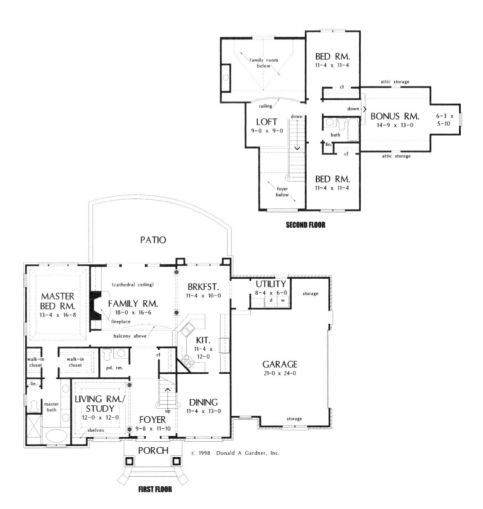

© 1998 Donald A. Gardner Architects, Inc.

© 1998 Donald A Gardner Architects, Inc.

plan #
HPT9600146

STYLE: FRENCH ECLECTIC
SQUARE FOOTAGE: 2,250
BEDROOMS: 3
BATHROOMS: 2½
WIDTH: 84' - 10"
DEPTH: 62' - 4"

SEARCH ONLINE @ EPLANS.COM

Stone and stucco accent the exterior of this dignified French Country home. A lovely courtyard precedes a grand French-door entry with an arched transom. The foyer, great room, and dining room feature stately 11-foot ceilings, and interior columns mark boundaries for the great room and dining room. The spacious kitchen features a pass-through to the great room, where built-in shelves flank the fireplace. Cozy side patios and a back porch add to this home's appeal. The master suite is magnificent with a double-door entry, an elegant tray ceiling, dual walk-in closets, and an extravagant bath.

© 2001 Donald A. Gardner, Inc.

plan
HPT9600147

STYLE: COLONIAL REVIVAL
SQUARE FOOTAGE: 2,461
BONUS SPACE: 397 SQ. FT.
BEDROOMS: 4
BATHROOMS: 2
WIDTH: 71' - 2"
DEPTH: 67' - 2"

SEARCH ONLINE @ EPLANS.COM

Turret-style bay windows, an arched entryway, and an elegant balustrade add timeless appeal to a remarkable facade, yet this refined exterior encompasses a very practical layout. Separated from the kitchen by an angled island, the great room features built-in shelves on both sides of the fireplace as well as French doors leading to the rear porch with a wet bar. Custom-style details include tray ceilings in the dining room and study/bedroom as well as columns in the foyer and master bath.

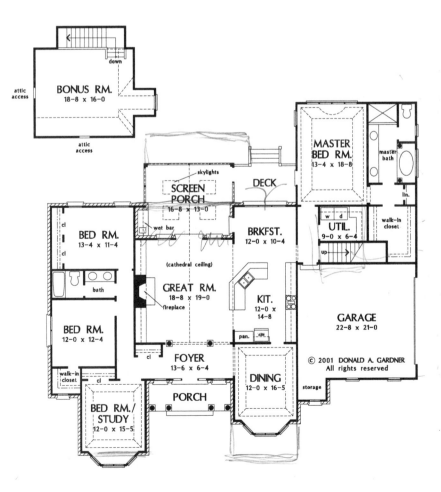

© 2001 DONALD A. GARDNER
All rights reserved

© 1998 Donald A. Gardner, Inc.

© 1998 Donald A Gardner, Inc.

plan
HPT9600148

STYLE: TRADITIONAL
SQUARE FOOTAGE: 2,262
BONUS SPACE: 388 SQ. FT.
BEDROOMS: 4
BATHROOMS: 2½
WIDTH: 77' - 4"
DEPTH: 62' - 0

SEARCH ONLINE @ EPLANS.COM

True tradition is exhibited in the brick-and-siding facade, hipped roof, and keystone arches of this spacious four-bedroom home. Stately columns framing the front entry are repeated in the home's formal foyer. The generous great room is exemplary, boasting a fireplace with flanking built-ins. A dramatic cathedral ceiling enhances the space and is continued out into the adjoining screened porch. The nearby breakfast area is enriched by dual skylights. Three family bedrooms, two with walk-in closets, share an impressive hall bath with dual-sink vanity. Secluded on the opposite side of the home, the master suite features rear-deck access, a walk-in closet, and a private bath with corner tub and separate vanities.

plan # HPT9600149

STYLE: TRANSITIONAL
SQUARE FOOTAGE: 2,041
BEDROOMS: 3
BATHROOMS: 2
WIDTH: 67' - 6"
DEPTH: 63' - 6"
FOUNDATION: BASEMENT
BASEMENT: 1,802 SQ. FT.

SEARCH ONLINE @ EPLANS.COM

Attention to detail and a touch of luxury create a home that showcases excellent taste, and provides an efficient floor plan. From the raised foyer, a striking view is offered of the great room with its elegantly styled windows and views of the deck. Split bedrooms provide privacy for the master suite, where a sitting area is topped by an exciting ceiling. A garden bath with a walk-in closet and whirlpool tub pampers the homeowner. An optional finished basement adds a recreation room, exercise room, and a guest bedroom.

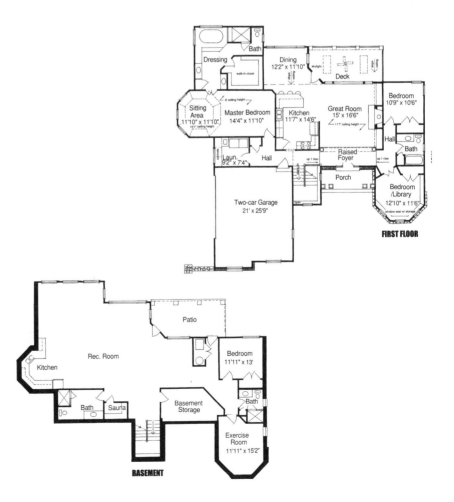

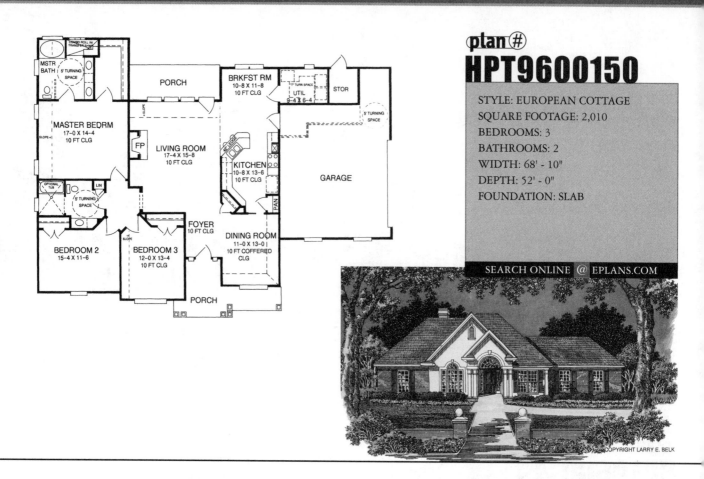

plan # HPT9600150

STYLE: EUROPEAN COTTAGE
SQUARE FOOTAGE: 2,010
BEDROOMS: 3
BATHROOMS: 2
WIDTH: 68' - 10"
DEPTH: 52' - 0"
FOUNDATION: SLAB

SEARCH ONLINE @ EPLANS.COM

COPYRIGHT LARRY E. BELK

plan # HPT9600151

STYLE: TRADITIONAL
SQUARE FOOTAGE: 2,193
BONUS SPACE: 400 SQ. FT.
BEDROOMS: 4
BATHROOMS: 2
WIDTH: 64' - 6"
DEPTH: 59' - 0"
FOUNDATION: SLAB, BASEMENT, CRAWLSPACE

SEARCH ONLINE @ EPLANS.COM

ORDER BLUEPRINTS 24 HOURS, 7 DAYS A WEEK, AT 1-800-521-6797

plan# HPT9600152

STYLE: TRANSITIONAL
SQUARE FOOTAGE: 2,398
BEDROOMS: 3
BATHROOMS: 2½
WIDTH: 58' - 0"
DEPTH: 76' - 0"
FOUNDATION: CRAWLSPACE, BASEMENT

SEARCH ONLINE @ EPLANS.COM

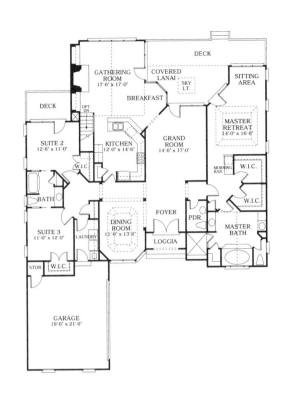

plan# HPT9600153

STYLE: TRADITIONAL
SQUARE FOOTAGE: 2,282
BONUS SPACE: 354 SQ. FT.
BEDROOMS: 4
BATHROOMS: 2½
WIDTH: 71' - 1"
DEPTH: 57' - 5"

SEARCH ONLINE @ EPLANS.COM

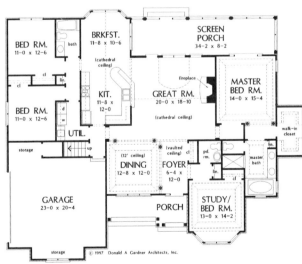

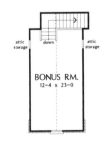

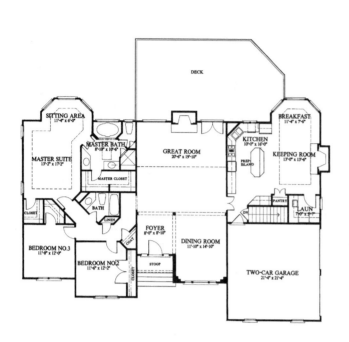

plan #
HPT9600154

STYLE: FRENCH ECLECTIC
SQUARE FOOTAGE: 2,295
BEDROOMS: 3
BATHROOMS: 2
WIDTH: 69' - 0"
DEPTH: 49' - 6"
FOUNDATION: WALKOUT
BASEMENT

SEARCH ONLINE @ EPLANS.COM

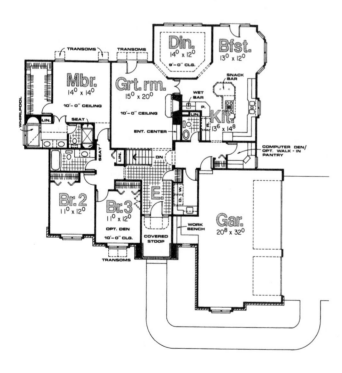

plan #
HPT9600155

STYLE: TRADITIONAL
SQUARE FOOTAGE: 2,186
BEDROOMS: 3
BATHROOMS: 2½
WIDTH: 64' - 0"
DEPTH: 66' - 0"

SEARCH ONLINE @ EPLANS.COM

ORDER BLUEPRINTS 24 HOURS, 7 DAYS A WEEK, AT 1-800-521-6797

plan
HPT9600156

STYLE: MEDITERRANEAN
SQUARE FOOTAGE: 2,491
BONUS SPACE: 588 SQ. FT.
BEDROOMS: 3
BATHROOMS: 2½
WIDTH: 64' - 0"
DEPTH: 72' - 4"
FOUNDATION: CRAWLSPACE,
BASEMENT, SLAB

SEARCH ONLINE @ EPLANS.COM

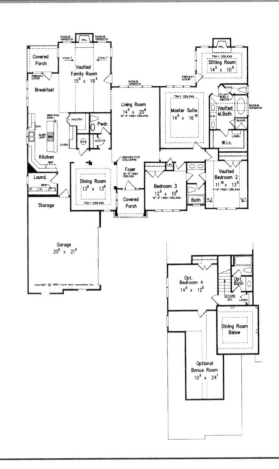

plan
HPT9600157

STYLE: FRENCH ECLECTIC
SQUARE FOOTAGE: 2,150
BEDROOMS: 3
BATHROOMS: 2½
WIDTH: 64' - 0"
DEPTH: 60' - 4"
FOUNDATION: WALKOUT
BASEMENT

SEARCH ONLINE @ EPLANS.COM

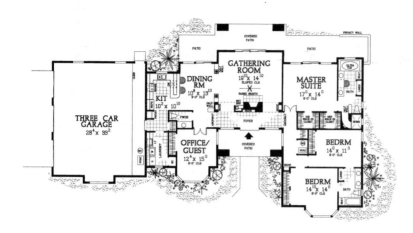

plan #
HPT9600158

STYLE: SPANISH COLONIAL
SQUARE FOOTAGE: 2,319
BEDROOMS: 4
BATHROOMS: 2½
WIDTH: 97' - 2"
DEPTH: 57' - 4"
FOUNDATION: SLAB

SEARCH ONLINE @ EPLANS.COM

ALTERNATIVE EXTERIOR

plan #
HPT9600159

STYLE: MEDITERRANEAN
SQUARE FOOTAGE: 2,352
BEDROOMS: 4
BATHROOMS: 3
WIDTH: 61' - 8"
DEPTH: 64' - 8"
FOUNDATION: SLAB

SEARCH ONLINE @ EPLANS.COM

ORDER BLUEPRINTS 24 HOURS, 7 DAYS A WEEK, AT 1-800-521-6797

plan
HPT9600160

STYLE: MEDITERRANEAN
SQUARE FOOTAGE: 2,253
BEDROOMS: 4
BATHROOMS: 3
WIDTH: 58' - 0"
DEPTH: 66' - 8"
FOUNDATION: SLAB

SEARCH ONLINE @ EPLANS.COM

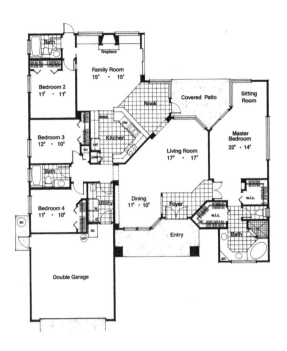

plan
HPT9600161

STYLE: MEDITERRANEAN
SQUARE FOOTAGE: 2,387
BEDROOMS: 3
BATHROOMS: 3
WIDTH: 53' - 6"
DEPTH: 94' - 6"
FOUNDATION: SLAB

SEARCH ONLINE @ EPLANS.COM

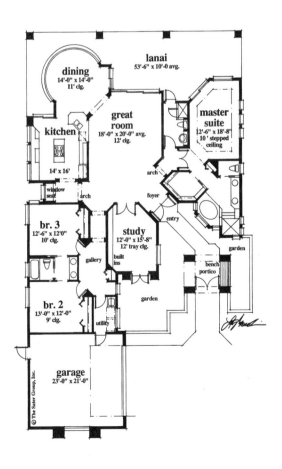

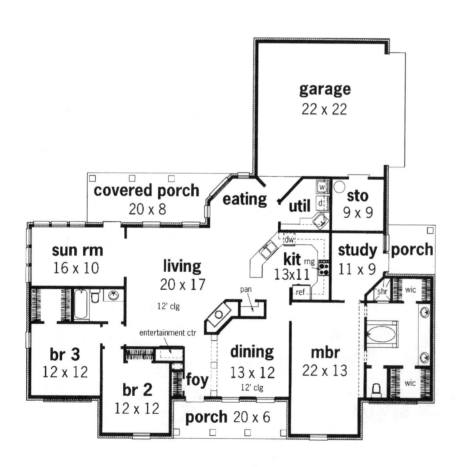

plan #
HPT9600162

STYLE: FRENCH ECLECTIC
SQUARE FOOTAGE: 2,160
BEDROOMS: 3
BATHROOMS: 2
WIDTH: 68' - 0"
DEPTH: 64' - 0"
FOUNDATION: CRAWLSPACE, SLAB

SEARCH ONLINE @ EPLANS.COM

Steep rooflines and columns make this home one to remember. Starburst windows align along the exterior and offer a nice touch of sophistication. Extra amenities run rampant through this one-story home. The sunroom can be enjoyed during every season. An eating nook right off the kitchen brightens the rear of the home. Utility and storage areas are also found at the rear of the home. A cozy study privately accesses the side porch. The master bedroom is complete with dual vanities and His and Hers closets. Two family bedrooms reside to the left of the plan.

ORDER BLUEPRINTS 24 HOURS, 7 DAYS A WEEK, AT 1-800-521-6797

plan
HPT9600163

STYLE: FRENCH ECLECTIC

FIRST FLOOR: 1,724 SQ. FT.

SECOND FLOOR: 700 SQ. FT.

TOTAL: 2,424 SQ. FT.

BEDROOMS: 3

BATHROOMS: 2½

WIDTH: 47' - 10"

DEPTH: 63' - 8"

FOUNDATION: WALKOUT
BASEMENT

SEARCH ONLINE @ EPLANS.COM

All the charm of gables, stonework, and multi-level rooflines combine to create this home. To the left of the foyer, you will see the dining room highlighted by a tray ceiling. This room and the living room flow together to form one large entertainment area. The gourmet kitchen holds a work island and adjoining octagonal breakfast room. The great room is a fantastic living space, featuring a pass-through wet bar, a fireplace, and bookcases. The master suite enjoys privacy at the rear of the home. An open-rail loft above the foyer leads to two additional bedrooms with walk-in closets, private vanities, and a shared bath.

FIRST FLOOR

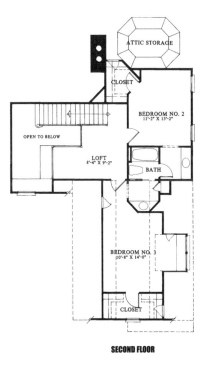

SECOND FLOOR

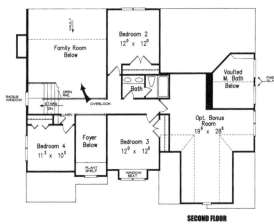

SECOND FLOOR

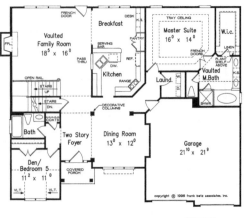

FIRST FLOOR

plan#
HPT9600164

STYLE: TRADITIONAL
FIRST FLOOR: 1,687 SQ. FT.
SECOND FLOOR: 694 SQ. FT.
TOTAL: 2,381 SQ. FT.
BONUS SPACE: 407 SQ. FT.
BEDROOMS: 5
BATHROOMS: 3
WIDTH: 55' - 10"
DEPTH: 44' - 6"
FOUNDATION: BASEMENT, CRAWLSPACE

SEARCH ONLINE @ EPLANS.COM

Classic clapboard siding with brick accents that add splash complement asymmetrical gables and a quaint covered porch on this 21st-Century traditional design. A cultivated interior starts with a two-story foyer that leads to a vaulted family room with an extended-hearth fireplace. The kitchen boasts a serving bar and ample pantry, and serves an elegant dining room with transom windows. An elegant master suite enjoys a private wing of the home and offers a vaulted bath with a whirlpool spa tub and a generous walk-in closet. Upstairs, three family bedrooms share a full bath and a hall with a balcony overlook.

plan#
HPT9600165

STYLE: TRADITIONAL
FIRST FLOOR: 1,688 SQ. FT.
SECOND FLOOR: 558 SQ. FT.
TOTAL: 2,246 SQ. FT.
BONUS SPACE: 269 SQ. FT.
BEDROOMS: 4
BATHROOMS: 3
WIDTH: 54' - 0"
DEPTH: 48' - 0"
FOUNDATION: CRAWLSPACE,
BASEMENT, SLAB

SEARCH ONLINE @ EPLANS.COM

Graceful details combine with a covered entryway to welcome friends and family to come on in. The canted bay sitting area in the master suite provides sunny respite and quiet solitude. To be the center of attention, invite everyone to party in the vaulted great room, which spills over into the big airy kitchen. Guests can make use of the optional study/bedroom. Upstairs, secondary bedrooms share a full bath and a balcony overlook. A spacious central hall leads to a bonus room that provides wardrobe space.

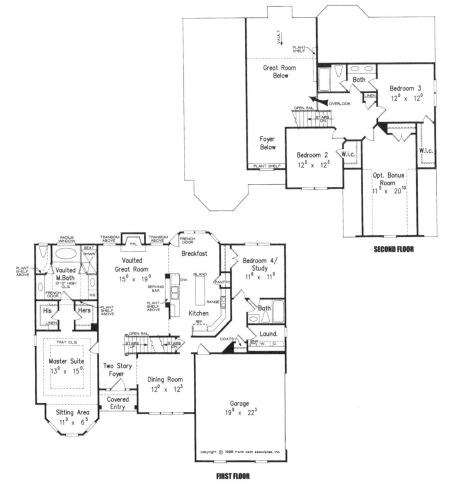

SECOND FLOOR

FIRST FLOOR

SECOND FLOOR

FIRST FLOOR

copyright © 1996 frank betz associates, inc.

plan#
HPT9600166

STYLE: TRADITIONAL
FIRST FLOOR: 1,290 SQ. FT.
SECOND FLOOR: 985 SQ. FT.
TOTAL: 2,275 SQ. FT.
BONUS SPACE: 186 SQ. FT.
BEDROOMS: 4
BATHROOMS: 3
WIDTH: 45' - 0"
DEPTH: 43' - 4"
FOUNDATION: CRAWLSPACE,
BASEMENT, SLAB

SEARCH ONLINE @ EPLANS.COM

This casually elegant European country-style home offers more than just a slice of everything you've always wanted: it is designed with room to grow. Formal living and dining rooms are defined by decorative columns and open from a two-story foyer, which leads to open family space. A two-story family room offers a fireplace and shares a French door to the rear property with the breakfast room. A gallery hall with a balcony overlook connects two sleeping wings upstairs. The master suite boasts a vaulted bath, and the family hall leads to bonus space.

ORDER BLUEPRINTS 24 HOURS, 7 DAYS A WEEK, AT 1-800-521-6797

plan #

HPT9600167

STYLE: TRADITIONAL

FIRST FLOOR: 1,761 SQ. FT.

SECOND FLOOR: 580 SQ. FT.

TOTAL: 2,341 SQ. FT.

BONUS SPACE: 276 SQ. FT.

BEDROOMS: 4

BATHROOMS: 3

WIDTH: 56' - 0"

DEPTH: 47' - 6"

FOUNDATION: CRAWLSPACE, SLAB, BASEMENT

SEARCH ONLINE @ EPLANS.COM

Decorative arches and quoins give this home a wonderful curb appeal that matches its comfortable interior. The two-story foyer is bathed in natural light as it leads to the formal dining room and beyond to the counter-filled kitchen and the vaulted breakfast nook. A den, or possible fourth bedroom, is tucked away at the rear for privacy and includes a full bath. Located on the first floor is a spacious master suite with a luxurious private bath. Two family bedrooms and a full bath reside on the second floor, as well as a balcony that looks down to the family room and the foyer. An optional bonus room is available for expanding at a later date.

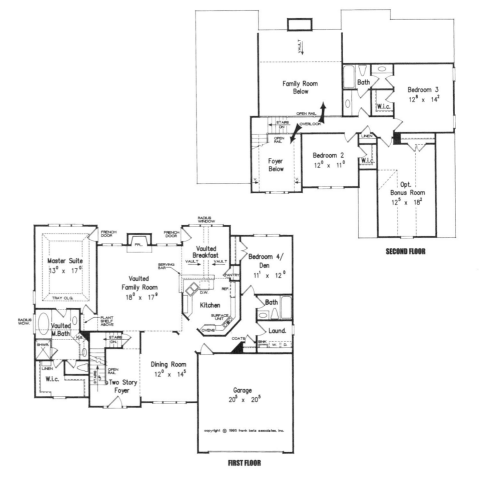

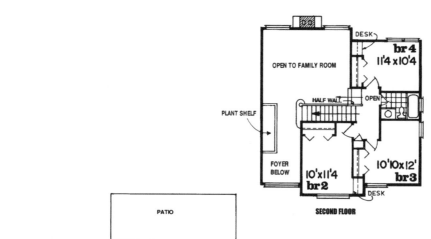

plan #
HPT9600168

STYLE: TRANSITIONAL
FIRST FLOOR: 1,445 SQ. FT.
SECOND FLOOR: 652 SQ. FT.
TOTAL: 2,097 SQ. FT.
BEDROOMS: 4
BATHROOMS: 2½
WIDTH: 56' - 8"
DEPTH: 48' - 4"
FOUNDATION: CRAWLSPACE,
BASEMENT

SEARCH ONLINE @ EPLANS.COM

A portico entry, graceful arches, and brick detailing provide appeal and a low-maintenance exterior for this design. A half-circle transom over the entry lights the two-story foyer, and a plant shelf lines the hallway to the sunken family room. This living space holds a vaulted ceiling, masonry fireplace, and French-door access to the railed patio. The nearby kitchen has a center prep island, built-in desk overlooking the family room, and extensive pantries in the breakfast area. The formal dining room has a tray ceiling and access to the foyer and the central hall. The master suite is on the first level for privacy and convenience. It features a walk-in closet and lavish bath with twin vanities, a whirlpool tub, and separate shower. Three family bedrooms, two of which feature built-in desks, are on the second floor.

ORDER BLUEPRINTS 24 HOURS, 7 DAYS A WEEK, AT 1-800-521-6797

plan ⊕
HPT9600169

STYLE: TRANSITIONAL

FIRST FLOOR: 1,566 SQ. FT.

SECOND FLOOR: 837 SQ. FT.

TOTAL: 2,403 SQ. FT.

BEDROOMS: 4

BATHROOMS: 3½

WIDTH: 116' - 3"

DEPTH: 55' - 1"

FOUNDATION: BASEMENT

SEARCH ONLINE @ EPLANS.COM

Be the owner of your own country estate-- this two-story home gives the look and feel of grand-style living without the expense of large square footage. The entry leads to a massive foyer and great hall. There's space enough here for living and dining areas. Two window seats in the great hall overlook the rear veranda. One fireplace warms the living area; another looks through the dining room to the kitchen and breakfast nook. A screened porch offers casual dining space for warm weather. The master suite has another fireplace and a window seat and adjoins a luxurious master bath with a separate tub and shower. The second floor contains three family bedrooms and two full baths. A separate apartment over the garage includes its own living room, kitchen, and bedroom.

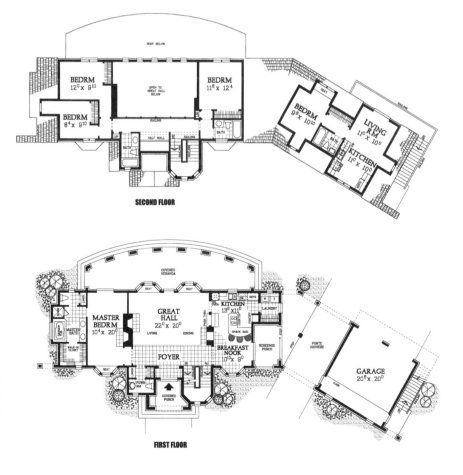

SECOND FLOOR

FIRST FLOOR

FIRST FLOOR

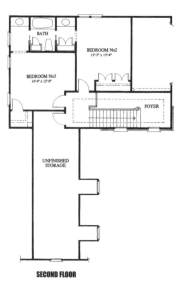

SECOND FLOOR

plan
HPT9600170

STYLE: TRADITIONAL
FIRST FLOOR: 1,580 SQ. FT.
SECOND FLOOR: 595 SQ. FT.
TOTAL: 2,175 SQ. FT.
BEDROOMS: 3
BATHROOMS: 2½
WIDTH: 50' - 2"
DEPTH: 70' - 11"
FOUNDATION: WALKOUT BASEMENT

SEARCH ONLINE @ EPLANS.COM

This home is a true Southern original. Inside, the spacious foyer leads directly to a large vaulted great room with its handsome fireplace. The dining room, just off the foyer, features a dramatic vaulted ceiling. The spacious kitchen offers both storage and large work areas opening up to the breakfast room. At the rear of the home, you will find the master suite with its garden bath, His and Hers vanities, and an oversize closet. The second floor provides two additional bedrooms with a shared bath and a balcony overlook to the foyer below.

plan #
HPT9600171

STYLE: TRADITIONAL
FIRST FLOOR: 1,847 SQ. FT.
SECOND FLOOR: 548 SQ. FT.
TOTAL: 2,395 SQ. FT.
BONUS SPACE: 395 SQ. FT.
BEDROOMS: 3
BATHROOMS: 2½
WIDTH: 60' - 0"
DEPTH: 66' - 4"
FOUNDATION: CRAWLSPACE,
BASEMENT

SEARCH ONLINE @ EPLANS.COM

Here is a truly elegant home with a striking exterior and an interior that uses diagonals to create comfort and space. The two-story foyer opens to the formal living/sitting room, which has a vaulted ceiling. A secluded master suite offers two walk-in closets and a vaulted bath with an angled corner tub. The family room reaches to the second story, where two bedrooms and an optional bonus room complete the plan.

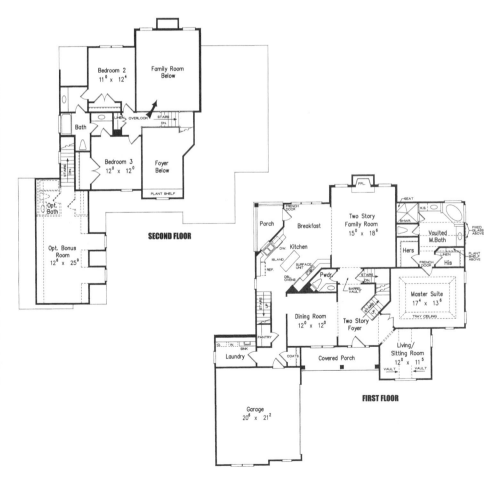

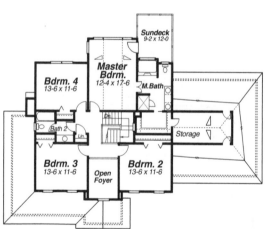

SECOND FLOOR

Sundeck
9-2 x 12-0

Master
Bdrm.
12-4 x 17-6

M.Bath

Bdrm. 4
13-6 x 11-6

Bath 2

Lin.

Storage

Bdrm. 3
13-6 x 11-6

Open
Foyer

Bdrm. 2
13-6 x 11-6

FIRST FLOOR

Sundeck
13-10 x 12-0

Screen
Porch
9-2 x 12-0

Brkfst.
12-4 x 11-6

Kit.
12-0 x 13-0

Family
13-10 x 19-6

Lav.

Butler's Pantry

Double Garage
21-8 x 23-4

Living
13-6 x 11-6

Open
Foyer
7-8 x 13-6

Dining
13-6 x 11-6

Covered Porch

plan
HPT9600172

STYLE: GEORGIAN FARMHOUSE
FIRST FLOOR: 1,250 SQ. FT.
SECOND FLOOR: 1,166 SQ. FT.
TOTAL: 2,416 SQ. FT.
BEDROOMS: 4
BATHROOMS: 2½
WIDTH: 64' - 0"
DEPTH: 52' - 0"
FOUNDATION: BASEMENT,
BASEMENT

SEARCH ONLINE @ EPLANS.COM

With its classic features, this home is reminiscent of Main Street, USA. The two-story foyer is flanked by the formal living and dining rooms, and the stairs are tucked back in the center of the house. Columns create a separation from the family room to the breakfast area, keeping that open feeling across the entire rear of the house. Corner windows in the kitchen look into the side yard and rear screened porch. The porch leads to the rear deck, which also ties into the side porch, creating outdoor living on three sides of the house. As you ascend the staircase to the second floor, you will pass a lighted panel of stained glass on the landing, creating the illusion of a window wall. The second floor features four bedrooms and a compartmented hall bath.

plan ⊕

HPT9600173

STYLE: TRADITIONAL

FIRST FLOOR: 1,744 SQ. FT.

SECOND FLOOR: 470 SQ. FT.

TOTAL: 2,214 SQ. FT.

BEDROOMS: 3

BATHROOMS: 2½

WIDTH: 53' - 0"

DEPTH: 44' - 0"

FOUNDATION: CRAWLSPACE

SEARCH ONLINE @ EPLANS.COM

Shingle and stucco accents enhance the striking facade of this contemporary plan. A thoughtful interior starts with a spacious foyer and central hall, which leads to a formal dining room and a den as well as to a private master suite. The second-floor balcony hall overlooks sections of space in the foyer and dining room. The gourmet kitchen has a corner pantry and a morning nook. To the rear of the plan, the master suite has a spa-style tub, a separate shower, and a walk-in closet. Upstairs, two additional bedrooms share a full bath with linen storage.

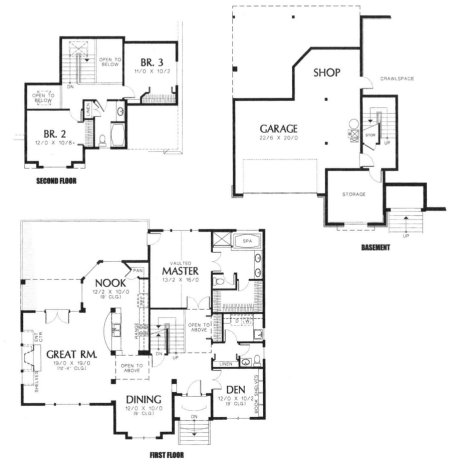

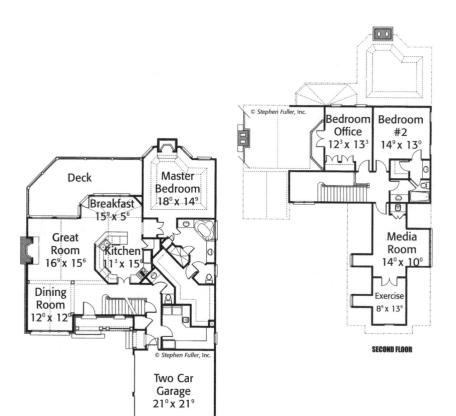

FIRST FLOOR

SECOND FLOOR

© Stephen Fuller, Inc.

plan #
HPT9600174

STYLE: TRADITIONAL
FIRST FLOOR: 1,746 SQ. FT.
SECOND FLOOR: 651 SQ. FT.
TOTAL: 2,397 SQ. FT.
BEDROOMS: 3
BATHROOMS: 2½
WIDTH: 50' - 0"
DEPTH: 75' - 4"
FOUNDATION: WALKOUT
BASEMENT

SEARCH ONLINE @ EPLANS.COM

At the heart of this home, a gourmet kitchen provides a snack counter and a walk-in pantry. Double doors open to a gallery hall that leads to the formal dining room--an enchanting retreat for chandelier-lit evenings—that provides a breathtaking view of the front yard. A classic great room is warmed by a cozy fireplace and illuminated by a wall of windows. The outdoor living area is spacious enough for grand events. The master suite is brightened by sweeping views of the backyard and a romantic fireplace just for two. Upstairs, the third bedroom is easily converted to a home office for the busy entrepreneur.

ORDER BLUEPRINTS 24 HOURS, 7 DAYS A WEEK, AT 1-800-521-6797

© 1999 Donald A. Gardner, Inc.

plan
HPT9600175

STYLE: TRADITIONAL
FIRST FLOOR: 1,668 SQ. FT.
SECOND FLOOR: 495 SQ. FT.
TOTAL: 2,163 SQ. FT.
BONUS SPACE: 327 SQ. FT.
BEDROOMS: 4
BATHROOMS: 3
WIDTH: 52' - 7"
DEPTH: 50' - 11"

SEARCH ONLINE @ EPLANS.COM

Four gables, a Palladian window, and an admirable transom with a sunburst are eye-catching additions to this plan's exterior. On the first floor, rounded columns present the dining room, which also sports a tray ceiling. The vaulted great room accesses the rear deck and features a warming fireplace. Set at an angle, the kitchen's serving bar allows the cook to keep up with activities in both the breakfast and great rooms. The master suite includes a walk-in closet, tray ceiling, and sumptuous bath. Note the triangular shape of the tub and separate shower. Upstairs, two family bedrooms share a full bath.

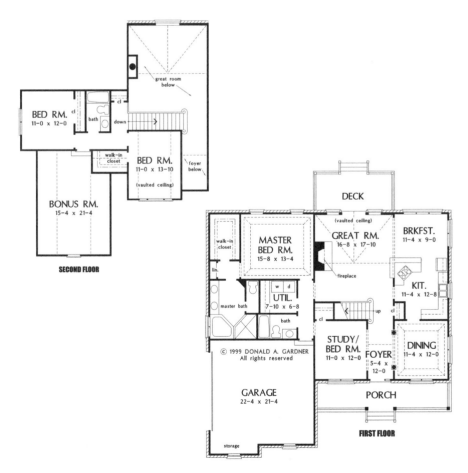

SECOND FLOOR

FIRST FLOOR

© 1999 DONALD A. GARDNER
All rights reserved

SECOND FLOOR

FIRST FLOOR

plan #

HPT9600176

STYLE: TRANSITIONAL
FIRST FLOOR: 1,501 SQ. FT.
SECOND FLOOR: 921 SQ. FT.
TOTAL: 2,422 SQ. FT.
BEDROOMS: 3
BATHROOMS: 2½
WIDTH: 52' - 0"
DEPTH: 36' - 0"
FOUNDATION: BASEMENT,
CRAWLSPACE

SEARCH ONLINE @ EPLANS.COM

The contemporary look of this modern country design is both impressive and unique. Enormous windows brighten and enliven every interior space. The vaulted family room features a fireplace, and a two-sided fireplace warms the formal living and dining rooms. The gourmet island kitchen is open to a nook. Double doors open to a den that accesses a front deck. Upstairs, the master bedroom features a private bath with linen storage and a walk-in closet. Two family bedrooms share a Jack-and-Jill bath. The two-car garage features a storage area on the lower level.

plan
HPT9600177

STYLE: TRADITIONAL

FIRST FLOOR: 1,720 SQ. FT.

SECOND FLOOR: 724 SQ. FT.

TOTAL: 2,444 SQ. FT.

BONUS SPACE: 212 SQ. FT.

BEDROOMS: 4

BATHROOMS: 3

WIDTH: 58' - 0"

DEPTH: 47' - 0"

FOUNDATION: CRAWLSPACE, BASEMENT

SEARCH ONLINE @ EPLANS.COM

Columns announce the front covered porch and entry of this comfortable home. An open arrangement of the interior allows vistas that extend from the two-story foyer to the rear property. A fireplace and two sets of radius windows define the vaulted great room, which allows passage to the casual breakfast area. The well-organized kitchen offers a serving bar, a planning desk, and an ample pantry. To the rear of the plan, a flex room offers the possibility of a guest suite or home office. The master suite offers a compartmented bath, separate vanities, and a walk-in closet. Upstairs, two secondary bedrooms share a gallery hall that ends in a computer nook.

DESIGNS FROM 2,000 TO 2,499 SQ. FT.

© 2001 Donald A. Gardner, Inc.

© 2001 DONALD A. GARDNER
All rights reserved

FIRST FLOOR

SECOND FLOOR

plan#
HPT9600178

STYLE: COUNTRY
FIRST FLOOR: 1,707 SQ. FT.
SECOND FLOOR: 514 SQ. FT.
TOTAL: 2,221 SQ. FT.
BONUS SPACE: 211 SQ. FT.
BEDROOMS: 4
BATHROOMS: 2½
WIDTH: 50' - 0"
DEPTH: 71' - 8"

SEARCH ONLINE @ EPLANS.COM

Stone and horizontal siding give a definite country flavor to this two-story home. The front study makes an ideal guest room with the adjoining powder room. The formal dining room is accented with decorative columns that define its perimeter. The great room boasts a fireplace, built-ins, and a magnificent view of the backyard beyond one of two rear porches. The master suite boasts two walk-in closets and a private bath. Two bedrooms share a full bath on the second floor.

© 1998 Donald A. Gardner, Inc.

plan ⊕

HPT9600179

STYLE: FARMHOUSE

FIRST FLOOR: 1,475 SQ. FT.

SECOND FLOOR: 730 SQ. FT.

TOTAL: 2,205 SQ. FT.

BONUS SPACE: 430 SQ. FT.

BEDROOMS: 3

BATHROOMS: 3½

WIDTH: 71' - 4"

DEPTH: 76' - 3"

SEARCH ONLINE @ EPLANS.COM

With a bonus room over the garage and a full wrapping porch on the exterior, this farmhouse is a true crowd-pleaser. The central foyer opens on the right to a formal dining room and then leads back to the great room. The master suite is located on the first floor and features a walk-in closet and a bath with a garden tub. Family bedrooms are on the second floor, separated by a loft area. Each family bedroom includes its own bath.

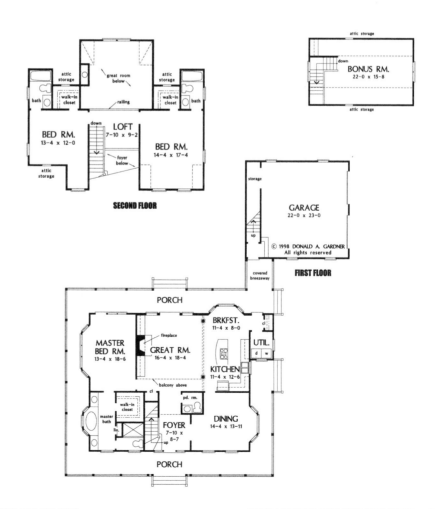

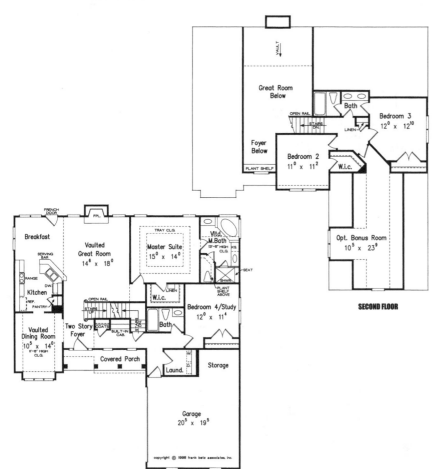

SECOND FLOOR

FIRST FLOOR

plan #
HPT9600180

STYLE: TRADITIONAL
FIRST FLOOR: 1,559 SQ. FT.
SECOND FLOOR: 475 SQ. FT.
TOTAL: 2,034 SQ. FT.
BONUS SPACE: 321 SQ. FT.
BEDROOMS: 4
BATHROOMS: 3
WIDTH: 50' - 0"
DEPTH: 56' - 4"
FOUNDATION: CRAWLSPACE,
BASEMENT

SEARCH ONLINE @ EPLANS.COM

A careful blend of siding and stone lends eye-catching appeal to this traditional plan. Vaulted ceilings grace the great room, master bath, and dining room. The efficient kitchen offers pantry storage and a serving bar to the breakfast room. The master suite features a tray ceiling and a deluxe private bath. A bedroom/study is located on the first floor. Two second-floor bedrooms easily access a full bath. An optional bonus room offers plenty of room to grow--making it perfect for a guest suite, home office, or exercise room.

plan (#)
HPT9600181

STYLE: NEOCLASSIC

FIRST FLOOR: 1,236 SQ. FT.

SECOND FLOOR: 1,120 SQ. FT.

TOTAL: 2,356 SQ. FT.

BONUS SPACE: 270 SQ. FT.

BEDROOMS: 3

BATHROOMS: 2½

WIDTH: 56' - 0"

DEPTH: 38' - 0"

FOUNDATION: CRAWLSPACE

SEARCH ONLINE @ EPLANS.COM

This gracious home integrates timeless traditional styling with a functional, cost-effective plan. An interesting feature is the two-story nook area with a bay window and a desk, set between the gourmet kitchen and the large family room. Warming fireplaces occupy both the family room and living area. Across from the bottom of the staircase sits a den with French doors. Upstairs, two bedrooms share a full bath that includes dual sinks. A conveniently located door in the upper hallway opens to the large bonus room over the two-car garage. Rounding out the upper floor, a sumptuous master suite makes its own private retreat over the entry with an enormous bath that contains a spa and separate shower.

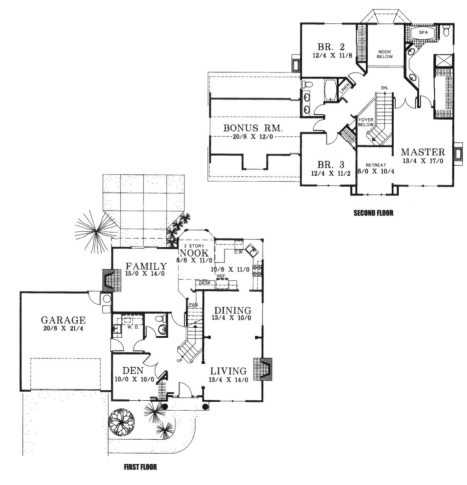

SECOND FLOOR

FIRST FLOOR

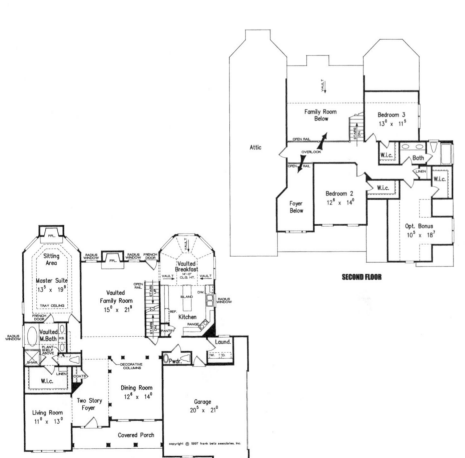

FIRST FLOOR

SECOND FLOOR

plan #
HPT9600182

STYLE: TRADITIONAL
FIRST FLOOR: 1,797 SQ. FT.
SECOND FLOOR: 654 SQ. FT.
TOTAL: 2,451 SQ. FT.
BONUS SPACE: 266 SQ. FT.
BEDROOMS: 3
BATHROOMS: 2½
WIDTH: 54' - 0"
DEPTH: 54' - 10"
FOUNDATION: CRAWLSPACE, BASEMENT

SEARCH ONLINE @ EPLANS.COM

Capstones and brick accents add a touch of class to this home. A vaulted breakfast bay fills a gourmet kitchen with natural light. The spacious family room enjoys radius windows and a French door to the back property; a private formal living room opens off the foyer. A fireplace flanked by windows dresses up the master suite, which also features a vaulted bath with a whirlpool tub. The second-floor bedrooms are connected by a balcony hall.

ORDER BLUEPRINTS 24 HOURS, 7 DAYS A WEEK, AT 1-800-521-6797

plan ⊕
HPT9600183

STYLE: TRADITIONAL

FIRST FLOOR: 1,082 SQ. FT.

SECOND FLOOR: 1,021 SQ. FT.

TOTAL: 2,103 SQ. FT.

BEDROOMS: 4

BATHROOMS: 2½

WIDTH: 50' - 0"

DEPTH: 40' - 0"

SEARCH ONLINE @ EPLANS.COM

A covered porch invites you into this country-style home. Handsome bookcases frame the fireplace in the spacious family room. Double doors off the entry provide the family room with added privacy. The kitchen features an island, a lazy Susan, and easy access to a walk-in laundry. The master bedroom features a boxed ceiling and separate entries to a walk-in closet and a pampering bath. The upstairs hall bath is compartmented, allowing maximum usage for today's busy family.

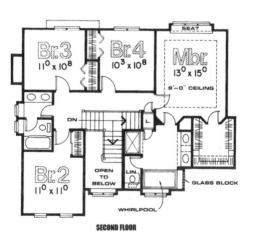

SECOND FLOOR

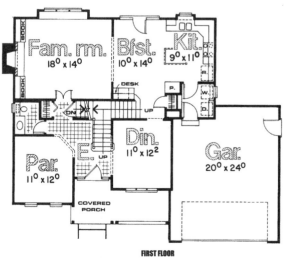

FIRST FLOOR

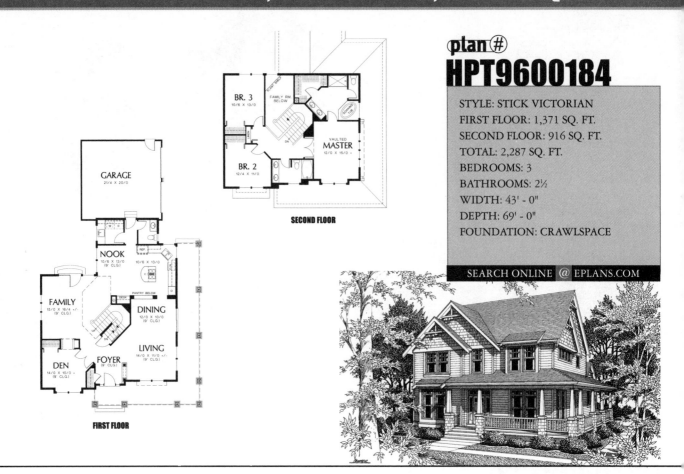

SECOND FLOOR

FIRST FLOOR

plan#
HPT9600184

STYLE: STICK VICTORIAN
FIRST FLOOR: 1,371 SQ. FT.
SECOND FLOOR: 916 SQ. FT.
TOTAL: 2,287 SQ. FT.
BEDROOMS: 3
BATHROOMS: 2½
WIDTH: 43' - 0"
DEPTH: 69' - 0"
FOUNDATION: CRAWLSPACE

SEARCH ONLINE @ EPLANS.COM

SECOND FLOOR

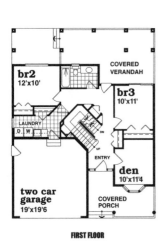

FIRST FLOOR

plan#
HPT9600185

STYLE: TRADITIONAL
FIRST FLOOR: 832 SQ. FT.
SECOND FLOOR: 1,331 SQ. FT.
TOTAL: 2,163 SQ. FT.
BEDROOMS: 3
BATHROOMS: 2½
WIDTH: 37' - 6"
DEPTH: 48' - 4"
FOUNDATION: BASEMENT

SEARCH ONLINE @ EPLANS.COM

plan #

HPT9600186

STYLE: VICTORIAN FARMHOUSE

FIRST FLOOR: 1,146 SQ. FT.

SECOND FLOOR: 943 SQ. FT.

TOTAL: 2,089 SQ. FT.

BONUS SPACE: 324 SQ. FT.

BEDROOMS: 3

BATHROOMS: 2½

WIDTH: 56' - 0"

DEPTH: 38' - 0"

FOUNDATION: BASEMENT

SEARCH ONLINE @ EPLANS.COM

This beautiful three-bedroom home boasts many attractive features. Two covered porches will entice you outside; inside, a special sunroom on the first floor brings the outdoors in. The foyer opens on the right to a comfortable family room that may be used as a home office. On the left, the living area is warmed by the sunroom and a cozy corner fireplace. A formal dining area lies adjacent to an efficient kitchen with a central island and breakfast nook overlooking the back porch. The second level offers two family bedrooms served by a full bath. A spacious master suite with a walk-in closet and luxurious bath completes the second floor.

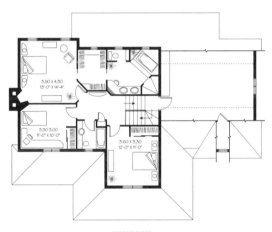

SECOND FLOOR

FIRST FLOOR

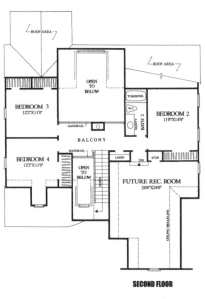

SECOND FLOOR

FIRST FLOOR

plan #
HPT9600187

STYLE: COUNTRY COTTAGE
FIRST FLOOR: 1,627 SQ. FT.
SECOND FLOOR: 783 SQ. FT.
TOTAL: 2,410 SQ. FT.
BONUS SPACE: 418 SQ. FT.
BEDROOMS: 4
BATHROOMS: 2½
WIDTH: 46' - 0"
DEPTH: 58' - 6"
FOUNDATION: CRAWLSPACE

SEARCH ONLINE @ EPLANS.COM

This "little jewel" of a home emanates a warmth and joy not soon forgotten. The two-story foyer leads to the formal living room, defined by graceful columns. A formal dining room opens off from the living room, making entertaining a breeze. A family room at the back features a fireplace and works well with the kitchen and breakfast areas. A lavish master suite is secluded on the first floor; three family bedrooms reside upstairs.

plan
HPT9600188

STYLE: COLONIAL REVIVAL

SQUARE FOOTAGE: 2,496

BONUS SPACE: 483 SQ. FT.

BEDROOMS: 4

BATHROOMS: 2½

WIDTH: 83' - 4"

DEPTH: 57' - 7"

FOUNDATION: SLAB, CRAWLSPACE

SEARCH ONLINE @ EPLANS.COM

This countryside estate boasts a quaint rustic charm. Inside, the dining room and study can be found on either side of the entryway—both feature bayed windows. A gallery separates the formal rooms from the great room, which offers a country fireplace. The master suite is enhanced by a vaulted ceiling and features a private master bath. The right side of the home hosts two additional family bedrooms. Upstairs, an unfinished bonus room with a sloped ceiling is reserved for future use.

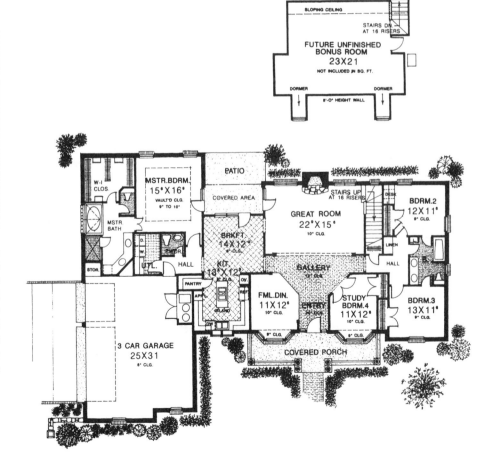

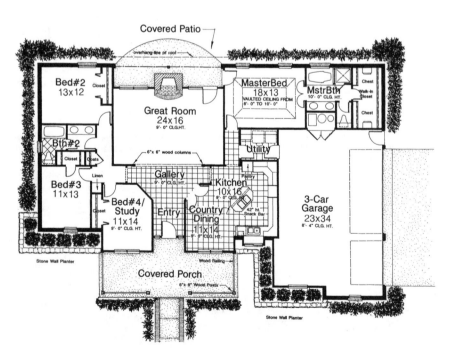

plan#

HPT9600189

STYLE: COLONIAL REVIVAL
SQUARE FOOTAGE: 2,078
BEDROOMS: 4
BATHROOMS: 2
WIDTH: 75' - 0"
DEPTH: 47' - 10"
FOUNDATION: SLAB

SEARCH ONLINE @ EPLANS.COM

Colonial style meets farmhouse charm in this plan, furnishing old-fashioned charisma with a flourish. From the entry, double doors open to the country dining room and a large island kitchen. Nearby, the spacious great room takes center stage and is warmed by a fireplace flanked by large windows. Tucked behind the three-car garage, the secluded master suite features a vaulted ceiling in the bedroom. The master bath contains a relaxing tub, double-bowl vanity, separate shower, and compartmented toilet. Beyond the bath is a huge walk-in closet with two built-in chests. Three family bedrooms—one doubles as a study or home office—full bath, and a utility room complete the plan.

plan
HPT9600190

STYLE: COLONIAL REVIVAL
SQUARE FOOTAGE: 2,387
BONUS SPACE: 400 SQ. FT.
BEDROOMS: 3
BATHROOMS: 2½
WIDTH: 69' - 6"
DEPTH: 68' - 11"
FOUNDATION: SLAB, CRAWLSPACE

SEARCH ONLINE @ EPLANS.COM

This three-bedroom home brings the past to life with Tuscan columns, dormers and fanlight windows. The entrance is flanked by the dining room and study. The great room boasts cathedral ceilings and a fireplace. The spacious kitchen adjoins a breakfast nook and accesses the rear covered veranda. The master bedroom enjoys a sitting area, access to the covered veranda, and a spacious bathroom. This home is complete with two family bedrooms.

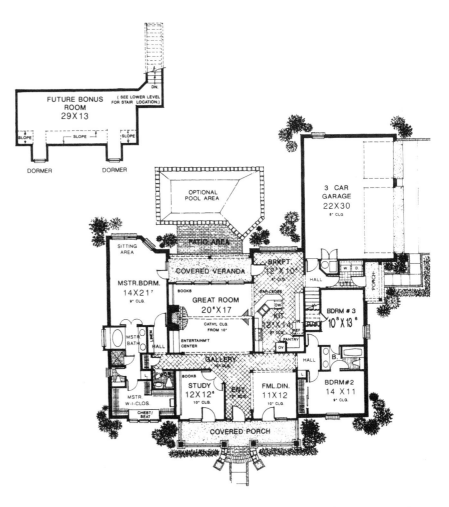

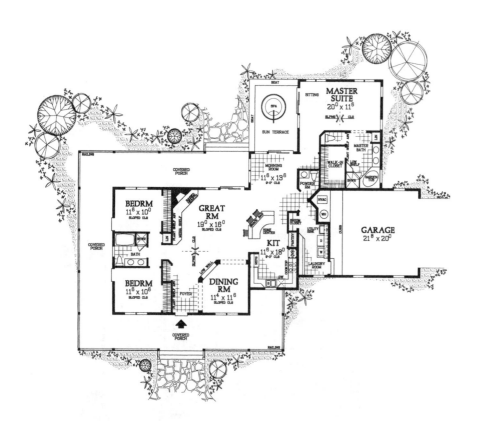

plan
HPT9600191

STYLE: FARMHOUSE

SQUARE FOOTAGE: 2,090

BEDROOMS: 3

BATHROOMS: 2½

WIDTH: 84' - 6"

DEPTH: 64' - 0"

FOUNDATION: CRAWLSPACE

SEARCH ONLINE @ EPLANS.COM

This classic farmhouse enjoys a wraparound porch that's perfect for enjoyment of the outdoors. To the rear of the plan, a sun terrace with a spa opens from the master suite and the morning room. A grand great room offers a sloped ceiling and a corner fireplace with a raised hearth. The formal dining room is defined by a low wall and graceful archways set off by decorative columns. The tiled kitchen has a centered island counter with a snack bar and adjoins a laundry area. Two family bedrooms reside to the side of the plan, and each enjoys private access to the covered porch. A secluded master suite nestles in its own wing and features a sitting area with access to the rear terrace and spa.

ORDER BLUEPRINTS 24 HOURS, 7 DAYS A WEEK, AT 1-800-521-6797

©2000 Donald A. Gardner, Inc.

B. NATHAN

plan #

HPT9600192

STYLE: VICTORIAN FARMHOUSE

FIRST FLOOR: 1,706 SQ. FT.

SECOND FLOOR: 776 SQ. FT.

TOTAL: 2,482 SQ. FT.

BONUS SPACE: 414 SQ. FT.

BEDROOMS: 4

BATHROOMS: 2½

WIDTH: 54' - 8"

DEPTH: 43' - 0"

SEARCH ONLINE @ EPLANS.COM

The small appearance of this country farmhouse belies the spaciousness that lies within. A large great room lies directly beyond the foyer and boasts a fireplace, shelves, a vaulted ceiling, and a door to the rear deck. A bayed breakfast room, located just off the kitchen, looks to a covered breezeway that leads from the house to the garage. The first-floor master bedroom is enhanced with a sitting area, walk-in closet, and full bath with a garden tub and dual sinks. The second floor overlooks the great room and includes three additional bedrooms, one with a cathedral ceiling.

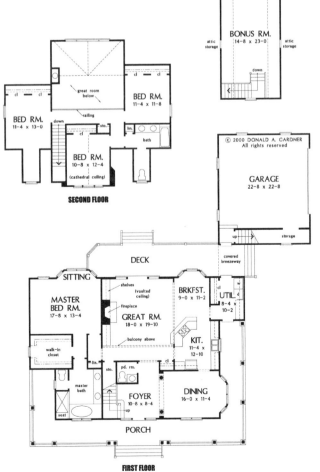

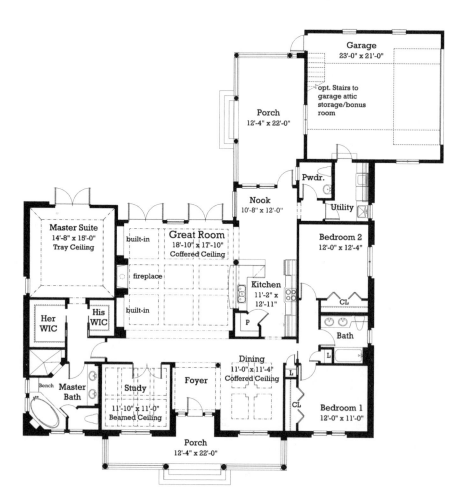

plan #
HPT9600193

STYLE: FARMHOUSE
SQUARE FOOTAGE: 2,329
BEDROOMS: 3
BATHROOMS: 2½
WIDTH: 72' - 6"
DEPTH: 73' - 4"
FOUNDATION: CRAWLSPACE

SEARCH ONLINE @ EPLANS.COM

Stately columns and bright windows grace the entry to this French farmhouse. Open rooms, French doors, and specialty ceilings add a sense of spaciousness throughout the home. Interior columns set the formal dining room apart. The great room boasts a fireplace, built-in cabinetry, and dazzling views. The master suite leads to His and Hers walk-in closets, a dual-sink vanity, a corner whirlpool tub, and an oversize corner shower. Two bedrooms with a shared bath sit in the right wing.

ORDER BLUEPRINTS 24 HOURS, 7 DAYS A WEEK, AT 1-800-521-6797

plan
HPT9600194

STYLE: FLORIDIAN
SQUARE FOOTAGE: 2,385
BONUS SPACE: 1,271 SQ. FT.
BEDROOMS: 3
BATHROOMS: 2½
WIDTH: 60' - 4"
DEPTH: 59' - 4"
FOUNDATION: PIER, BLOCK

SEARCH ONLINE @ EPLANS.COM

REAR EXTERIOR

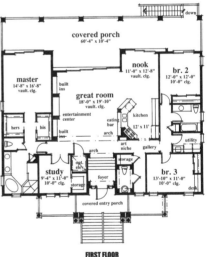

FIRST FLOOR

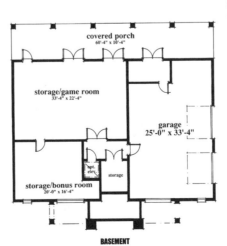

BASEMENT

A classic pediment and low-pitched roof are topped by a cupola on this gorgeous coastal design, influenced by 19th-Century Caribbean plantation houses. Savory style blended with a contemporary seaside spirit invites entertaining as well as year-round living—plus room to grow. The beauty and warmth of natural light splash the spacious living area with a sense of the outdoors and a touch of joie de vivre. The great room features a wall of built-ins designed for even the most technology-savvy entertainment buff. Dazzling views through walls of glass are enlivened by the presence of a breezy porch. The master suite features a luxurious bath, a dressing area, and two walk-in closets. Glass doors open to the porch and provide generous views of the seascape; a nearby study offers an indoor retreat.

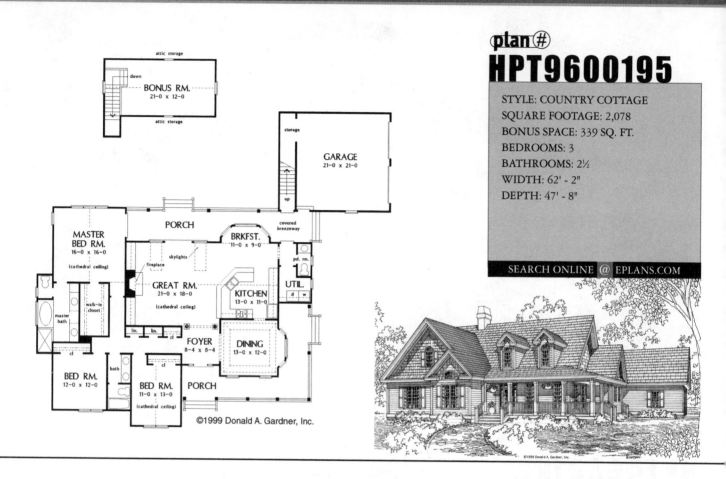

plan#
HPT9600195

STYLE: COUNTRY COTTAGE
SQUARE FOOTAGE: 2,078
BONUS SPACE: 339 SQ. FT.
BEDROOMS: 3
BATHROOMS: 2½
WIDTH: 62' - 2"
DEPTH: 47' - 8"

SEARCH ONLINE @ EPLANS.COM

©1999 Donald A. Gardner, Inc.

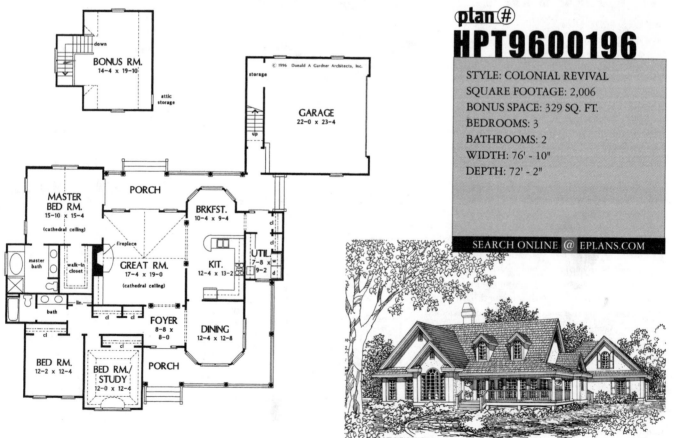

plan#
HPT9600196

STYLE: COLONIAL REVIVAL
SQUARE FOOTAGE: 2,006
BONUS SPACE: 329 SQ. FT.
BEDROOMS: 3
BATHROOMS: 2
WIDTH: 76' - 10"
DEPTH: 72' - 2"

SEARCH ONLINE @ EPLANS.COM

© 1997 Donald A. Gardner Architects, Inc.

B. NATHAN

plan #

HPT9600197

STYLE: FARMHOUSE
SQUARE FOOTAGE: 2,273
BONUS SPACE: 342 SQ. FT.
BEDROOMS: 4
BATHROOMS: 2½
WIDTH: 74' - 8"
DEPTH: 75' - 10"

SEARCH ONLINE @ EPLANS.COM

With an exciting blend of styles, this home features the wrapping porch of a country farmhouse with a brick-and-siding exterior for a uniquely pleasing effect. The great room shares its cathedral ceiling with an open kitchen, and the octagonal dining room is complemented by a tray ceiling. Built-ins flank the great room's fireplace for added convenience. The master suite features a full bath, a walk-in closet, and access to the rear porch. Two additional bedrooms share a full hall bath; a third can be converted into a study. Skylit bonus space is available above the garage, which is connected to the home by a covered breezeway.

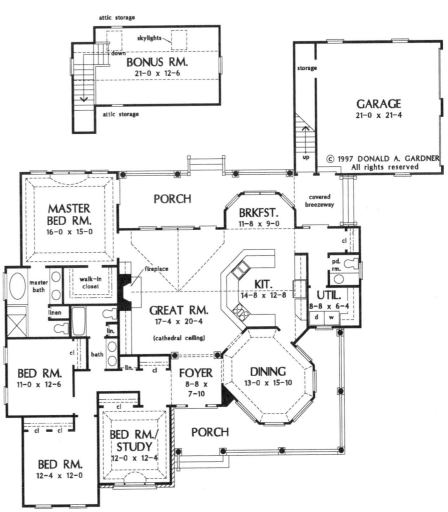

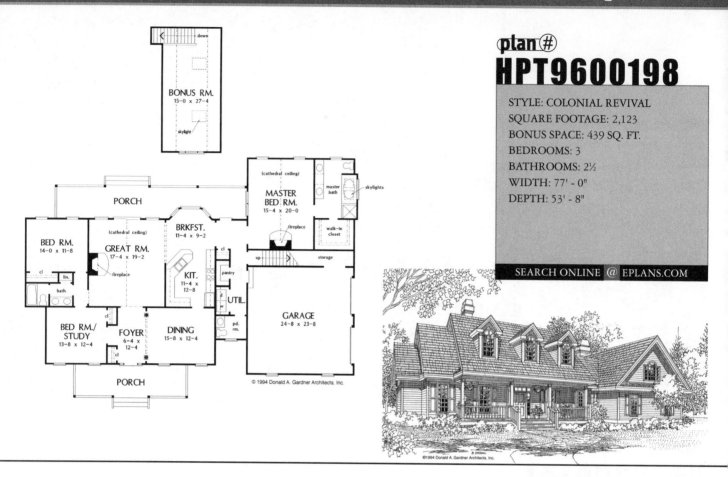

plan #
HPT9600198

STYLE: COLONIAL REVIVAL
SQUARE FOOTAGE: 2,123
BONUS SPACE: 439 SQ. FT.
BEDROOMS: 3
BATHROOMS: 2½
WIDTH: 77' - 0"
DEPTH: 53' - 8"

SEARCH ONLINE @ EPLANS.COM

© 1994 Donald A. Gardner Architects, Inc.

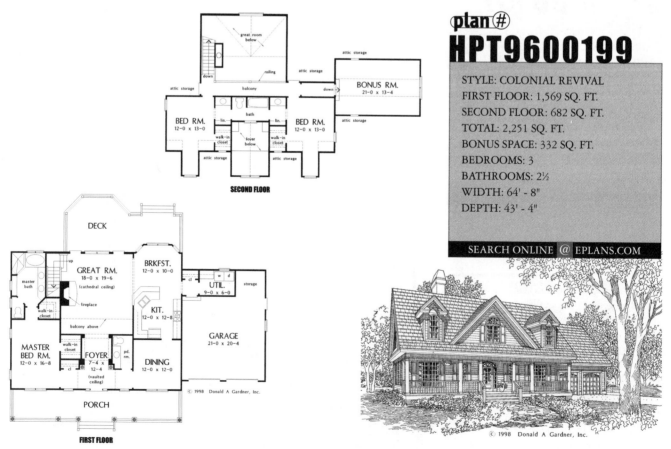

plan #
HPT9600199

STYLE: COLONIAL REVIVAL
FIRST FLOOR: 1,569 SQ. FT.
SECOND FLOOR: 682 SQ. FT.
TOTAL: 2,251 SQ. FT.
BONUS SPACE: 332 SQ. FT.
BEDROOMS: 3
BATHROOMS: 2½
WIDTH: 64' - 8"
DEPTH: 43' - 4"

SEARCH ONLINE @ EPLANS.COM

© 1998 Donald A Gardner, Inc.

ORDER BLUEPRINTS 24 HOURS, 7 DAYS A WEEK, AT 1-800-521-6797

© 1998 Donald A. Gardner, Inc.

plan # HPT9600200

STYLE: COLONIAL REVIVAL

SQUARE FOOTAGE: 2,487

BEDROOMS: 4

BATHROOMS: 3

WIDTH: 86' - 2"

DEPTH: 51' - 8"

SEARCH ONLINE @ EPLANS.COM

A trio of dormers and a front porch adorn the facade of this sprawling four-bedroom country home. Illuminated by the center dormer, the vaulted foyer gives way to the dining room with a tray ceiling and the spacious great room with a cathedral ceiling, a fireplace, and built-in shelves. A split-bedroom layout provides privacy for homeowners in a generous master suite with a tray ceiling and private bath. Three additional bedrooms reside on the opposite side of the home.

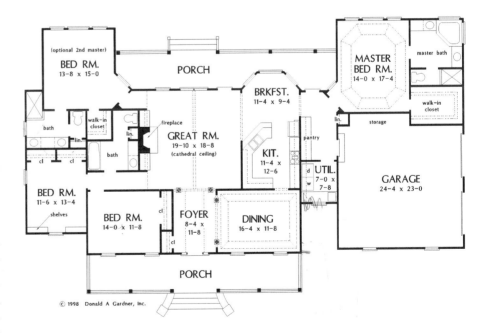

© 1998 Donald A. Gardner, Inc.

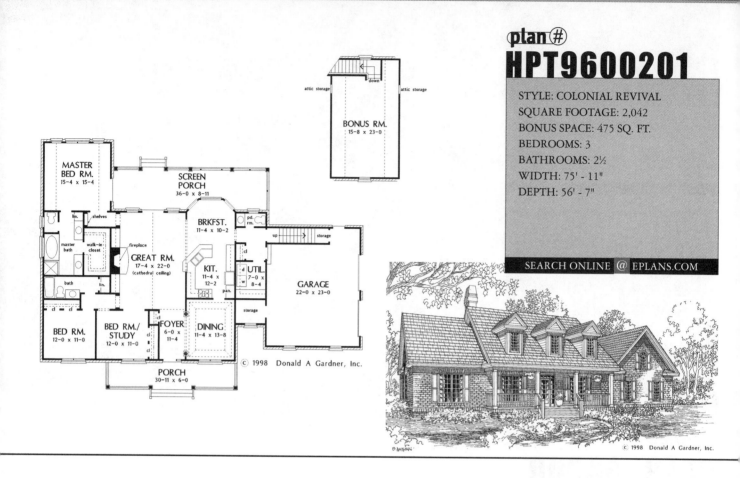

BONUS RM.
15-8 x 23-0

attic storage   down   attic storage

MASTER
BED RM.
15-4 x 15-4

SCREEN
PORCH
36-0 x 8-11

BRKFST.
11-4 x 10-2

pd. rm.

shelves
lin.

master
bath

walk-in
closet

fireplace

GREAT RM.
17-4 x 22-0
(cathedral ceiling)

KIT.
11-4 x
12-2

UTIL.
7-0 x
8-4

up   storage

GARAGE
22-0 x 23-0

bath

lin.

pan.

storage

cl   cl

BED RM.
12-0 x 11-0

BED RM./
STUDY
12-0 x 11-0

cl

FOYER
6-0 x
11-4

cl

DINING
11-4 x 13-8

PORCH
30-11 x 6-0

© 1998   Donald A Gardner, Inc.

ptan#
HPT9600201

STYLE: COLONIAL REVIVAL
SQUARE FOOTAGE: 2,042
BONUS SPACE: 475 SQ. FT.
BEDROOMS: 3
BATHROOMS: 2½
WIDTH: 75' - 11"
DEPTH: 56' - 7"

SEARCH ONLINE @ EPLANS.COM

© 1998   Donald A Gardner, Inc.

Master
Bedroom
15⁶x14⁰

Porch

Bedroom
No. 2
11⁸x12⁰

Great
Room
16⁸x24³

Bedroom
No. 3
10⁸x14⁰

Kitchen
12⁸x9⁰

Dining
Room
9⁸x16³

Stoop

Unfinished
Loft
16⁸x24⁰

Open to
Below

W.I.C.

OPTIONAL LAYOUT

ptan#
HPT9600202

STYLE: VACATION
SQUARE FOOTAGE: 2,019
BEDROOMS: 3
BATHROOMS: 2
WIDTH: 56' - 0"
DEPTH: 56' - 3"
FOUNDATION: CRAWLSPACE

SEARCH ONLINE @ EPLANS.COM

REAR EXTERIOR

plan
HPT9600203

STYLE: FARMHOUSE
FIRST FLOOR: 1,618 SQ. FT.
SECOND FLOOR: 570 SQ. FT.
TOTAL: 2,188 SQ. FT.
BONUS SPACE: 495 SQ. FT.
BEDROOMS: 3
BATHROOMS: 2½
WIDTH: 87' - 0"
DEPTH: 57' - 0"

SEARCH ONLINE @ EPLANS.COM

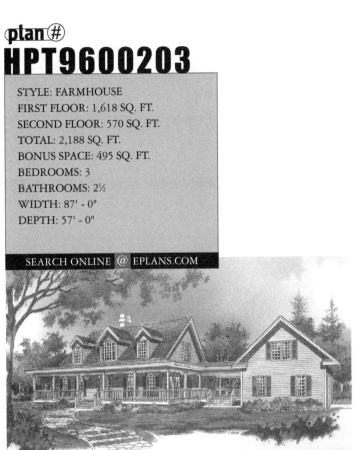

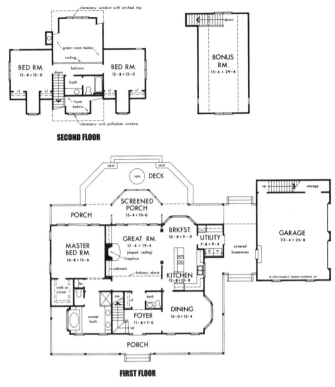

SECOND FLOOR

FIRST FLOOR

plan
HPT9600204

STYLE: COLONIAL REVIVAL
SQUARE FOOTAGE: 2,267
BEDROOMS: 4
BATHROOMS: 2½
WIDTH: 71' - 2"
DEPTH: 62' - 0"
FOUNDATION: BASEMENT,
CRAWLSPACE, SLAB

SEARCH ONLINE @ EPLANS.COM

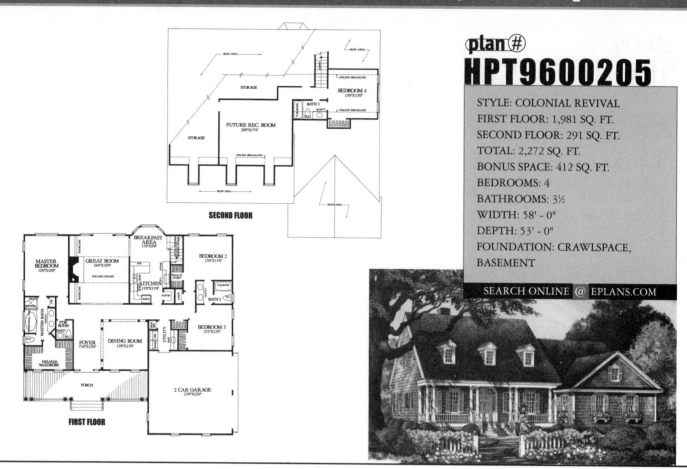

SECOND FLOOR

FIRST FLOOR

plan # HPT9600205

STYLE: COLONIAL REVIVAL
FIRST FLOOR: 1,981 SQ. FT.
SECOND FLOOR: 291 SQ. FT.
TOTAL: 2,272 SQ. FT.
BONUS SPACE: 412 SQ. FT.
BEDROOMS: 4
BATHROOMS: 3½
WIDTH: 58' - 0"
DEPTH: 53' - 0"
FOUNDATION: CRAWLSPACE,
BASEMENT

SEARCH ONLINE @ EPLANS.COM

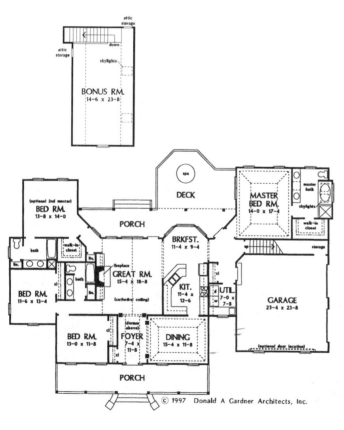

© 1997 Donald A Gardner Architects, Inc.

plan # HPT9600206

STYLE: COLONIAL REVIVAL
SQUARE FOOTAGE: 2,349
BONUS SPACE: 435 SQ. FT.
BEDROOMS: 4
BATHROOMS: 3
WIDTH: 83' - 2"
DEPTH: 56' - 4"

SEARCH ONLINE @ EPLANS.COM

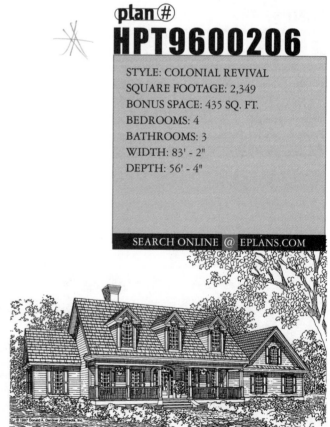

ORDER BLUEPRINTS 24 HOURS, 7 DAYS A WEEK, AT 1-800-521-6797

plan
HPT9600207

STYLE: COLONIAL REVIVAL
SQUARE FOOTAGE: 2,465
BEDROOMS: 4
BATHROOMS: 2½
WIDTH: 65' - 1"
DEPTH: 73' - 7"
FOUNDATION: SLAB,
BASEMENT, CRAWLSPACE

SEARCH ONLINE @ EPLANS.COM

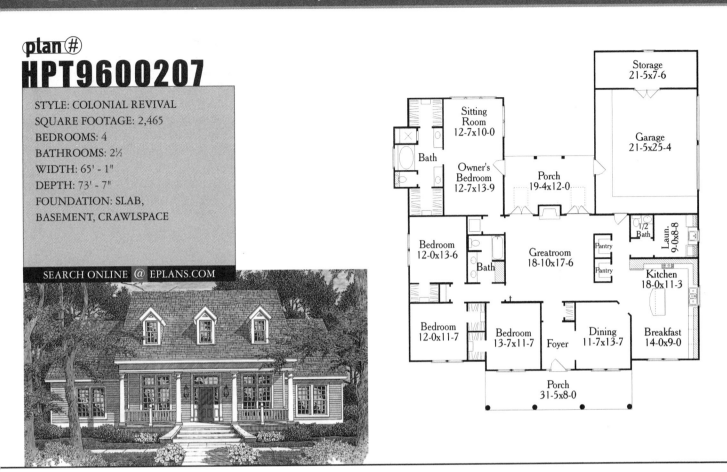

plan
HPT9600208

STYLE: COLONIAL REVIVAL
FIRST FLOOR: 1,870 SQ. FT.
SECOND FLOOR: 500 SQ. FT.
TOTAL: 2,370 SQ. FT.
BONUS SPACE: 222 SQ. FT.
BEDROOMS: 3
BATHROOMS: 3
WIDTH: 65' - 2"
DEPTH: 51' - 9"
FOUNDATION: CRAWLSPACE,
BASEMENT

SEARCH ONLINE @ EPLANS.COM

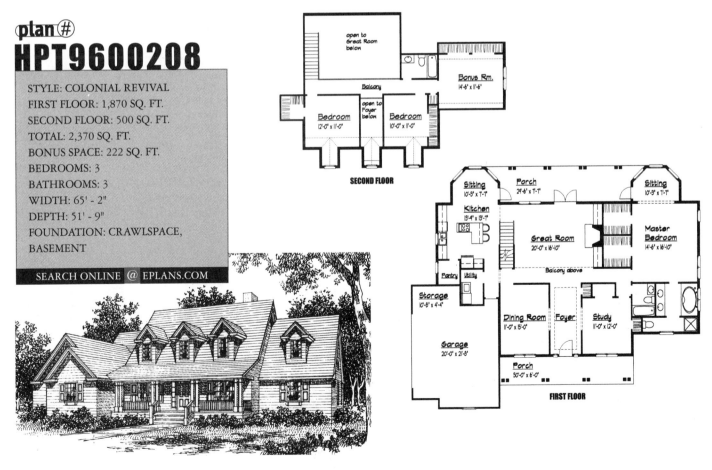

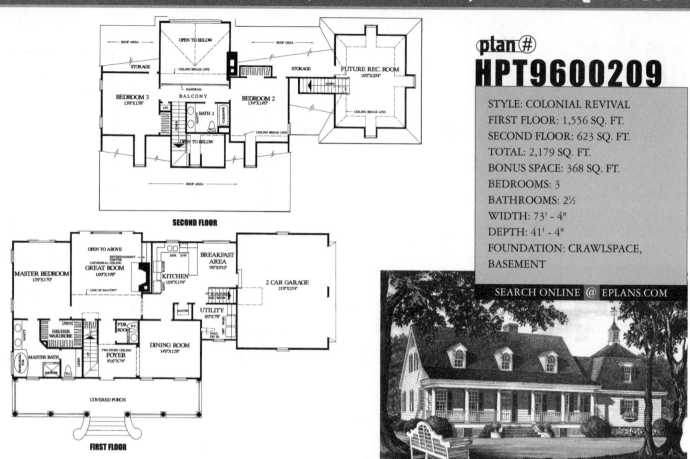

plan #

HPT9600209

STYLE: COLONIAL REVIVAL
FIRST FLOOR: 1,556 SQ. FT.
SECOND FLOOR: 623 SQ. FT.
TOTAL: 2,179 SQ. FT.
BONUS SPACE: 368 SQ. FT.
BEDROOMS: 3
BATHROOMS: 2½
WIDTH: 73' - 4"
DEPTH: 41' - 4"
FOUNDATION: CRAWLSPACE,
BASEMENT

SEARCH ONLINE @ EPLANS.COM

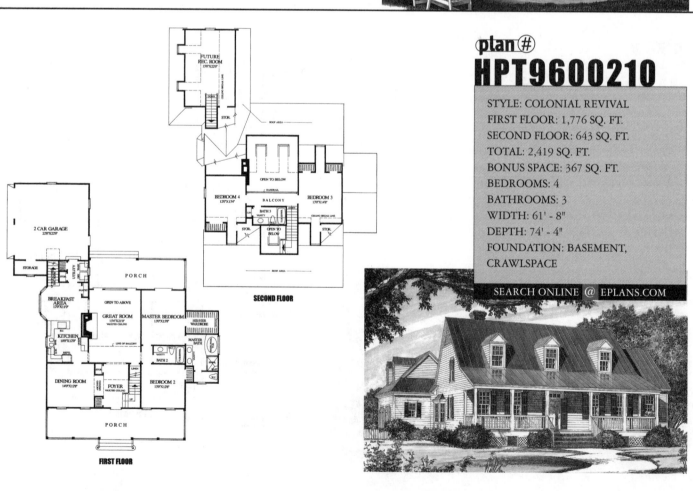

plan #

HPT9600210

STYLE: COLONIAL REVIVAL
FIRST FLOOR: 1,776 SQ. FT.
SECOND FLOOR: 643 SQ. FT.
TOTAL: 2,419 SQ. FT.
BONUS SPACE: 367 SQ. FT.
BEDROOMS: 4
BATHROOMS: 3
WIDTH: 61' - 8"
DEPTH: 74' - 4"
FOUNDATION: BASEMENT,
CRAWLSPACE

SEARCH ONLINE @ EPLANS.COM

ORDER BLUEPRINTS 24 HOURS, 7 DAYS A WEEK, AT 1-800-521-6797

plan # HPT9600211

STYLE: COLONIAL REVIVAL
SQUARE FOOTAGE: 2,215
BEDROOMS: 3
BATHROOMS: 3
WIDTH: 69' - 10"
DEPTH: 62' - 6"
FOUNDATION: CRAWLSPACE,
BASEMENT

SEARCH ONLINE @ EPLANS.COM

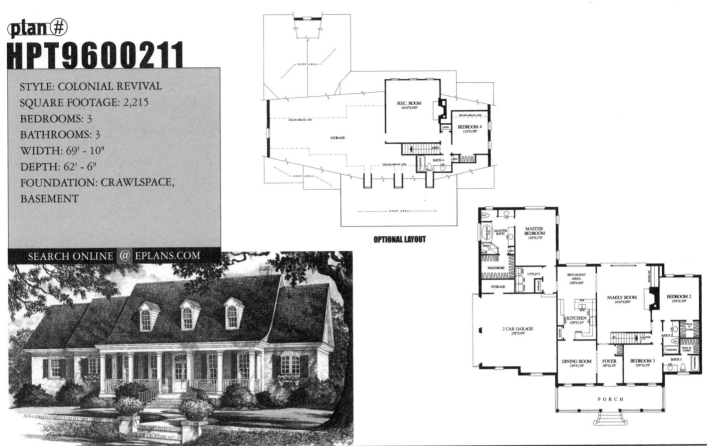

OPTIONAL LAYOUT

plan # HPT9600212

STYLE: COLONIAL REVIVAL
FIRST FLOOR: 1,376 SQ. FT.
SECOND FLOOR: 695 SQ. FT.
TOTAL: 2,071 SQ. FT.
BEDROOMS: 3
BATHROOMS: 2½
WIDTH: 47' - 0"
DEPTH: 49' - 8"
FOUNDATION: BASEMENT

SEARCH ONLINE @ EPLANS.COM

SECOND FLOOR

FIRST FLOOR

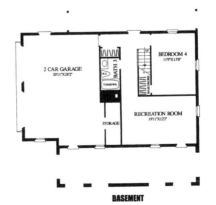

BASEMENT

OPTIONAL LAYOUT

Great Room
LINEN
W.I.c.
LINEN

TRAY CEILING
Master Suite
15⁹ x 15⁰
FRENCH DOORS
RADIUS WINDOW
FRENCH DOOR
PLANT SHELF ABOVE
Vaulted M.Bath
LINEN
W.I.c.
LINEN
RADIUS WINDOW
SHWR.
Bath
Bedroom 3
13⁵ x 12⁰
Bedroom 2
12¹⁰ x 11⁹
COATS
DECORATIVE COLUMNS
Foyer
11'-9" HIGH CEILING
BUILT-IN CAB. AND BOOKSHELVES
Great Room
17⁸ x 20²
11'-9" HIGH CEILING
SERVING BAR
DW.
ISLAND
REF.
DBL. OVEN
PANTRY
Dining Room
13⁰ x 13⁰
Kitchen
SURF. UNIT
Breakfast
FRENCH DOOR
Laund.
Study/ Bedroom 4
11⁰ x 11⁰
Bath
Storage
Garage
20⁹ x 19¹⁰
Covered Porch

plan #
HPT9600213

STYLE: COLONIAL REVIVAL
SQUARE FOOTAGE: 2,306
BEDROOMS: 4
BATHROOMS: 3
WIDTH: 72' - 0"
DEPTH: 56' - 1"
FOUNDATION: CRAWLSPACE, BASEMENT

SEARCH ONLINE @ EPLANS.COM

plan #
HPT9600214

STYLE: TRANSITIONAL
SQUARE FOOTAGE: 2,046
BEDROOMS: 3
BATHROOMS: 2½
WIDTH: 68' - 2"
DEPTH: 57' - 4"
FOUNDATION: CRAWLSPACE, SLAB, BASEMENT

Porch
32-2x8-0
Breakfast
11-8x10-6
Master Bedroom
14-0x17-6
Bath
9-0x15-3
Bedroom
11-10x11-6
Greatroom
17-6x17-6
Kitchen
11-8x14-11
Bath
Laundry
11-6x7-6
shelving linen shelving
Storage
11-6x7-10
Bedroom
11-10x11-6
Foyer
Dining
13-0x11-6
1/2 Bath
Garage
23-4x21-8
Porch
36-4x8-0

SEARCH ONLINE @ EPLANS.COM

ORDER BLUEPRINTS 24 HOURS, 7 DAYS A WEEK, AT 1-800-521-6797

plan # HPT9600215

STYLE: TRADITIONAL
SQUARE FOOTAGE: 2,098
BEDROOMS: 3
BATHROOMS: 2
WIDTH: 64' - 0"
DEPTH: 69' - 8"
FOUNDATION: BASEMENT

SEARCH ONLINE @ EPLANS.COM

plan # HPT9600216

STYLE: TRADITIONAL
SQUARE FOOTAGE: 2,018
BEDROOMS: 3
BATHROOMS: 2
WIDTH: 74' - 11"
DEPTH: 49' - 2"
FOUNDATION: CRAWLSPACE,
SLAB, BASEMENT

SEARCH ONLINE @ EPLANS.COM

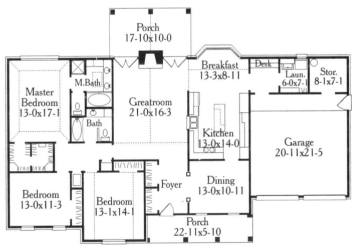

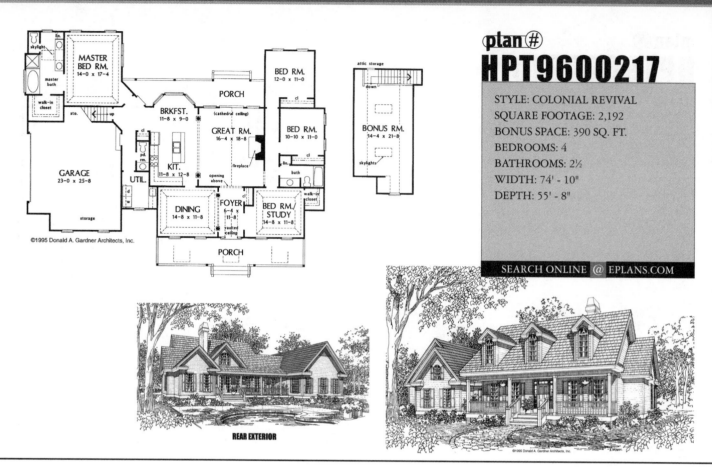

plan#
HPT9600217

STYLE: COLONIAL REVIVAL
SQUARE FOOTAGE: 2,192
BONUS SPACE: 390 SQ. FT.
BEDROOMS: 4
BATHROOMS: 2½
WIDTH: 74' - 10"
DEPTH: 55' - 8"

SEARCH ONLINE @ EPLANS.COM

REAR EXTERIOR

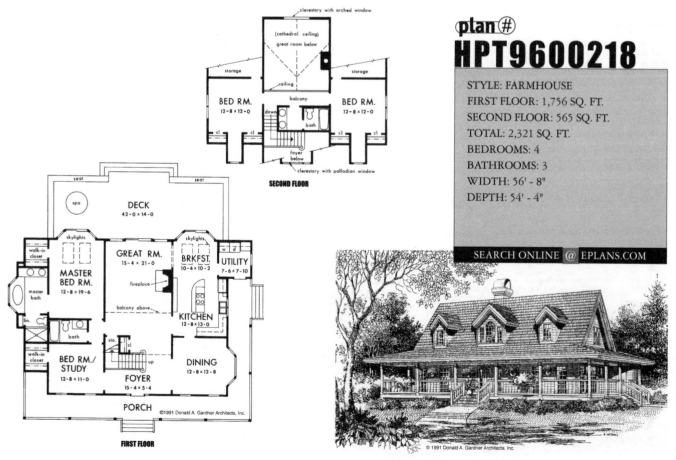

plan#
HPT9600218

STYLE: FARMHOUSE
FIRST FLOOR: 1,756 SQ. FT.
SECOND FLOOR: 565 SQ. FT.
TOTAL: 2,321 SQ. FT.
BEDROOMS: 4
BATHROOMS: 3
WIDTH: 56' - 8"
DEPTH: 54' - 4"

SEARCH ONLINE @ EPLANS.COM

SECOND FLOOR

FIRST FLOOR

ORDER BLUEPRINTS 24 HOURS, 7 DAYS A WEEK, AT 1-800-521-6797

plan
HPT9600219

STYLE: TRADITIONAL
SQUARE FOOTAGE: 2,170
BEDROOMS: 4
BATHROOMS: 3
WIDTH: 62' - 0"
DEPTH: 61' - 6"
FOUNDATION: WALKOUT
BASEMENT

SEARCH ONLINE @ EPLANS.COM

plan
HPT9600220

STYLE: COUNTRY
FIRST FLOOR: 1,324 SQ. FT.
SECOND FLOOR: 688 SQ. FT.
TOTAL: 2,012 SQ. FT.
BEDROOMS: 4
BATHROOMS: 2
WIDTH: 55' - 0"
DEPTH: 41' - 0"
FOUNDATION: BASEMENT

SEARCH ONLINE @ EPLANS.COM

SECOND FLOOR

FIRST FLOOR

REAR EXTERIOR

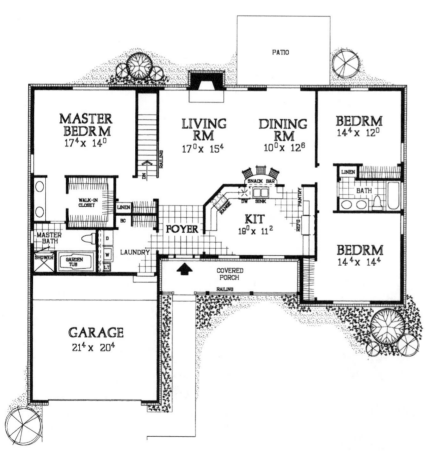

plan #

HPT9600221

STYLE: RANCH
SQUARE FOOTAGE: 2,076
BEDROOMS: 3
BATHROOMS: 2
WIDTH: 64' - 8"
DEPTH: 54' - 7"
FOUNDATION: BASEMENT

SEARCH ONLINE @ EPLANS.COM

Multipane windows, mock shutters, and a covered front porch exhibit the charm of this home's facade. Inside, the foyer is flanked by a spacious, efficient kitchen to the right and a large, convenient laundry room to the left. The living room features a warming fireplace. To the right of the living room is the formal dining room; both rooms share a snack bar and direct access to the kitchen. Sleeping quarters are split, with two family bedrooms and a full bath on the right side of the plan and the deluxe master suite on the left. The private master bath offers such luxuries as a walk-in closet, a twin-sink vanity, a garden tub, and a separate shower.

ORDER BLUEPRINTS 24 HOURS, 7 DAYS A WEEK, AT 1-800-521-6797

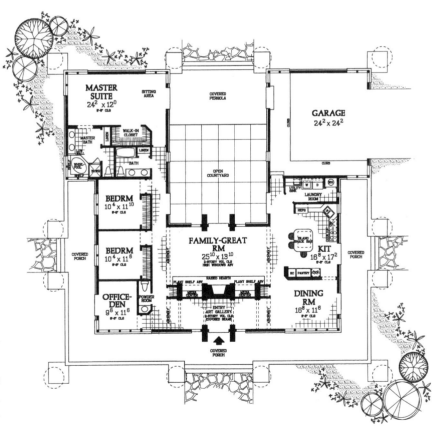

plan
HPT9600222

STYLE: PRAIRIE

SQUARE FOOTAGE: 2,626

BEDROOMS: 3

BATHROOMS: 2½

WIDTH: 75' - 10"

DEPTH: 69' - 4"

FOUNDATION: CRAWLSPACE

SEARCH ONLINE @ EPLANS.COM

Frank Lloyd Wright had a knack for enhancing the environment with the homes he designed. This adaptation reflects his purest Prairie style complemented by a brick exterior, a multitude of windows, and a low-slung hip roof. The foyer introduces a gallery wall to display your artwork. To the right, an archway leads to a formal dining room lined with a wall of windows. Nearby, the spacious kitchen features an island snack bar. The two-story family/great room provides an ideal setting for formal or informal gatherings. If philosophical discussions heat up, they can be continued in the open courtyard. The left wing contains the sleeping quarters and an office/den. The private master suite includes a sitting area, a walk-in closet, and a lavish master bath.

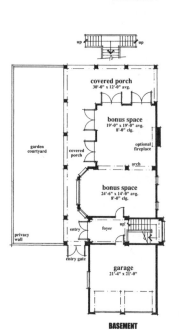

REAR EXTERIOR

covered porch
30'-0" x 12'-0" avg.

bonus space
19'-0" x 19'-0" avg.
8'-0" clg.

optional
fireplace

garden
courtyard

covered
porch

bonus space
24'-6" x 14'-0" avg.
8'-0" clg.

privacy
wall

entry

foyer

up

entry gate

garage
21'-4" x 21'-0"

BASEMENT

covered porch
30'-0" x 12'-0" avg.

down

great room
19'-0" x 19'-0"
10'-0" clg.

built
ins

fireplace

built
ins

covered
porch

arch

arch

eating
bar

dining
11'-4" x 14'-0"
10'-0" clg.

kitchen

arch

arch

arch

gallery

up

down

arch

study
10'-4" x 11'-4"
10'-0" clg.

util.

FIRST FLOOR

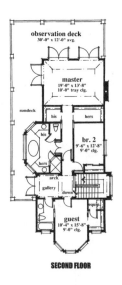

observation deck
30'-0" x 12'-0" avg.

master
19'-0" x 13'-8"
10'-0" tray clg.

sundeck

his

hers

his

br. 2
9'-6" x 12'-8"
9'-0" clg.

hers

arch

gallery

down

equip.

guest
10'-4" x 15'-8"
9'-0" clg.

SECOND FLOOR

plan
HPT9600223

STYLE: TIDEWATER

FIRST FLOOR: 1,305 SQ. FT.

SECOND FLOOR: 1,215 SQ. FT.

TOTAL: 2,520 SQ. FT.

BONUS SPACE: 935 SQ. FT.

BEDROOMS: 3

BATHROOMS: 2½

WIDTH: 30' - 6"

DEPTH: 72' - 2"

FOUNDATION: SLAB, BASEMENT

SEARCH ONLINE @ EPLANS.COM

Louvered shutters, balustered railings, and a slate-style roof complement a stucco-and-siding blend on this narrow design. Entry stairs lead up to the living areas, defined by arches and columns. A wall of built-ins and a fireplace highlight the contemporary great room; four sets of French doors expand the living area to the wraparound porch. Second-floor sleeping quarters include a guest suite with a bayed sitting area, an additional bedroom, and a full bath. The master suite features two walk-in closets, separate vanities, and French doors to a private observation deck. The lower level offers bonus space for future use and another porch.

plan # HPT9600224

STYLE: VICTORIAN

FIRST FLOOR: 1,362 SQ. FT.

SECOND FLOOR: 1,270 SQ. FT.

TOTAL: 2,632 SQ. FT.

BEDROOMS: 4

BATHROOMS: 2½

WIDTH: 79' - 0"

DEPTH: 44' - 0"

FOUNDATION: BASEMENT, CRAWLSPACE

SEARCH ONLINE @ EPLANS.COM

Rich with Victorian details—scalloped shingles, a wraparound veranda, and turrets—this beautiful facade conceals a modern floor plan. Archways announce a distinctive tray-ceilinged living room and help define the dining room. An octagonal den across from the foyer provides a private spot for reading or studying. The U-shaped island kitchen holds an octagonal breakfast bay and a pass-through breakfast bar to the family room. Upstairs, three family bedrooms share a hall bath--one bedroom is within a turret. The master suite is complete with a sitting room with a bay window, along with a fancy bath set in another of the turrets.

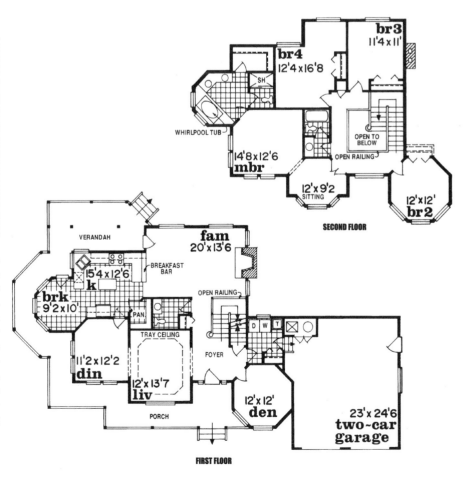

SECOND FLOOR

M.Bath

Bath

Bedroom
13-8x10-0

Master
Bedroom
13-4x19-6

Playroom
14-0x11-0

Bedroom
10-0x14-0

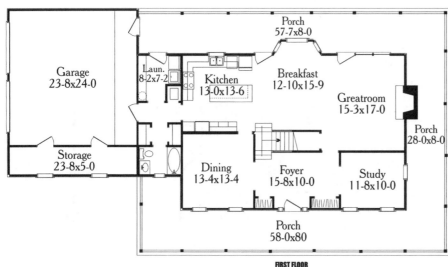

FIRST FLOOR

Garage
23-8x24-0

Laun.
8-2x7-2

Kitchen
13-0x13-6

Porch
57-7x8-0

Breakfast
12-10x15-9

Greatroom
15-3x17-0

Porch
28-0x8-0

Storage
23-8x5-0

Dining
13-4x13-4

Foyer
15-8x10-0

Study
11-8x10-0

Porch
58-0x80

plan #
HPT9600225

STYLE: VICTORIAN FARMHOUSE
FIRST FLOOR: 1,370 SQ. FT.
SECOND FLOOR: 1,212 SQ. FT.
TOTAL: 2,582 SQ. FT.
BEDROOMS: 3
BATHROOMS: 3
WIDTH: 74' - 0"
DEPTH: 44' - 0"
FOUNDATION: BASEMENT,
CRAWLSPACE, SLAB

SEARCH ONLINE @ EPLANS.COM

Charming dormer windows and a wraparound
porch make this country home a prize. The great
room offers porch views and a fireplace to warm
guests and family alike. The dining room features
a bumped-out wall of windows and easy service
from the nearby kitchen. The master suite is pampered by a walk-in closet and lavish bath.
Upstairs, two family bedrooms enjoy plenty of
closet space and share a full bath.

© 1990 Donald A. Gardner Architects, Inc.

B·NATHAN·

plan
HPT9600226

STYLE: FARMHOUSE

FIRST FLOOR: 1,734 SQ. FT.

SECOND FLOOR: 958 SQ. FT.

TOTAL: 2,692 SQ. FT.

BEDROOMS: 4

BATHROOMS: 3½

WIDTH: 55' - 0"

DEPTH: 59' - 10"

SEARCH ONLINE @ EPLANS.COM

A wraparound covered porch at the front and sides of this home and the open deck with a spa and seating provide plenty of outside living area. A central great room features a vaulted ceiling, fireplace, and clerestory windows above. The loft/study on the second floor overlooks this gathering area. Besides a formal dining room, kitchen, breakfast room, and sunroom on the first floor, there is also a generous master suite with a garden tub. Three second-floor bedrooms complete the sleeping accommodations.

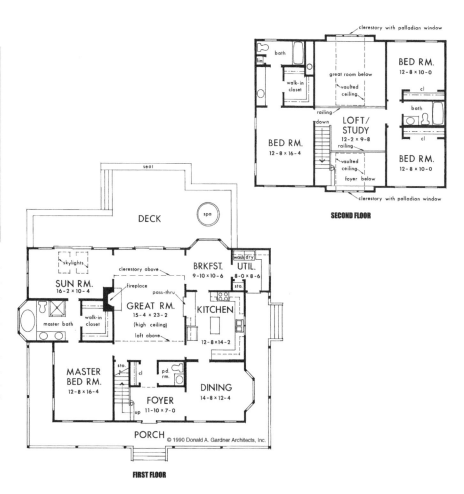

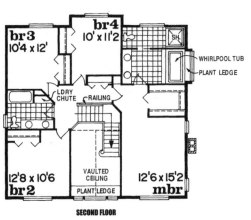

SECOND FLOOR

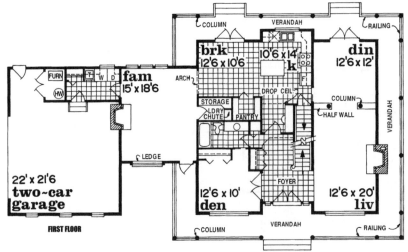

FIRST FLOOR

plan#
HPT9600227

STYLE: VICTORIAN FARMHOUSE
FIRST FLOOR: 1,639 SQ. FT.
SECOND FLOOR: 1,158 SQ. FT.
TOTAL: 2,797 SQ. FT.
BEDROOMS: 4
BATHROOMS: 3
WIDTH: 80' - 0"
DEPTH: 44' - 0"
FOUNDATION: CRAWLSPACE,
BASEMENT

SEARCH ONLINE @ EPLANS.COM

This grand farmhouse design is anything but ordinary. Its lovely details—a Palladian window, a covered veranda, and shutters—put it a cut above the rest. The interior features classic floor planning with a vaulted center-hall foyer and staircase to the second floor. Formal areas—a living room and a dining room—reside on the right; a cozy den and the large family room are on the left. A full bath sits near the den so that it can double as guest space. Four bedrooms on the second floor include a luxurious master suite.

ORDER BLUEPRINTS 24 HOURS, 7 DAYS A WEEK, AT 1-800-521-6797

© 1992 Donald A. Gardner Architects, Inc.

plan
HPT9600228

STYLE: FARMHOUSE
FIRST FLOOR: 1,357 SQ. FT.
SECOND FLOOR: 1,204 SQ. FT.
TOTAL: 2,561 SQ. FT.
BEDROOMS: 4
BATHROOMS: 2½
WIDTH: 80' - 0"
DEPTH: 57' - 0"

SEARCH ONLINE @ EPLANS.COM

This grand farmhouse features a double-gabled roof, a Palladian window, and an intricately detailed brick chimney. The foyer opens to the living room for formal entertaining, and the family room offers a fireplace, wet bar, and direct access to the porch. The lavish kitchen boasts a cooking island and serves the dining room, breakfast nook, and porch. The master suite on the second level has a large walk-in closet and a master bath with a whirlpool tub, separate shower, and double-bowl vanity. Three additional bedrooms share a full bath.

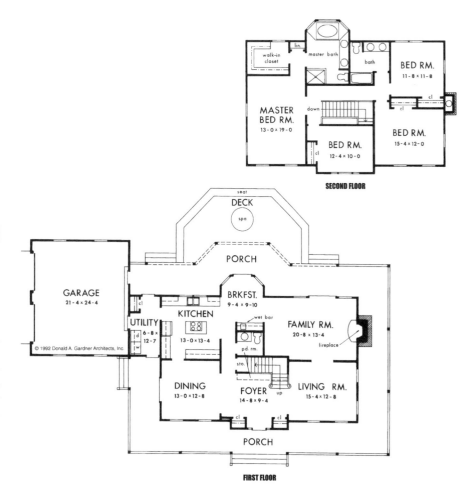

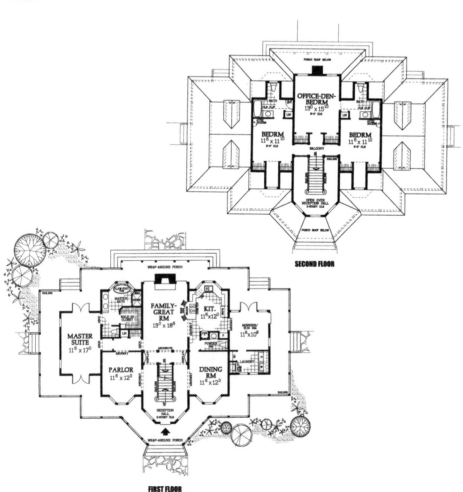

SECOND FLOOR

FIRST FLOOR

plan #

HPT9600229

STYLE: VICTORIAN FARMHOUSE
FIRST FLOOR: 1,752 SQ. FT.
SECOND FLOOR: 906 SQ. FT.
TOTAL: 2,658 SQ. FT.
BEDROOMS: 4
BATHROOMS: 3½
WIDTH: 74' - 0"
DEPTH: 51' - 7"
FOUNDATION: BASEMENT

SEARCH ONLINE @ EPLANS.COM

Delightfully proportioned and superbly symmetrical, this Victorian farmhouse has lots of curb appeal. The wraparound porch offers rustic columns and railings, and broad steps present easy access to the front, rear, and side yards. Archways, display niches, and columns help define the great room, which offers a fireplace framed by views to the rear property. A formal parlor and a dining room flank the reception hall, and each offers a bay window. The master suite boasts two sets of French doors to the wraparound porch and a private bath with a clawfoot tub, twin lavatories, a walk-in closet, and a stall shower. Upstairs, a spacious office/den adjoins two family bedrooms, each with a private bath.

ORDER BLUEPRINTS 24 HOURS, 7 DAYS A WEEK, AT 1-800-521-6797

© 1994 Donald A. Gardner Architects, Inc.

plan
HPT9600230

STYLE: VICTORIAN FARMHOUSE
FIRST FLOOR: 1,821 SQ. FT.
SECOND FLOOR: 956 SQ. FT.
TOTAL: 2,777 SQ. FT.
BEDROOMS: 4
BATHROOMS: 3
WIDTH: 77' - 0"
DEPTH: 58' - 8"

SEARCH ONLINE @ EPLANS.COM

With its long wraparound porches and expansive informal living spaces stretching across the back, this farmhouse projects a graceful, relaxed attitude. Nine-foot ceilings on the first level with a vaulted ceiling in the great room, ventilating skylights in the sunroom, a two-level foyer, and bay windows combine to make this home feel more like 3,000 square feet. The first-floor bedroom can double as a study, and the master bedroom upstairs features double vanities and a large walk-in closet.

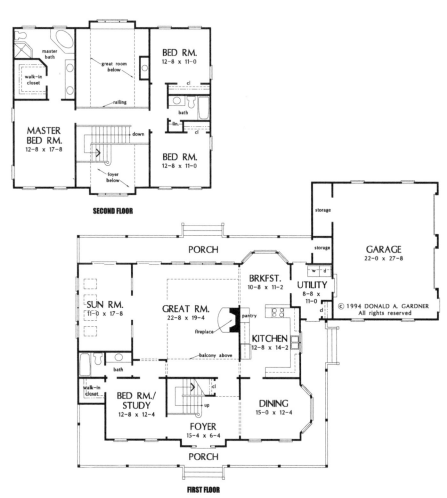

© 1993 Donald A. Gardner Architects, Inc.

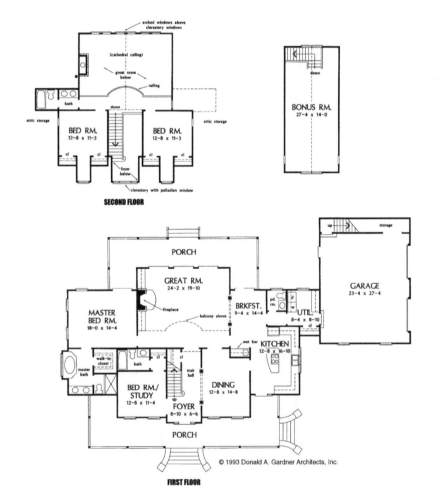

arched windows above clerestory windows

(cathedral ceiling)

great room below

railing

bath

attic storage

BED RM. 12-8 x 11-3

BED RM. 12-8 x 11-3

attic storage

cl   cl

cl   cl

down

foyer below

clerestory with palladian window

SECOND FLOOR

down

BONUS RM. 27-4 x 14-0

PORCH

GREAT RM. 24-2 x 19-10

fireplace

balcony above

MASTER BED RM. 18-0 x 14-4

master bath

walk-in closet

bath

BRKFST. 9-4 x 14-4

pd. rm.

UTIL. 8-4 x 8-10

cl

wet bar

KITCHEN 12-8 x 16-10

stair hall

BED RM./ STUDY 12-8 x 11-4

DINING 12-8 x 14-8

FOYER 8-10 x 6-6

up

PORCH

up

storage

GARAGE 23-4 x 27-4

© 1993 Donald A. Gardner Architects, Inc.

FIRST FLOOR

plan
HPT9600231

STYLE: FARMHOUSE
FIRST FLOOR: 2,064 SQ. FT.
SECOND FLOOR: 594 SQ. FT.
TOTAL: 2,658 SQ. FT.
BONUS SPACE: 483 SQ. FT.
BEDROOMS: 4
BATHROOMS: 3½
WIDTH: 92' - 0"
DEPTH: 57' - 8"

SEARCH ONLINE @ EPLANS.COM

Meandering through this four-bedroom farmhouse with its wraparound porch, you'll find country living at its best. A front Palladian dormer window, and rear clerestory windows in the great room add exciting visual elements to the exterior and provide natural light to the interior. The large great room boasts a fireplace, bookshelves, and a raised cathedral ceiling, allowing a curved balcony overlook above. The great room, master bedroom, and breakfast room are accessible to the rear porch for greater circulation and flexibility. Special features such as the large cooktop island in the kitchen, the wet bar, the bedroom/study, the generous bonus room over the garage, and ample storage space set this plan apart.

ORDER BLUEPRINTS 24 HOURS, 7 DAYS A WEEK, AT 1-800-521-6797

© 1993 Donald A. Gardner Architects, Inc.

B. NATHAN

plan
HPT9600232

STYLE: FARMHOUSE

FIRST FLOOR: 1,871 SQ. FT.

SECOND FLOOR: 731 SQ. FT.

TOTAL: 2,602 SQ. FT.

BONUS SPACE: 402 SQ. FT.

BEDROOMS: 4

BATHROOMS: 3

WIDTH: 77' - 6"

DEPTH: 70' - 0"

SEARCH ONLINE @ EPLANS.COM

This fetching four-bedroom country home has porches and dormers at both front and rear to offer a welcoming touch. The spacious great room enjoys a large fireplace, a cathedral ceiling and an arched clerestory window. An efficient kitchen is centrally located in order to provide service to the dining room and bayed breakfast area and includes a cooktop island. The expansive master suite is located on the first floor with a generous walk-in closet and a luxurious private bath. A front bedroom would make a lovely study or guest room. The second level is highlighted by a balcony hall that leads to two family bedrooms sharing a full bath.

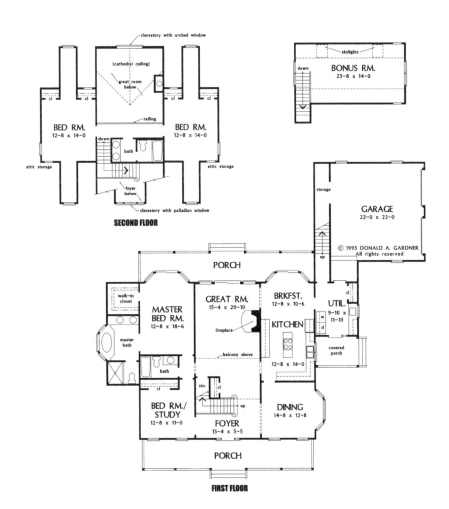

© 1994 Donald A. Gardner Architects, Inc.   B. NATHAN.

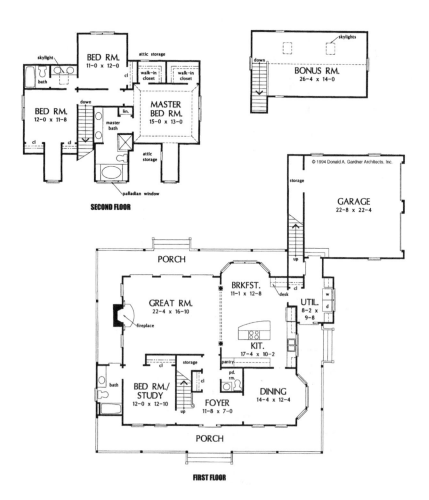

SECOND FLOOR

FIRST FLOOR

plan #
HPT9600233

STYLE: FARMHOUSE
FIRST FLOOR: 1,576 SQ. FT.
SECOND FLOOR: 947 SQ. FT.
TOTAL: 2,523 SQ. FT.
BEDROOMS: 4
BATHROOMS: 3½
WIDTH: 71' - 4"
DEPTH: 66' - 0"

SEARCH ONLINE @ EPLANS.COM

Enjoy balmy breezes as you relax on the wrap-around porch of this delightful country farmhouse. The foyer introduces a dining room to the right and a bedroom or study to the left. The expansive great room—with its cozy fireplace—has direct access to the rear porch. Columns define the kitchen and breakfast area. The house gourmet will enjoy preparing meals at the island cooktop, which also allows for additional eating space. A built-in pantry and a desk are additional popular features in the well-planned kitchen/breakfast room combination. A powder room and a utility room are located nearby. The master bedroom features a tray ceiling and a luxurious bath. Two additional bedrooms share a skylit bath.

ORDER BLUEPRINTS 24 HOURS, 7 DAYS A WEEK, AT 1-800-521-6797

© 1994 Donald A. Gardner Architects, Inc.

plan
HPT9600234

STYLE: FARMHOUSE

FIRST FLOOR: 1,907 SQ. FT.

SECOND FLOOR: 656 SQ. FT.

TOTAL: 2,563 SQ. FT.

BONUS SPACE: 467 SQ. FT.

BEDROOMS: 4

BATHROOMS: 2½

WIDTH: 89' - 10"

DEPTH: 53' - 4"

SEARCH ONLINE @ EPLANS.COM

Sunny bay windows splash this favorite farmhouse with style and create a charming facade that's set off by an old-fashioned country porch. Inside, the two-story foyer opens to a formal dining room and to a study, which could be used as a guest suite. The casual living area enjoys a fireplace with an extended hearth and access to an expansive screened porch. The sensational master suite offers a walk-in closet and a bath with a bumped-out bay tub, a double-sink vanity, and a separate shower. The two family bedrooms share a full bath

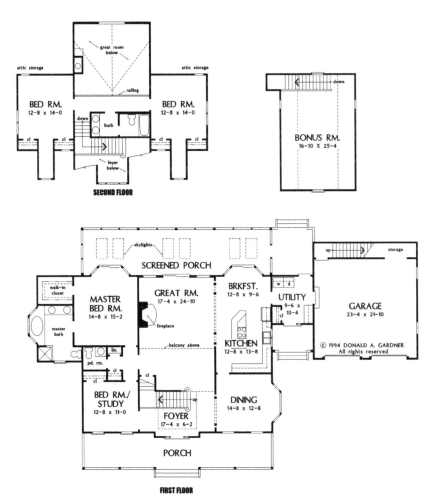

© 1998 Donald A. Gardner Architects, Inc.

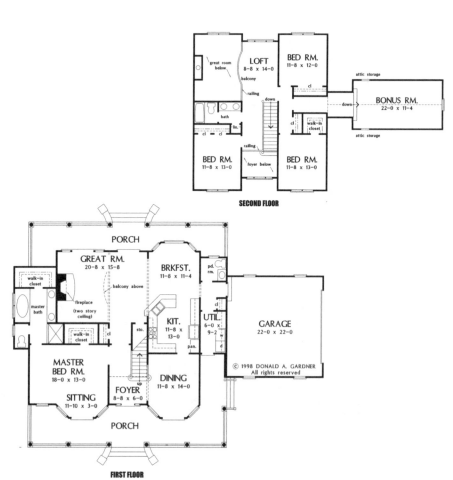

SECOND FLOOR

FIRST FLOOR

plan #

HPT9600235

STYLE: COLONIAL REVIVAL

FIRST FLOOR: 1,614 SQ. FT.

SECOND FLOOR: 892 SQ. FT.

TOTAL: 2,506 SQ. FT.

BONUS SPACE: 341 SQ. FT.

BEDROOMS: 4

BATHROOMS: 2½

WIDTH: 71' - 10"

DEPTH: 50' - 0"

SEARCH ONLINE @ EPLANS.COM

At the front of this farmhouse design, the master suite includes a sitting bay, two walk-in closets, a door to the front porch, and a compartmented bath with a double-bowl vanity. The formal dining room in the second bay also features a door to the front porch. Access the rear porch from the great room, which opens to the breakfast room under the balcony. On the second floor, three family bedrooms share a bath that has a double-bowl vanity. One of the family bedrooms offers a walk-in closet. A bonus room over the garage can be used as a study or game room.

ORDER BLUEPRINTS 24 HOURS, 7 DAYS A WEEK, AT 1-800-521-6797

© 1997 Donald A. Gardner Architects, Inc.

plan#
HPT9600236

STYLE: COLONIAL REVIVAL

FIRST FLOOR: 1,939 SQ. FT.

SECOND FLOOR: 657 SQ. FT.

TOTAL: 2,596 SQ. FT.

BONUS SPACE: 386 SQ. FT.

BEDROOMS: 4

BATHROOMS: 3

WIDTH: 80' - 10"

DEPTH: 55' - 8"

SEARCH ONLINE @ EPLANS.COM

This country farmhouse offers an inviting wrap-around porch for comfort and three gabled dormers for style. The foyer leads to a generous great room with an extended-hearth fireplace, vaulted ceiling, and access to the back covered porch. The first-floor master suite enjoys a sunny bay window and features a private bath with a cathedral ceiling, large oval tub set near a window, separate shower, and dual-vanity sinks. Upstairs, two family bedrooms share an elegant bath that has a cathedral ceiling. An optional bonus room over the garage allows plenty of room to grow.

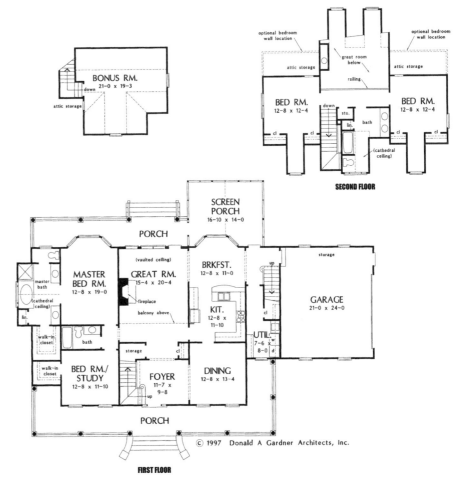

FUTURE REC. ROOM
22'-0" X 18'-10"

9' CEILING BREAKLINE

DOWN

ROOF AREA

ROOF AREA

BATH 2

WARDROBE
5'-8" X 4'-4"

OPEN TO BELOW

BEDROOM 3
11'-0" X 14'-8"

HANDRAIL

BALCONY

LINEN

BEDROOM 2
12'-0" X 14'-0"

BATH 3

STUDY LOFT

BEDROOM 4
13'-6" X 12'-0"

ROOF AREA

SECOND FLOOR

2 CAR GARAGE
22'-0" X 22'-0"

WORK BENCH

STORAGE

PORCH

UTIL

TERRACE AREA

BREAKFAST
10'-8" X 11'-4"

GREAT ROOM
17'-0" X 22'-0"

MASTER BATH

ISLAND

KITCHEN
10'-0" X 15'-0"

PANTRY

LINEN

LINE OF BALCONY ABOVE

WARDROBE
9'-6" X 7'-0"

DINING ROOM
12'-0" X 14'-0"

FOYER
8'-0" X 9'-10"

PDR ROOM

MASTER BEDROOM
13'-6" X 16'-0"

GAZEBO

PORCH

FIRST FLOOR

plan
HPT9600237

STYLE: COLONIAL REVIVAL
FIRST FLOOR: 1,734 SQ. FT.
SECOND FLOOR: 1,091 SQ. FT.
TOTAL: 2,825 SQ. FT.
BONUS SPACE: 488 SQ. FT.
BEDROOMS: 4
BATHROOMS: 3½
WIDTH: 57' - 6"
DEPTH: 80' - 11"
FOUNDATION: CRAWLSPACE,
BASEMENT

SEARCH ONLINE @ EPLANS.COM

Wonderful Victorian charm combines with the flavor of country in this delightful two-story home. A wraparound porch with a gazebo corner welcomes you into the foyer, where the formal dining room waits to the left and a spacious, two-story great room is just ahead. Here, a fireplace, built-ins, and backyard access add to the charm. The L-shaped kitchen features a work-top island, a walk-in pantry, and a breakfast area. Located on the first floor for privacy, the master suite offers a large walk-in closet and a pampering bath. Upstairs, three bedrooms—one with a private bath—share access to a study loft.

ORDER BLUEPRINTS 24 HOURS, 7 DAYS A WEEK, AT 1-800-521-6797

ptan
HPT9600238

STYLE: COUNTRY COTTAGE

FIRST FLOOR: 1,804 SQ. FT.

SECOND FLOOR: 1,041 SQ. FT.

TOTAL: 2,845 SQ. FT.

BEDROOMS: 4

BATHROOMS: 3½

WIDTH: 57' - 3"

DEPTH: 71' - 0"

FOUNDATION: WALKOUT BASEMENT

SEARCH ONLINE @ EPLANS.COM

There's a feeling of old Charleston in this stately home—particularly on the quiet side porch that wraps around the kitchen and breakfast room. The interior of this home revolves around a spacious great room with a welcoming fireplace. The left wing is dedicated to the master suite, which boasts wide views of the rear property. A corner kitchen easily serves planned events in the formal dining room, as well as family meals in the breakfast area. Three family bedrooms, one with a private bath and the others sharing a bath, are tucked upstairs.

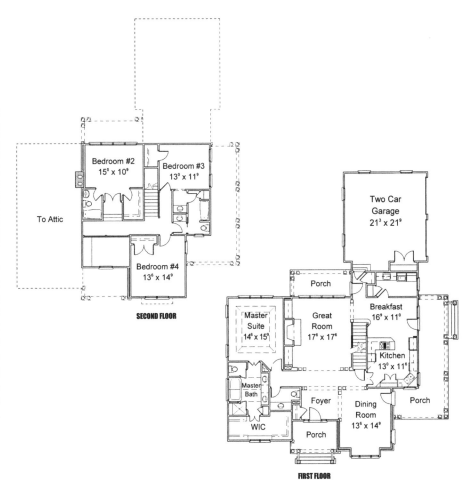

SECOND FLOOR

FIRST FLOOR

© Stephen Fuller, Inc.

plan
HPT9600239

STYLE: GEORGIAN
FIRST FLOOR: 1,650 SQ. FT.
SECOND FLOOR: 1,060 SQ. FT.
TOTAL: 2,710 SQ. FT.
BEDROOMS: 4
BATHROOMS: 3½
WIDTH: 53' - 0"
DEPTH: 68' - 2"
FOUNDATION: WALKOUT
BASEMENT

SEARCH ONLINE @ EPLANS.COM

This home features keystone arches that frame the arched front door and windows. Inside, the foyer opens directly to the large great room with a fireplace and French doors that lead outside. Just off the foyer, the dining room is defined by columns. Adjacent to the breakfast room is the keeping room, which includes a corner fireplace and more French doors to the large rear porch. The master suite has dual vanities and a spacious walk-in closet. Upstairs, two family bedrooms enjoy separate access to a shared bath; down the hall a fourth bedroom includes a private bath.

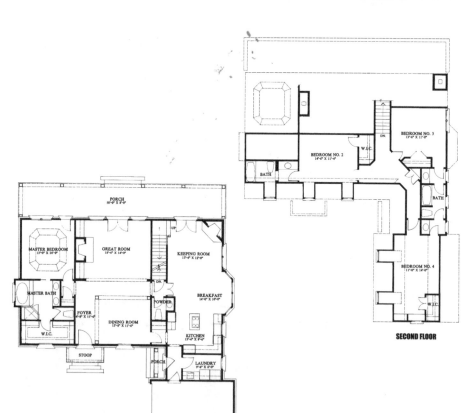

SECOND FLOOR

FIRST FLOOR

plan(#)
HPT9600240

STYLE: COLONIAL

FIRST FLOOR: 1,960 SQ. FT.

SECOND FLOOR: 905 SQ. FT.

TOTAL: 2,865 SQ. FT.

BONUS SPACE: 297 SQ. FT.

BEDROOMS: 4

BATHROOMS: 3½

WIDTH: 61' - 0"

DEPTH: 70' - 6"

FOUNDATION: WALKOUT
BASEMENT

SEARCH ONLINE @ EPLANS.COM

Traditionalists will appreciate the classic styling of this Colonial home. The foyer opens to both a banquet-sized dining room and formal living room with a fireplace. Just beyond is the two-story great room. The entire right side of the main level is taken up by the enchanting master suite. The other side of the main level includes a large kitchen and a breakfast room just steps away from the detached garage. Upstairs, each bedroom features ample closet space and direct access to a bath. The detached garage features an unfinished office or studio on its second level.

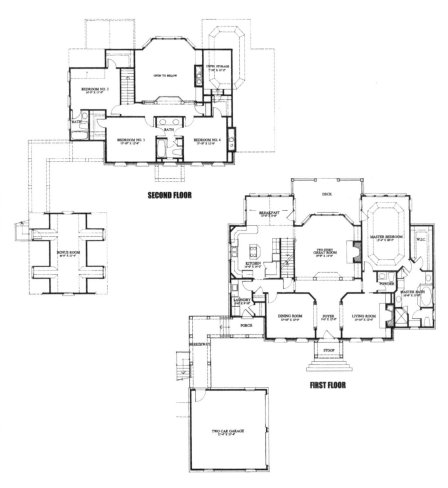

SECOND FLOOR

FIRST FLOOR

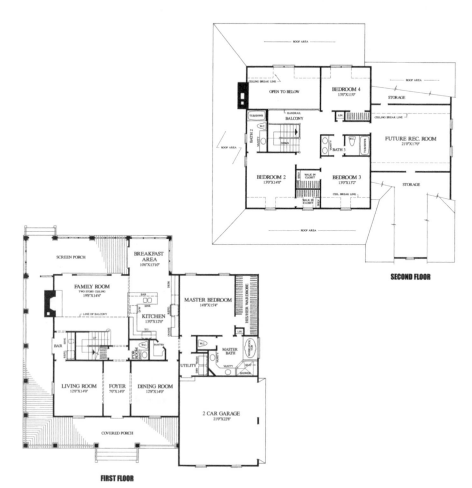

SECOND FLOOR

FIRST FLOOR

plan
HPT9600241

STYLE: FARMHOUSE
FIRST FLOOR: 1,913 SQ. FT.
SECOND FLOOR: 997 SQ. FT.
TOTAL: 2,910 SQ. FT.
BONUS SPACE: 377 SQ. FT.
BEDROOMS: 4
BATHROOMS: 3½
WIDTH: 63' - 0"
DEPTH: 59' - 4"
FOUNDATION: CRAWLSPACE,
BASEMENT, SLAB

SEARCH ONLINE @ EPLANS.COM

This enchanting farmhouse brings the past to life with plenty of modern amenities. An open-flow kitchen/breakfast area and family room combination is the heart of the home, opening up to the screen porch and enjoying the warmth of a fireplace. For more formal occasions, the foyer is flanked by a living room on the left and a dining room on the right. An elegant master bedroom, complete with a super-size walk-in closet, is tucked away quietly behind the garage. Three more bedrooms reside upstairs, along with two full baths and a future recreation room.

ORDER BLUEPRINTS 24 HOURS, 7 DAYS A WEEK, AT 1-800-521-6797

plan#
HPT9600242

STYLE: SOUTHERN COLONIAL
FIRST FLOOR: 1,273 SQ. FT.
SECOND FLOOR: 1,358 SQ. FT.
TOTAL: 2,631 SQ. FT.
BEDROOMS: 4
BATHROOMS: 3½
WIDTH: 54' - 10"
DEPTH: 48' - 6"
FOUNDATION: CRAWLSPACE

SEARCH ONLINE @ EPLANS.COM

This two-story home suits the needs of each household member. Family gatherings won't be crowded in the spacious family room, which is adjacent to the kitchen and the breakfast area. Just beyond the foyer, the dining and living rooms view the front yard. The master suite features its own full bath with dual vanities, a whirlpool tub, and separate shower. Three family bedrooms are available upstairs—one with a walk-in closet—and two full hall baths. Extra storage space is found in the two-car garage.

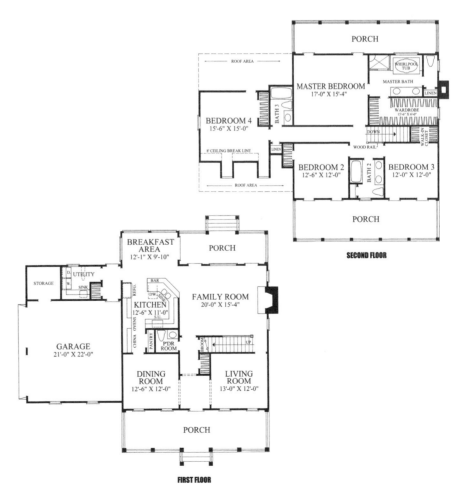

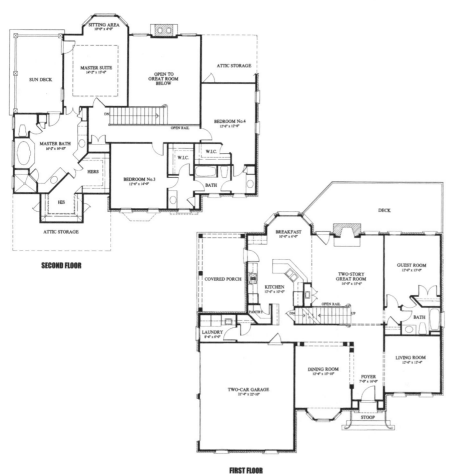

SECOND FLOOR

FIRST FLOOR

plan #
HPT9600243

STYLE: NORMAN
FIRST FLOOR: 1,581 SQ. FT.
SECOND FLOOR: 1,415 SQ. FT.
TOTAL: 2,996 SQ. FT.
BEDROOMS: 4
BATHROOMS: 3
WIDTH: 55' - 0"
DEPTH: 52' - 0"
FOUNDATION: WALKOUT
BASEMENT

SEARCH ONLINE @ EPLANS.COM

Classical details and a stately brick exterior accentuate the grace and timeless elegance of this home. Inside, the foyer opens to a large banquet-sized dining room and an adjacent formal living room. Just beyond, the two-story great room awaits, featuring a wet bar and warming fireplace. A large covered porch off the kitchen completes the family center. Upstairs, the master suite features an unusual bay-window design, private sundeck, garden tub, His and Hers vanities and walk-in closets, and a compartmented toilet. Two bedrooms with a connecting bath complete the second floor.

ORDER BLUEPRINTS 24 HOURS, 7 DAYS A WEEK, AT 1-800-521-6797

ROD DENT 95

plan #

HPT9600244

STYLE: TRADITIONAL

FIRST FLOOR: 1,932 SQ. FT.

SECOND FLOOR: 807 SQ. FT.

TOTAL: 2,739 SQ. FT.

BEDROOMS: 4

BATHROOMS: 2½

WIDTH: 63' - 0"

DEPTH: 51' - 6"

FOUNDATION: WALKOUT BASEMENT

SEARCH ONLINE @ EPLANS.COM

This sensational country Colonial exterior is set off by a cozy covered porch, just right for enjoying cool evenings outside. A two-story foyer opens to a quiet study with a centered fireplace and to the formal dining room with views to the front property. The gourmet kitchen features an island cooktop counter and a charming bayed breakfast nook. The great room soars two stories high but is made cozy with an extended-hearth fireplace. Two walk-in closets, a garden tub, and a separate shower highlight the master bath; a coffered ceiling decorates the master bedroom. Three family bedrooms, each with a walk-in closet, share a full bath upstairs.

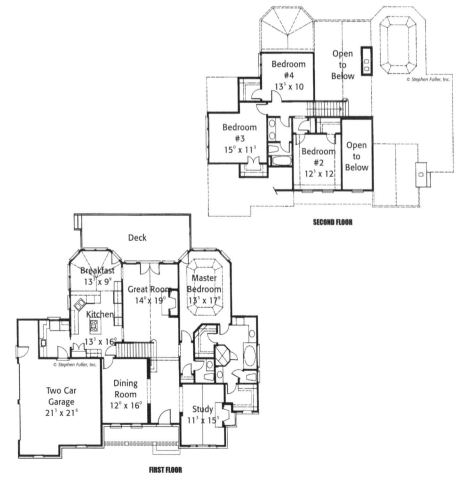

© 1997 Donald A. Gardner Architects, Inc.

B. NATHAN.

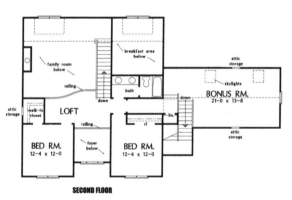

SECOND FLOOR

plan #
HPT9600245

STYLE: COLONIAL REVIVAL
FIRST FLOOR: 1,914 SQ. FT.
SECOND FLOOR: 597 SQ. FT.
TOTAL: 2,511 SQ. FT.
BONUS SPACE: 487 SQ. FT.
BEDROOMS: 3
BATHROOMS: 2½
WIDTH: 79' - 2"
DEPTH: 51' - 6"

SEARCH ONLINE @ EPLANS.COM

Filled with the charm of farmhouse details, such as twin dormers and bay windows, this design begins with a classic covered porch. The entry leads to a foyer flanked by columns that separate it from the formal dining and living rooms. The U-shaped kitchen separates the dining room from the bayed breakfast room. The first-floor master suite features a bedroom with a tray ceiling and a luxurious private bath.

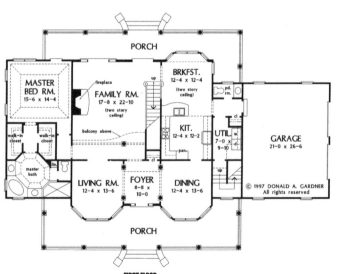

FIRST FLOOR

ORDER BLUEPRINTS 24 HOURS, 7 DAYS A WEEK, AT 1-800-521-6797

plan
HPT9600246

STYLE: TRADITIONAL

FIRST FLOOR: 1,930 SQ. FT.

SECOND FLOOR: 791 SQ. FT.

TOTAL: 2,721 SQ. FT.

BEDROOMS: 4

BATHROOMS: 3

WIDTH: 64' - 4"

DEPTH: 62' - 0"

FOUNDATION: BASEMENT, CRAWLSPACE, SLAB

SEARCH ONLINE @ EPLANS.COM

A delightful facade with a flared roof captures the eye and provides just the right touch for this inviting home. Inside, an angled foyer with a volume ceiling directs attention to the enormous great room. The detailed dining room includes massive round columns connected by arches and shares a through-fireplace with the great room. The master suite includes an upscale bath and access to a private covered porch. Nearby, Bedroom 2 is perfect for a nursery or home office/study. The kitchen features a large cooktop island and walk-in pantry. The second floor is dominated by an oversized game room. Two family bedrooms, a bath, and a linen closet complete the upstairs.

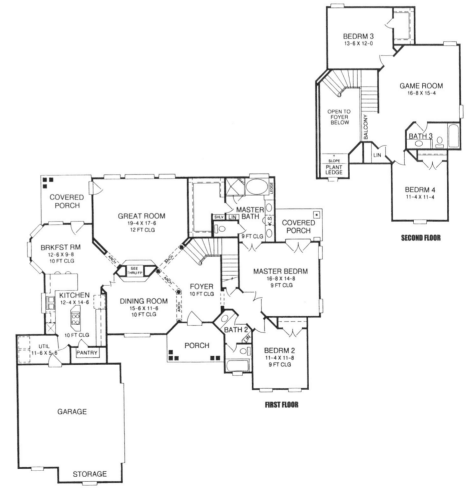

B. NATHAN.

© 1997 Donald A. Gardner Architects, Inc.

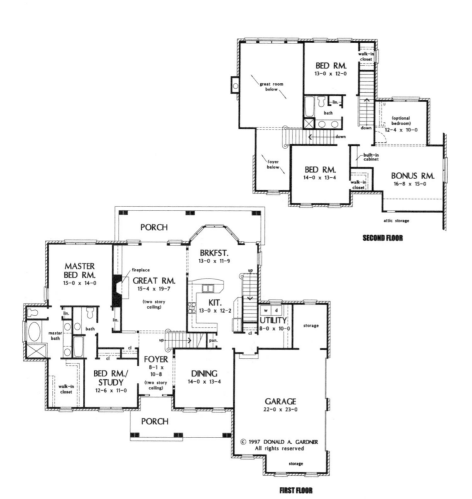

SECOND FLOOR

great room below

BED RM.
13-0 x 12-0

walk-in closet

lin.

bath

(optional bedroom)
12-4 x 10-0

down

down

foyer below

built-in cabinet

BED RM.
14-0 x 13-4

BONUS RM.
16-8 x 15-0

walk-in closet

attic storage

FIRST FLOOR

PORCH

MASTER BED RM.
15-0 x 14-0

fireplace

BRKFST.
13-0 x 11-9

GREAT RM.
15-4 x 19-7

(two story ceiling)

KIT.
13-0 x 12-2

up

lin.

master bath

bath

lin.

w d

UTILITY
8-0 x 10-0

storage

cl

walk-in closet

cl

cl

FOYER
8-1 x 10-8

(two story ceiling)

pan.

up

BED RM./
STUDY
12-6 x 11-0

DINING
14-0 x 13-4

GARAGE
22-0 x 23-0

PORCH

© 1997 DONALD A. GARDNER
All rights reserved

storage

plan
HPT9600247

STYLE: TRADITIONAL
FIRST FLOOR: 2,067 SQ. FT.
SECOND FLOOR: 615 SQ. FT.
TOTAL: 2,682 SQ. FT.
BONUS SPACE: 394 SQ. FT.
BEDROOMS: 4
BATHROOMS: 3
WIDTH: 73' - 0"
DEPTH: 60' - 6"

SEARCH ONLINE @ EPLANS.COM

Multiple gables, columns, and a balustrade add stature to the facade of this four-bedroom traditional home. Both the foyer and great room have impressive two-story ceilings and clerestory windows. The great room is highlighted by built-in bookshelves and French doors that lead to the back porch. The breakfast bay features a rear staircase to the upstairs bedrooms and the bonus room. Downstairs, the master suite enjoys an indulgent bath with a large walk-in closet; a nearby bedroom/study offers flexibility.

ORDER BLUEPRINTS 24 HOURS, 7 DAYS A WEEK, AT 1-800-521-6797

plan
HPT9600248

STYLE: TRADITIONAL

FIRST FLOOR: 2,028 SQ. FT.

SECOND FLOOR: 558 SQ. FT.

TOTAL: 2,586 SQ. FT.

BONUS SPACE: 272 SQ. FT.

BEDROOMS: 4

BATHROOMS: 3

WIDTH: 64' - 10"

DEPTH: 61' - 0"

FOUNDATION: CRAWLSPACE,
SLAB, BASEMENT

SEARCH ONLINE @ EPLANS.COM

Double columns and an arch-top clerestory window create an inviting entry to this fresh interpretation of traditional style. Decorative columns and arches open to the formal dining room and to the octagonal great room, which has a 10-foot tray ceiling. The U-shaped kitchen looks over an angled counter to a breakfast bay that brings in the outdoors and shares a through-fireplace with the great room. A sitting area and a lavish bath set off the secluded master suite. A nearby secondary bedroom with its own bath could be used as a guest suite. Upstairs, two family bedrooms share a full bath and a hall that leads to an expandable area.

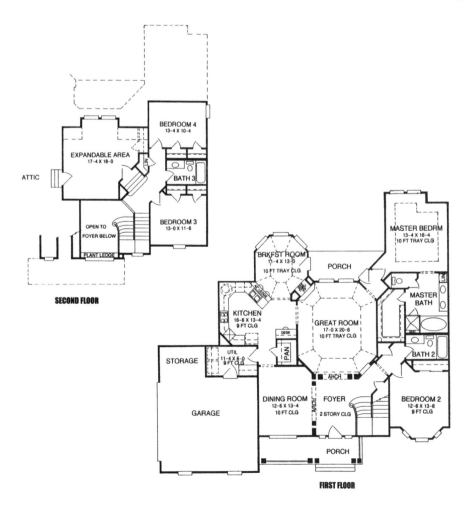

SECOND FLOOR

SUITE 2
12'-6" x 12'-0"

BATH

W.I.C.

MASTER
BATH

MASTER
SUITE
19'-0" x 14'-6"

LIN

SUITE 3
12'-8" x 11'-6"

SUITE 4
11'-4" x 13'-4"

LAUN.

BONUS
ROOM
12'-2" x 14'-0"

OPEN
TO
BELOW

FIRST FLOOR

DECK

KITCHEN
13'-0" x 17'-6"

BREAKFAST
10'-0" x 13'-0"

FAMILY
ROOM
18'-0" x 14'-6"

DINING
ROOM
12'-0" x 14'-6"

PDR.

STOR.

LIVING
ROOM
12'-8" x 14'-0"

LIBRARY
11'-4" x 10'-2"

FOYER

GARAGE
20'-6" x 20'-8"

PORITICO

plan(#)

HPT9600249

STYLE: TRANSITIONAL
FIRST FLOOR: 1,426 SQ. FT.
SECOND FLOOR: 1,315 SQ. FT.
TOTAL: 2,741 SQ. FT.
BONUS SPACE: 200 SQ. FT.
BEDROOMS: 4
BATHROOMS: 2½
WIDTH: 57' - 7"
DEPTH: 44' - 10"
FOUNDATION: CRAWLSPACE

SEARCH ONLINE @ EPLANS.COM

The handsome facade of this outstanding two-story traditional home is equaled by its efficient interior design. A library with multipane windows sits to the right of the entryway. The living room on the left adjoins a formal dining room with an octagonal tray ceiling. The island kitchen fills a bay window that looks out to the rear deck. A large breakfast room is adjacent to the family room with a fireplace and hearth. The master suite, with a cove ceiling, private bath, and walk-in closet resides on the second floor. Three family bedrooms and a bonus room complete this floor.

plan
HPT9600250

STYLE: TRADITIONAL

FIRST FLOOR: 1,333 SQ. FT.

SECOND FLOOR: 1,280 SQ. FT.

TOTAL: 2,613 SQ. FT.

BONUS SPACE: 294 SQ. FT.

BEDROOMS: 4

BATHROOMS: 3½

WIDTH: 58' - 0"

DEPTH: 44' - 4"

SEARCH ONLINE @ EPLANS.COM

Classic lines define the statuesque look of this four-bedroom home. The formal rooms flank the foyer and provide views to the front. An angled snack bar in the kitchen serves the breakfast area that is bathed in natural light. Connecting the spacious family room and living room is a wet bar that has the option of being used as a computer den. Upstairs, Bedrooms 3 and 4 share a bath, and Bedroom 2 offers a private bath, making it a fine guest suite. The master bedroom is sure to please with His and Hers walk-in closets, a whirlpool tub, and a tray ceiling. Completing this level is a large bonus room available for future expansion.

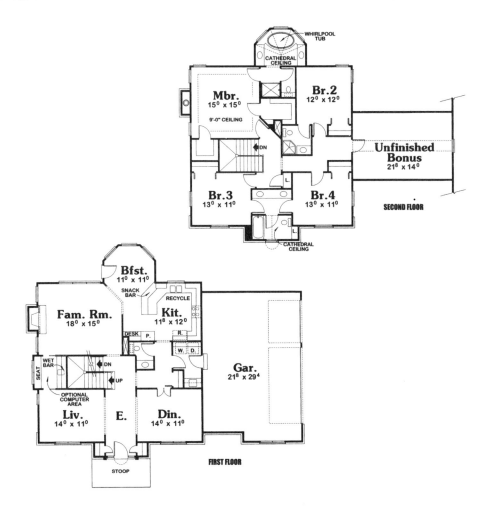

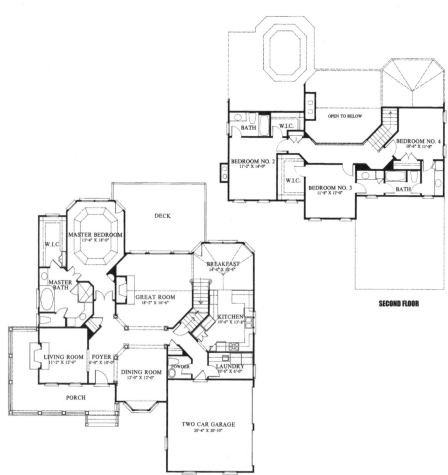

SECOND FLOOR

FIRST FLOOR

plan#
HPT9600251

STYLE: FARMHOUSE
FIRST FLOOR: 1,840 SQ. FT.
SECOND FLOOR: 950 SQ. FT.
TOTAL: 2,790 SQ. FT.
BEDROOMS: 4
BATHROOMS: 3½
WIDTH: 58' - 6"
DEPTH: 62' - 0"
FOUNDATION: WALKOUT
BASEMENT

SEARCH ONLINE @ EPLANS.COM

The appearance of this early American home brings the past to mind with its wraparound porch, wood siding, and flower-box detailing. Inside, columns frame the great room and the dining room. Left of the foyer lies the living room with a warming fireplace. The angular kitchen joins a sunny breakfast nook. The master bedroom has a spacious private bath and a walk-in closet. Stairs to the second level lead from the breakfast area to an open landing overlooking the great room. Three family bedrooms—two with walk-in closets and all three with private access to a bath—complete this level.

plan
HPT9600252

STYLE: COUNTRY COTTAGE
FIRST FLOOR: 1,475 SQ. FT.
SECOND FLOOR: 1,460 SQ. FT.
TOTAL: 2,935 SQ. FT.
BEDROOMS: 4
BATHROOMS: 3½
WIDTH: 57' - 6"
DEPTH: 46' - 6"
FOUNDATION: WALKOUT
BASEMENT

SEARCH ONLINE @ EPLANS.COM

Quaint keystones and shutters offer charming accents to the stucco-and-stone exterior of this stately English Country home. The two-story foyer opens through decorative columns to the formal living room, which offers a wet bar. The nearby media room shares a through-fireplace with the two-story great room, which has double doors that lead to the rear deck. A bumped-out bay holds a breakfast area that shares its light with an expansive cooktop-island kitchen. This area opens to the formal dining room through a convenient butler's pantry. One wing of the second floor is dedicated to the rambling master suite, which boasts unusual amenities with angled walls, a tray ceiling, and a bumped-out bay with a sitting area in the bedroom.

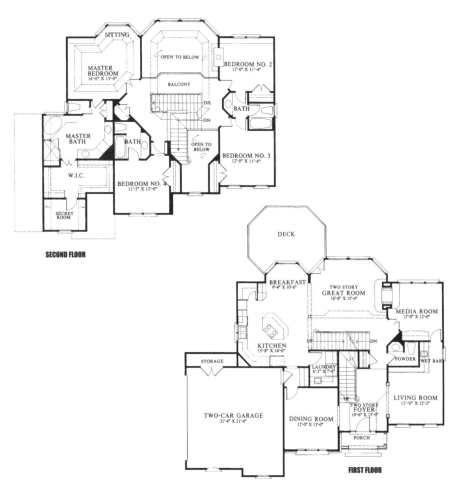

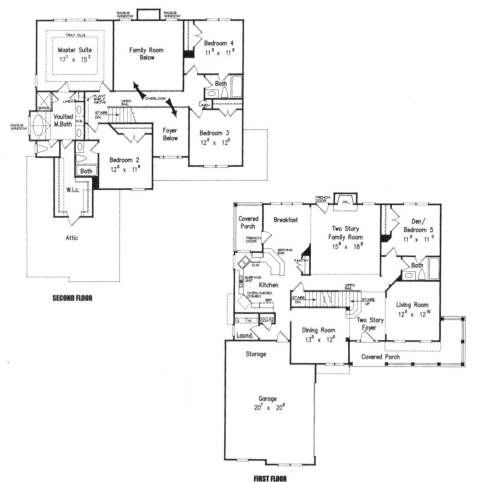

SECOND FLOOR

FIRST FLOOR

plan #
HPT9600253

STYLE: TRADITIONAL
FIRST FLOOR: 1,409 SQ. FT.
SECOND FLOOR: 1,300 SQ. FT.
TOTAL: 2,709 SQ. FT.
BEDROOMS: 5
BATHROOMS: 4
WIDTH: 54' - 6"
DEPTH: 59' - 4"
FOUNDATION: BASEMENT

SEARCH ONLINE @ EPLANS.COM

Feel like royalty in this stunning two-story home! The two-story foyer leads to a massive two-story family room, which features a cozy fireplace and a French door accessing the outside. To the right of the home is a living room and a den/bedroom sharing a full bath. To the opposite side of the home is the gourmet kitchen featuring an oven and microwave combo, a pantry, a serving bar, and a breakfast area with another French door accessing a side covered porch. Upstairs, four large bedrooms easily access three baths and a balcony overlook. The elegant master suite boasts a tray ceiling and a private bath with a large walk-in closet and a pampering soaking tub.

plan
HPT9600254

STYLE: TRANSITIONAL

FIRST FLOOR: 2,044 SQ. FT.

SECOND FLOOR: 896 SQ. FT.

TOTAL: 2,940 SQ. FT.

BONUS SPACE: 197 SQ. FT.

BEDROOMS: 4

BATHROOMS: 3½

WIDTH: 63' - 0"

DEPTH: 54' - 0"

FOUNDATION: BASEMENT, CRAWLSPACE, SLAB

SEARCH ONLINE @ EPLANS.COM

A gracious front porch off the formal dining room and a two-story entry set the tone for this elegant home. The living room is set to the front of the plan, thoughtfully separated from casual family areas that radiate from the kitchen. The two-story family room is framed by a balcony hall and accented with a fireplace and serving bar. The first-floor master suite features a sitting area, lush bath, and walk-in closet. Upstairs, two family bedrooms share a full bath; a third enjoys a private bath.

SECOND FLOOR

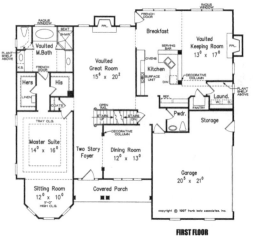

FIRST FLOOR

plan
HPT9600255

STYLE: EUROPEAN COTTAGE
FIRST FLOOR: 1,972 SQ. FT.
SECOND FLOOR: 579 SQ. FT.
TOTAL: 2,551 SQ. FT.
BONUS SPACE: 256 SQ. FT.
BEDROOMS: 3
BATHROOMS: 2½
WIDTH: 57' - 4"
DEPTH: 51' - 2"
FOUNDATION: CRAWLSPACE,
BASEMENT, SLAB

SEARCH ONLINE @ EPLANS.COM

A beautiful one-story turret is accompanied by arched windows and a stucco facade. A terrific casual combination of kitchen, breakfast area, and a vaulted keeping room provide space for family gatherings. Both the keeping room and great room sport cheery fireplaces. The master suite is secluded on the first floor. This relaxing retreat offers a sitting room, His and Hers walk-in closets, dual vanities, and compartmented toilet. Two family bedrooms share a full bath on the second floor. An optional bonus room can be used as a game room or home office.

ORDER BLUEPRINTS 24 HOURS, 7 DAYS A WEEK, AT 1-800-521-6797

plan #

HPT9600256

STYLE: TRADITIONAL

FIRST FLOOR: 2,015 SQ. FT.

SECOND FLOOR: 628 SQ. FT.

TOTAL: 2,643 SQ. FT.

BONUS SPACE: 315 SQ. FT.

BEDROOMS: 4

BATHROOMS: 3

WIDTH: 56' - 0"

DEPTH: 52' - 6"

FOUNDATION: CRAWLSPACE, BASEMENT

SEARCH ONLINE @ EPLANS.COM

Traditional architecture creates a feeling of timelessness that fits in established neighborhoods with ease. The formal living room opens directly off the vaulted foyer. An efficient kitchen serves the family room, vaulted breakfast room, and the dining room. A secluded study can double as a guest suite; the master suite enjoys privacy at the rear of the first floor. A full bath and two family bedrooms with walk-in closets are located on the second floor. The optional bonus room is available for future expansion.

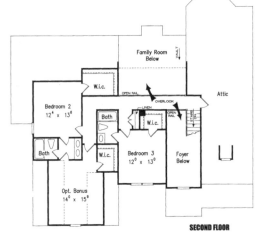

SECOND FLOOR

FIRST FLOOR

plan #
HPT9600257

STYLE: TRADITIONAL
FIRST FLOOR: 2,026 SQ. FT.
SECOND FLOOR: 726 SQ. FT.
TOTAL: 2,752 SQ. FT.
BONUS SPACE: 277 SQ. FT.
BEDROOMS: 4
BATHROOMS: 4½
WIDTH: 61' - 6"
DEPTH: 56' - 0"
FOUNDATION: CRAWLSPACE,
SLAB, BASEMENT

SEARCH ONLINE @ EPLANS.COM

This charming two-story traditional home welcomes in abundant natural light with its multitude of windows. The two-story foyer with its grand staircase is flanked by the dining room to the left and the living room to the right. The vaulted family room to the rear delights with picturesque views and a warming fireplace. The angled kitchen will easily serve the dining room, breakfast area, and family room. A study/bedroom is tucked away to the left, and the master suite finds privacy to the right. Two additional bedrooms and optional space for a third are located on the second floor along with two full baths.

ORDER BLUEPRINTS 24 HOURS, 7 DAYS A WEEK, AT 1-800-521-6797

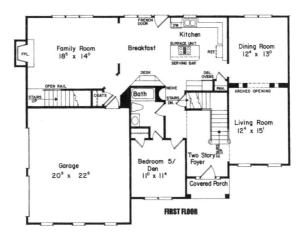

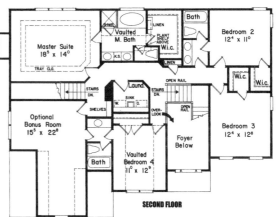

plan #

HPT9600258

STYLE: NEO-ECLECTIC

FIRST FLOOR: 1,447 SQ. FT.

SECOND FLOOR: 1,325 SQ. FT.

TOTAL: 2,772 SQ. FT.

BEDROOMS: 5

BATHROOMS: 4

WIDTH: 56' - 4"

DEPTH: 41' - 0"

FOUNDATION: CRAWLSPACE, BASEMENT

SEARCH ONLINE @ EPLANS.COM

Keystones, stucco arches, and shutters add a gentle European flavor to this traditional home. Inside, formal rooms are defined by decorative columns and a lovely arched opening. An additional bedroom or den to the front of the plan offers an adjacent bath. Open planning allows the breakfast area to enjoy the fireplace in the family room. The gourmet kitchen centers around a cooktop island counter and includes its own French door to the back property. On the second floor, a deluxe master suite enjoys a vaulted bath with a plant shelf, a walk-in closet, and garden tub.

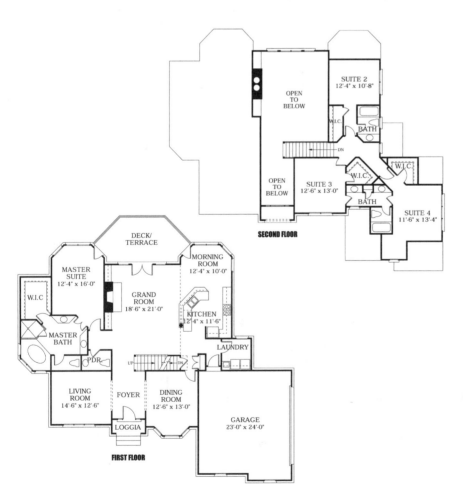

SECOND FLOOR

FIRST FLOOR

plan#
HPT9600259

STYLE: TRANSITIONAL

FIRST FLOOR: 1,878 SQ. FT.

SECOND FLOOR: 886 SQ. FT.

TOTAL: 2,764 SQ. FT.

BEDROOMS: 4

BATHROOMS: 3½

WIDTH: 67' - 10"

DEPTH: 56' - 4"

FOUNDATION: BASEMENT

SEARCH ONLINE @ EPLANS.COM

This distinguished brick home with traditional stucco accents includes a spectacular two-story foyer and grand room featuring a dramatic Palladian window. The grand room also opens to the kitchen and morning room. The master suite and morning room create matching bay wings to form a beautiful rear facade. A deck/terrace is accessible from both wings. The master suite features a tray ceiling in the bedroom, a large walk-in closet, and a bath with dual vanities and a garden tub. Upstairs, three additional suites share two baths. This design offers a basement plan that includes a guest suite and recreation area.

ORDER BLUEPRINTS 24 HOURS, 7 DAYS A WEEK, AT 1-800-521-6797

© 1997 Donald A. Gardner Architects, Inc.

plan #

HPT9600260

STYLE: TRANSITIONAL
FIRST FLOOR: 2,249 SQ. FT.
SECOND FLOOR: 620 SQ. FT.
TOTAL: 2,869 SQ. FT.
BONUS SPACE: 308 SQ. FT.
BEDROOMS: 4
BATHROOMS: 3½
WIDTH: 69' - 6"
DEPTH: 52' - 0"

SEARCH ONLINE @ EPLANS.COM

An impressive two-story entrance welcomes you to this stately home. Massive chimneys and pillars and varying rooflines add interest to the stucco exterior. The foyer, lighted by a clerestory window, opens to the formal living and dining rooms. The living room—which could also serve as a study—features a fireplace, as does the family room. Both rooms access the patio. The L-shaped island kitchen opens to a bay-windowed breakfast nook, which is echoed by the sitting area in the master suite. A room next to the kitchen could serve as a bedroom or a home office. The second floor contains two family bedrooms plus a bonus room for future expansion.

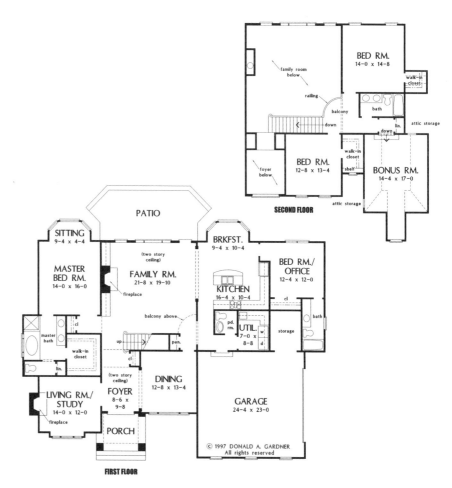

BEDROOM NO. 4
13'-4" X 11'-4"

OPEN TO BELOW

BEDROOM NO. 3
15'-0" X 17'-0"

BATH

OPEN TO BELOW

BEDROOM NO. 2
12'-4" X 13'-6"

SECOND FLOOR

DECK

BREAKFAST
15'-4" X 12'-6"

MASTER BEDROOM
13'-4" X 17'-10"

KITCHEN
13'-4" X 16'-0"

GREAT ROOM
14'-6" X 19'-0"

LAUNDRY
8'-0" X 9'-0"

W.I.C.

MASTER BATH
10'-8" X 16'-4"

W.I.C.

TWO CAR GARAGE
21'-4" X 21'-6"

DINING ROOM
12'-0" X 16'-0"

FOYER
7'-0" X 13'-6"

STUDY
11'-4" X 15'-2"

FIRST FLOOR

plan
HPT9600261

STYLE: FRENCH
FIRST FLOOR: 1,900 SQ. FT.
SECOND FLOOR: 800 SQ. FT.
TOTAL: 2,700 SQ. FT.
BEDROOMS: 4
BATHROOMS: 2½
WIDTH: 63' - 0"
DEPTH: 51' - 0"
**FOUNDATION: WALKOUT
BASEMENT**

SEARCH ONLINE @ EPLANS.COM

A perfect blend of stucco and stacked stone sets off keystones, transoms, and arches in this French Country facade to inspire an elegant spirit. The foyer is flanked by the spacious dining room and study, accented by a vaulted ceiling and a fireplace. A great room with a full wall of glass connects the interior with the outdoors. A first-floor master suite offers both style and intimacy with a coffered ceiling and a secluded bath.

ORDER BLUEPRINTS 24 HOURS, 7 DAYS A WEEK, AT 1-800-521-6797

plan #

HPT9600262

STYLE: NORMAN

FIRST FLOOR: 1,374 SQ. FT.

SECOND FLOOR: 1,311 SQ. FT.

TOTAL: 2,685 SQ. FT.

BEDROOMS: 4

BATHROOMS: 3

WIDTH: 57' - 4"

DEPTH: 42' - 0"

FOUNDATION: BASEMENT, SLAB

SEARCH ONLINE @ EPLANS.COM

Charming French accents create an inviting facade on this country home. An arched opening set off by decorative columns introduces a two-story family room with a fireplace and a radius window. The gourmet kitchen features an island cooktop counter, a planning desk, and a roomy breakfast area with a French door to the back property. The second-floor master suite offers a secluded sitting room, a tray ceiling in the bedroom, and a lavish bath with an oversize corner shower. Two family bedrooms share a gallery hall with a balcony overlook to the family room.

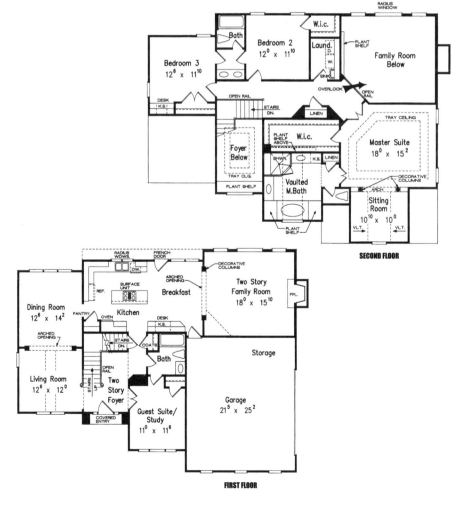

OSCAR THOMPSON, PHOTO COURTESY OF: SATER DESIGN COLLECTION
THIS HOME, AS SHOWN IN THE PHOTOGRAPH, MAY DIFFER FROM THE ACTUAL BLUEPRINTS.

REAR EXTERIOR

spa

deck

3 sided fireplace

master suite
20'-0" x 16'-0"
vaulted clg.

open to grand room below

elev. gallery walkway

storage

w.l.c.

open to below

down

SECOND FLOOR

screened verandah
50'-0" x 12'-0" avg.

grill

kitchen

nook

study
12'-8" x 13'-4"
vaulted clg.

grand room
17'-6" x 18'-0"
2 story clg.

dining
11'-6" x 14'-0"
8'-6" clg.

18' x 14'

3 sided fireplace

wetbar

elev.

up   down

br. 3
10'-10" x 15'-0"
8'-6" clg.

utility

foyer

br. 2
12'-8" x 14'-0"
8'-6" clg.

entry

down

balcony

FIRST FLOOR

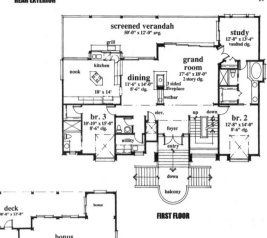

deck
50'-0" x 12'-0"

bonus

bonus
36'-0" x 17'-0"

garage
23'-0" x 27'-0"

opt. elev.

storage

bonus

BASEMENT

plan
HPT9600263

STYLE: FLORIDIAN
FIRST FLOOR: 2,066 SQ. FT.
SECOND FLOOR: 810 SQ. FT.
TOTAL: 2,876 SQ. FT.
BONUS SPACE: 1,260 SQ. FT.
BEDROOMS: 3
BATHROOMS: 3½
WIDTH: 64' - 0"
DEPTH: 45' - 0"
FOUNDATION: PIER

SEARCH ONLINE | @ EPLANS.COM

If entertaining is your passion, then this is the design for you. With a large, open floor plan and an array of amenities, every gathering will be a success. The foyer embraces living areas accented by a glass fireplace and a wet bar. The grand room and dining room each access a screened veranda for outside enjoyments. The gourmet kitchen delights with its openness to the rest of the house. A morning nook here also adds a nice touch. Two bedrooms and a study radiate from the first-floor living areas. Upstairs—or use the elevator—is a masterful master suite. It contains a huge walk-in closet, a whirlpool tub, and a private sundeck with a spa.

plan
HPT9600264

STYLE: TRANSITIONAL
SQUARE FOOTAGE: 2,946
BEDROOMS: 4
BATHROOMS: 3
WIDTH: 94' - 1"
DEPTH: 67' - 4"
FOUNDATION: SLAB

SEARCH ONLINE @ EPLANS.COM

This home's varying hipped-roof planes make a strong statement. Exquisite classical detailing includes delightfully proportioned columns below a modified pedimented gable and masses of brick punctuated by corner quoins. The central foyer, with its high ceiling, leads to interesting traffic patterns. This extremely functional floor plan fosters flexible living patterns. There are formal and informal living areas, which are well defined by the living and family rooms. The sunken family room, wonderfully spacious with its high, sloping ceiling, contains a complete media-center wall and a fireplace flanked by doors to the entertainment patio. Occupying the isolated end of the floor plan, the master suite includes an adjacent office/den with a private porch.

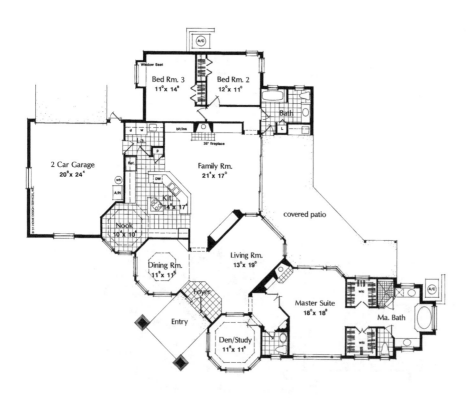

plan #
HPT9600265

STYLE: FLORIDIAN
SQUARE FOOTAGE: 2,656
BEDROOMS: 3
BATHROOMS: 2½
WIDTH: 92' - 0"
DEPTH: 69' - 0"
FOUNDATION: SLAB

SEARCH ONLINE @ EPLANS.COM

A graceful design sets this charming home apart from the ordinary and transcends the commonplace. From the foyer, the dining room branches off the sunny living room, setting a lovely backdrop for entertaining. Casual living is the focus in the oversized family room, where sliding doors open to the patio and the eat-in, gourmet kitchen is open for easy conversation. Two family bedrooms and a cabana bath are just off the family room. The master suite has a cozy fireplace in the sitting area, twin closets, and a compartmented bath. A large covered patio adds to the living area.

   ORDER BLUEPRINTS 24 HOURS, 7 DAYS A WEEK, AT 1-800-521-6797

plan
HPT9600266

STYLE: MEDITERRANEAN
SQUARE FOOTAGE: 2,597
BEDROOMS: 4
BATHROOMS: 3
WIDTH: 96' - 6"
DEPTH: 50' - 0"
FOUNDATION: SLAB

SEARCH ONLINE @ EPLANS.COM

The angles in this home create unlimited views and space. Majestic columns of brick add warmth to a striking facade. Inside, the foyer commands a special perspective on living areas including the living room, dining room, and den. The island kitchen serves the breakfast nook and the family room. A large pantry provides ample space for food storage. Nearby, in the master suite, mitered glass and a private bath set the tone for simple luxury. Two secondary bedrooms share privacy and quiet at the front of the house. The den may also convert to a fourth bedroom, if desired.

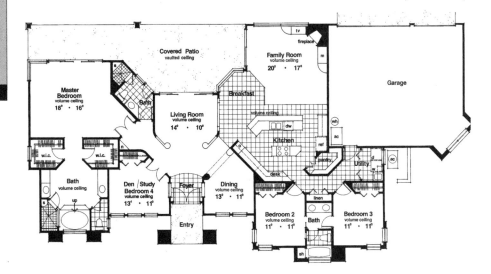

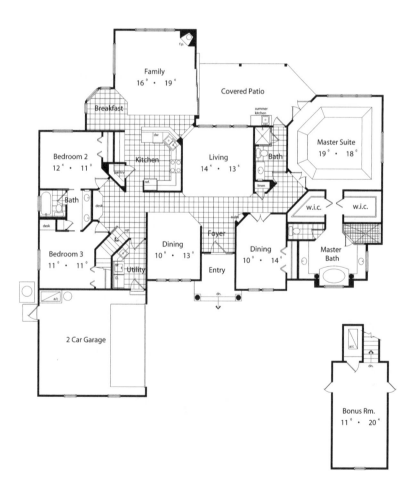

ptan #

HPT9600267

STYLE: MEDITERRANEAN
SQUARE FOOTAGE: 2,551
BONUS SPACE: 287 SQ. FT.
BEDROOMS: 4
BATHROOMS: 3
WIDTH: 69' - 8"
DEPTH: 71' - 4"
FOUNDATION: SLAB

SEARCH ONLINE @ EPLANS.COM

Shutters and multipane windows dress up the exterior of this lovely Mediterranean home. Formal and informal areas flow easily, beginning with the dining room sized to accommodate large parties and function with the adjacent living room. A gourmet kitchen is complete with a walk-in pantry and a cozy breakfast nook. Double doors lead to the spacious master suite. The lavish master bath features His and Hers walk-in closets, a tub framed by a columned archway, and an oversized shower. Off the angular hallway, two bedrooms share a Pullman-style bath and a study desk. A bonus room over the garage provides additional space.

J.N. HANSEN P.T.L.

plan
HPT9600268

STYLE: TRANSITIONAL

SQUARE FOOTAGE: 2,931

BEDROOMS: 3

BATHROOMS: 3

WIDTH: 70' - 8"

DEPTH: 83' - 0"

FOUNDATION: SLAB

SEARCH ONLINE @ EPLANS.COM

Quoins and keystone accents lend a French Country flavor to this stucco exterior. A tiled foyer leads to a gracefully curved gallery hall. The heart of the plan is the vaulted living room, which overlooks the covered patio and rear grounds, but friends may want to gather in the family room, where a centered fireplace offers cozy niches. A gourmet kitchen is designed to handle casual meals as well as planned occasions, with a service kitchen on the patio for outdoor events.

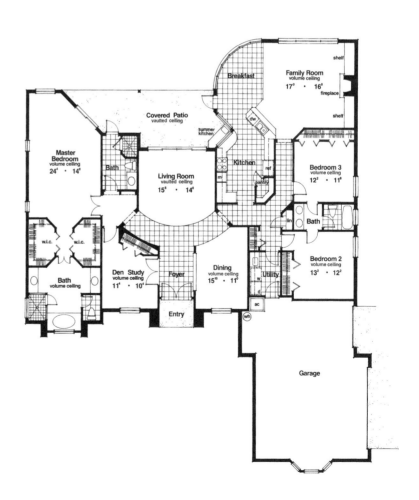

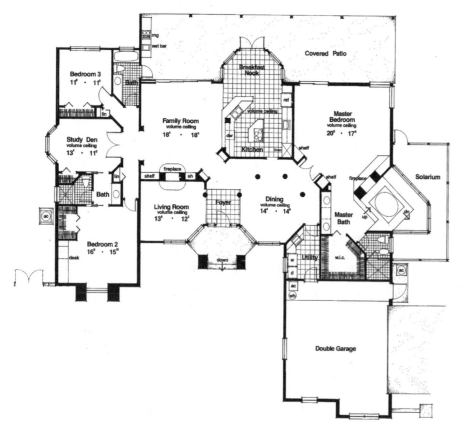

plan #

HPT9600269

STYLE: MEDITERRANEAN
SQUARE FOOTAGE: 2,987
BEDROOMS: 3
BATHROOMS: 3
WIDTH: 74' - 4"
DEPTH: 82' - 4"
FOUNDATION: SLAB

SEARCH ONLINE @ EPLANS.COM

Classic columns, a tiled roof, and beautiful arched windows herald a gracious interior for this fine home. Arched windows also mark the entrance into the vaulted living room with a tiled fireplace. The dining room opens off the vaulted foyer. Filled with light from a wall of sliding glass doors, the family room leads to the covered patio—note the wet bar and range that enhance outdoor living. The kitchen features a vaulted ceiling and unfolds into the roomy nook, which boasts French doors to the patio. The master bedroom also has patio access and shares a dual fireplace with the master bath—a solarium lights this space. A vaulted study/den sits between two additional bedrooms.

ORDER BLUEPRINTS 24 HOURS, 7 DAYS A WEEK, AT 1-800-521-6797

© The Sater Group, Inc.

plan
HPT9600270

STYLE: MEDITERRANEAN

SQUARE FOOTAGE: 2,794

BEDROOMS: 3

BATHROOMS: 3

WIDTH: 70' - 0"

DEPTH: 98' - 0"

FOUNDATION: SLAB

SEARCH ONLINE @ EPLANS.COM

Classic columns, circle-head windows, and a bay-windowed study give this stucco home a wonderful street presence. The foyer leads to the formal living and dining areas. An arched buffet server separates these rooms and contributes an open feeling. The kitchen, nook, and leisure room are grouped for informal living. A desk/message center in the island kitchen, art niches in the nook, and a fireplace with an entertainment center and shelves add custom touches. Two secondary suites have guest baths and offer full privacy from the master wing. The master suite hosts a private garden area; the bath features a walk-in shower that overlooks the garden and a water closet room with space for books or a television. Large His and Hers walk-in closets complete these private quarters.

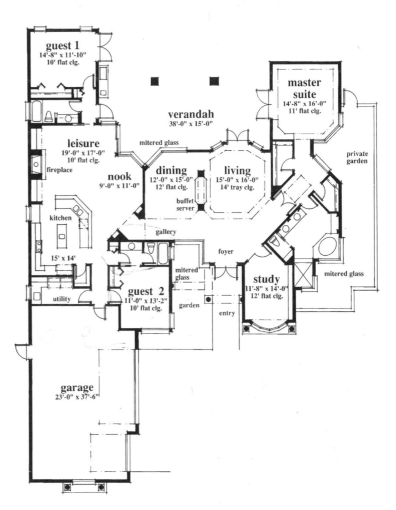

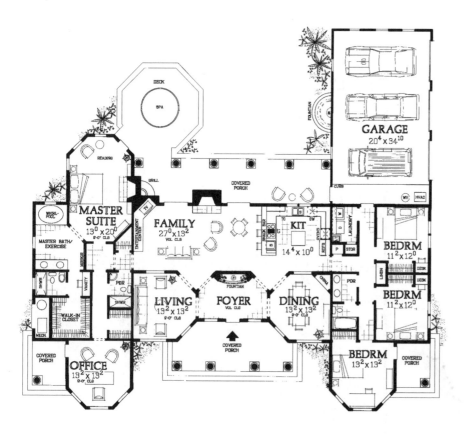

plan #

HPT9600271

STYLE: MEDITERRANEAN

SQUARE FOOTAGE: 2,831

BEDROOMS: 4

BATHROOMS: 3

WIDTH: 84' - 0"

DEPTH: 77' - 0"

FOUNDATION: SLAB

SEARCH ONLINE @ EPLANS.COM

Besides great curb appeal, this home has a wonderful floor plan. The foyer features a fountain that greets visitors and leads to a formal dining room on the right and a living room on the left. A large family room at the rear has a built-in entertainment center and a fireplace. The U-shaped kitchen is perfectly located for servicing all living and dining areas. To the right of the plan, away from the central entertaining spaces, are three family bedrooms sharing a full bath. On the left side, with solitude and comfort for the master suite, are a large sitting area, an office, and an amenity-filled bath. A deck with a spa sits outside the master suite.

ptan⊕
HPT9600272

STYLE: MEDITERRANEAN
SQUARE FOOTAGE: 2,660
BEDROOMS: 4
BATHROOMS: 3
WIDTH: 66' - 4"
DEPTH: 74' - 4"
FOUNDATION: SLAB

SEARCH ONLINE @ EPLANS.COM

Circle-top windows are beautifully showcased in this magnificent home. The double-door entry leads into the foyer and welcomes guests into a formal living and dining room area with wonderful views. As you approach the entrance to the master suite, you pass the den/study, which can easily become a guest or bedroom suite. A gently bowed soffit and stepped ceiling treatments add excitement to the master bedroom, with floor-length windows framing the bed. The bay-window sitting area further enhances the opulence of the suite. The master bath comes complete with a double vanity, a make-up area, and a soaking tub balanced by the large shower and private toilet chamber. The walk-in closet caps off this well-appointed space with ample hanging and built-in areas.

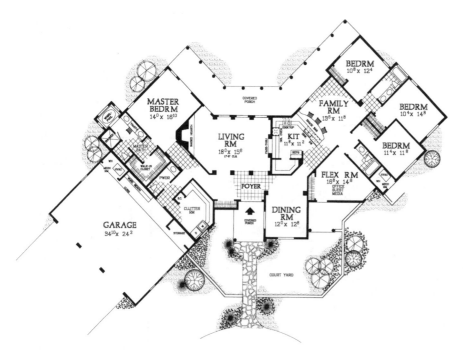

plan
HPT9600273

STYLE: SW CONTEMPORARY
SQUARE FOOTAGE: 2,966
BEDROOMS: 4
BATHROOMS: 3½
WIDTH: 114' - 10"
DEPTH: 79' - 2"
FOUNDATION: SLAB

SEARCH ONLINE @ EPLANS.COM

The dramatic entrance of this grand Sun Country home gives way to interesting angles and optimum livability inside. Columns frame the formal living room, which provides views of the rear grounds from the foyer. The private master bedroom is contained on the left portion of the plan. Here, a relaxing master bath provides an abundance of amenities that include a walk-in closet, a bumped-out whirlpool tub, a separate shower, and a double-bowl vanity. A clutter room and powder room complete this wing. Centrally located for efficiency, the kitchen easily serves the living room—via a pass-through—as well as the formal dining room, family room, and flex room. Three secondary bedrooms share two full baths.

ORDER BLUEPRINTS 24 HOURS, 7 DAYS A WEEK, AT 1-800-521-6797

© American Home Gallery, Ltd.

plan #

HPT9600274

STYLE: FRENCH COLONIAL
SQUARE FOOTAGE: 2,697
BEDROOMS: 3
BATHROOMS: 2½
WIDTH: 65' - 3"
DEPTH: 67' - 3"
FOUNDATION: WALKOUT BASEMENT

SEARCH ONLINE @ EPLANS.COM

Dual chimneys (one a false chimney created to enhance the aesthetic effect) and a double stairway to the covered entry of this home create a balanced architectural statement. The sunlit foyer leads straight into the spacious great room, where French doors provide a generous view of the covered veranda in back. The great room features a tray ceiling and a fireplace, bordered by twin bookcases. Another great view is offered from the spacious kitchen with a breakfast bar and a roomy work island. The master suite provides a large balanced bath and a spacious closet.

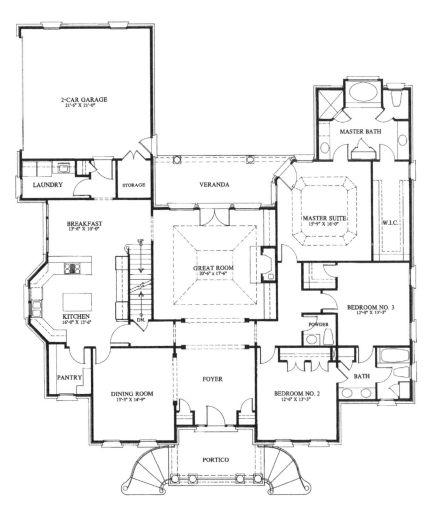

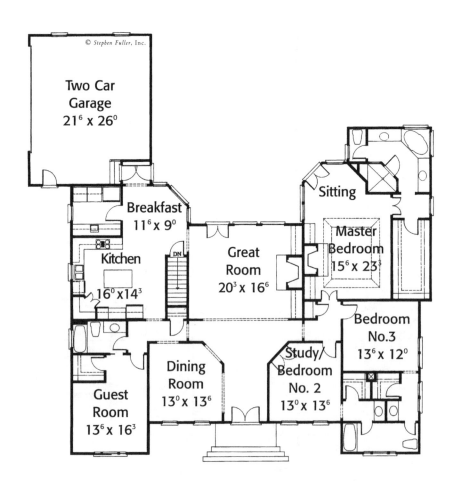

© Stephen Fuller, Inc.

Two Car Garage
21⁶ x 26⁰

Breakfast
11⁶ x 9⁰

Kitchen
16⁰ x 14³

Great Room
20³ x 16⁶

Sitting

Master Bedroom
15⁶ x 23³

Bedroom No.3
13⁶ x 12⁰

Dining Room
13⁰ x 13⁶

Study/ Bedroom No. 2
13⁰ x 13⁶

Guest Room
13⁶ x 16³

plan #
HPT9600275

STYLE: FRENCH ECLECTIC
SQUARE FOOTAGE: 2,785
BEDROOMS: 4
BATHROOMS: 3
WIDTH: 72' - 0"
DEPTH: 72' - 0"
FOUNDATION: WALKOUT BASEMENT

SEARCH ONLINE @ EPLANS.COM

This elegant Colonial design boasts many European influences such as the stucco facade, corner quoins, and arched windows. The foyer is flanked by a formal dining room and a study, which converts to an additional bedroom. Straight ahead, the great room, featuring a fireplace and built-ins, accesses the rear yard. The island kitchen opens to a breakfast nook for casual occasions. The master suite on the opposite side of the home boasts wondrous amenities such as a private fireplace, a bayed sitting area accessing the rear, a lavish bath, and an enormous walk-in closet.

plan
HPT9600276

STYLE: FRENCH ECLECTIC
SQUARE FOOTAGE: 2,500
BEDROOMS: 3
BATHROOMS: 2½
WIDTH: 73' - 0"
DEPTH: 65' - 10"
FOUNDATION: CRAWLSPACE

SEARCH ONLINE @ EPLANS.COM

Triple dormers highlight the roofline of this distinctive single-level French Country design. Double doors enhance the covered entryway, which leads to a grand open area with graceful columns. The large family room with a fireplace leads through double doors to the rear terrace. An L-shaped island kitchen opens to a breakfast area with a bay window. The master suite fills one wing and features a bay window, vaulted ceilings, and access to the terrace. Two additional bedrooms share a full bath.

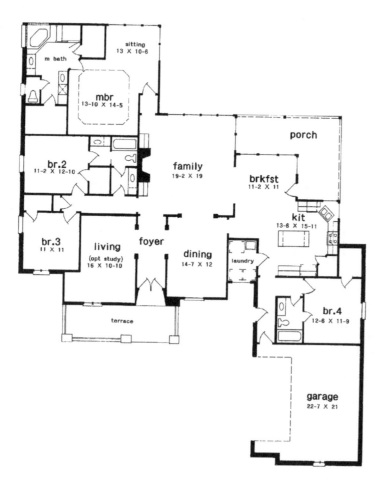

plan #

HPT9600277

STYLE: FRENCH ECLECTIC
SQUARE FOOTAGE: 2,678
BEDROOMS: 4
BATHROOMS: 3
WIDTH: 69' - 4"
DEPTH: 84' - 8"
FOUNDATION: SLAB

SEARCH ONLINE @ EPLANS.COM

In true French Country style, this home begins with a lovely terrace that announces the double-door entry. The main foyer separates formal living and dining areas and leads back to a large family room with a fireplace and built-ins. The breakfast room overlooks a wrapping porch and opens to the island kitchen. Three bedrooms are found on the left side of the plan—two family bedrooms sharing a full bath and a master suite with a sitting area. A fourth bedroom is tucked behind the two-car garage and features a private bath.

plan #

HPT9600278

STYLE: FRENCH ECLECTIC
SQUARE FOOTAGE: 2,618
BEDROOMS: 4
BATHROOMS: 3½
WIDTH: 71' - 1"
DEPTH: 74' - 0"
FOUNDATION: SLAB

SEARCH ONLINE @ EPLANS.COM

This delightful French chateau features high rooflines and a stucco and brick exterior. The floor plan is open, with columns defining the formal living and dining rooms and separating them from the family room. Two family bedrooms share a full bath on the right side of the plan, and an additional bedroom with full bath is located behind the garage—a perfect hideaway for guests. The master suite is amenity-filled and features a tray ceiling.

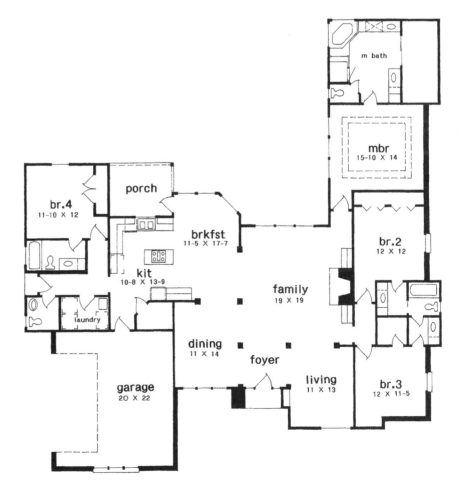

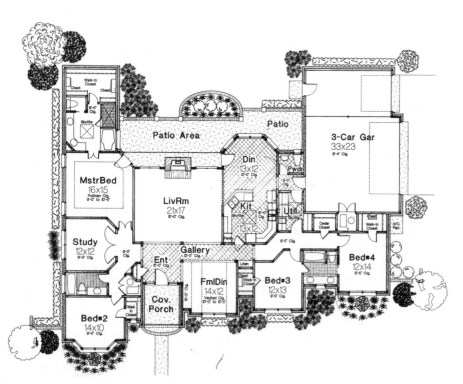

plan #
HPT9600279

STYLE: TRANSITIONAL
SQUARE FOOTAGE: 2,696
BEDROOMS: 4
BATHROOMS: 3½
WIDTH: 80' - 0"
DEPTH: 64' - 1"
FOUNDATION: SLAB

SEARCH ONLINE @ EPLANS.COM

A brick archway covers the front porch of this European-style home, creating a truly grand entrance. Situated beyond the entry, the living room takes center stage with a fireplace flanked by tall windows. To the right is a bayed eating area and an efficient kitchen. Steps away is the formal dining room. Skillful planning creates flexibility for the master suite. If you wish, use Bedroom 2 as a secondary bedroom or guest room, with the adjacent study accessible to everyone. Or if you prefer, combine the master suite with the study and use it as a private retreat with Bedroom 2 as a nursery, creating a wing that provides complete privacy. Completing this clever plan are two family bedrooms, a powder room, and a utility room.

ORDER BLUEPRINTS 24 HOURS, 7 DAYS A WEEK, AT 1-800-521-6797

plan #

HPT9600280

STYLE: FRENCH ECLECTIC

SQUARE FOOTAGE: 2,985

BEDROOMS: 4

BATHROOMS: 3½

WIDTH: 80' - 0"

DEPTH: 68' - 0"

FOUNDATION: SLAB

SEARCH ONLINE @ EPLANS.COM

A brick exterior, cast-stone trim, and corner quoins make up this attractive single-living-area design. The entry introduces a formal dining room to the right and a living room with a wall of windows to the left. The hearth-warmed family room opens to the kitchen/dinette, both with 10-foot ceilings. A large bay window enhances the dinette with a full glass door to the covered patio. A large master suite with vaulted ceilings features a bayed sitting area, a luxurious bath with double sinks, and an oversize walk-in closet.

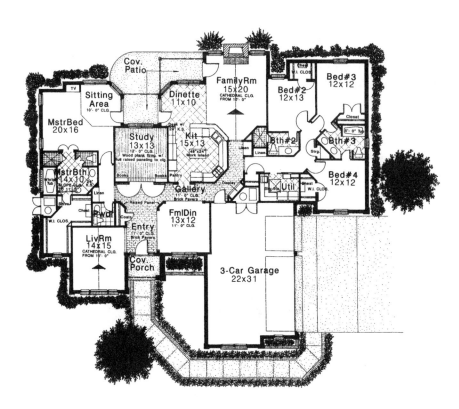

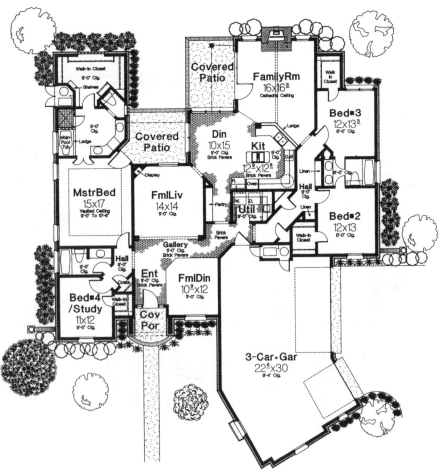

plan #
HPT9600281

STYLE: FRENCH
SQUARE FOOTAGE: 2,526
BEDROOMS: 4
BATHROOMS: 3
WIDTH: 64' - 0"
DEPTH: 81' - 7"
FOUNDATION: SLAB

SEARCH ONLINE @ EPLANS.COM

Interesting angles and creative detailing characterize the exterior of this brick cottage. Inside, the formal dining room is just off the foyer for ease in entertaining. A gallery hall leads to the island kitchen, which opens to an informal dining area with access to two covered patios. Sleeping quarters include two family bedrooms to the right of the plan and another bedroom, which could be used as a study, on the left. The left wing is dedicated to a lavish master suite complete with a vaulted ceiling and sumptuous bath with a whirlpool tub and separate shower.

plan#
HPT9600282

STYLE: FRENCH

SQUARE FOOTAGE: 2,590

BEDROOMS: 4

BATHROOMS: 3½

WIDTH: 73' - 6"

DEPTH: 64' - 10"

FOUNDATION: SLAB

SEARCH ONLINE @ EPLANS.COM

With a solid exterior of rough cedar and stone, this new French Country design will stand the test of time. A wood-paneled study in the front features a large bay window. The heart of the house is found in a large open great room with a built-in entertainment center. The spacious master bedroom features a corner reading area and access to an adjacent covered patio. A three-car garage and three additional bedrooms complete this generous family home.

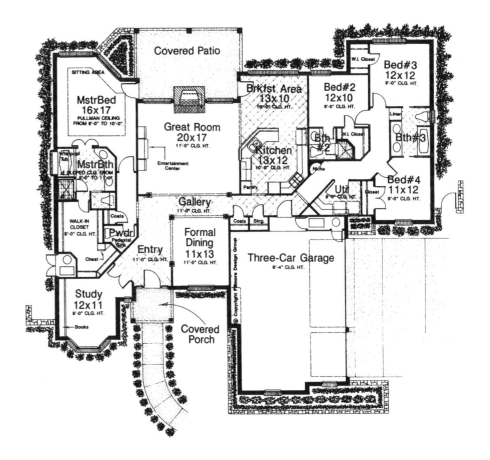

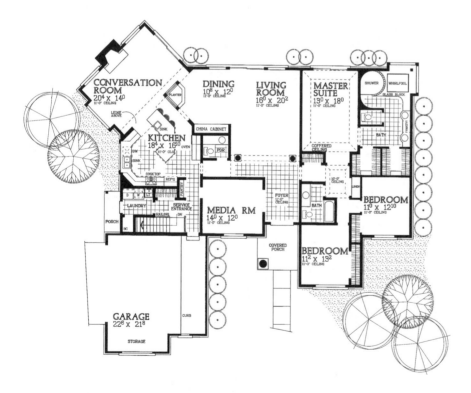

plan
HPT9600283

STYLE: TRADITIONAL

SQUARE FOOTAGE: 2,881

BEDROOMS: 3

BATHROOMS: 2½

WIDTH: 77' - 11"

DEPTH: 73' - 11"

FOUNDATION: BASEMENT

SEARCH ONLINE @ EPLANS.COM

The high, massive hipped roof of this home creates an impressive facade, andvarying roof planes and projecting gables further enhance appeal. A central foyer routes traffic efficiently to the sleeping, formal, and informal zones of the house. Note the sliding glass doors that provide access to outdoor living facilities. A built-in china cabinet and planter unit are fine decor features. In the angular kitchen, a high ceiling and efficient work design set the pace. The conversation room may act as a multipurpose room. Sleeping quarters take off in the spacious master suite, with a tray ceiling and sliding doors to the rear yard. Two sizable bedrooms accommodate family members or guests.

ORDER BLUEPRINTS 24 HOURS, 7 DAYS A WEEK, AT 1-800-521-6797

plan #

HPT9600284

STYLE: TRANSITIONAL

SQUARE FOOTAGE: 2,585

BONUS SPACE: 519 SQ. FT.

BEDROOMS: 3

BATHROOMS: 2½

WIDTH: 61' - 0"

DEPTH: 80' - 0"

FOUNDATION: CRAWLSPACE, BASEMENT

SEARCH ONLINE @ EPLANS.COM

Designed to take full advantage of panoramic rear vistas, this home possesses some great visual effects of its own. Its unusual and creative use of space includes an angled gathering room, expansive grand room, and continuous covered lanai. High ceilings throughout create an air of spaciousness. A tray ceiling reflects the pentagonal shape of the open dining room. The master retreat features a sitting area and a bath that includes both His and Hers vanities and walk-in closets. A private staircase leads to a large bonus room.

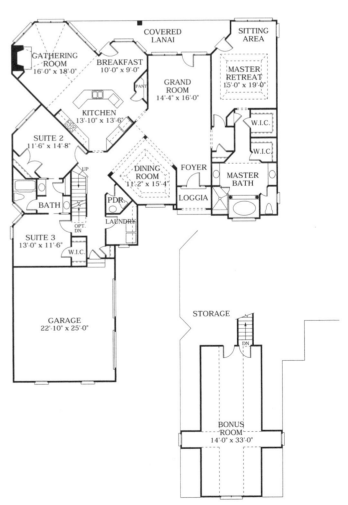

REAR EXTERIOR

plan
HPT9600285

STYLE: TRADITIONAL
SQUARE FOOTAGE: 2,770
BEDROOMS: 3
BATHROOMS: 2½
WIDTH: 73' - 6"
DEPTH: 78' - 0"
FOUNDATION: WALKOUT
BASEMENT

SEARCH ONLINE @ EPLANS.COM

This English cottage with a cedar shake exterior displays the best qualities of traditional design. With the bay window and recessed entry, visitors will feel warmly welcomed. The foyer opens to both the dining room and the great room with its fireplace and built-in cabinetry. Surrounded by windows, the breakfast room opens to a gourmet kitchen and a laundry room conveniently located near the garage entrance. To the right of the foyer is a hall powder room. Two bedrooms with large closets are joined by a full bath with individual vanities and a window seat. Through double doors at the end of a short hall, the master suite awaits with a tray ceiling and an adjoining sunlit sitting room. The master bath includes His and Hers closets, separate vanities, an individual shower, and a garden tub with a bay window.

plan#

HPT9600286

STYLE: COLONIAL REVIVAL

FIRST FLOOR: 1,676 SQ. FT.

SECOND FLOOR: 851 SQ. FT.

TOTAL: 2,527 SQ. FT.

BEDROOMS: 5

BATHROOMS: 2½

WIDTH: 55' - 0"

DEPTH: 50' - 0"

FOUNDATION: SLAB

SEARCH ONLINE @ EPLANS.COM

Muntin windows and gentle arches decorate the exterior of this traditional home. Living spaces consist of a formal dining room, a kitchen with an adjacent breakfast bay, and a great room with access to the rear veranda. A private study or guest suite in the rear left corner of the plan offers its own door to the veranda. The master suite enjoys a spacious bath with twin lavatories, a dressing area, and two walk-in closets. A gallery hall on the second floor leads to a computer loft with built-ins for books and software.

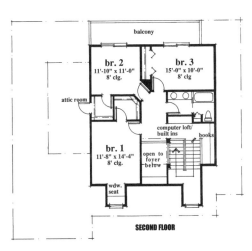

SECOND FLOOR

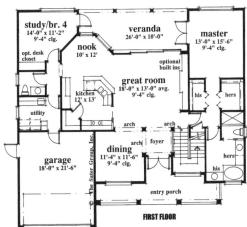

FIRST FLOOR

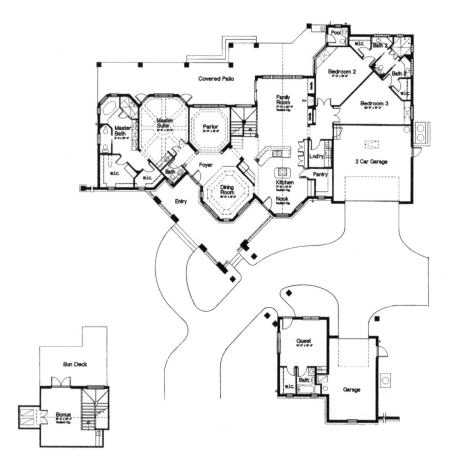

plan #
HPT9600287

STYLE: COUNTRY COTTAGE
SQUARE FOOTAGE: 2,816
BONUS SPACE: 290 SQ. FT.
BEDROOMS: 3
BATHROOMS: 3½ + ½
WIDTH: 94' - 0"
DEPTH: 113' - 5"
FOUNDATION: SLAB

SEARCH ONLINE @ EPLANS.COM

Though designed as a grand estate, this home retains the warmth of a country manor with intimate details, on the inside and out. A one-of-a-kind drive court leads to private parking and ends in a two-car garage; a separate guest house is replete with angled walls and sculptured ceilings. A continuous vault follows from the family room through the kitchen and nook. The vault soars even higher in the bonus room with a sundeck upstairs. Two exquisitely appointed family bedrooms with window seats and walk-in closets share a full bath. The master suite has pampering details such as a juice bar and media wall, walk-in closets, and covered patio access.

plan#
HPT9600288

STYLE: PLANTATION

FIRST FLOOR: 1,969 SQ. FT.

SECOND FLOOR: 660 SQ. FT.

TOTAL: 2,629 SQ. FT.

BONUS SPACE: 360 SQ. FT.

BEDROOMS: 4

BATHROOMS: 3

WIDTH: 90' - 8"

DEPTH: 80' - 4"

FOUNDATION: BASEMENT

SEARCH ONLINE @ EPLANS.COM

Varying roof planes, gables, and dormers help create the unique character of this house. Inside, the family/great room gains attention with its high ceiling, fireplace/media-center wall, view of the upstairs balcony, and French doors to the sunroom. In the U-shaped kitchen, an island work surface, a planning desk, and a pantry are added conveniences. The spacious master suite can function with the home office, library, or private sitting room. Its direct access to the huge raised veranda provides an ideal private outdoor haven for relaxation. The second floor contains two bedrooms and a bath. The garage features a workshop area and stairway to a second-floor storage or multipurpose room.

REAR EXTERIOR

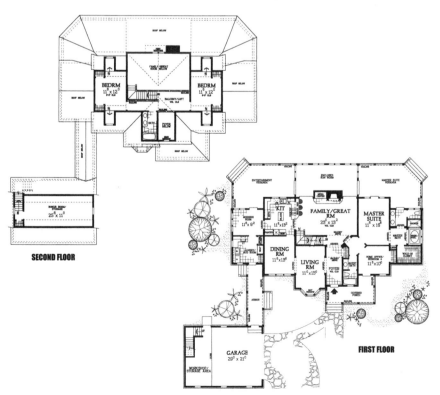

SECOND FLOOR

FIRST FLOOR

© 1998 Donald A. Gardner Architects, Inc.

REAR EXTERIOR

© 1998 Donald A. Gardner Architects, Inc.

MAIN LEVEL

LOWER LEVEL

plan #

HPT9600289

STYLE: COUNTRY
MAIN LEVEL: 1,472 SQ. FT.
LOWER LEVEL: 1,211 SQ. FT.
TOTAL: 2,683 SQ. FT.
BEDROOMS: 3
BATHROOMS: 2½
WIDTH: 54' - 0"
DEPTH: 40' - 8"

SEARCH ONLINE @ EPLANS.COM

A stone-and-stucco exterior and exquisite window detailing give this home its Mediterranean appeal. A covered porch connects the garage to the main house via the breakfast room. The master suite includes two walk-in closets and a bath with separate vanities. Two family bedrooms in the lower level feature walk-in closets and share a compartmented bath and a media/recreation room. Both bedrooms offer private access to the patio. A utility room and storage room complete this level.

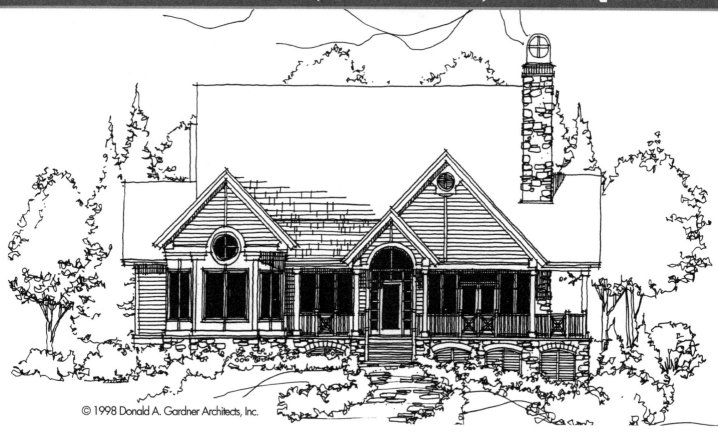

© 1998 Donald A. Gardner Architects, Inc.

plan
HPT9600290

STYLE: NEO-ECLECTIC
FIRST FLOOR: 1,896 SQ. FT.
SECOND FLOOR: 692 SQ. FT.
TOTAL: 2,588 SQ. FT.
BEDROOMS: 3
BATHROOMS: 2½
WIDTH: 60' - 0"
DEPTH: 84' - 10"

SEARCH ONLINE @ EPLANS.COM

This fine three-bedroom home is full of amenities and will surely be a family favorite! A covered porch leads into the great room/dining room. Here, a fireplace reigns at one end, casting its glow throughout the room. A private study is tucked away, perfect for a home office or computer study. The master bedroom suite offers a bayed sitting area, large walk-in closet, and pampering bath. With plenty of counter and cabinet space and an adjacent breakfast area, the kitchen will be a favorite gathering place for casual mealtimes. The family sleeping zone is upstairs and includes two bedrooms, a full bath, a loft/study area, and a huge storage room.

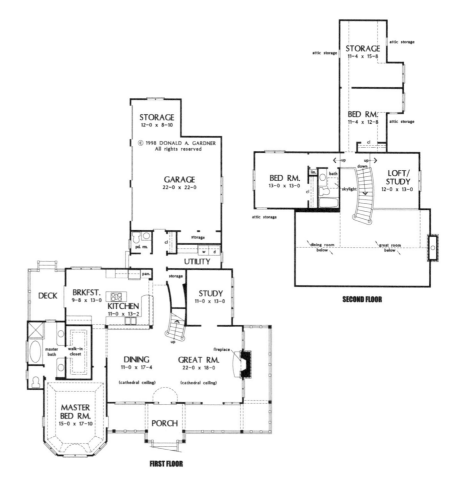

© 1999 DAG
All rights reserved

DECK

DECK

fireplace

SCREEN PORCH
10-0 x 14-0

DINING
12-0 x 14-0

GREAT RM.
16-0 x 20-2
(cathedral ceiling)

MASTER BED RM.
14-0 x 16-0

down

BRKFST.
10-0 x 12-0

KITCHEN
14-4 x 12-0

FOYER
9-8 x 12-0

cl

walk-in closet

bath

walk-in closet

walk-in closet

UTILITY
10-0 x 6-0

storage

d w

PORCH

BED RM./ STUDY
12-0 x 12-2

master bath

GARAGE
22-4 x 20-0

© 1999 DONALD A. GARDNER
All rights reserved

storage

MAIN LEVEL

PATIO

BED RM.
11-2 x 14-0

REC. RM.
16-0 x 19-6

fireplace

sto.

up

BED RM.
13-2 x 14-2

walk-in closet

storage

bath

lin.

cl   cl

LOWER LEVEL

plan
HPT9600291

STYLE: NEO-ECLECTIC

MAIN LEVEL: 1,901 SQ. FT.

LOWER LEVEL: 1,075 SQ. FT.

TOTAL: 2,976 SQ. FT.

BEDROOMS: 4

BATHROOMS: 3

WIDTH: 64' - 0"

DEPTH: 62' - 4"

SEARCH ONLINE @ EPLANS.COM

The vaulted foyer receives light from two clerestory dormer windows and includes a niche for displaying collectibles. The generous great room enjoys a dramatic cathedral ceiling, a rear wall of windows, access to two rear decks, a fireplace, and built-in bookshelves. A recreation room is located on the basement level. Two bedrooms can be found on the main floor, and two more flank the rec room downstairs. The master suite boasts an elegant tray ceiling, His and Hers walk-in closets, and a luxurious bath with dual vanities, a garden tub, and separate shower.

ORDER BLUEPRINTS 24 HOURS, 7 DAYS A WEEK, AT 1-800-521-6797

© 1999 Donald A. Gardner, Inc.

plan
HPT9600292

STYLE: STICK VICTORIAN
MAIN LEVEL: 1,662 SQ. FT.
UPPER LEVEL: 706 SQ. FT.
LOWER LEVEL: 585 SQ. FT.
TOTAL: 2,953 SQ. FT.
BONUS SPACE: 575 SQ. FT.
BEDROOMS: 4
BATHROOMS: 3½
WIDTH: 81' - 4"
DEPTH: 68' - 8"

SEARCH ONLINE @ EPLANS.COM

A stunning center dormer with an arched window embellishes the exterior of this Craftsman-style home. The dormer's arched window allows light into the foyer and built-in niche. The second-floor hall is a balcony that overlooks both the foyer and great room. A generous back porch extends the great room, which features an impressive vaulted ceiling and fireplace; a tray ceiling adorns the formal dining room. The master suite, which includes a tray ceiling as well, enjoys back-porch access, a built-in cabinet, generous walk-in closet, and private bath. Two more bedrooms are located upstairs; a fourth can be found in the basement along with a family room.

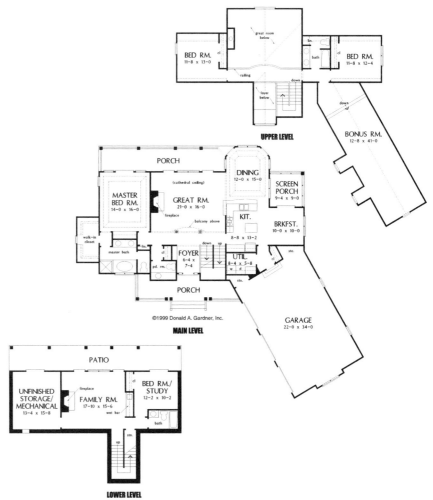

plan #

HPT9600293

STYLE: NEO-ECLECTIC
SQUARE FOOTAGE: 2,555
BEDROOMS: 3
BATHROOMS: 2½
WIDTH: 70' - 6"
DEPTH: 76' - 6"
FOUNDATION: CRAWLSPACE

SEARCH ONLINE @ EPLANS.COM

Shingles, stone, and sturdy porch pillars make this farmhouse an eye-catching retreat. Inside, the foyer is flanked by formal rooms—a dining room with a stepped ceiling and a study with a beamed ceiling and built-in bookshelves. Family living space is to the center of the plan—the kitchen includes a built-in planning desk and an adjoining breakfast nook. The great room features a coffered ceiling, a fireplace, built-in shelves, and three sets of French doors that open to the rear porch. The split-bedroom plan—family bedrooms to the right, and the master suite to the left—allows everyone plenty of privacy.

© 1994 Donald A. Gardner Architects, Inc.

plan #

HPT9600294

STYLE: TRADITIONAL

SQUARE FOOTAGE: 2,625

BONUS SPACE: 447 SQ. FT.

BEDROOMS: 4

BATHROOMS: 2½

WIDTH: 63' - 1"

DEPTH: 90' - 2"

SEARCH ONLINE @ EPLANS.COM

This stately brick facade features a columned, covered porch that ushers visitors into the large foyer. An expansive great room with a fireplace and access to a covered rear porch awaits. The centrally located kitchen is within easy reach of the great room, formal dining room, and skylit breakfast area. Split-bedroom planning places the master bedroom and elegant master bath to the right of the home. Two bedrooms with abundant closet space are placed to the left; an optional bedroom or study with a Palladian window faces the front. A large bonus room is located above the garage.

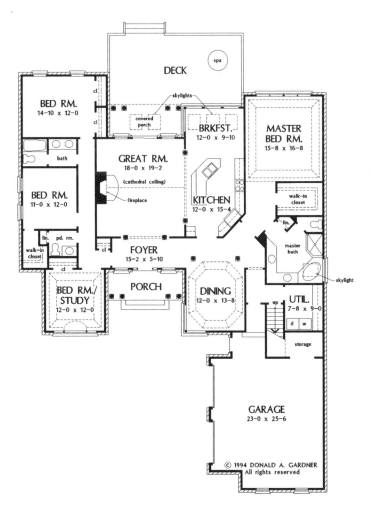

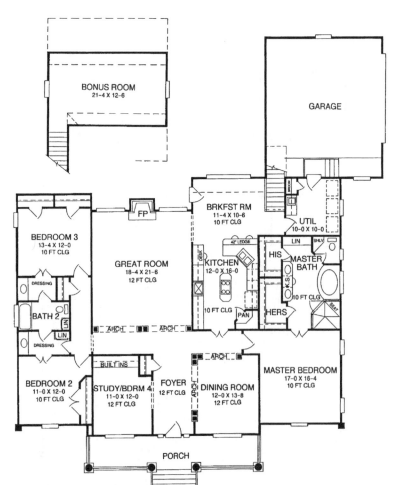

plan #

HPT9600295

STYLE: SOUTHERN COLONIAL
SQUARE FOOTAGE: 2,648
BONUS SPACE: 293 SQ. FT.
BEDROOMS: 4
BATHROOMS: 2
WIDTH: 68' - 10"
DEPTH: 77' - 10"
FOUNDATION: CRAWLSPACE,
SLAB, BASEMENT

SEARCH ONLINE @ EPLANS.COM

This Southern-style design looks cozy but lives large, with an interior layout and amenities preferred by today's homeowners. Inside, 12-foot ceilings and graceful columns and arches lend an aura of hospitality throughout the formal rooms and the living space in the great room. Double doors open to the gourmet kitchen, which offers a built-in desk, a snack counter for easy meals, and a breakfast room with a picture window. The secluded master suite features His and Hers walk-in closets, a whirlpool tub, and a knee-space vanity.

ORDER BLUEPRINTS 24 HOURS, 7 DAYS A WEEK, AT 1-800-521-6797

plan
HPT9600296

STYLE: COLONIAL REVIVAL

SQUARE FOOTAGE: 2,506

BEDROOMS: 4

BATHROOMS: 2½

WIDTH: 72' - 2"

DEPTH: 66' - 4"

FOUNDATION: CRAWLSPACE, SLAB, BASEMENT

SEARCH ONLINE @ EPLANS.COM

A porch full of columns gives a relaxing emphasis to this country home. To the right of the foyer, the dining area resides conveniently near the efficient kitchen. The kitchen island, walk-in pantry, and serving bar add plenty of work space to the food-preparation zone. Natural light fills the breakfast nook through a ribbon of windows. Escape to the relaxing master suite featuring a private sunroom/retreat and a luxurious bath set between His and Hers walk-in closets. The great room features a warming fireplace and built-ins.

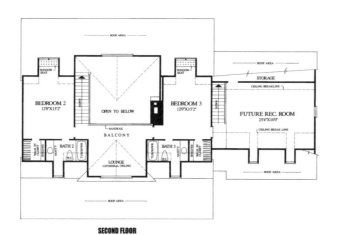

SECOND FLOOR

FIRST FLOOR

plan #
HPT9600297

STYLE: COLONIAL REVIVAL
FIRST FLOOR: 1,694 SQ. FT.
SECOND FLOOR: 874 SQ. FT.
TOTAL: 2,568 SQ. FT.
BONUS SPACE: 440 SQ. FT.
BEDROOMS: 3
BATHROOMS: 3½
WIDTH: 74' - 2"
DEPTH: 46' - 8"
FOUNDATION: BASEMENT,
SLAB, CRAWLSPACE

SEARCH ONLINE @ EPLANS.COM

A welcoming front porch lined by graceful columns introduces this fine farmhouse. Inside, the foyer leads through an elegant arch to the spacious great room, which features a fireplace and built-ins. The formal dining room and sunny breakfast room flank a highly efficient kitchen—complete with a pantry and a serving bar. Located on the first floor for privacy, the master suite is filled with pampering amenities. Upstairs, two large bedrooms each provide a private bath and walk-in closet.

ORDER BLUEPRINTS 24 HOURS, 7 DAYS A WEEK, AT 1-800-521-6797

plan
HPT9600298

STYLE: COLONIAL REVIVAL
SQUARE FOOTAGE: 2,777
BONUS SPACE: 424 SQ. FT.
BEDROOMS: 3
BATHROOMS: 2½
WIDTH: 75' - 6"
DEPTH: 60' - 2"
FOUNDATION: CRAWLSPACE, BASEMENT

SEARCH ONLINE @ EPLANS.COM

This home is an absolute dream when it comes to living space! Whether formal or casual, there's a room for every occasion. The foyer opens to the formal dining room on the left; straight ahead lies the magnificent hearth-warmed living room. The island kitchen opens not only to a breakfast nook, but to a huge family/sunroom surrounded by two walls of windows! The right wing of the plan holds the sleeping quarters— two family bedrooms sharing a bath, and a majestic master suite. The second floor holds an abundance of expandable space.

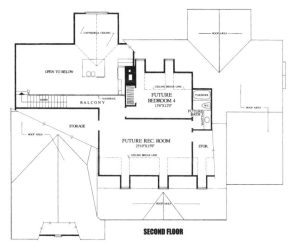

SECOND FLOOR

FIRST FLOOR

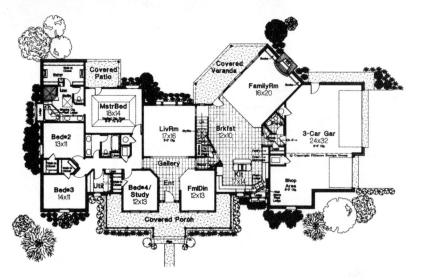

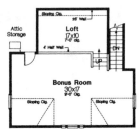

plan
HPT9600299

STYLE: VICTORIAN FARMHOUSE
SQUARE FOOTAGE: 2,787
BONUS SPACE: 636 SQ. FT.
BEDROOMS: 4
BATHROOMS: 2½
WIDTH: 101' - 0"
DEPTH: 58' - 8"
FOUNDATION: CRAWLSPACE, SLAB

SEARCH ONLINE @ EPLANS.COM

plan
HPT9600300

STYLE: VICTORIAN FARMHOUSE
SQUARE FOOTAGE: 2,539
BONUS SPACE: 636 SQ. FT.
BEDROOMS: 4
BATHROOMS: 3
WIDTH: 98' - 0"
DEPTH: 53' - 11"
FOUNDATION: SLAB

SEARCH ONLINE @ EPLANS.COM

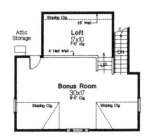

ORDER BLUEPRINTS 24 HOURS, 7 DAYS A WEEK, AT 1-800-521-6797

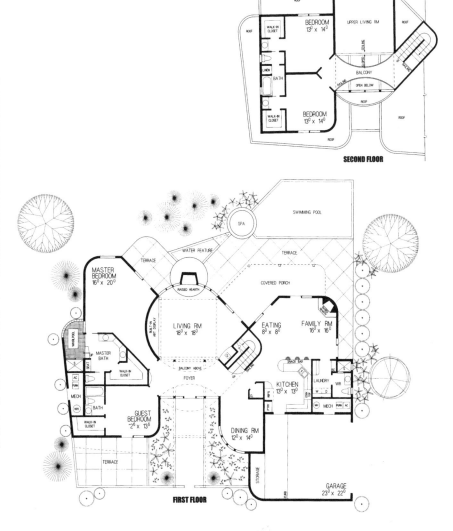

ptan ⊕
HPT9600301

STYLE: INTERNATIONAL

FIRST FLOOR: 2,422 SQ. FT.

SECOND FLOOR: 714 SQ. FT.

TOTAL: 3,136 SQ. FT.

BEDROOMS: 4

BATHROOMS: 4

WIDTH: 77' - 6"

DEPTH: 62' - 0"

FOUNDATION: SLAB

SEARCH ONLINE @ EPLANS.COM

This Southwestern contemporary home offers a distinctive look for any neighborhood—both inside and out. The formal living areas are concentrated in the center of the plan, perfect for entertaining. To the right, the kitchen and family room function well together as a working and living area. The first-floor sleeping wing includes a guest suite and a master suite. Upstairs, two family bedrooms are reached by a balcony overlooking the living room. Each bedroom has a walk-in closet and a dressing area with a vanity; they share a compartmented bath that includes a linen closet.

plan #

HPT9600302

STYLE: SW CONTEMPORARY
FIRST FLOOR: 2,401 SQ. FT.
SECOND FLOOR: 927 SQ. FT.
TOTAL: 3,328 SQ. FT.
BEDROOMS: 4
BATHROOMS: 3
WIDTH: 104' - 9"
DEPTH: 62' - 5"
FOUNDATION: SLAB

SEARCH ONLINE @ EPLANS.COM

Honored traditions are echoed throughout this warm and inviting Santa Fe home. A large, two-story gathering room with a beehive fireplace provides a soothing atmosphere for entertaining or quiet interludes. A gallery leads to the kitchen and breakfast area where abundant counter space and a work island will please the fussiest of cooks. A nearby laundry room provides entry to the three-car garage. On the right side of the plan, the master suite offers a private study, a fireplace, and a luxurious bath with dual lavatories, a whirlpool tub, and a curved shower. On the second floor, a reading loft with built-in bookshelves complements three family bedrooms.

ORDER BLUEPRINTS 24 HOURS, 7 DAYS A WEEK, AT 1-800-521-6797

plan
HPT9600303

STYLE: SW CONTEMPORARY

SQUARE FOOTAGE: 3,144

BEDROOMS: 4

BATHROOMS: 3

WIDTH: 139' - 10"

DEPTH: 63' - 8"

FOUNDATION: SLAB

SEARCH ONLINE @ EPLANS.COM

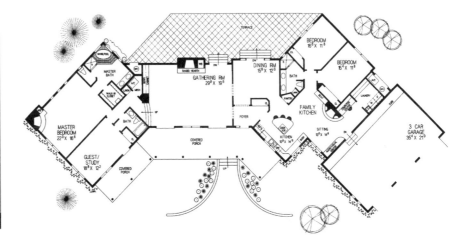

In classic Santa Fe style, this home strikes a beautiful combination of historic exterior detailing and open floor planning on the inside. A covered porch running the width of the facade leads to an entry foyer that connects to a huge gathering room with a fireplace and a formal dining room. The family kitchen allows special space for casual gatherings. The right wing of the home holds two family bedrooms and a full bath. The left wing is devoted to the master suite and a guest room or study.

SECOND FLOOR

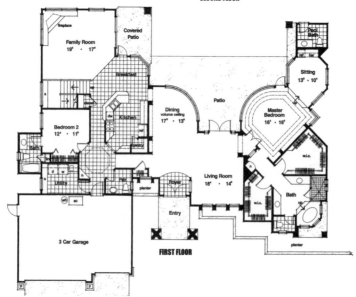

FIRST FLOOR

plan #
HPT9600304

STYLE: PRAIRIE
FIRST FLOOR: 2,531 SQ. FT.
SECOND FLOOR: 669 SQ. FT.
TOTAL: 3,200 SQ. FT.
BEDROOMS: 4
BATHROOMS: 3½ + ½
WIDTH: 82' - 4"
DEPTH: 72' - 0"
FOUNDATION: SLAB

SEARCH ONLINE @ EPLANS.COM

This exquisite brick-and-stucco contemporary home takes its cue from the tradition of Frank Lloyd Wright. The formal living and dining areas combine to provide a spectacular view of the rear grounds. "Unique" best describes the private master suite, highlighted by a multitude of amenities. The family living area encompasses the left portion of the plan, featuring a spacious family room with a corner fireplace, access to the covered patio from the breakfast area, and a step-saving kitchen. Bedroom 2 connects to a private bath. Upstairs, two bedrooms share a balcony, a sitting room, and a full bath.

plan #

HPT9600305

STYLE: PRAIRIE
SQUARE FOOTAGE: 3,278
BEDROOMS: 4
BATHROOMS: 3½
WIDTH: 75' - 10"
DEPTH: 69' - 4"
FOUNDATION: CRAWLSPACE

SEARCH ONLINE @ EPLANS.COM

Form follows function as dual gallery halls lead from formal areas to split sleeping quarters in this Prairie adaptation. At the heart of the plan, the grand-scale great room offers a raised-hearth fireplace framed by built-in cabinetry and plant shelves. Open planning combines the country kitchen with an informal dining space and adds an island counter with a snack bar. A lavish master suite harbors a sitting area with private access to the covered pergola. The secondary sleeping wing includes a spacious guest suite. A fifth bedroom or home office offers its own door to the wraparound porch.

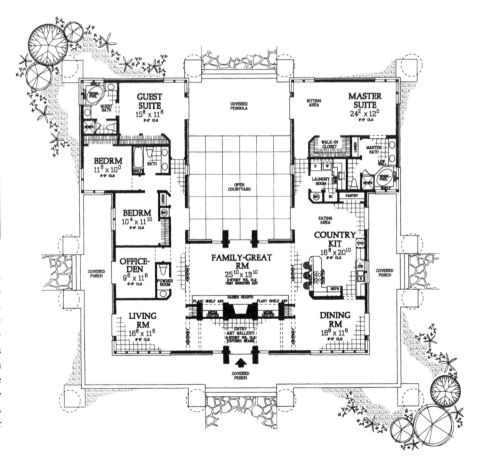

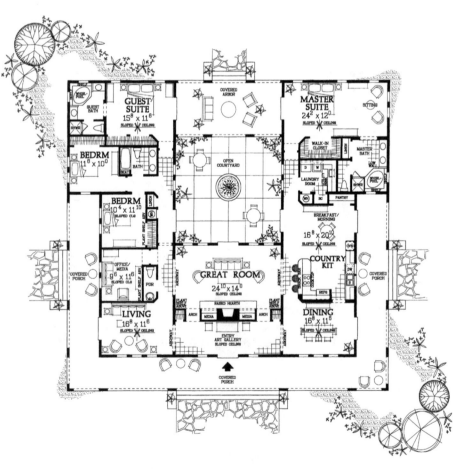

plan #

HPT9600306

STYLE: MEDITERRANEAN
SQUARE FOOTAGE: 3,163
BEDROOMS: 4
BATHROOMS: 3½
WIDTH: 75' - 2"
DEPTH: 68' - 8"
FOUNDATION: SLAB

SEARCH ONLINE @ EPLANS.COM

An open courtyard takes center stage in this home, providing a happy marriage of indoor/outdoor relationships. Art collectors will appreciate the gallery that enhances the entry and showcases their favorite works. The centrally located great room supplies the nucleus for formal and informal entertaining. A raised-hearth fireplace flanked by built-in media centers adds a special touch. The master suite provides a private retreat where you may relax—try the sitting room or retire to the private bath for a pampering soak in the corner whirlpool tub.

ORDER BLUEPRINTS 24 HOURS, 7 DAYS A WEEK, AT 1-800-521-6797

plan
HPT9600307

STYLE: FLORIDIAN
SQUARE FOOTAGE: 3,477
BEDROOMS: 3
BATHROOMS: 3½
WIDTH: 95' - 0"
DEPTH: 88' - 8"
FOUNDATION: SLAB

SEARCH ONLINE @ EPLANS.COM

Make dreams come true with this fine sunny design. An octagonal study provides a nice focal point both inside and out. The living areas remain open to each other and access outdoor areas. A wet bar makes entertaining a breeze, especially with a window pass-through to a grill area on the lanai. The kitchen enjoys shared space with a lovely breakfast nook and a bright leisure room. Two bedrooms are located near the family living center. In the master bedroom suite, luxury abounds with a two-way fireplace, a morning kitchen, two walk-in closets, and a compartmented bath. Another full bath accommodates a pool area.

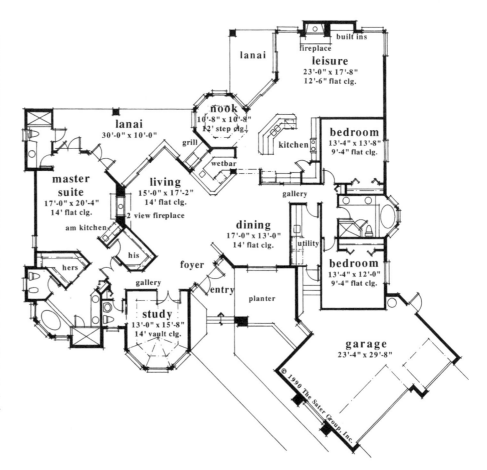

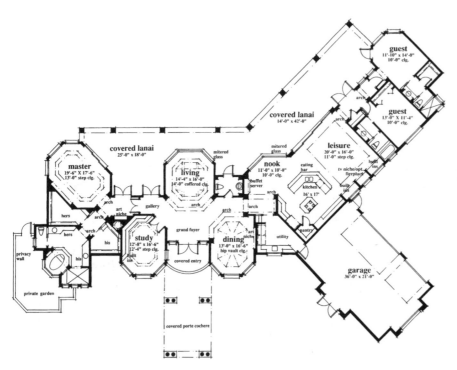

plan #
HPT9600308

STYLE: MEDITERRANEAN
SQUARE FOOTAGE: 3,398
BEDROOMS: 3
BATHROOMS: 3½
WIDTH: 121' - 5"
DEPTH: 96' - 2"
FOUNDATION: SLAB

SEARCH ONLINE @ EPLANS.COM

Bringing the outdoors in through a multitude of bay windows is what this design is all about. The grand foyer opens to the living room with a magnificent view to the covered lanai. The study and dining room flank the foyer. The master suite is found on the left with an opulent private bath and views of the private garden. To the right, the kitchen adjoins the nook that boasts a mitered-glass bay window overlooking the lanai. Beyond the leisure room are two guest rooms, each with a private bath.

plan
HPT9600309

STYLE: TRANSITIONAL

SQUARE FOOTAGE: 3,190

BONUS SPACE: 769 SQ. FT.

BEDROOMS: 3

BATHROOMS: 2½

WIDTH: 91' - 0"

DEPTH: 83' - 0"

FOUNDATION: SLAB

SEARCH ONLINE @ EPLANS.COM

Plentiful amenities abound in this charming design. Family bedrooms and a dining room flank the foyer. A fireplace warms the formal living area, which features a wall of double doors opening to the rear pool and patio. The kitchen features an island workstation and is open to the breakfast room. Courtyards to the left and right of the plan encourage outdoor enjoyment. The master suite offers an exquisite private bath and roomy walk-in closet. The two-car garage and recreation room are appealing additions to the floor plan. Optional space above the garage is reserved for future use.

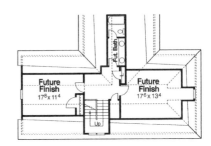

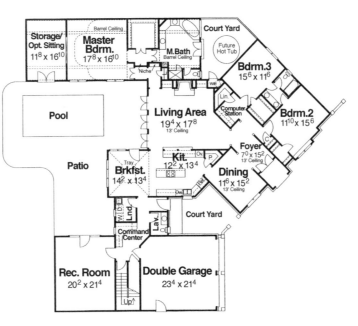

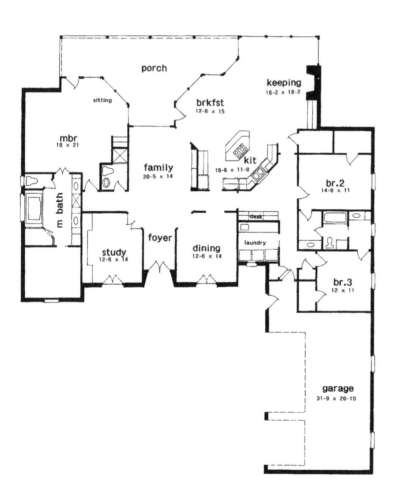

plan #
HPT9600310

STYLE: FRENCH
SQUARE FOOTAGE: 3,032
BEDROOMS: 3
BATHROOMS: 3
WIDTH: 73' - 0"
DEPTH: 87' - 8"
FOUNDATION: SLAB

SEARCH ONLINE @ EPLANS.COM

This country estate is bedecked with all the details that pronounce its French origins. They include the study, family room, and keeping room. Dine in one of two areas--the formal dining room or the casual breakfast room. A large porch to the rear can be reached through the breakfast room or the master suite's sitting area. All three bedrooms in the plan have walk-in closets. Bedrooms 2 and 3 share a full bath that includes private vanities.

ptan
HPT9600311

STYLE: FRENCH ECLECTIC

SQUARE FOOTAGE: 3,268

BEDROOMS: 4

BATHROOMS: 3

WIDTH: 98' - 0"

DEPTH: 67' - 3"

FOUNDATION: SLAB

SEARCH ONLINE @ EPLANS.COM

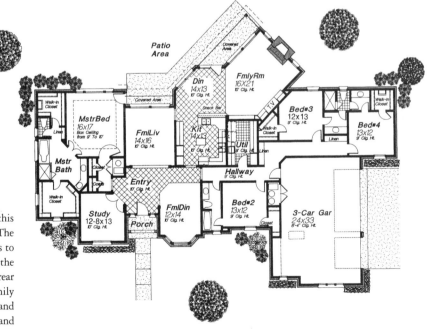

Brick, with accents of stone, define the stately facade of this home. It gives some hint of the grand floor plan inside. The entry hall is centrally located to provide convenient access to the study (or make it a bedroom), the formal dining room, the formal living room, and the kitchen. Living spaces to the rear include a breakfast nook with snack bar and the angled family room with great views to the rear yard. Across the back and connecting to the formal living room, casual dining area, and family room is a covered porch/patio area. Three family bedrooms dominate the right side of the plan--one has a private bath. The master suite is on the left side and has access to the rear patio and an amenity-filled bath with two walk-in closets, whirlpool tub, shower, and double sinks.

SECOND FLOOR

FIRST FLOOR

ptan#
HPT9600312

STYLE: FRENCH ECLECTIC

FIRST FLOOR: 2,438 SQ. FT.

SECOND FLOOR: 882 SQ. FT.

TOTAL: 3,320 SQ. FT.

BONUS SPACE: 230 SQ. FT.

BEDROOMS: 4

BATHROOMS: 4½

WIDTH: 70' - 0"

DEPTH: 63' - 2"

FOUNDATION: SLAB, BASEMENT

SEARCH ONLINE @ EPLANS.COM

Wonderful rooflines top a brick exterior with cedar and stone accents and lots of English Country charm. The two-story entry reveals a graceful curving staircase and opens to the formal living and dining rooms. Fireplaces are found in the living room as well as the great room, which also boasts built-in bookcases and access to the rear patio. The kitchen and breakfast room add to the informal area and include a snack bar. A private patio is part of the master suite, which also offers a lavish bath, a large walk-in closet, and a nearby study. Three family bedrooms and a bonus room complete the second floor.

plan
HPT9600313

STYLE: FRENCH

FIRST FLOOR: 2,302 SQ. FT.

SECOND FLOOR: 1,177 SQ. FT.

TOTAL: 3,479 SQ. FT.

BEDROOMS: 4

BATHROOMS: 3½

WIDTH: 66' - 3"

DEPTH: 57' - 9"

FOUNDATION: WALKOUT
BASEMENT

SEARCH ONLINE @ EPLANS.COM

Gently arched cornices and keystones call up a sense of history with this traditional home. Formal rooms flank the two-story foyer, which leads to comfortably elegant living space with an extended-hearth fireplace. A sizable kitchen serves the formal dining room through a butler's pantry and overlooks the breakfast room. A secluded home office is a quiet place for business conversations. The master suite nestles to the rear of the plan and offers luxurious amenities. Upstairs, Bedrooms 3 and 4 share a full bath that includes two lavatories, while Bedroom 2 enjoys a private bath.

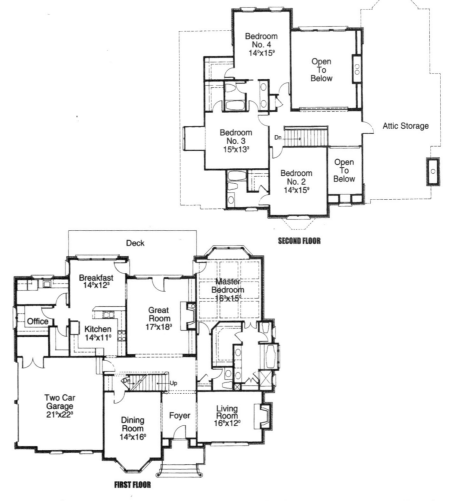

SECOND FLOOR

FIRST FLOOR

plan #
HPT9600314

STYLE: FRENCH COUNTRY
FIRST FLOOR: 2,174 SQ. FT.
SECOND FLOOR: 877 SQ. FT.
TOTAL: 3,051 SQ. FT.
BEDROOMS: 4
BATHROOMS: 3½
WIDTH: 76' - 0"
DEPTH: 56' - 0"
FOUNDATION: BASEMENT

SEARCH ONLINE @ EPLANS.COM

This two-story French Country home welcomes guests and owners. Imagine the possibilities of four bedrooms, a three-car garage, and over 3,000 square feet of livable space. French doors open to a study with a tray ceiling just off the entry. On the other side of the entry sits a formal dining room. Straight ahead, the vaulted two-story ceiling, fireplace, built-in shelves, and stunning windows that overlook the backyard enhance the great room. The nearby kitchen features a pantry, work island, and snack bar. Also on the main floor of this home is a spectacular master bedroom. A cathedral ceiling adorns the master bath, which includes a spacious walk-in closet with a built-in bench. Upstairs, three family bedrooms and two full baths complete the design.

plan
HPT9600315

STYLE: TRADITIONAL
FIRST FLOOR: 2,454 SQ. FT.
SECOND FLOOR: 986 SQ. FT.
TOTAL: 3,440 SQ. FT.
BEDROOMS: 4
BATHROOMS: 3½
WIDTH: 73' - 4"
DEPTH: 59' - 4"

SEARCH ONLINE @ EPLANS.COM

This traditional design fits well into a country-side setting and boasts an abundance of amenities. Inside, the great room and hearth room offer fireplaces. The kitchen features a snack bar and walk-in pantry. The master suite provides a sitting area, whirlpool bath and walk-in closet. A den off the foyer easily flexes to a library or home office. Upstairs, each of three secondary bedrooms provides a walk-in closet.

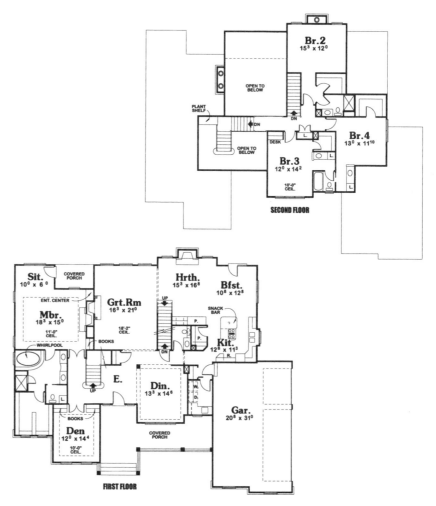

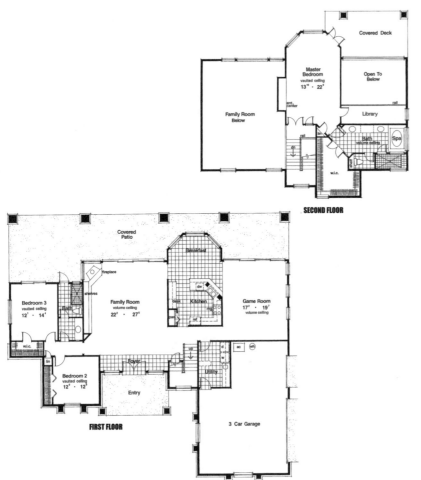

SECOND FLOOR

FIRST FLOOR

plan
HPT9600316

STYLE: TRANSITIONAL
FIRST FLOOR: 2,136 SQ. FT.
SECOND FLOOR: 1,046 SQ. FT.
TOTAL: 3,182 SQ. FT.
BEDROOMS: 3
BATHROOMS: 2
WIDTH: 74' - 0"
DEPTH: 67' - 2"
FOUNDATION: SLAB

SEARCH ONLINE @ EPLANS.COM

Varied textures and rooflines, combined with a grand entrance, give this contemporary home plenty of curb appeal. Inside, the foyer opens directly into the family room, which is graced by a corner fireplace, built-in shelves and a wall of sliding glass doors. The efficient kitchen and oversized nook conveniently separate the family room from the game room, providing ease in serving either room. Two family bedrooms share a pool bath and complete this level. Upstairs, privacy is ensured with the master suite reigning supreme and enjoying a private covered deck. The master bath features a huge walk-in closet, spa tub, large separate shower, and dual-bowl vanity. A loft library is a fine finishing touch to this level.

ORDER BLUEPRINTS 24 HOURS, 7 DAYS A WEEK, AT 1-800-521-6797

plan
HPT9600317

STYLE: TRANSITIONAL

MAIN LEVEL: 1,887 SQ. FT.

LOWER LEVEL: 1,338 SQ. FT.

TOTAL: 3,225 SQ. FT.

BEDROOMS: 3

BATHROOMS: 2½

WIDTH: 65' - 4"

DEPTH: 52' - 8"

SEARCH ONLINE @ EPLANS.COM

A majestic window and a brick exterior provide an extra measure of style to this handsome traditional home. Straight ahead, upon entering the foyer, is the spacious great room. The kitchen and breakfast area are integrated with the gathering room. Entertaining is easy in the adjacent dining room. The large master suite is highlighted by double doors opening to the private dressing area. The lower level features a fabulous family room and two family bedrooms and offers a second fireplace.

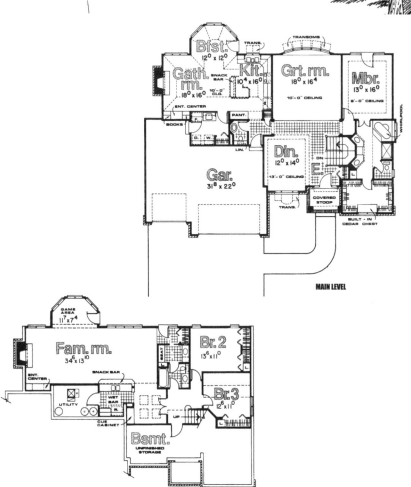

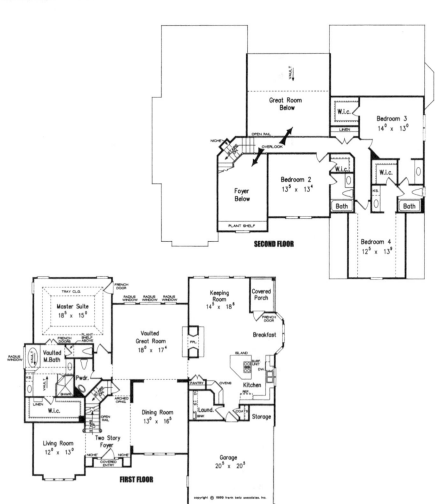

SECOND FLOOR

Great Room Below

W.i.c.

Bedroom 3
14⁰ x 13⁰

LINEN

NICHE

OPEN RAIL

OVERLOOK

W.i.c.

W.i.c.

Bedroom 2
13⁵ x 13⁴

Foyer Below

Bath

Bath

PLANT SHELF

Bedroom 4
12⁵ x 13⁹

FIRST FLOOR

TRAY CLG.

FRENCH DOOR

Master Suite
18⁵ x 15⁰

RADIUS WINDOW

RADIUS WINDOW

RADIUS WINDOW

Keeping Room
14⁵ x 18⁵

Covered Porch

FRENCH DOORS ABOVE

PLANT SHELF ABOVE

Vaulted Great Room
18⁰ x 17⁴

FRENCH DOOR

Breakfast

RADIUS WINDOW

Vaulted M.Bath

VAULT

PWDR.

ISLAND

Kitchen

Pwdr.

PANTRY

OVENS

ARCHED OPNG.

Linen

W.i.c.

DINING ROOM
13⁰ x 16⁵

Laund.

COATS

Storage

OPEN RAIL

Two Story Foyer

Living Room
12⁰ x 13⁰

NICHE

COVERED ENTRY

NICHE

Garage
20⁵ x 20⁵

copyright © 1999 frank betz associates, inc.

plan #
HPT9600318

STYLE: TRADITIONAL
FIRST FLOOR: 2,182 SQ. FT.
SECOND FLOOR: 956 SQ. FT.
TOTAL: 3,138 SQ. FT.
BEDROOMS: 4
BATHROOMS: 3½
WIDTH: 62' - 0"
DEPTH: 54' - 0"
FOUNDATION: CRAWLSPACE, BASEMENT

SEARCH ONLINE @ EPLANS.COM

Arched windows, shutters, and lintels add a touch of European flavor to this two-story, four-bedroom home. To the right of the two-story foyer is a living room, and to the left a spacious dining area. The vaulted great room is immense and includes a see-through fireplace to the cooktop-island kitchen and the keeping room. A bayed breakfast area—accessible to a covered porch—is also included in this area of the home. The master bedroom features a tray ceiling and French doors opening to a luxurious private bath and a vast walk-in closet. Upstairs, each family bedroom is complete with individual walk-in closets—one bedroom also contains a private full bath.

plan #

HPT9600319

STYLE: STICK VICTORIAN

FIRST FLOOR: 2,514 SQ. FT.

SECOND FLOOR: 975 SQ. FT.

TOTAL: 3,489 SQ. FT.

BEDROOMS: 4

BATHROOMS: 3½

WIDTH: 74' - 8"

DEPTH: 64' - 8"

FOUNDATION: BASEMENT

SEARCH ONLINE @ EPLANS.COM

You are sure to fall in love with what this traditional French Country two-story design has to offer. The great room offers a fireplace surrounded by built-in cabinets, a two-story ceiling, and striking arched windows. The study will provide you with a corner of the house to yourself with a view out the front and side. The master bedroom enjoys plenty of space and walk-in closets. The master bathroom features a welcoming arch over the bathtub and large shower.

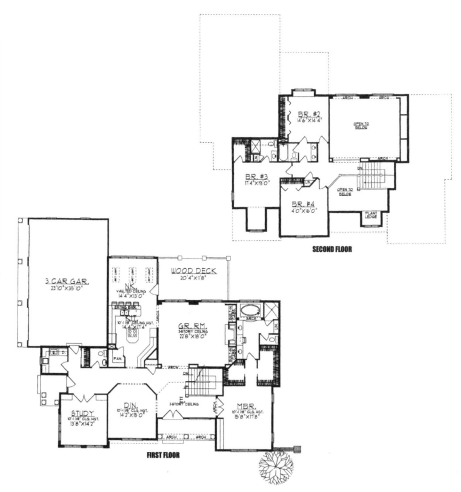

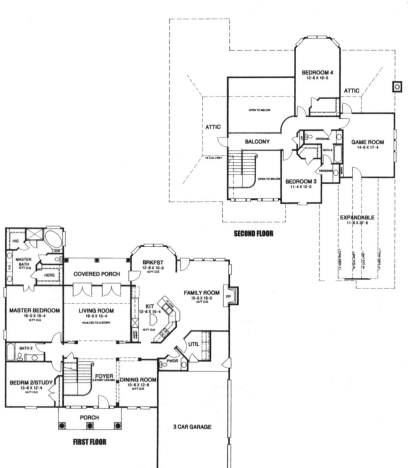

SECOND FLOOR

ATTIC

BEDROOM 4
12-6 X 16-0

ATTIC

OPEN TO BELOW

BALCONY

GAME ROOM
14-6 X 17-4

DRESSING

BATH 3

DRESSING

OPEN TO BELOW

BEDROOM 3
11-4 X 12-0

EXPANDABLE
11-6 X 20'-6

FIRST FLOOR

HIS

MASTER BATH

HERS

COVERED PORCH

BRKFST
12-6 X 10-8

FAMILY ROOM
15-0 X 19-0

FP

MASTER BEDROOM
16-0 X 15-4

LIVING ROOM
19-0 X 15-4
VAULTED TO 2 STORY

KIT
12-6 X 15-4

BATH 2

UTIL

PWDR

BEDRM 2/STUDY
13-8 X 12-4

FOYER
2 STORY CEILING

DINING ROOM
10-8 X 12-8

PORCH

3 CAR GARAGE

plan
HPT9600320

STYLE: NEO-ECLECTIC
FIRST FLOOR: 2,469 SQ. FT.
SECOND FLOOR: 1,025 SQ. FT.
TOTAL: 3,494 SQ. FT.
BONUS SPACE: 320 SQ. FT.
BEDROOMS: 4
BATHROOMS: 3½
WIDTH: 67' - 8"
DEPTH: 74' - 2"
FOUNDATION: BASEMENT,
CRAWLSPACE, SLAB

SEARCH ONLINE @ EPLANS.COM

A lovely double arch gives this European-style home a commanding presence. Once inside, a two-story foyer provides an open view directly through the formal living room to the rear grounds beyond. The spacious kitchen with a work island and the bayed breakfast area share space with the family room. The private master suite features dual sinks, twin walk-in closets, a corner garden tub, and a separate shower. A large game room completes this wonderful family home.

SECOND FLOOR

plan ⊕
HPT9600321

STYLE: NEO-ECLECTIC
FIRST FLOOR: 2,508 SQ. FT.
SECOND FLOOR: 960 SQ. FT.
TOTAL: 3,468 SQ. FT.
BEDROOMS: 4
BATHROOMS: 3½
WIDTH: 79' - 8"
DEPTH: 70' - 0"
FOUNDATION: BASEMENT

SEARCH ONLINE @ EPLANS.COM

At first sight, the charm of this home will invite you inside. You will adore the traditional French style of this two-story, three-car garage, 3,468 square-foot home. You can't help but love the balcony that stretches from a second-floor bedroom. You are sure to appreciate the uniqueness of a music room with a generous arched window. You will also be pleased with the French doors that welcome you to a study that overlooks the backyard. Certainly, you will be enticed by the arched soffit that invites you into the great room. An astonishing fireplace, built-in cabinets, and an enormous arched window overlooks the backyard from the great room. The kitchen provides great use of space with a built-in desk, island workstation, and walk-in pantry. The screened porch is accessible from the nook and the deck. The master bedroom leaves nothing to be desired and includes built-in cabinets with French doors that open to the master bathroom.

FIRST FLOOR

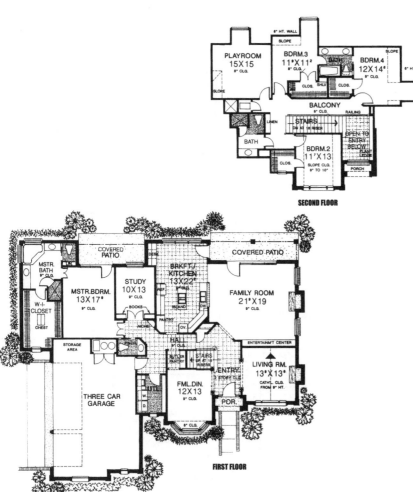

SECOND FLOOR

FIRST FLOOR

plan
HPT9600322

STYLE: FRENCH
FIRST FLOOR: 2,223 SQ. FT.
SECOND FLOOR: 1,163 SQ. FT.
TOTAL: 3,386 SQ. FT.
BEDROOMS: 4
BATHROOMS: 3½
WIDTH: 68' - 10"
DEPTH: 58' - 1"
FOUNDATION: CRAWLSPACE, SLAB

SEARCH ONLINE @ EPLANS.COM

This beautiful European estate, with corner quoins, high arched windows, and a grand brick facade, will be the envy of any neighborhood. The entry is bordered by the bayed dining room and the living room, with a cathedral ceiling and a warming fireplace. The family room is ideal for entertaining; a fireplace, entertainment center, and covered-patio access will please family and guests. In the island kitchen, space enough for two exuberant chefs makes meal preparation fun and easy. Past the study, French doors lead to the master suite, luxurious with private patio access and a spa bath. Upstairs, three generous bedrooms and a playroom will delight.

FOR MORE DETAILED INFORMATION, PLEASE CHECK THE FLOOR PLANS CAREFULLY.

plan #

HPT9600323

STYLE: TRANSITIONAL

FIRST FLOOR: 2,198 SQ. FT.

SECOND FLOOR: 1,028 SQ. FT.

TOTAL: 3,226 SQ. FT.

BONUS SPACE: 466 SQ. FT.

BEDROOMS: 4

BATHROOMS: 3½

WIDTH: 72' - 8"

DEPTH: 56' - 6"

FOUNDATION: CRAWLSPACE

SEARCH ONLINE @ EPLANS.COM

Designed for active lifestyles, this home caters to homeowners who enjoy dinner guests, privacy, luxurious surroundings, and open spaces. The foyer, parlor, and dining hall are defined by sets of columns and share a gallery hall that runs through the center of the plan. The grand room opens to the deck/terrace, which is also accessed from the sitting area and morning room. The right wing of the plan contains the well-appointed kitchen. The left wing is dominated by the master suite with its sitting bay, fireplace, two walk-in closets, and compartmented bath.

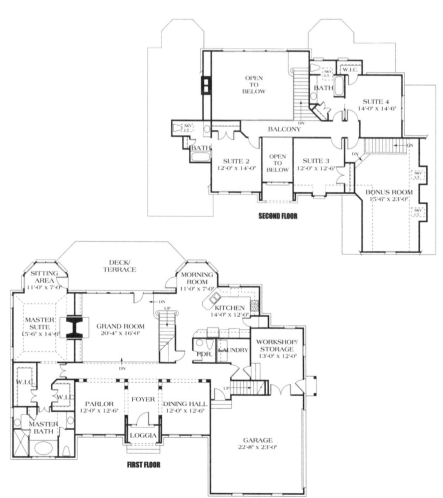

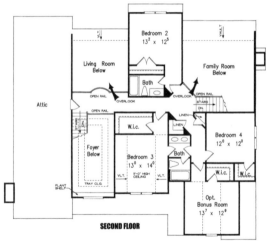

SECOND FLOOR

FIRST FLOOR

plan #
HPT9600324

STYLE: FRENCH ECLECTIC
FIRST FLOOR: 2,384 SQ. FT.
SECOND FLOOR: 1,050 SQ. FT.
TOTAL: 3,434 SQ. FT.
BONUS SPACE: 228 SQ. FT.
BEDROOMS: 4
BATHROOMS: 3½
WIDTH: 63' - 4"
DEPTH: 57' - 0"
FOUNDATION: CRAWLSPACE,
BASEMENT

SEARCH ONLINE @ EPLANS.COM

The covered front porch of this stucco home opens to a two-story foyer and one of two staircases. Arched openings lead into both the formal dining room and the vaulted living room. The efficient kitchen features a walk-in pantry, built-in desk, work island, and separate snack bar. Nearby, the large breakfast area opens to the family room. Lavish in its amenities, the master suite offers a separate, vaulted sitting room with a fireplace, among other luxuries. Three bedrooms, along with optional bonus space and attic storage, are found on the second floor.

plan
HPT9600325

STYLE: EUROPEAN COTTAGE
FIRST FLOOR: 1,583 SQ. FT.
SECOND FLOOR: 1,632 SQ. FT.
TOTAL: 3,215 SQ. FT.
BEDROOMS: 5
BATHROOMS: 4½
WIDTH: 58' - 4"
DEPTH: 50' - 0"
FOUNDATION: CRAWLSPACE,
BASEMENT

SEARCH ONLINE @ EPLANS.COM

From outside to inside, the decorative details on this stucco two-story make it very special. Ceiling adornments are particularly interesting: the two-story foyer and the master bedroom have tray ceilings. The dining room and living room are separated by columns; another column graces the two-story family room. A den is reached through double doors just to the left of the foyer. Use it for an additional bedroom if needed—it has a private bath. There are four upstairs bedrooms in this plan. The master suite includes a fireplace in the vaulted sitting room.

plan #

HPT9600326

STYLE: TRANSITIONAL
FIRST FLOOR: 2,270 SQ. FT.
SECOND FLOOR: 788 SQ. FT.
TOTAL: 3,058 SQ. FT.
BONUS SPACE: 397 SQ. FT.
BEDROOMS: 3
BATHROOMS: 3½
WIDTH: 84' - 9"
DEPTH: 76' - 2"
FOUNDATION: CRAWLSPACE

SEARCH ONLINE @ EPLANS.COM

Dramatic on the highest level, this spectacular plan offers a recessed entry, double rows of multi-pane windows, and two dormers over the garage. On the inside, formal living and dining areas reside to the right of the foyer and are separated from it by columns. A private den is also accessed from the foyer through double doors. The family room with a fireplace is to the rear and adjoins the breakfast nook and attached island kitchen. The master suite sits on the first floor to separate it from family bedrooms. Bonus space over the garage can be developed at a later time.

plan #

HPT9600327

STYLE: FRENCH ECLECTIC

FIRST FLOOR: 2,398 SQ. FT.

SECOND FLOOR: 657 SQ. FT.

TOTAL: 3,055 SQ. FT.

BONUS SPACE: 374 SQ. FT.

BEDROOMS: 4

BATHROOMS: 3½

WIDTH: 72' - 8"

DEPTH: 69' - 1"

FOUNDATION: CRAWLSPACE, BASEMENT

SEARCH ONLINE @ EPLANS.COM

European formality meets a bold American spirit in this splendid transitional plan. Perfect for a lake or golf course setting, this home offers walls of windows in the living areas. Soak up the scenery in the sunroom, which opens from the breakfast nook and leads to a rear terrace or deck. Ten-foot ceilings throughout the main level provide interior vistas and add volume to the rooms. The library features a tray ceiling and an arched window and would make an excellent home office or guest suite. Classical columns divide the great room and dining room, which has a see-through wet bar. The deluxe master suite uses defining columns between the bedroom and the lavish bath and walk-in closet. Upstairs, there are two additional suites and a bonus room.

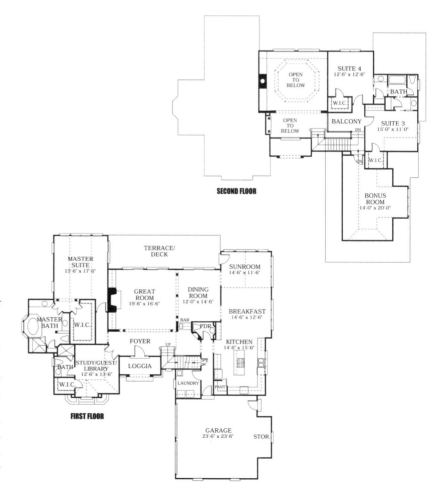

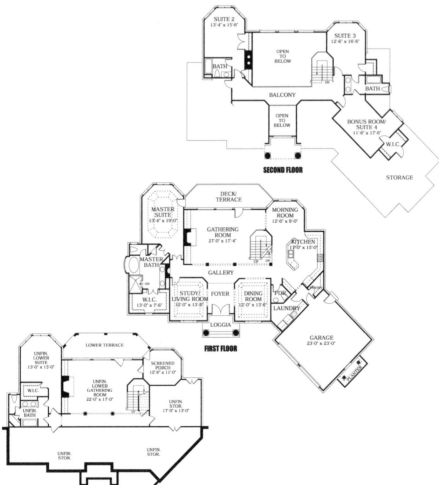

SECOND FLOOR

SUITE 2
13'-4" x 15'-6"

SUITE 3
12'-6" x 16'-6"

OPEN TO BELOW

BATH

BALCONY

OPEN TO BELOW

BATH

BONUS ROOM/
SUITE 4
11'-6" x 17'-6"

W.I.C.

STORAGE

FIRST FLOOR

DECK/
TERRACE

MASTER SUITE
13'-4" x 19'-0"

GATHERING ROOM
27'-0" x 17'-4"

MORNING ROOM
12'-6" x 9'-0"

KITCHEN
17'-0" x 15'-0"

MASTER BATH

GALLERY

W.I.C.
13'-0" x 7'-6"

STUDY/
LIVING ROOM
12'-0" x 13'-6"

FOYER

DINING ROOM
12'-0" x 13'-6"

PDR.

LAUNDRY

LOGGIA

GARAGE
23'-0" x 23'-0"

BASEMENT

UNFIN. LOWER SUITE
13'-0" x 15'-0"

LOWER TERRACE

SCREENED PORCH
12'-6" x 11'-0"

W.I.C.

UNFIN. LOWER GATHERING ROOM
22'-0" x 17'-0"

UNFIN. STOR.
17'-0" x 13'-0"

UNFIN. BATH

UNFIN. STOR.

UNFIN. STOR.

plan
HPT9600328

STYLE: TRANSITIONAL
FIRST FLOOR: 2,293 SQ. FT.
SECOND FLOOR: 901 SQ. FT.
TOTAL: 3,194 SQ. FT.
BONUS SPACE: 265 SQ. FT.
BEDROOMS: 3
BATHROOMS: 3½
WIDTH: 82' - 6"
DEPTH: 67' - 2"
FOUNDATION: BASEMENT

SEARCH ONLINE @ EPLANS.COM

From its dramatic front entry to its rear twin-bay turret, this design is as traditional as it is historic. A two-story foyer opens through a gallery to an expansive gathering room, which shares its natural light with a bumped-out morning nook. A formal living room or study offers a coffered ceiling and a private door to the gallery hall that leads to the master suite. The dining room opens to more casual living space, including the kitchen with its angled island counter. Bonus space may be developed later.

ORDER BLUEPRINTS 24 HOURS, 7 DAYS A WEEK, AT 1-800-521-6797

plan #
HPT9600329

STYLE: TRANSITIONAL
FIRST FLOOR: 2,188 SQ. FT.
SECOND FLOOR: 1,110 SQ. FT.
TOTAL: 3,298 SQ. FT.
BEDROOMS: 4
BATHROOMS: 4½
WIDTH: 69' - 0"
DEPTH: 64' - 8"
FOUNDATION: SLAB

SEARCH ONLINE @ EPLANS.COM

This European-style, brick-and-stucco home showcases an arched entry and presents a commanding presence from the curb. Inside, the living room, the dining room, and the family room are located at the rear of the home to provide wide-open views of the rear grounds beyond. A colonnade with connecting arches defines the space for a living room with a fireplace and the dining room. The spacious master suite features a relaxing sitting area, His and Hers closets, and His and Hers baths. On the second floor, three bedrooms, two baths, and a game room complete the home.

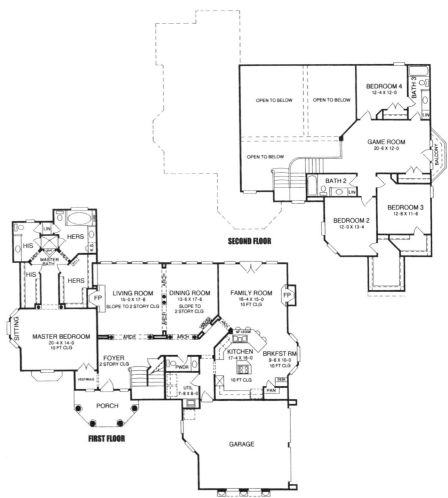

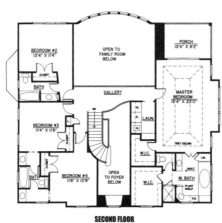

SECOND FLOOR

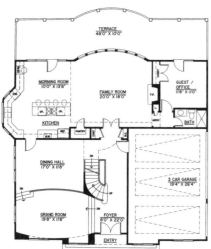

FIRST FLOOR

plan
HPT9600330

STYLE: CLASSICAL REVIVAL
FIRST FLOOR: 1,593 SQ. FT.
SECOND FLOOR: 1,480 SQ. FT.
TOTAL: 3,073 SQ. FT.
BEDROOMS: 4
BATHROOMS: 3½
WIDTH: 51' - 0"
DEPTH: 46' - 6"
FOUNDATION: BASEMENT

SEARCH ONLINE @ EPLANS.COM

Symmetry is exhibited though the use of brick details, shutters, and graceful columns on this design. Inside, to the left of the two-story foyer and down a few steps, is the grand room, which is slightly oval. A spacious dining hall is just up three steps and offers direct access from the huge island kitchen. The family room, located to the rear of the home, features a bowed wall of windows and a warming fireplace. A guest room or office accesses the rear deck as well as a full bath. Upstairs, the master bedroom is full of amenities, including wo walk-in closets, a private porch, and a lavish bath. Three family bedrooms, each with direct access to a bath, finish out this floor.

ORDER BLUEPRINTS 24 HOURS, 7 DAYS A WEEK, AT 1-800-521-6797

C. Rosario

plan
HPT9600331

STYLE: GEORGIAN
FIRST FLOOR: 2,253 SQ. FT.
SECOND FLOOR: 890 SQ. FT.
TOTAL: 3,143 SQ. FT.
BEDROOMS: 4
BATHROOMS: 3½
WIDTH: 61' - 6"
DEPTH: 64' - 0"
FOUNDATION: BASEMENT

SEARCH ONLINE @ EPLANS.COM

This grand Georgian home begins with a double-door entry topped by a beautiful arched window. Inside, the foyer opens to the two-story living room, which has a wide bow window overlooking the rear property. Double doors open to a study warmed by a fireplace. The kitchen features a walk-in pantry and serves both the formal dining room and the breakfast area, which adjoins the bright keeping room. The master suite, secluded on the first floor, is large and opulent. Three more bedrooms and two baths are upstairs for family and friends.

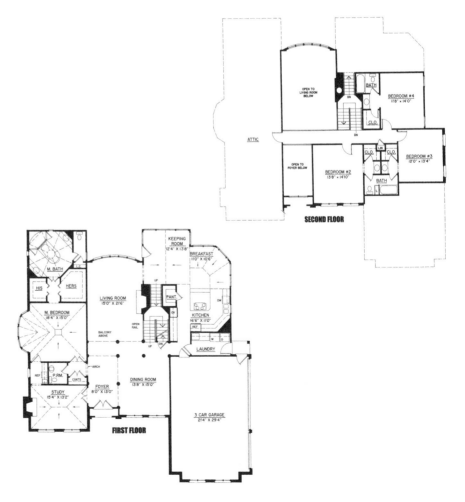

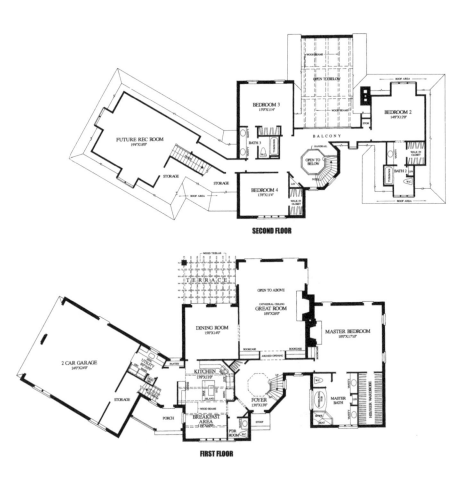

SECOND FLOOR

FIRST FLOOR

plan# HPT9600332

STYLE: FRENCH
FIRST FLOOR: 2,272 SQ. FT.
SECOND FLOOR: 1,154 SQ. FT.
TOTAL: 3,426 SQ. FT.
BONUS SPACE: 513 SQ. FT.
BEDROOMS: 4
BATHROOMS: 3½
WIDTH: 102' - 8"
DEPTH: 49' - 6"
FOUNDATION: CRAWLSPACE,
BASEMENT

SEARCH ONLINE @ EPLANS.COM

The gracious façade of this French home engages refinement and fantasy. The foyer is housed within the turret, which holds an elegant spiral staircase. To the left, gourmet entertaining can be had with the spacious island kitchen that serves both the casual breakfast room and the formal dining room. Enjoy a nightcap in front of a relaxing fire in the great room. With comfort in mind, the master suite features a fireplace and a sumptuous bath. The upper floor creates a space for guests and family members with three secondary bedrooms—one with a private bath—and a future recreation room.

plan
HPT9600333

STYLE: FRENCH ECLECTIC
FIRST FLOOR: 2,216 SQ. FT.
SECOND FLOOR: 1,192 SQ. FT.
TOTAL: 3,408 SQ. FT.
BONUS SPACE: 458 SQ. FT.
BEDROOMS: 4
BATHROOMS: 3½
WIDTH: 67' - 10"
DEPTH: 56' - 10"
FOUNDATION: CRAWLSPACE

SEARCH ONLINE @ EPLANS.COM

This elegant, tasteful chateau charms and delights, with an Old World flavor and a balcony that will inspire Shakespearean soliloquies. The foyer is flanked by the formal living room and dining room. The expansive kitchen is conveniently situated to serve both dining and breakfast areas with ease. The comforting family room offers a marvelous view and an enchanting fireplace. The master suite finds privacy on the first floor near a secondary stairway on the left. An additional bedroom suite is found on the second floor, along with two more bedrooms, a full bath, and space for a future rec room.

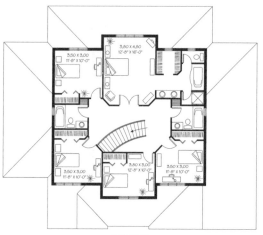

SECOND FLOOR

FIRST FLOOR

plan
HPT9600334

STYLE: MEDITERRANEAN
FIRST FLOOR: 1,700 SQ. FT.
SECOND FLOOR: 1,300 SQ. FT.
TOTAL: 3,000 SQ. FT.
BEDROOMS: 6
BATHROOMS: 4½
WIDTH: 60' - 0"
DEPTH: 43' - 4"
FOUNDATION: BASEMENT

SEARCH ONLINE @ EPLANS.COM

This stunning Mediterranean-influenced design features a spacious first-floor media room that doubles as a convenient home office. The formal living room adjoins the dining room, creating a fine area for entertaining. Nearby, the kitchen offers space for a dining table and access to the family room, which opens to the backyard. A luxurious master suite with a walk-in closet, dual vanities, and a soothing tub completes the first floor. A gently curved staircase leads up to five additional bedrooms, one of them a roomy guest suite with a private dual-vanity bath. The remaining four bedrooms access two full baths.

ORDER BLUEPRINTS 24 HOURS, 7 DAYS A WEEK, AT 1-800-521-6797

FOR MORE DETAILED INFORMATION, PLEASE CHECK THE FLOOR PLANS CAREFULLY.

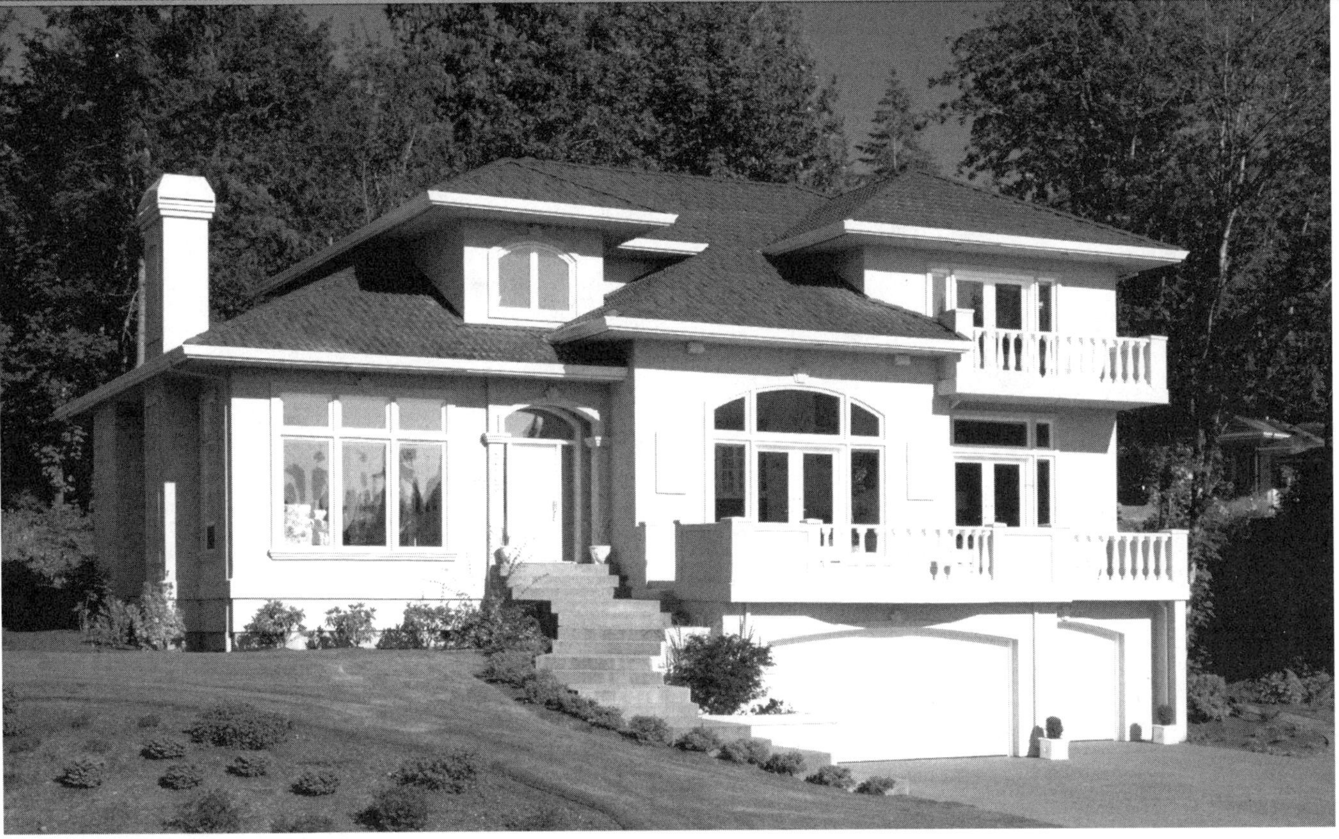

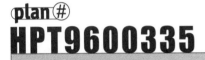

plan #

HPT9600335

STYLE: NEO-ECLECTIC
FIRST FLOOR: 1,989 SQ. FT.
SECOND FLOOR: 1,349 SQ. FT.
TOTAL: 3,338 SQ. FT.
BONUS SPACE: 487 SQ. FT.
BEDROOMS: 3
BATHROOMS: 2½
WIDTH: 63' - 0"
DEPTH: 48' - 0"
FOUNDATION: BASEMENT

SEARCH ONLINE @ EPLANS.COM

Dramatic balconies and spectacular window treatments enhance this stunning luxury home. Inside, a through-fireplace warms the formal living room and a restful den. Both living spaces open to a balcony that invites quiet reflection on starry nights. The banquet-sized dining room is easily served from the adjacent kitchen. Here, space is shared with an eating nook that provides access to the rear grounds and a family room with a corner fireplace—perfect for casual gatherings. The upper level contains two family bedrooms and a luxurious master suite that enjoys its own private balcony. The lower level accommodates a shop and a bonus room for future development.

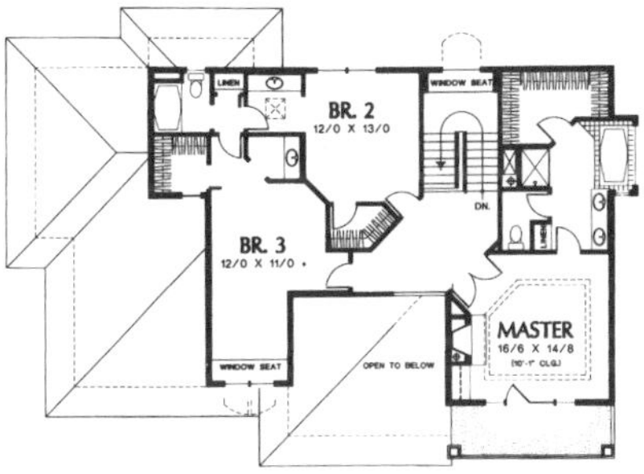

SECOND FLOOR

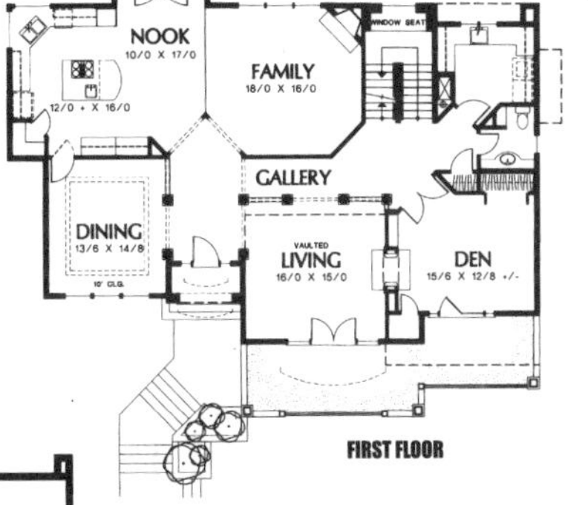

FIRST FLOOR

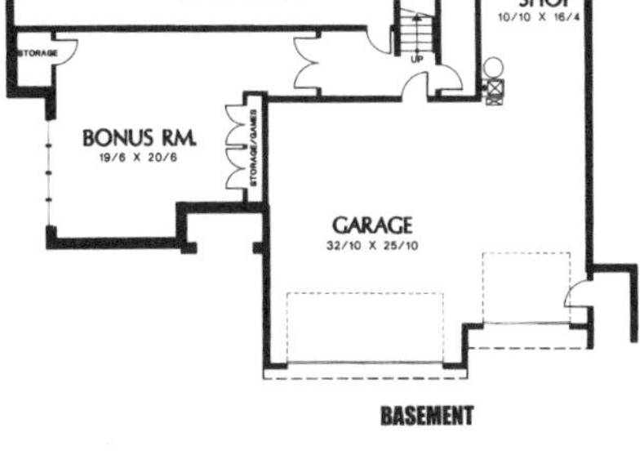

BASEMENT

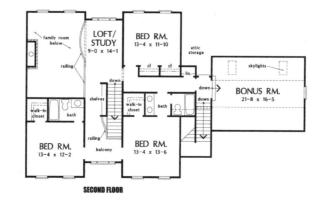

LOFT/ STUDY 9-0 x 14-1

family room below

railing

BED RM. 13-4 x 11-10

attic storage

down

skylights

BONUS RM. 21-8 x 16-5

walk-in closet

bath

shelves

walk-in closet

bath

down

down

BED RM. 13-4 x 12-2

railing

balcony

BED RM. 13-4 x 13-6

SECOND FLOOR

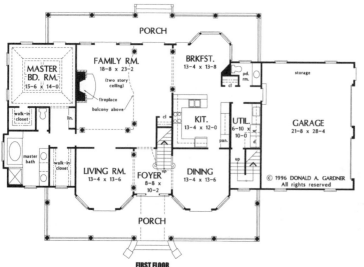

PORCH

MASTER BD. RM. 15-6 x 14-0

FAMILY RM. 18-8 x 23-2
(two story ceiling)
fireplace
balcony above

BRKFST. 13-4 x 13-8

pd. rm.

storage

walk-in closet

lin.

cl

KIT. 13-4 x 12-0

UTIL. 6-10 x 10-0

GARAGE 21-8 x 28-4

master bath

walk-in closet

LIVING RM. 13-4 x 13-6

FOYER 8-8 x 10-2

up

DINING 13-4 x 13-6

pan.

up

© 1996 DONALD A. GARDNER
All rights reserved

PORCH

FIRST FLOOR

ptan
HPT9600336

STYLE: VICTORIAN FARMHOUSE
FIRST FLOOR: 2,086 SQ. FT.
SECOND FLOOR: 1,077 SQ. FT.
TOTAL: 3,163 SQ. FT.
BONUS SPACE: 403 SQ. FT.
BEDROOMS: 4
BATHROOMS: 3½
WIDTH: 81' - 10"
DEPTH: 51' - 8"

SEARCH ONLINE @ EPLANS.COM

This beautiful farmhouse, with its prominent twin gables and bays, adds just the right amount of country style. The master suite is quietly tucked away downstairs with no rooms directly above. The family cook will love the spacious U-shaped kitchen and adjoining bayed breakfast nook. A bonus room awaits expansion on the second floor, where three large bedrooms share two full baths. Storage space abounds with walk-ins, half-shelves, and linen closets. A curved balcony borders a versatile loft/study, which overlooks the stunning two-story family room.

ORDER BLUEPRINTS 24 HOURS, 7 DAYS A WEEK, AT 1-800-521-6797

© 2001 Donald A. Gardner, Inc.

plan #
HPT9600337

STYLE: VICTORIAN FARMHOUSE

FIRST FLOOR: 2,194 SQ. FT.

SECOND FLOOR: 973 SQ. FT.

TOTAL: 3,167 SQ. FT.

BONUS SPACE: 281 SQ. FT.

BEDROOMS: 4

BATHROOMS: 3½

WIDTH: 71' - 11"

DEPTH: 54' - 4"

SEARCH ONLINE @ EPLANS.COM

This updated farmhouse has been given additional custom-styled features. Twin gables, sidelights, and an arched entryway accent the facade, and decorative ceiling treatments, bay windows, and French doors adorn the interior. From an abundance of counter space and large walk-in pantry to the built-ins and storage areas, this design makes the most of space. Supported by columns, a curved balcony overlooks the stunning two-story great room. The powder room is easily accessible from the common rooms, and angled corners soften the dining room.

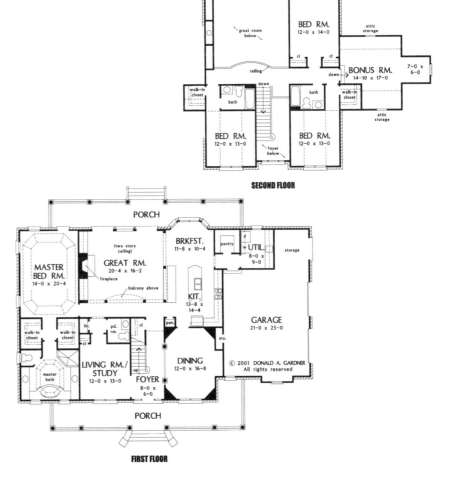

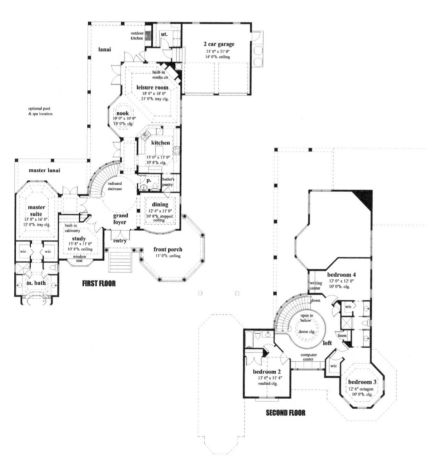

plan #

HPT9600338

STYLE: TIDEWATER
FIRST FLOOR: 2,083 SQ. FT.
SECOND FLOOR: 1,013 SQ. FT.
TOTAL: 3,096 SQ. FT.
BEDROOMS: 4
BATHROOMS: 3½
WIDTH: 74' - 0"
DEPTH: 88' - 0"
FOUNDATION: SLAB

SEARCH ONLINE @ EPLANS.COM

This beautiful design is accented by the circular front porch and the abundance of windows. The entry leads into a grand foyer, where a radius staircase presents itself. Most of the rooms in this house are graced with tray, stepped, or vaulted ceilings, adding a sense of spaciousness to the plan. The first-floor master suite boasts many amenities including a private lanai, His and Hers walk-in closets, a bayed tub area, and a separate shower. Other unique features on the first-floor include a study, with a window seat and built-in cabinetry, a breakfast nook, butler's pantry, utility room, and outdoor kitchen, among others. The upstairs houses three family bedrooms and two full baths. Bedroom 3 boasts an octagonal ceiling, and the ceiling of Bedroom 2 is vaulted. A computer center, linen area, and loft completes the second floor.

J.N.HANSEN S.D.G.

plan
HPT9600339

STYLE: VICTORIAN

FIRST FLOOR: 2,041 SQ. FT.

SECOND FLOOR: 1,098 SQ. FT.

TOTAL: 3,139 SQ. FT.

BONUS SPACE: 385 SQ. FT.

BEDROOMS: 4

BATHROOMS: 3½

WIDTH: 76' - 6"

DEPTH: 62' - 2"

FOUNDATION: SLAB

SEARCH ONLINE @ EPLANS.COM

The turret and the circular covered porch of this Victorian home make a great impression. The foyer carries you past a library and dining room to the hearth-warmed family room. A spacious kitchen with an island acts as a passageway to the nook and dining area. The master bedroom is located on the first floor and offers its own French doors to the rear covered porch. The master bath is designed to cater to both His and Hers needs with two walk-in closets, separate vanities, a garden tub, and separate shower. The second-floor balcony looks to the family room below.

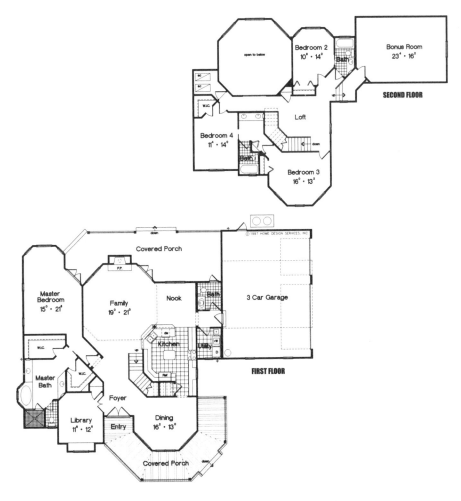

SECOND FLOOR

SECOND FLOOR:
- BEDRM 12² x 10⁶
- BEDRM 16⁸ x 10⁶
- LOFT 14⁸ x 11⁰
- BEDRM 15⁸ x 11⁰
- BATH

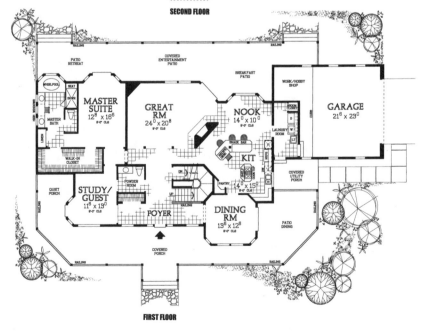

FIRST FLOOR

FIRST FLOOR:
- PATIO RETREAT
- COVERED ENTERTAINMENT PATIO
- BREAKFAST PATIO
- WORK/HOBBY SHOP
- MASTER SUITE 12⁸ x 18⁶
- GREAT RM 24⁰ x 20⁸
- NOOK 14⁰ x 10⁰
- GARAGE 21⁸ x 29⁰
- MASTER BATH
- WALK-IN CLOSET
- LAUNDRY ROOM
- KIT 14⁰ x 15⁰
- SNACK BAR
- QUIET PORCH
- STUDY/GUEST 11⁸ x 19⁰
- POWDER ROOM
- FOYER
- DINING RM 15⁸ x 12⁶
- COVERED UTILITY PORCH
- PATIO DINING
- PANTRY
- COVERED PORCH

plan # HPT9600340

STYLE: FARMHOUSE
FIRST FLOOR: 2,347 SQ. FT.
SECOND FLOOR: 1,087 SQ. FT.
TOTAL: 3,434 SQ. FT.
BEDROOMS: 4
BATHROOMS: 2½
WIDTH: 93' - 6"
DEPTH: 61' - 0"
FOUNDATION: BASEMENT

SEARCH ONLINE @ EPLANS.COM

Dutch-gable rooflines and a gabled wraparound porch provide an extra measure of farmhouse style. The foyer opens on the left to the study or guest bedroom that leads to the master suite. To the right is the formal dining room; the massive great room is in the center. The kitchen combines with the great room, the breakfast nook, and the dining room for entertaining options. The master suite includes access to the covered patio, a spacious walk-in closet, and a full bath with a whirlpool tub.

© 1993 Donald A. Gardner Architects, Inc.

B·NATHAN·

plan⊕ HPT9600341

STYLE: FARMHOUSE

FIRST FLOOR: 2,176 SQ. FT.

SECOND FLOOR: 861 SQ. FT.

TOTAL: 3,037 SQ. FT.

BONUS SPACE: 483 SQ. FT.

BEDROOMS: 4

BATHROOMS: 2½

WIDTH: 94' - 0"

DEPTH: 58' - 4"

SEARCH ONLINE @ EPLANS.COM

Country living is at its best in this spacious four-bedroom farmhouse with a wraparound porch. A front Palladian window dormer and rear clerestory windows in the great room add exciting visual elements to the exterior, while providing natural light to the interior. In the great room, a fireplace, bookshelves, a cathedral ceiling, and a balcony overlook create a comfortable atmosphere. The formal dining room is open to the foyer, and the living room could be used as a study instead. Special features such as a large cooktop island in the kitchen, a wet bar, a generous bonus room over the garage and ample storage space set this plan apart from others. You'll also love the fact that the master suite, the great room, and the breakfast room all directly access the rear porch.

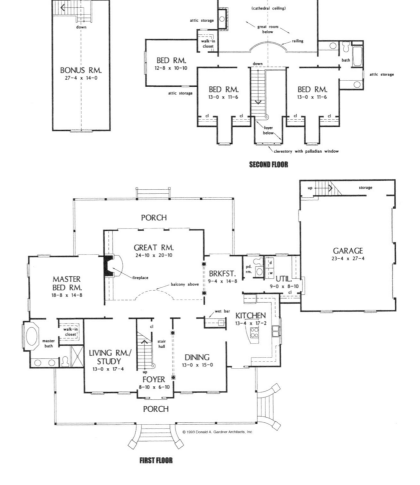

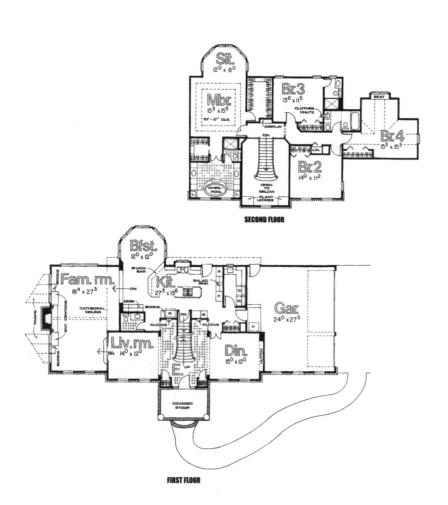

SECOND FLOOR

FIRST FLOOR

plan #
HPT9600342

STYLE: COLONIAL REVIVAL
FIRST FLOOR: 1,717 SQ. FT.
SECOND FLOOR: 1,518 SQ. FT.
TOTAL: 3,235 SQ. FT.
BEDROOMS: 4
BATHROOMS: 3½
WIDTH: 78' - 0"
DEPTH: 42' - 0"

SEARCH ONLINE @ EPLANS.COM

Stately columns highlight the facade of this beautiful Southern Colonial home. The open entry allows for views into formal areas and up the tapering staircase. The dining room joins the kitchen through double doors. The living room can be divided from the sunken family room by pocket doors. Step down into the huge family room to find large windows, a fireplace, a built-in entertainment center, and bookcases. The kitchen features a gazebo breakfast area, serving bar, and cooktop island. Upstairs, three family bedrooms share two full baths. The private master suite features a tiered ceiling, two walk-in closets, and a roomy bayed sitting area.

plan# HPT9600343

STYLE: NEO-ECLECTIC

FIRST FLOOR: 2,219 SQ. FT.

SECOND FLOOR: 1,085 SQ. FT.

TOTAL: 3,304 SQ. FT.

BONUS SPACE: 404 SQ. FT.

BEDROOMS: 4

BATHROOMS: 3½

WIDTH: 91' - 0"

DEPTH: 52' - 8"

FOUNDATION: SLAB

SEARCH ONLINE @ EPLANS.COM

This home features two levels of pampering luxury filled with the most up-to-date amenities. Touches of Mediterranean detail add to the striking facade. A wrapping front porch welcomes you inside to a formal dining room and two-story great room warmed by a fireplace. Double doors from the master suite, great room, and breakfast nook access the rear veranda. The first-floor master suite enjoys a luxury bath, roomy walk-in closet, and close access to the front-facing office/study. Three additional bedrooms reside upstairs. The bonus room above the garage is great for an apartment or storage space.

SECOND FLOOR

FIRST FLOOR

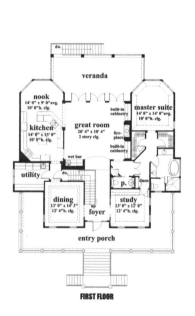

FIRST FLOOR

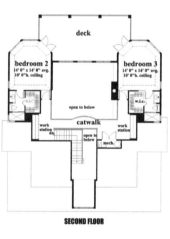

SECOND FLOOR

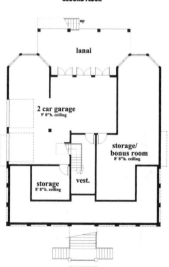

BASEMENT

plan#
HPT9600344

STYLE: TIDEWATER
FIRST FLOOR: 2,146 SQ. FT.
SECOND FLOOR: 952 SQ. FT.
TOTAL: 3,098 SQ. FT.
BEDROOMS: 3
BATHROOMS: 3½
WIDTH: 52' - 0"
DEPTH: 65' - 4"
FOUNDATION: BASEMENT

SEARCH ONLINE @ EPLANS.COM

Outdoor spaces, such as the inviting wrap-around porch and the rear veranda, are the living areas of this cottage. French doors, a fireplace, and built-in cabinets adorn the great room. A private hall leads to the first-floor master suite. The upper level boasts a catwalk that overlooks the great room and the foyer. A secluded master wing enjoys a bumped-out window, a stunning tray ceiling, and two walk-in closets. The island kitchen conveniently accesses the nook, dining area, and the wet bar.

plan#
HPT9600345

STYLE: NEO-ECLECTIC
FIRST FLOOR: 2,083 SQ. FT.
SECOND FLOOR: 1,013 SQ. FT.
TOTAL: 3,096 SQ. FT.
BEDROOMS: 4
BATHROOMS: 3½
WIDTH: 59' - 6"
DEPTH: 88' - 0"
FOUNDATION: SLAB

SEARCH ONLINE @ EPLANS.COM

This dream cabin captures the finest historic details in rooms furnished with comfort and style. A grand foyer features a radius staircase that decks out the entry hall and defines the wide-open interior. A formal dining room is served through a butler's pantry by a well-equipped kitchen. Casual space includes a leisure room that sports a corner fireplace, tray ceiling, and built-in media center. An outdoor kitchen makes it easy to enjoy life outside on the wraparound porch. The main-level master suite is suited with a spacious bedroom, two walk-in closets, and a lavish bath with separate vanities and a bumped-out whirlpool tub. Upstairs, two family bedrooms share a compartmented bath, and a guest suite boasts a roomy bath.

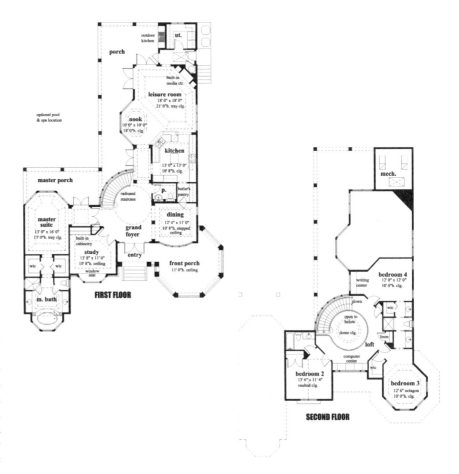

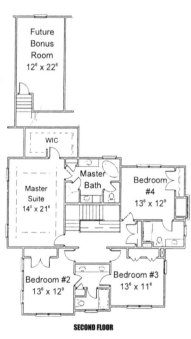

Future Bonus Room
12⁶ x 22⁶

WIC

Master Suite
14⁰ x 21⁶

Master Bath

Bedroom #4
13⁶ x 12⁹

Bedroom #2
13⁶ x 12⁹

Bedroom #3
13⁶ x 11⁶

SECOND FLOOR

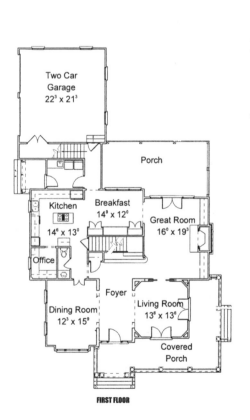

Two Car Garage
22³ x 21³

Porch

Kitchen
14⁶ x 13⁰

Breakfast
14⁹ x 12⁰

Great Room
16⁰ x 19³

Office

Foyer

Dining Room
12³ x 15⁹

Living Room
13⁶ x 13⁶

Covered Porch

FIRST FLOOR

plan
HPT9600346

STYLE: FARMHOUSE
FIRST FLOOR: 1,652 SQ. FT.
SECOND FLOOR: 1,460 SQ. FT.
TOTAL: 3,112 SQ. FT.
BONUS SPACE: 256 SQ. FT.
BEDROOMS: 4
BATHROOMS: 3½
WIDTH: 48' - 0"
DEPTH: 78' - 4"
FOUNDATION: BASEMENT

SEARCH ONLINE @ EPLANS.COM

Distinctive windows, round columns, and well-planned projections lend a touch of grandeur to the charming front porch of this alluring home. Horizontal siding and a stone chimney provide captivating complements to the exterior. The living room opens to the great room and includes two sets of doors to the front porch. The great room features built-in bookshelves and a fireplace. A large kitchen, adjacent to a compact office, easily serves the breakfast room and the dining room. Upstairs, a spacious master suite features a tray ceiling and a walk-in closet. Three additional bedrooms and a bonus room with access to a rear staircase complete the upper floor.

ORDER BLUEPRINTS 24 HOURS, 7 DAYS A WEEK, AT 1-800-521-6797

THIS HOME, AS SHOWN IN THE PHOTOGRAPH, MAY DIFFER FROM THE ACTUAL BLUEPRINTS. FOR MORE DETAILED INFORMATION, PLEASE CHECK THE FLOOR PLANS CAREFULLY.

plan
HPT9600347

STYLE: TRADITIONAL
FIRST FLOOR: 2,642 SQ. FT.
SECOND FLOOR: 603 SQ. FT.
TOTAL: 3,245 SQ. FT.
BONUS SPACE: 255 SQ. FT.
BEDROOMS: 4
BATHROOMS: 3½ + ½
WIDTH: 80' - 0"
DEPTH: 61' - 0"
FOUNDATION: CRAWLSPACE

SEARCH ONLINE @ EPLANS.COM

In this three-bedroom design, the casual areas are free-flowing, open, and soaring, and the formal areas are secluded and well defined. The two-story foyer with a clerestory window leads to a quiet parlor with a vaulted ceiling and a Palladian window. The formal dining room opens from the foyer through decorative columns and is served by a spacious gourmet kitchen. The family room, defined by columns, has an angled corner hearth and is open to the kitchen and breakfast nook. The master suite is full of interesting angles, from the triangular bedroom and multi-angled walk-in closet to the corner tub in the sumptuous master bath. A nearby den has its own bathroom and could serve as a guest room. Upstairs, two additional bedrooms share a full bath and a balcony hall.

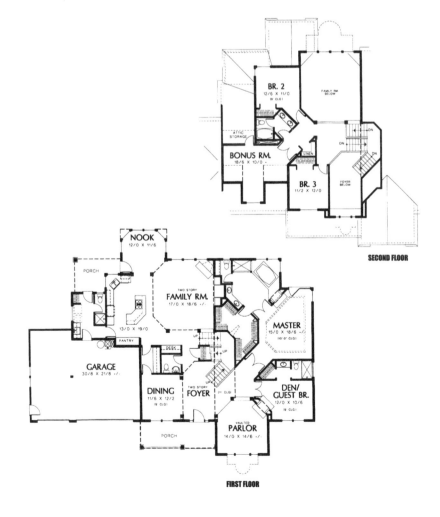

SECOND FLOOR

FIRST FLOOR

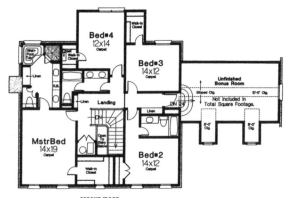

SECOND FLOOR

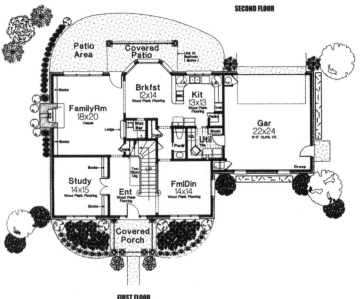

FIRST FLOOR

plan #

HPT9600348

STYLE: COLONIAL REVIVAL
FIRST FLOOR: 1,573 SQ. FT.
SECOND FLOOR: 1,449 SQ. FT.
TOTAL: 3,022 SQ. FT.
BONUS SPACE: 375 SQ. FT.
BEDROOMS: 4
BATHROOMS: 3½
WIDTH: 65' - 10"
DEPTH: 38' - 10"
FOUNDATION: SLAB, BASEMENT

SEARCH ONLINE @ EPLANS.COM

A lovely facade graces this striking four-bedroom traditional home with double columns supporting the impressive gabled entry. The hardwood floor in the foyer continues through double doors into a large study with built-in bookshelves and extends to the right into the formal dining room. The bright open area across the back holds the family room with a fireplace, the breakfast room with a bay window, and the U-shaped kitchen with a pantry. The master bedroom on the second level features a corner whirlpool tub. Three family or guest bedrooms access two additional full baths. A large well-lighted bonus room over the garage awaits future development.

plan #
HPT9600349

STYLE: FRENCH COUNTRY
SQUARE FOOTAGE: 3,049
BONUS SPACE: 868 SQ. FT.
BEDROOMS: 3
BATHROOMS: 2½
WIDTH: 72' - 6"
DEPTH: 78' - 10"
FOUNDATION: BASEMENT,
CRAWLSPACE

SEARCH ONLINE @ EPLANS.COM

This charming home, with its brick exterior and Old World accents, seems to have been plucked from the English countryside. The arched entry opens to the two-story foyer with a balcony overlook. The formal dining room sits on the left, and the living room is on the right. Beyond the elegant staircase, the family room offers a magnificent view of the backyard. Off to the left is the sunny breakfast alcove and the adjoining kitchen. A split-bedroom design places the master suite on the left and two family bedrooms on the right. An optional second floor allows for two more bedrooms, two additional baths, and a recreation room.

SECOND FLOOR

Bedroom #2
13'⁶ x 15'⁶

Bath

Bedroom #3
14'⁶ x 11'⁶

Bath

Bedroom #4
13'⁶ x 14'⁶

Open to Below

FIRST FLOOR

Two Car Garage
21'⁶ x 21'⁶

Deck

Breakfast
14'⁶ x 10'⁶

Family Room
17'⁶ x 18'⁶

Master Bath

Kitchen
17'⁶ x 13'⁶

Master Bedroom
14'⁶ x 16'⁶

Pwd.

Lndy.

Dining Room
14'⁶ x 15'⁶

Foyer

Living Room
13'⁶ x 14'⁶

Porch

plan #

HPT9600350

STYLE: FARMHOUSE
FIRST FLOOR: 2,210 SQ. FT.
SECOND FLOOR: 1,070 SQ. FT.
TOTAL: 3,280 SQ. FT.
BEDROOMS: 4
BATHROOMS: 3½
WIDTH: 60' - 6"
DEPTH: 58' - 6"
FOUNDATION: BASEMENT

SEARCH ONLINE @ EPLANS.COM

A standing-seam roof, dormer windows, and a generous front porch enhance the exterior of this welcoming farmhouse. Double doors open to the living room, which has its own fireplace. The family room boasts its own fireplace and French doors that open to a rear deck. The gourmet kitchen features an island cooktop and adjoins a breakfast room brightened by a ribbon of windows. The master suite includes a divided walk-in closet and an angled shower. Upstairs, two additional bedrooms share a full bath that provides two vanities. A third bedroom offers a private bath and a walk-in closet.

plan
HPT9600351

STYLE: COLONIAL REVIVAL
FIRST FLOOR: 1,570 SQ. FT.
SECOND FLOOR: 1,630 SQ. FT.
TOTAL: 3,200 SQ. FT.
BEDROOMS: 4
BATHROOMS: 3½
WIDTH: 59' - 10"
DEPTH: 43' - 4"
FOUNDATION: WALKOUT
BASEMENT

SEARCH ONLINE @ EPLANS.COM

This classic Americana design employs wood siding, a variety of window styles, and a detailed front porch. Inside, the large two-story foyer flows into the formal dining room with arched window accents and the living room highlighted by a bay window. A short passage with a wet bar accesses the family room with its wall of windows, French doors, and fireplace. The large breakfast area and open island kitchen are spacious and airy as well as efficient. Upstairs, the master suite's sleeping and sitting rooms feature architectural details including columns, tray ceilings, and a fireplace. The elegant private bath contains a raised oval tub, dual vanities, and a separate shower. A generous walk-in closet is located beyond the bath. Additional bedrooms are complete with closets and a variety of bath combinations.

SECOND FLOOR

FIRST FLOOR

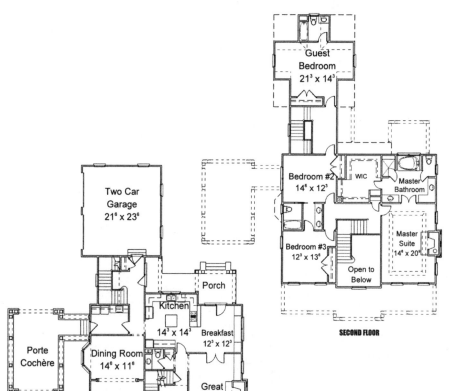

Guest Bedroom
21³ x 14³

Bedroom #2
14⁶ x 12³

WIC

Master Bathroom

Bedroom #3
12³ x 13⁶

Master Suite
14⁶ x 20⁶

Open to Below

SECOND FLOOR

Two Car Garage
21⁶ x 23⁶

Porch

Kitchen
14³ x 14³

Breakfast
12³ x 12³

Porte Cochère

Dining Room
14⁶ x 11⁶

Living Room
14⁶ x 13⁶

Foyer

Great Room
14⁶ x 20⁹

Porch

FIRST FLOOR

plan
HPT9600352

STYLE: GEORGIAN
FIRST FLOOR: 1,670 SQ. FT.
SECOND FLOOR: 1,741 SQ. FT.
TOTAL: 3,411 SQ. FT.
BEDROOMS: 4
BATHROOMS: 3½
WIDTH: 64' - 0"
DEPTH: 78' - 2"
FOUNDATION: BASEMENT

SEARCH ONLINE @ EPLANS.COM

Symmetry is everything in the Georgian style, and this home is a classic Georgian in both plan and exterior. The facade as a whole balances a one-story extended porch under a two-story hipped roof box. Inside, a traditional foyer with a central staircase is flanked by the living/dining rooms on one side and the great room on the other. Rear stairs allow private access to a secluded guest suite over the garage.

plan
HPT9600353

STYLE: FEDERAL

FIRST FLOOR: 2,432 SQ. FT.

SECOND FLOOR: 903 SQ. FT.

TOTAL: 3,335 SQ. FT.

BEDROOMS: 4

BATHROOMS: 3½

WIDTH: 90' - 0"

DEPTH: 53' - 10"

FOUNDATION: CRAWLSPACE,
SLAB, BASEMENT

SEARCH ONLINE @ EPLANS.COM

The elegant symmetry of this four-bedroom Southern traditional plan makes it a joy to own. Six columns frame the covered porch, and two chimneys add interest to the exterior roofline. The two-story foyer opens to the right to a formal living room with a built-in wet bar and a fireplace. A massive family room with a cathedral ceiling leads outside to a large covered patio or to the breakfast room and kitchen. A side-entry, three-car garage provides room for a golf cart and separate workshop area. The first-floor master bedroom features vaulted ceilings, a secluded covered patio, and a plant ledge in the master bath. The three bedrooms upstairs share two baths.

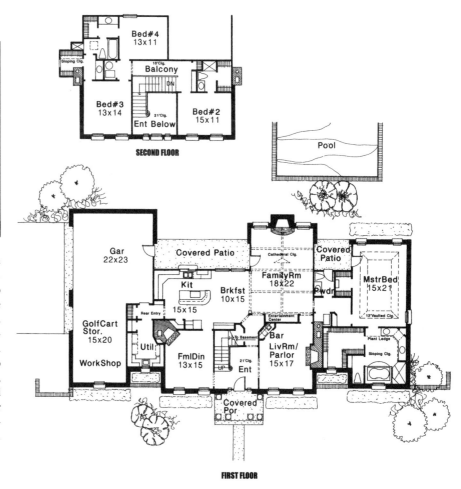

SECOND FLOOR

FIRST FLOOR

plan
HPT9600354

STYLE: GEORGIAN
FIRST FLOOR: 1,455 SQ. FT.
SECOND FLOOR: 1,649 SQ. FT.
TOTAL: 3,104 SQ. FT.
BEDROOMS: 4
BATHROOMS: 3½
WIDTH: 54' - 4"
DEPTH: 46' - 0"
FOUNDATION: WALKOUT
BASEMENT

SEARCH ONLINE @ EPLANS.COM

The double wings, twin chimneys, and center portico of this home work in concert to create a classic architectural statement. The two-story foyer is flanked by the spacious dining room and formal living room, each containing its own fireplace. A large family room with a full wall of glass opens conveniently to the kitchen and breakfast room. The master suite features a tray ceiling and French doors that open to a covered porch. A grand master bath completes the master suite. Two family bedrooms share a bath; another has a private bath. Bedroom 4 features a nook for sitting or reading.

ORDER BLUEPRINTS 24 HOURS, 7 DAYS A WEEK, AT 1-800-521-6797

plan ⊕
HPT9600355

STYLE: SOUTHERN COLONIAL
FIRST FLOOR: 1,598 SQ. FT.
SECOND FLOOR: 1,675 SQ. FT.
TOTAL: 3,273 SQ. FT.
BONUS SPACE: 534 SQ. FT.
BEDROOMS: 4
BATHROOMS: 3½
WIDTH: 54' - 8"
DEPTH: 68' - 0"

SEARCH ONLINE @ EPLANS.COM

First- and second-level covered porches, accompanied by intricate detailing, and many multipane windows create a splendid Southern mansion. The prominent entry opens to formal dining and living rooms. The grand family room is warmed by a fireplace and views a screened porch with a cozy window seat. The roomy breakfast area provides access to the porch and the three-car garage. French doors open to the second-floor master suite, which features decorative ceiling details, His and Hers walk-in closets, a large dressing area, dual vanities, a whirlpool bath, and a separate shower area.

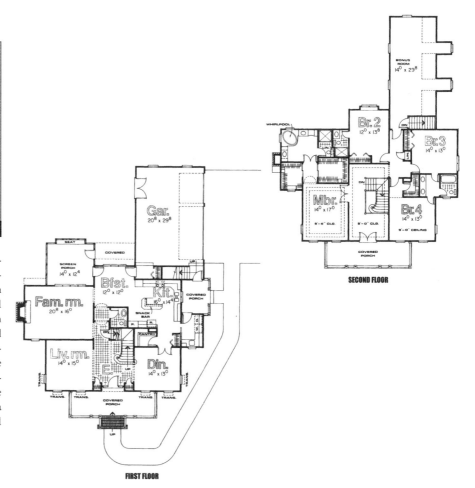

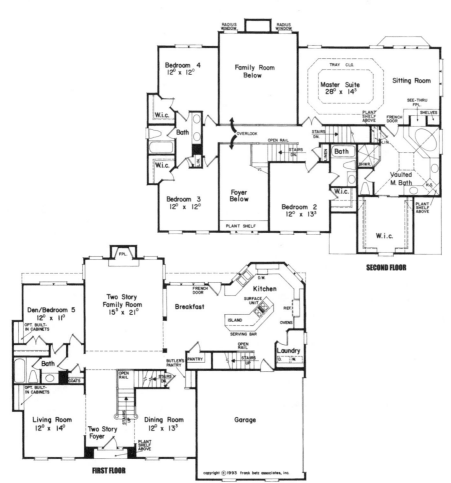

SECOND FLOOR

FIRST FLOOR

copyright © 1993 frank betz associates, inc.

plan#
HPT9600356

STYLE: COLONIAL REVIVAL
FIRST FLOOR: 1,665 SQ. FT.
SECOND FLOOR: 1,554 SQ. FT.
TOTAL: 3,219 SQ. FT.
BEDROOMS: 5
BATHROOMS: 4
WIDTH: 58' - 6"
DEPTH: 44' - 10"
FOUNDATION: CRAWLSPACE,
BASEMENT

SEARCH ONLINE @ EPLANS.COM

This stately transitional home focuses on family living. The formal living areas are traditionally placed flanking the two-story foyer. The two-story family room has a lovely fireplace and windows to the rear yard. The remarkable kitchen features wraparound counters, a breakfast nook, and a cooktop island/serving bar. A bedroom and full bath would make a comfortable guest suite or a quiet den. A balcony hall leads to two bedrooms that share a bath; a third bedroom has its own bath and walk-in closet. The master suite is designed with a tray ceiling and a sitting room with a through-fireplace to the vaulted bath.

ORDER BLUEPRINTS 24 HOURS, 7 DAYS A WEEK, AT 1-800-521-6797

ptan#

HPT9600357

STYLE: GEORGIAN

FIRST FLOOR: 1,554 SQ. FT.

SECOND FLOOR: 1,648 SQ. FT.

TOTAL: 3,202 SQ. FT.

BEDROOMS: 4

BATHROOMS: 3½

WIDTH: 60' - 0"

DEPTH: 43' - 0"

FOUNDATION: WALKOUT BASEMENT

SEARCH ONLINE @ EPLANS.COM

The classic styling of this brick American traditional home will be respected for years to come. The formidable, double-door, transomed entry and a Palladian window reveal the shining foyer within. The spacious dining room and the formal study or living room flank the foyer, and a large family room with a full wall of glass conveniently opens to the breakfast room and the kitchen. The master suite features a spacious sitting area with its own fireplace and a tray ceiling. Two additional bedrooms share a bath; a fourth bedroom has its own private bath.

SECOND FLOOR

SITTING AREA

MASTER SUITE
14'-0" x 19'-2"

MASTER BATH

HERS   HIS

BEDROOM No.3
11'-10" x 12'-0"

FUTURE OFFICE/ BONUS ROOM
17'-2" x 10'-8"

BATH

BEDROOM No.2
11'-8" x 10'

OPEN RAIL

OPEN TO BELOW

BATH

BEDROOM No.4
11'-10" x 12'-0"

FIRST FLOOR

DECK

BREAKFAST
10'-10" x 7'-0"

KITCHEN
14'-0" x

GREAT ROOM
17'-2" x 19'-2"

GUEST ROOM
17'-0" x 12'-0"

LAUNDRY
10'-3" x 5'-6"

STORAGE

TWO-CAR GARAGE
21'-4" x 21'-4"

DINING ROOM
11'-0" x

FOYER
11'-10" x 17'-2"

LIVING ROOM
14'-0" x 13'-6"

STOOP

plan
HPT9600358

STYLE: COLONIAL REVIVAL
FIRST FLOOR: 1,700 SQ. FT.
SECOND FLOOR: 1,585 SQ. FT.
TOTAL: 3,285 SQ. FT.
BONUS SPACE: 176 SQ. FT.
BEDROOMS: 5
BATHROOMS: 4
WIDTH: 60' - 0"
DEPTH: 47' - 6"
FOUNDATION: WALKOUT BASEMENT

SEARCH ONLINE @ EPLANS.COM

The covered front stoop of this two-story traditionally styled home gives way to the foyer and formal areas inside. A cozy living room with a fireplace sits on the right, and an elongated dining room is on the left. For fine family living, a great room and a kitchen/breakfast area account for the rear of the first-floor plan. A guest room with a nearby full bath finishes off the accommodations. Upstairs, four bedrooms include a master suite fit for royalty. A bonus room rests near Bedroom 3 and would make a great office or additional bedroom.

ORDER BLUEPRINTS 24 HOURS, 7 DAYS A WEEK, AT 1-800-521-6797

plan
HPT9600359

STYLE: GEORGIAN

FIRST FLOOR: 2,081 SQ. FT.

SECOND FLOOR: 940 SQ. FT.

TOTAL: 3,021 SQ. FT.

BEDROOMS: 4

BATHROOMS: 3½

WIDTH: 69' - 9"

DEPTH: 65' - 0"

FOUNDATION: WALKOUT BASEMENT

SEARCH ONLINE @ EPLANS.COM

This Georgian country-style home displays an impressive appearance. The front porch and columns frame the elegant elliptical entrance. Georgian symmetry balances the living room and dining room off the foyer. The first floor continues into the two-story great room, which offers built-in cabinetry, a fireplace, and a large bay window that overlooks the rear deck. A dramatic tray ceiling, a wall of glass, and access to the rear deck complete the master bedroom. To the left of the great room, a large kitchen opens to a breakfast area with walls of windows. Upstairs, each of three family bedrooms features ample closet space as well as direct access to a bathroom.

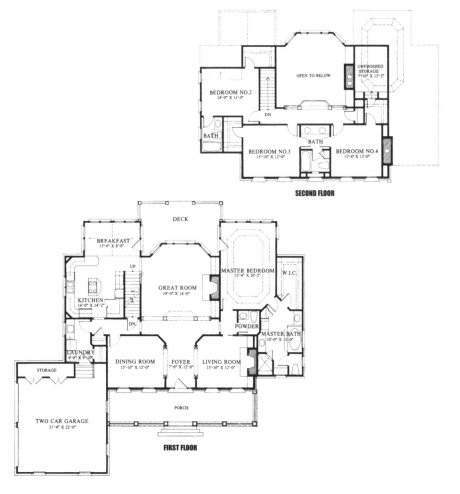

SECOND FLOOR

FIRST FLOOR

plan
HPT9600360

STYLE: GEORGIAN
FIRST FLOOR: 2,168 SQ. FT.
SECOND FLOOR: 1,203 SQ. FT.
TOTAL: 3,371 SQ. FT.
BONUS SPACE: 452 SQ. FT.
BEDROOMS: 4
BATHROOMS: 4½
WIDTH: 71' - 2"
DEPTH: 63' - 4"
FOUNDATION: CRAWLSPACE,
BASEMENT

SEARCH ONLINE @ EPLANS.COM

This stately two-story beauty offers the utmost in style and livability. The grand columned entryway is topped by a railed roof, making it the centerpiece of the facade. Formal space resides at the front of the plan, with a living room and dining room flanking the foyer. Secluded behind the staircase is the elegant master suite, with a huge walk-in closet and swanky private bath. The hearth-warmed family room flows into the island kitchen and breakfast nook, making this space the comfortable hub of home life. A laundry room and half-bath are convenient to this area. Upstairs, three bedrooms all have access to separate baths and share space with a future recreation room.

plan #

HPT9600361

STYLE: COLONIAL
FIRST FLOOR: 1,338 SQ. FT.
SECOND FLOOR: 1,200 SQ. FT.
THIRD FLOOR: 506 SQ. FT.
TOTAL: 3,044 SQ. FT.
BEDROOMS: 4
BATHROOMS: 2½
WIDTH: 72' - 0"
DEPTH: 38' - 0"
FOUNDATION: BASEMENT

SEARCH ONLINE @ EPLANS.COM

This is clearly a pleasing Georgian. Its facade features a front porch with a roof supported by 12" diameter wooden columns. The garage wing has a sheltered service entry and brick facing, which complements the design. Sliding glass doors link the terrace and family room, providing an indoor/outdoor area for entertaining as pictured in the rear elevation. The floor plan has been designed to serve the family efficiently. The stairway in the foyer leads to four second-floor bedrooms. The third floor is windowed and can be used as a studio and study.

SECOND FLOOR

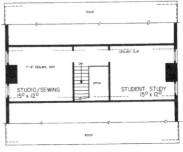

THIRD FLOOR

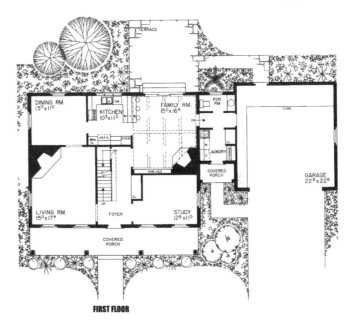

FIRST FLOOR

SECOND FLOOR

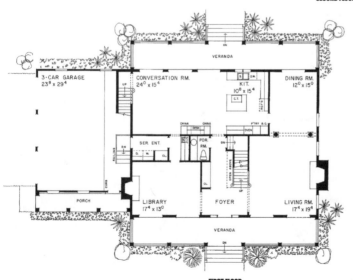

FIRST FLOOR

plan # HPT9600362

STYLE: SOUTHERN COLONIAL
FIRST FLOOR: 1,778 SQ. FT.
SECOND FLOOR: 1,663 SQ. FT.
TOTAL: 3,441 SQ. FT.
BONUS SPACE: 442 SQ. FT.
BEDROOMS: 4
BATHROOMS: 3½
WIDTH: 72' - 0"
DEPTH: 50' - 0"
FOUNDATION: BASEMENT

SEARCH ONLINE @ EPLANS.COM

Spring breezes and summer nights will be a joy to take in on the verandas and balcony of this gorgeous Southern Colonial home. Or, if you prefer, sit back and enjoy a good book in the library, or invite a friend over for a chat in the conversation room. The first floor also includes formal dining and living rooms, a service entry with a laundry and a three-car garage. You'll find a bonus room over the garage; you may decide to turn it into a media room or an exercise room. The master bedroom sports a fireplace, two walk-in closets, a double-bowl vanity, a shower, and a whirlpool tub. Three other bedrooms occupy the second floor—one has its own full bath. Of course, the balcony is just a step away.

plan
HPT9600363

STYLE: COLONIAL REVIVAL

FIRST FLOOR: 1,995 SQ. FT.

SECOND FLOOR: 1,062 SQ. FT.

TOTAL: 3,057 SQ. FT.

BONUS SPACE: 459 SQ. FT.

BEDROOMS: 4

BATHROOMS: 3½

WIDTH: 71' - 0"

DEPTH: 57' - 4"

FOUNDATION: BASEMENT

SEARCH ONLINE @ EPLANS.COM

Wood siding, muntin window dormers, and a double-decker porch exemplify Southern country style in this welcoming plan. Slide off your porch swing and enter through the foyer, flanked by the bayed living room and dining room. The family room flows effortlessly into the breakfast area and the kitchen, complete with an island. The master bedroom wows with a closet designed for a true clotheshorse. Three upstairs bedrooms enjoy access to the upper porch and space for a future recreation room.

SECOND FLOOR

FIRST FLOOR

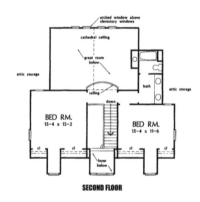

arched window above
clerestory windows

cathedral ceiling

great room
below

attic storage

attic storage

bath

railing

down

BED RM.
15-4 x 15-2

BED RM.
15-4 x 11-6

cl

cl

cl

foyer
below

SECOND FLOOR

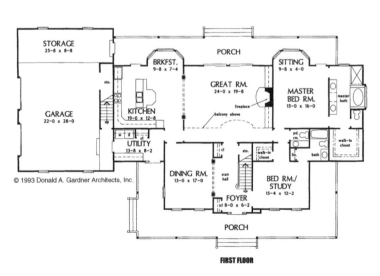

STORAGE
25-8 x 8-8

PORCH

BRKFST.
9-8 x 7-4

SITTING
9-8 x 4-0

GREAT RM.
24-0 x 19-8

MASTER
BED RM.
15-0 x 16-0

master
bath

GARAGE
22-0 x 28-0

KITCHEN
19-0 x 12-8

fireplace

balcony above

walk-in
closet

UTILITY
13-8 x 8-2

pd.
rm.

walk-in
closet

© 1993 Donald A. Gardner Architects, Inc.

DINING RM.
13-0 x 17-0

cl

sto.

lin.

bath

stair
hall

BED RM./
STUDY
15-4 x 12-2

FOYER
8-0 x 6-2

up

PORCH

FIRST FLOOR

plan
HPT9600364

STYLE: FARMHOUSE
FIRST FLOOR: 2,316 SQ. FT.
SECOND FLOOR: 721 SQ. FT.
TOTAL: 3,037 SQ. FT.
BONUS SPACE: 545 SQ. FT.
BEDROOMS: 4
BATHROOMS: 3½
WIDTH: 95' - 4"
DEPTH: 54' - 10"

SEARCH ONLINE @ EPLANS.COM

Three dormers top a very welcoming covered wraparound porch on this attractive country home. The entrance enjoys a Palladian clerestory window, lending an abundance of natural light to the foyer. The great room furthers this feeling of airiness with a balcony above and two sets of sliding glass doors leading to the back porch. For privacy, the master suite occupies the right side of the first floor. With a sitting bay and all the amenities of a modern master bath, this lavish retreat will be a welcome haven for the home-owner. Two family bedrooms reside upstairs, sharing a balcony overlook into the great room.

ORDER BLUEPRINTS 24 HOURS, 7 DAYS A WEEK, AT 1-800-521-6797

plan
HPT9600365

STYLE: COLONIAL REVIVAL

FIRST FLOOR: 2,142 SQ. FT.

SECOND FLOOR: 960 SQ. FT.

TOTAL: 3,102 SQ. FT.

BONUS SPACE: 327 SQ. FT.

BEDROOMS: 4

BATHROOMS: 3½

WIDTH: 75' - 8"

DEPTH: 53' - 0"

FOUNDATION: CRAWLSPACE

SEARCH ONLINE @ EPLANS.COM

Imagine driving up to this cottage beauty at the end of a long week. The long wraparound porch, hipped rooflines, and shuttered windows will transport you. Inside, the foyer is flanked by a living room on the left and a formal dining room on the right. Across the gallery hall, the hearth-warmed family room will surely become the hub of the home. To the right, the spacious kitchen boasts a worktop island counter, ample pantry space, and a breakfast area. A short hallway opens to the utility room and the two-car garage. The master suite takes up the entire left wing of the home, enjoying an elegant private bath and a walk-in closet that goes on and on. Upstairs, three more bedrooms reside, sharing two full baths. Expandable future space awaits on the right.

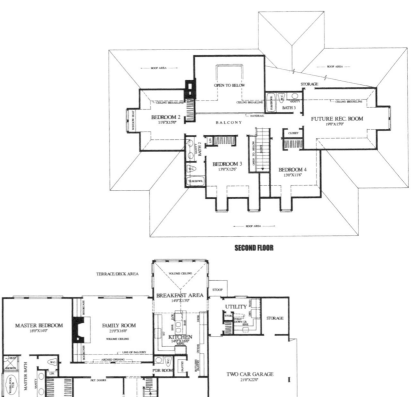

SECOND FLOOR

FIRST FLOOR

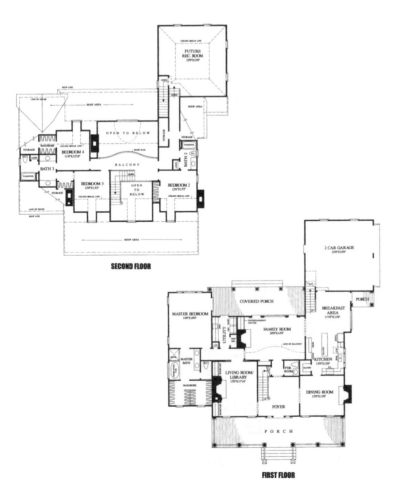

SECOND FLOOR

FIRST FLOOR

plan #
HPT9600366

STYLE: COLONIAL REVIVAL
FIRST FLOOR: 2,200 SQ. FT.
SECOND FLOOR: 1,001 SQ. FT.
TOTAL: 3,201 SQ. FT.
BONUS SPACE: 674 SQ. FT.
BEDROOMS: 4
BATHROOMS: 3½
WIDTH: 70' - 4"
DEPTH: 74' - 4"
FOUNDATION: CRAWLSPACE

SEARCH ONLINE @ EPLANS.COM

A wide, welcoming front porch and three dormer windows lend Southern flair to this charming farmhouse. Inside, three fireplaces—found in the living, dining, and family rooms—create a cozy atmosphere. The family room opens to the covered rear porch, and the breakfast area opens to a small side porch. Sleeping quarters include a luxurious first-floor master suite—with a private bath and two walk-in closets—as well as three family bedrooms upstairs.

ORDER BLUEPRINTS 24 HOURS, 7 DAYS A WEEK, AT 1-800-521-6797

plan
HPT9600367

STYLE: COLONIAL REVIVAL
FIRST FLOOR: 2,191 SQ. FT.
SECOND FLOOR: 1,220 SQ. FT.
TOTAL: 3,411 SQ. FT.
BONUS SPACE: 280 SQ. FT.
BEDROOMS: 4
BATHROOMS: 3½
WIDTH: 75' - 8"
DEPTH: 54' - 4"
FOUNDATION: CRAWLSPACE,
BASEMENT, SLAB

SEARCH ONLINE @ EPLANS.COM

This Colonial farmhouse will be the showpiece of
your neighborhood. Come in from the wide front
porch through French doors topped by a sunburst
window. Continue past the formal dining and
living rooms to a columned gallery and a large
family room with a focal fireplace. The kitchen
astounds with a unique layout, an island, and
abundant counter and cabinet space. The master
bath balances luxury with efficiency. Three
upstairs bedrooms enjoy amenities such as dormer
windows or walk-in closets. Bonus space is ready
for expansion as your needs change.

© 1998 Donald A. Gardner, Inc.

SECOND FLOOR

LIBRARY 9-10 x 9-8

BONUS RM. 13-0 x 23-0

attic storage

storage

linen

bath

living room below

down

railing

walk-in closet

BED RM. 12-0 x 13-0

foyer below

attic storage

walk-in closet

bath

BED RM. 12-0 x 13-0

FIRST FLOOR

PORCH

fireplace

FAMILY RM. 16-0 x 22-0 (cathedral ceiling)

shelves

BRKFST. 9-4 x 9-0

KIT. 16-0 x 15-4

pantry

PATIO

LIVING RM. 18-0 x 15-10 (cathedral ceiling)

shelves

up

fireplace

SITTING 9-0 x 9-0

shelves

PORCH

fireplace

MASTER BED RM. 18-0 x 14-0 (cathedral ceiling)

walk-in closet

cl

lin.

pd. rm.

lin.

cl

FOYER 10-8 x 8-0 (two story ceiling)

shelves

walk-in closet

master bath

UTIL. 8-0 x 8-4

DINING 12-0 x 14-0

STUDY 12-0 x 14-4

d w

GARAGE 22-0 x 23-0

PORCH

© 1998 Donald A Gardner, Inc.

storage

plan #
HPT9600368

STYLE: COUNTRY
FIRST FLOOR: 2,755 SQ. FT.
SECOND FLOOR: 735 SQ. FT.
TOTAL: 3,490 SQ. FT.
BONUS SPACE: 481 SQ. FT.
BEDROOMS: 3
BATHROOMS: 3½
WIDTH: 92' - 6"
DEPTH: 69' - 10"

SEARCH ONLINE @ EPLANS.COM

Dormers, gables with wood brackets, a double-door entry, and a stone-and-siding exterior lend charm and sophistication to this Craftsman estate. Cathedral ceilings and fireplaces are standard in the living room, family room, and master bedroom; the living room, family room, and study feature built-in bookshelves. The spacious kitchen with a cooktop island and walk-in pantry opens completely to the family room and breakfast area. The master suite excels with a private sitting room, access to its own porch, two over-sized walk-in closets, and a lavish bath. Overlooking both the foyer and the living room, the second-floor balcony connects two bedrooms, a library, and a bonus room.

plan
HPT9600369

STYLE: COLONIAL REVIVAL

SQUARE FOOTAGE: 3,270

BEDROOMS: 4

BATHROOMS: 3½

WIDTH: 101' - 0"

DEPTH: 48' - 1"

FOUNDATION: CRAWLSPACE, SLAB

SEARCH ONLINE @ EPLANS.COM

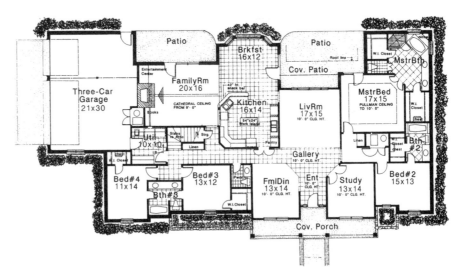

A distinctive exterior, complete with siding, stone and brick, presents a welcoming facade on this four-bedroom home. The large family room includes a cathedral ceiling, a fireplace, and built-ins. The island kitchen has plenty of work space and direct access to a sunny, bay-windowed breakfast room. A study and formal dining room flank the tiled entryway, which leads straight into a formal living room. Three family bedrooms are arranged across the front of the house. The master suite offers plenty of seclusion as well as two walk-in closets, a lavish bath, and direct access to the rear patio. A stairway leads to the attic.

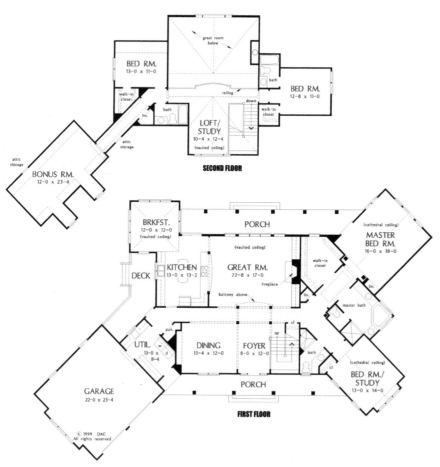

SECOND FLOOR

FIRST FLOOR

© 1999 DAC
All rights reserved

plan #
HPT9600370

STYLE: STICK VICTORIAN
FIRST FLOOR: 2,477 SQ. FT.
SECOND FLOOR: 742 SQ. FT.
TOTAL: 3,219 SQ. FT.
BONUS SPACE: 419 SQ. FT.
BEDROOMS: 4
BATHROOMS: 4
WIDTH: 100' - 0"
DEPTH: 66' - 2"

SEARCH ONLINE @ EPLANS.COM

A prominent center gable with an arched window accents the facade of this custom Craftsman home, which features an exterior of cedar shakes, siding, and stone. An open floor plan with generously proportioned rooms contributes to the spacious and relaxed atmosphere. The vaulted great room boasts a rear wall of windows, a fireplace bordered by built-in cabinets, and convenient access to the kitchen. A second-floor loft overlooks the great room for added drama. The master suite is completely secluded and enjoys a cathedral ceiling, back-porch access, a large walk-in closet, and a luxurious bath. The home includes three additional bedrooms and baths as well as a vaulted loft/study and a bonus room.

ORDER BLUEPRINTS 24 HOURS, 7 DAYS A WEEK, AT 1-800-521-6797

©1998 Donald A. Gardner, Inc.

plan
HPT9600371

STYLE: COUNTRY
MAIN LEVEL: 2,065 SQ. FT.
LOWER LEVEL: 1,216 SQ. FT.
TOTAL: 3,281 SQ. FT.
BEDROOMS: 4
BATHROOMS: 3½
WIDTH: 82' - 2"
DEPTH: 43' - 6"

SEARCH ONLINE @ EPLANS.COM

Stone, siding, and multiple gables combine beautifully on the exterior of this hillside home. Taking advantage of rear views, the home's most oft-used rooms are oriented at the back with plenty of windows. Augmented by a cathedral ceiling, the great room features a fireplace, built-in shelves, and access to the rear deck. Twin walk-in closets and a private bath infuse the master suite with luxury. The nearby powder room offers an optional full-bath arrangement, allowing the study to double as a bedroom. Downstairs, a large media/recreation room with a wet bar and fireplace separates two more bedrooms, each with a full bath and walk-in closet.

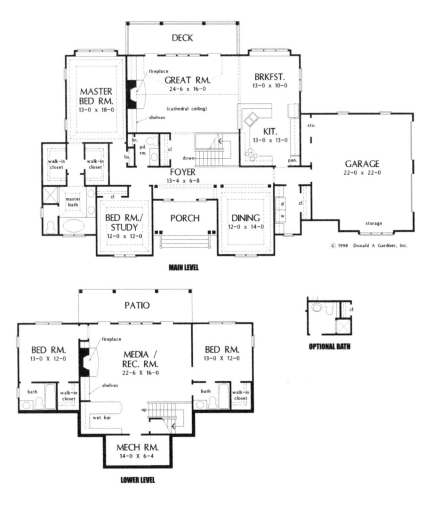

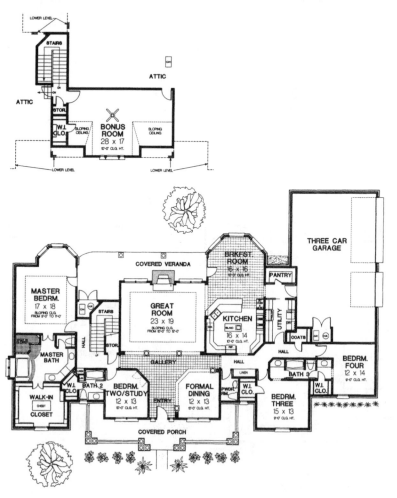

plan #

HPT9600372

STYLE: VICTORIAN FARMHOUSE
SQUARE FOOTAGE: 3,439
BONUS SPACE: 514 SQ. FT.
BEDROOMS: 4
BATHROOMS: 3½
WIDTH: 100' - 0"
DEPTH: 67' - 11"
FOUNDATION: CRAWLSPACE,
SLAB, BASEMENT

SEARCH ONLINE @ EPLANS.COM

This gigantic country farmhouse is accented by exterior features that really stand out—a steep roof gable, shuttered muntin windows, stone siding, and the double-columned, covered front porch. Inside, the entry is flanked by the study/Bedroom 2 and the dining room. Across the tiled gallery, the great room provides an impressive fireplace and overlooks the rear veranda. The island kitchen opens to a bayed breakfast room. The right side of the home includes a utility room and a three-car garage, and two family bedrooms that share a bath. The master wing of the home enjoys a bayed sitting area, a sumptuous bath, and an enormous walk-in closet. The second-floor bonus room is cooled by a ceiling fan and is perfect for a guest suite.

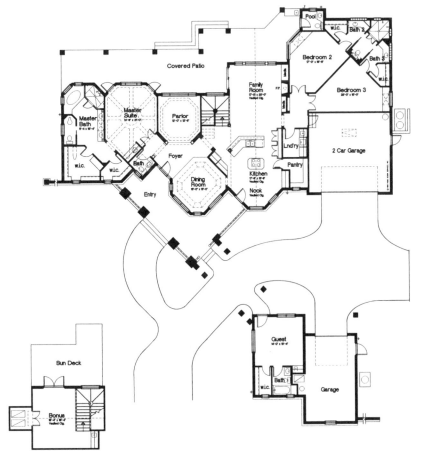

plan
HPT9600373

STYLE: NEO-ECLECTIC
SQUARE FOOTAGE: 3,436
BONUS SPACE: 290 SQ. FT.
BEDROOMS: 3
BATHROOMS: 3½
WIDTH: 94' - 0"
DEPTH: 114' - 0"
FOUNDATION: SLAB

SEARCH ONLINE @ EPLANS.COM

A striking front-facing pediment, bold columns, and varying rooflines set this design apart from the rest. An angled entry leads to the foyer, flanked on one side by the dining room with a tray ceiling and on the other by a lavish master suite. This suite is enhanced with a private bath, two large walk-in closets, a garden tub, a compartmented toilet and bidet, and access to the covered patio. The parlor also enjoys rear-yard views. The vaulted ceilings provide a sense of spaciousness from the breakfast nook and kitchen to the family room. A laundry room and roomy pantry are accessible from the kitchen area. Two family bedrooms reside on the right side of the plan; each has its own full bath and both are built at interesting angles. An upstairs, vaulted bonus room includes French doors opening to a second-floor sundeck.

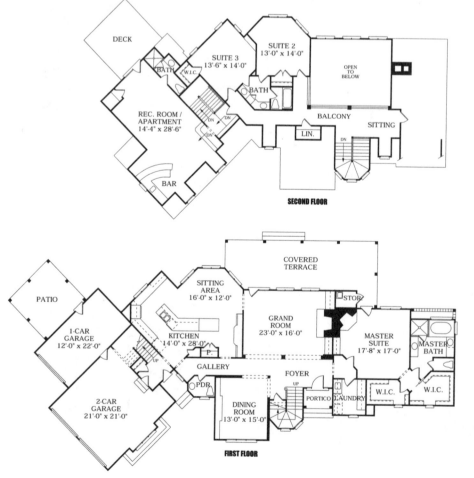

DECK

SUITE 3
13'-6" x 14'-0"

SUITE 2
13'-0" x 14'-0"

BATH

W.I.C.

OPEN TO BELOW

BATH

REC. ROOM / APARTMENT
14'-4" x 28'-6"

DN
DN

BALCONY

LIN.

SITTING

DN

BAR

SECOND FLOOR

COVERED TERRACE

SITTING AREA
16'-0" x 12'-0"

STOR.

PATIO

KITCHEN
14'-0" x 28'-0"

GRAND ROOM
23'-0" x 16'-0"

1-CAR GARAGE
12'-0" x 22'-0"

P.

MASTER SUITE
17'-8" x 17'-0"

MASTER BATH

UP

GALLERY

FOYER

PDR

UP

2-CAR GARAGE
21'-0" x 21'-0"

DINING ROOM
13'-0" x 15'-0"

PORTICO

LAUNDRY

W.I.C.

W.I.C.

FIRST FLOOR

plan #

HPT9600374

STYLE: FRENCH ECLECTIC
FIRST FLOOR: 2,391 SQ. FT.
SECOND FLOOR: 1,071 SQ. FT.
TOTAL: 3,462 SQ. FT.
BEDROOMS: 3
BATHROOMS: 3½
WIDTH: 113' - 7"
DEPTH: 57' - 5"
FOUNDATION: CRAWLSPACE

SEARCH ONLINE @ EPLANS.COM

If you've ever dreamed of living in a castle, this could be the home for you. The interior is also fit for royalty, from the formal dining room to the multipurpose grand room to the comfortable sitting area off the kitchen. The master suite has its own fireplace, two walk-in closets, and a compartmented bath with dual vanities and a garden tub. Two stairways lead to the second floor. One, housed in the turret, leads to a sitting area and a balcony overlooking the grand room. The balcony leads to two more bedrooms and a recreation room (or apartment) with a deck.

ptan#
HPT9600375

STYLE: FRENCH COUNTRY
FIRST FLOOR: 2,390 SQ. FT.
SECOND FLOOR: 765 SQ. FT.
TOTAL: 3,155 SQ. FT.
BONUS SPACE: 433 SQ. FT.
BEDROOMS: 4
BATHROOMS: 3½
WIDTH: 87' - 11"
DEPTH: 75' - 2"
FOUNDATION: CRAWLSPACE

SEARCH ONLINE @ EPLANS.COM

The grand exterior of this Normandy country design features a steeply pitched gable roofline. Arched dormers repeat the window accents. Inside, the promise of space is fulfilled with a large gathering room that fills the center of the house and opens to a long trellised veranda. The den or guest suite with a fireplace, the adjacent powder room, and the master suite with a vaulted ceiling and access to the veranda reside in the right wing. Two additional bedrooms with two baths and a loft overlooking the gathering room are upstairs. A large bonus room is found over the garage and can be developed later as office or hobby space.

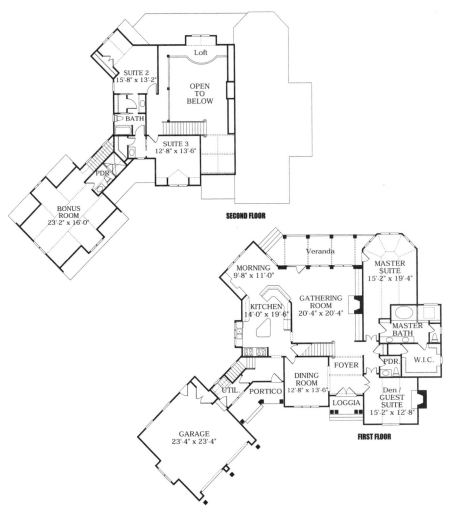

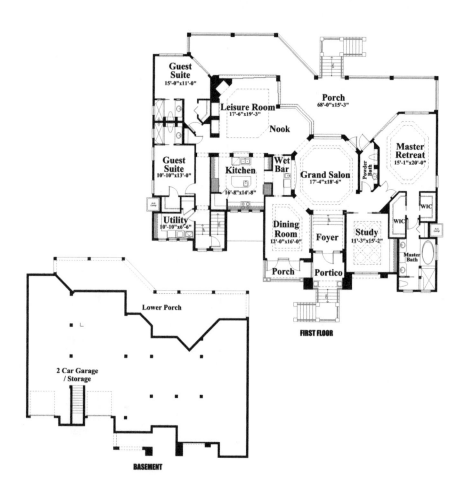

FIRST FLOOR

Guest Suite 15'-0"x11'-0"

Leisure Room 17'-6"x19'-3"

Nook

Porch 68'-0"x15'-3"

Master Retreat 15'-1"x20'-0"

Guest Suite 10'-10"x13'-0"

Kitchen

Wet Bar

Grand Salon 17'-4"x18'-6"

Powder Bath

Utility 10'-10"x6'-6"

Dining Room 12'-0"x16'-0"

Foyer

Study 11'-3"x15'-2"

WIC

WIC

Master Bath

Porch

Portico

Lower Porch

2 Car Garage / Storage

BASEMENT

plan#
HPT9600376

STYLE: TIDEWATER

SQUARE FOOTAGE: 3,074

BEDROOMS: 3

BATHROOMS: 3½

WIDTH: 77' - 0"

DEPTH: 66' - 8"

FOUNDATION: BASEMENT

SEARCH ONLINE @ EPLANS.COM

Symmetry and the perfect blend of past and future comprise this home. A steeply pitched roof caps a collection of Prairie-style windows and elegant columns. The portico leads to a midlevel foyer, which rises to the grand salon. A wide-open leisure room hosts a corner fireplace that's ultra cozy. The master wing sprawls from the front portico to the rear covered porch, rich with luxury amenities and plenty of secluded space.

ORDER BLUEPRINTS 24 HOURS, 7 DAYS A WEEK, AT 1-800-521-6797

plan
HPT9600377

STYLE: SPANISH TERRITORIAL

SQUARE FOOTAGE: 3,505

BEDROOMS: 3

BATHROOMS: 2½

WIDTH: 110' - 7"

DEPTH: 66' - 11"

FOUNDATION: SLAB

SEARCH ONLINE @ EPLANS.COM

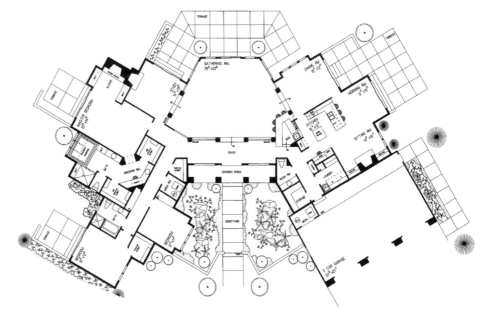

Loaded with custom features, this plan is designed to delight the imagination. The foyer enters directly into the commanding sunken gathering room. Framed by an elegant railing, this centerpiece for entertaining is open to both the study and the formal dining room and offers sliding glass doors to the terrace. A full bar further extends the entertaining possibilities of this room. The country-style kitchen contains an efficient work area, as well as a morning room and sitting area—ideal for family gatherings around the cozy fireplace. The grand master suite has a private terrace, fireplace alcove with built-in seats and a huge spa-style bath. Two nicely sized bedrooms and a hall bath round out the plan.

plan
HPT9600378

STYLE: PUEBLO
SQUARE FOOTAGE: 3,838
BEDROOMS: 4
BATHROOMS: 3½
WIDTH: 127' - 6"
DEPTH: 60' - 10"
FOUNDATION: SLAB

SEARCH ONLINE @ EPLANS.COM

This diamond in the desert gives new meaning to old style. A courtyard leads to a covered porch with nooks for sitting and open-air dining. The gracious living room is highlighted by a corner fireplace; the formal dining room comes with an adjacent butler's pantry and access to the porch dining area. Two sleeping zones are luxurious with whirlpool tubs and separate showers. The master suite also boasts an exercise room and a nearby private office. A guest suite includes a private entrance and another corner fireplace.

ORDER BLUEPRINTS 24 HOURS, 7 DAYS A WEEK, AT 1-800-521-6797

plan
HPT9600379

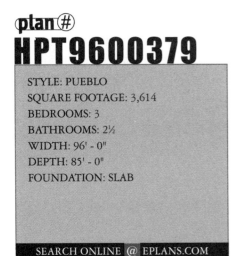

STYLE: PUEBLO

SQUARE FOOTAGE: 3,614

BEDROOMS: 3

BATHROOMS: 2½

WIDTH: 96' - 0"

DEPTH: 85' - 0"

FOUNDATION: SLAB

SEARCH ONLINE @ EPLANS.COM

Come home to a bold Santa Fe design that is made for entertaining! The plan begins with a gated courtyard, surrounded by privacy walls. A fountain and columned loggia join an outdoor fireplace for effortless regaling. Although four rooms access the loggia, the main entrance is to the right, presenting an impressive foyer. A living room greets guests; family bedrooms are located nearby, with patio access. The vast family room is topped with vigas and warmed by a beehive hearth. Just ahead, a gourmet kitchen serves at least five hungry family members at the island bar. Casual meals can also be enjoyed in the light-filled nook; the dining room is ready to host with a wet bar and decorative columns. The master suite is a dream come true, complete with a step-up tub, spiral shower, and massive walk-in closet.

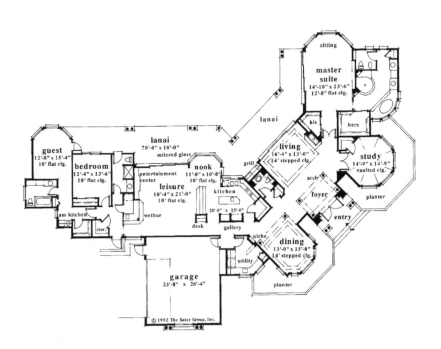

plan #

HPT9600380

STYLE: MEDITERRANEAN
SQUARE FOOTAGE: 3,866
BEDROOMS: 3
BATHROOMS: 3½
WIDTH: 120' - 0"
DEPTH: 89' - 0"
FOUNDATION: CRAWLSPACE

SEARCH ONLINE @ EPLANS.COM

This modern home adds a contemporary twist to the typical ranch-style plan. The turret study and bayed dining room add a sensuous look from the streetscape. The main living areas open up to the lanai and offer broad views to the rear through large expanses of glass and doors. The family kitchen, nook, and leisure room focus on the lanai, the entertainment center, and an ale bar. The guest suites have separate baths and also access the lanai. The master bath features a curved-glass shower, whirlpool tub, and private toilet and bidet room. Dual walk-in closets and an abundance of light further the appeal of this suite.

© 91 HOME DESIGN SERVICES, INC.

plan #
HPT9600381

STYLE: FLORIDIAN
SQUARE FOOTAGE: 3,743
BEDROOMS: 4
BATHROOMS: 3½
WIDTH: 86' - 8"
DEPTH: 95' - 0"
FOUNDATION: SLAB

SEARCH ONLINE @ EPLANS.COM

A central foyer gives way to an expansive design. Straight ahead, the living room features French doors set in a bay area. To the left, columns and a coffered ceiling offset the exquisite formal dining room. A fireplace warms the large family room, which adjoins the breakfast nook. Traffic flows easily through the ample kitchen with cooktop island and pass-through to the patio. The master bedroom features a tray ceiling, walk-in closet, and sumptuous bath with shower and step-up tub overlooking a private garden. Two bedrooms are joined by an optional media room and optional study, which could bring the count up to five bedrooms if necessary.

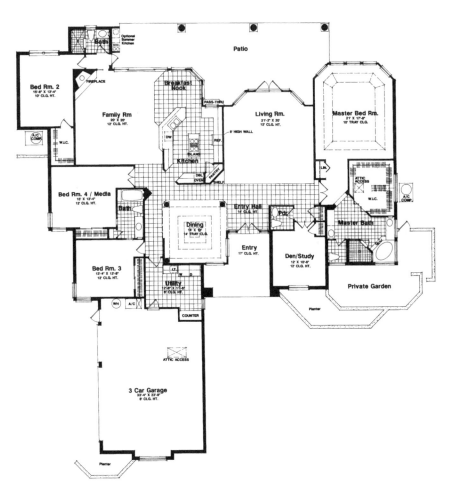

© The Sater Design Collection, Inc.

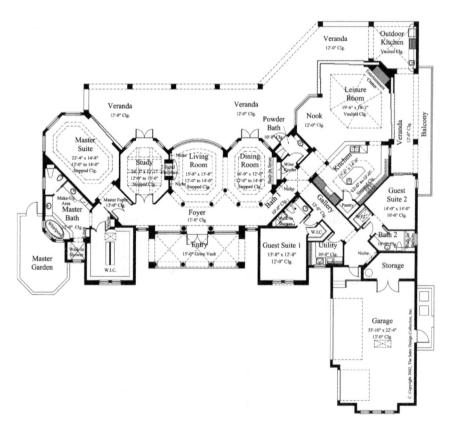

plan#

HPT9600382

STYLE: MEDITERRANEAN
SQUARE FOOTAGE: 3,640
BEDROOMS: 3
BATHROOMS: 3½
WIDTH: 106' - 4"
DEPTH: 102' - 4"
FOUNDATION: SLAB

SEARCH ONLINE @ EPLANS.COM

Come home to luxurious living—all on one level—with this striking Mediterranean plan. Unique ceiling treatments highlight the living areas—the living and dining rooms, as well as the study, feature stepped ceilings, and the leisure room soars with a vaulted ceiling. The gourmet kitchen includes a spacious center island; another kitchen, this one outdoors, can be accessed from the leisure room. The master suite boasts plenty of amenities: a large, skylit walk-in closet, a bath with a whirlpool tub and walk-in shower, and private access to a charming garden area. Two suites, both with private baths, sit to the right of the plan.

ORDER BLUEPRINTS 24 HOURS, 7 DAYS A WEEK, AT 1-800-521-6797

plan
HPT9600383

STYLE: MEDITERRANEAN

SQUARE FOOTAGE: 3,566

BEDROOMS: 3

BATHROOMS: 2½

WIDTH: 88' - 0"

DEPTH: 70' - 8"

FOUNDATION: BASEMENT

SEARCH ONLINE @ EPLANS.COM

Symmetrically grand, this home features large windows, which flood the interior with natural light. The massive sunken great room with a vaulted ceiling includes an exciting balcony overlook of the towering atrium window wall. The open breakfast nook and hearth room adjoin the kitchen. Four fireplaces throughout the house create an overall sense of warmth. A colonnade, a private entrance to the rear deck, and a sunken tub with a fireplace complement the master suite. Two family bedrooms share a dual-vanity bath.

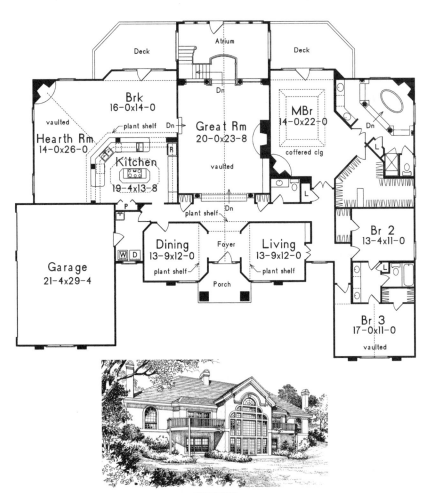

REAR EXTERIOR

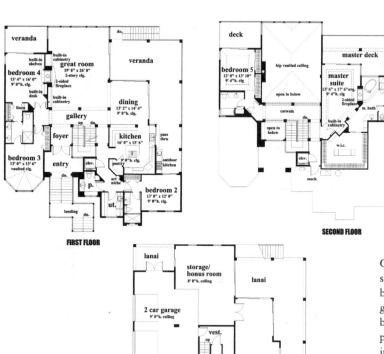

FIRST FLOOR

SECOND FLOOR

BASEMENT

plan #
HPT9600384

STYLE: ITALIANATE

FIRST FLOOR: 2,491 SQ. FT.

SECOND FLOOR: 1,290 SQ. FT.

TOTAL: 3,781 SQ. FT.

BEDROOMS: 5

BATHROOMS: 4½

WIDTH: 62' - 0"

DEPTH: 67' - 0"

FOUNDATION: BASEMENT

SEARCH ONLINE @ EPLANS.COM

Chic and glamorous, this Mediterranean facade pairs ancient shapes, such as square columns, with a refined disposition set off by radius windows. A magnificent entry leads to an interior gallery and the great room. This extraordinary space is warmed by a two-sided fireplace and defined by extended views of the rear property. Sliding glass doors to a wraparound veranda create great indoor/outdoor flow. The gourmet kitchen easily serves any occasion and provides a pass-through to the outdoor kitchen. A powder room accommodates visitors, and an elevator leads to the sleeping quarters upstairs. Double doors open to the master suite, which features a walk-in closet, two-sided fireplace, and angled whirlpool bath. The master bedroom boasts a tray ceiling and doors to a spacious deck. The upper-level catwalk leads to a bedroom suite that can easily accommodate a guest or live-in relative. The basement level features future space and a two-car garage.

ORDER BLUEPRINTS 24 HOURS, 7 DAYS A WEEK, AT 1-800-521-6797

plan#
HPT9600385

STYLE: ITALIANATE
FIRST FLOOR: 2,391 SQ. FT.
SECOND FLOOR: 1,539 SQ. FT.
TOTAL: 3,930 SQ. FT.
BEDROOMS: 3
BATHROOMS: 3½
WIDTH: 71' - 0"
DEPTH: 69' - 0"
FOUNDATION: BASEMENT

SEARCH ONLINE @ EPLANS.COM

Impressive pillars, keystone lintel arches, a covered carport, an abundance of windows, and an alluring fountain are just a few of the decorative touches of this elegant design. The two-story foyer leads to a two-story great room, which enjoys built-in cabinetry, a two-sided fireplace, and spectacular views to the rear property. To the left of the great room is the dining area, with a wet bar, island kitchen, and nearby bayed breakfast nook. Bedroom 2 boasts a semicircular wall of windows, a full bath, and a walk-in closet. The second-floor master suite is filled with amenities, including a two-sided fireplace.

SECOND FLOOR

FIRST FLOOR

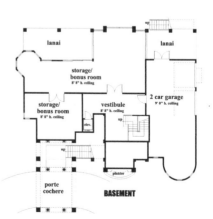

BASEMENT

© The Sater Design Collection, Inc.

SECOND FLOOR

FIRST FLOOR

plan #
HPT9600386

STYLE: NEO-ECLECTIC
FIRST FLOOR: 2,834 SQ. FT.
SECOND FLOOR: 1,143 SQ. FT.
TOTAL: 3,977 SQ. FT.
BEDROOMS: 4
BATHROOMS: 3½
WIDTH: 85' - 0"
DEPTH: 76' - 8"
FOUNDATION: SLAB

SEARCH ONLINE @ EPLANS.COM

Mediterranean accents enhance the facade of this contemporary estate home. Two fanciful turret bays add a sense of grandeur to the exterior. Double doors open inside to a grand two-story foyer. A two-sided fireplace warms the study and living room, with a two-story coffered ceiling. To the right, the master suite includes a private bath, two walk-in closets, and double-door access to the sweeping rear veranda. Casual areas of the home include the gourmet island kitchen, breakfast nook, and leisure room warmed by a fireplace. A spiral staircase leads upstairs, where a second-floor balcony separates two family bedrooms from the luxurious guest suite.

© The Sater Group, Inc.

plan #
HPT9600387

STYLE: NEO-ECLECTIC
FIRST FLOOR: 2,841 SQ. FT.
SECOND FLOOR: 1,052 SQ. FT.
TOTAL: 3,893 SQ. FT.
BEDROOMS: 4
BATHROOMS: 3½
WIDTH: 85' - 0"
DEPTH: 76' - 8"
FOUNDATION: CRAWLSPACE

SEARCH ONLINE @ EPLANS.COM

Ensure an elegant lifestyle with this luxurious plan. A turret, two-story bay windows, and plenty of arched glass impart a graceful style to the exterior, and rich amenities inside furnish contentment. A grand foyer decked with columns introduces the living room with curved-glass windows viewing the rear gardens. The study and living room share a through-fireplace. The master suite enjoys a tray ceiling, two walk-in closets, a separate shower, and a garden tub set in a bay window. Informal entertainment will be a breeze with a rich leisure room adjoining the kitchen and breakfast nook and opening to a rear veranda. Upstairs, two family bedrooms and a guest suite with a private deck complete the plan.

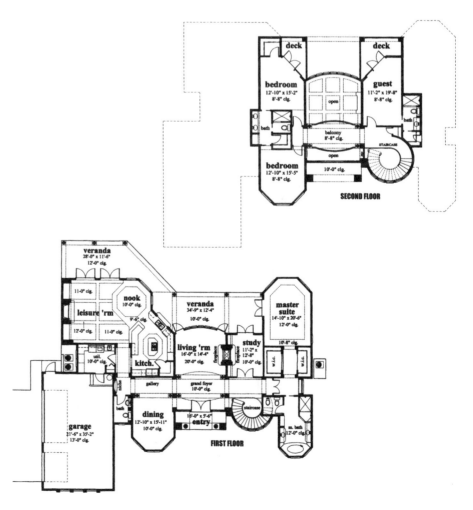

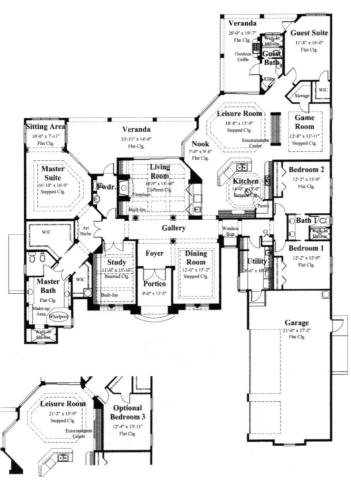

plan#

HPT9600388

STYLE: MEDITERRANEAN
SQUARE FOOTAGE: 3,790
BEDROOMS: 4
BATHROOMS: 3½
WIDTH: 80' - 0"
DEPTH: 107' - 8"
FOUNDATION: SLAB

SEARCH ONLINE @ EPLANS.COM

A majestic desert oasis, this well-planned home puts family comfort and privacy first. Enter under a keystone portico to the foyer; a dramatic dining room opens to the right. Just ahead, the living room is an inviting place to relax by the fireplace under the coffered ceiling. A unique kitchen supports gourmet meals or a quick snack enjoyed in the sunny nook. An entertainment center separates the leisure room and game room—or finish the space to include a fourth bedroom. The rear guest suite offers a private bath and access to the veranda, featuring an outdoor grill. For the ultimate in luxury, the master suite is peerless; a light-filled sitting area, angled bedroom, and indulgent bath make an inviting retreat for any homeowner.

plan
HPT9600389

STYLE: TRANSITIONAL
MAIN LEVEL: 2,157 SQ. FT.
LOWER LEVEL: 1,754 SQ. FT.
TOTAL: 3,911 SQ. FT.
BEDROOMS: 4
BATHROOMS: 3½
WIDTH: 80' - 0"
DEPTH: 61' - 0"
FOUNDATION: BASEMENT

SEARCH ONLINE @ EPLANS.COM

Homeowners will look forward to coming home to this plan. A spacious gallery hall welcomes you inside. The lower level holds two family bedrooms, a game room, and a media room; the main level includes the kitchen, dining room, great room, and master suite. Thoughtful built-ins like a wet bar make this home a prize. Other special amenities such as the corner fireplace in the great room and island workstation in the kitchen are just some of the modern additions found throughout the home. A spacious three-car garage completes the plan.

MAIN LEVEL

LOWER LEVEL

plan
HPT9600390

STYLE: TRANSITIONAL
MAIN LEVEL: 1,854 SQ. FT.
LOWER LEVEL: 1,703 SQ. FT.
TOTAL: 3,557 SQ. FT.
BEDROOMS: 3
BATHROOMS: 2½
WIDTH: 87' - 6"
DEPTH: 56' - 0"

SEARCH ONLINE @ EPLANS.COM

There's room to spare in this grand hillside design. And the plan is made to seem even larger than it is, due to a high roofline that allows for extended ceilings in the main-level rooms. Beyond the columned gallery are a dining room with a tray ceiling and a great room with a tray ceiling and corner fireplace. The kitchen/nook area has deck access and an island work counter with space for casual dining. The master suite is on the main level and is reached through a skylit hall. The master bath is also skylit and offers a spa tub, walk-in closet, and double sinks. Family bedrooms are on the lower level along with a media room and an additional space that may be used as a family room or den.

ORDER BLUEPRINTS 24 HOURS, 7 DAYS A WEEK, AT 1-800-521-6797

plan#
HPT9600391

STYLE: TRANSITIONAL
FIRST FLOOR: 1,912 SQ. FT.
SECOND FLOOR: 1,630 SQ. FT.
TOTAL: 3,542 SQ. FT.
BONUS SPACE: 300 SQ. FT.
BEDROOMS: 4
BATHROOMS: 3½
WIDTH: 71' - 0"
DEPTH: 58' - 6"
FOUNDATION: CRAWLSPACE

SEARCH ONLINE @ EPLANS.COM

A sunlit two-story foyer leads to all areas of this exceptional contemporary home. Enter the formal combined living and dining areas highlighted by glass walls and interior columns. The adjacent kitchen blends well with an octagonal nook and a family room with a corner fireplace. A den, a powder room, and a utility room complete the first floor. Upstairs, the master suite features a curved-glass wall, a uniquely styled bath, and a huge walk-in closet. Three additional bedrooms, two full baths, and a bonus room complete the second floor.

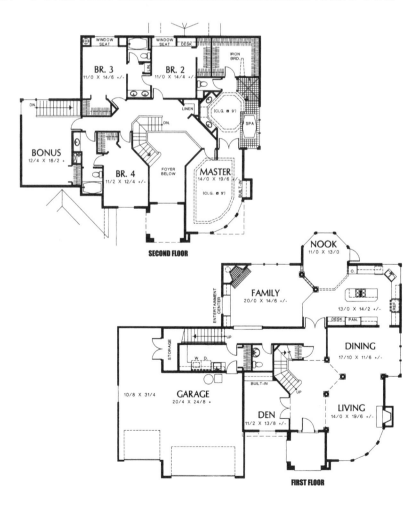

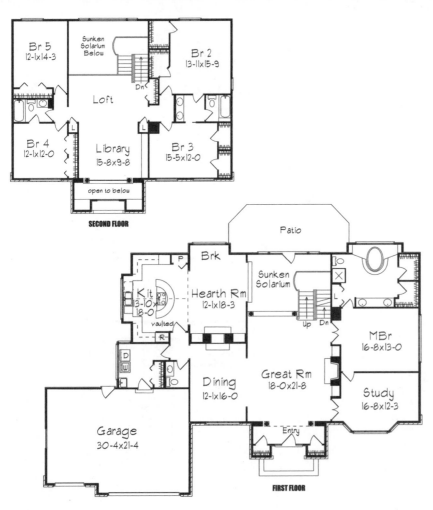

SECOND FLOOR

Br 5
12-1x14-3

Sunken Solarium Below

Br 2
13-11x15-9

Loft

Br 4
12-1x12-0

Library
15-8x9-8

Br 3
15-5x12-0

open to below

FIRST FLOOR

Brk

Kit
13-10x18-0

Hearth Rm
12-1x18-3

Sunken Solarium

Patio

MBr
16-8x13-0

vaulted

Dining
12-1x16-0

Great Rm
18-0x21-8

Study
16-8x12-3

Garage
30-4x21-4

Entry

plan #
HPT9600392

STYLE: TRANSITIONAL
FIRST FLOOR: 2,306 SQ. FT.
SECOND FLOOR: 1,544 SQ. FT.
TOTAL: 3,850 SQ. FT.
BEDROOMS: 5
BATHROOMS: 3½
WIDTH: 80' - 8"
DEPTH: 51' - 8"
FOUNDATION: BASEMENT

SEARCH ONLINE @ EPLANS.COM

The detailed keystone arch highlights the grand entryway of this home. The vast windows flood the home with natural light throughout. The entry leads into a splendid great room with a sunken solarium. The solarium features U-shaped stairs and a balcony with an arched window. The secluded master suite includes a luxurious bath and a large study with a bay window. A loft, the library, and four family bedrooms occupy the second floor.

ORDER BLUEPRINTS 24 HOURS, 7 DAYS A WEEK, AT 1-800-521-6797

plan
HPT9600393

STYLE: TRANSITIONAL
MAIN LEVEL: 2,196 SQ. FT.
LOWER LEVEL: 1,542 SQ. FT.
TOTAL: 3,738 SQ. FT.
BEDROOMS: 4
BATHROOMS: 2½
WIDTH: 71' - 0"
DEPTH: 56' - 0"
FOUNDATION: CRAWLSPACE,
BASEMENT

SEARCH ONLINE @ EPLANS.COM

This refined hillside home is designed for lots that fall off toward the rear and works especially well with a view out the back. The kitchen and eating nook wrap around the vaulted family room where arched transom windows flank the fireplace. Formal living is graciously centered in the living room that's directly off the foyer and the adjoining dining room. A grand master suite is located on the main level for convenience and privacy. Downstairs, three family bedrooms share a compartmented hall bath.

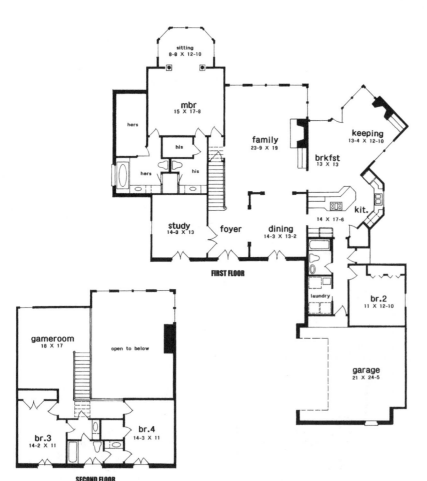

plan #
HPT9600394

STYLE: FRENCH
FIRST FLOOR: 2,780 SQ. FT.
SECOND FLOOR: 878 SQ. FT.
TOTAL: 3,658 SQ. FT.
BEDROOMS: 4
BATHROOMS: 4
WIDTH: 68' - 3"
DEPTH: 89' - 1"
FOUNDATION: SLAB

SEARCH ONLINE @ EPLANS.COM

The symmetrical front of this home conceals an imaginatively asymmetrical floor plan beyond. A keeping room, a sitting area in the master bedroom, and a second bedroom all jut out from this home, forming interesting angles and providing extra window space. Two fireplaces, a game room, a study, and His and Hers bathrooms in the master suite are interesting elements in this home. The bayed kitchen, with a walk-in pantry and a center island with room for seating, is sure to lure guests and family alike. The open floor plan and two-story ceilings in the family room add a contemporary touch.

plan #

HPT9600395

STYLE: FRENCH REVIVAL

FIRST FLOOR: 2,346 SQ. FT.

SECOND FLOOR: 1,260 SQ. FT.

TOTAL: 3,606 SQ. FT.

BEDROOMS: 4

BATHROOMS: 3½

WIDTH: 68' - 11"

DEPTH: 58' - 9"

FOUNDATION: WALKOUT BASEMENT

SEARCH ONLINE @ EPLANS.COM

The European character of this home is enhanced through the use of stucco and stone on the exterior, giving this French Country estate home its charm and beauty. The foyer leads to the dining room and study/living room. The two-story family room is positioned for convenient access to the back staircase, kitchen, wet bar, and deck area. The master bedroom is privately located on the right side of the home with an optional entry to the study and a large garden bath. Upstairs are three additional large bedrooms; two have a shared bath and private vanities and one has a full private bath. All bedrooms conveniently access the back staircase and have open-rail views to the family room below.

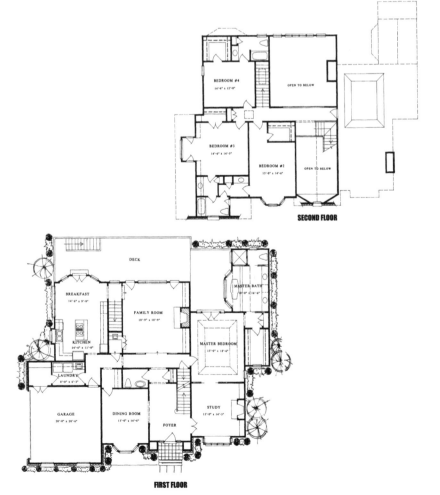

SECOND FLOOR

FIRST FLOOR

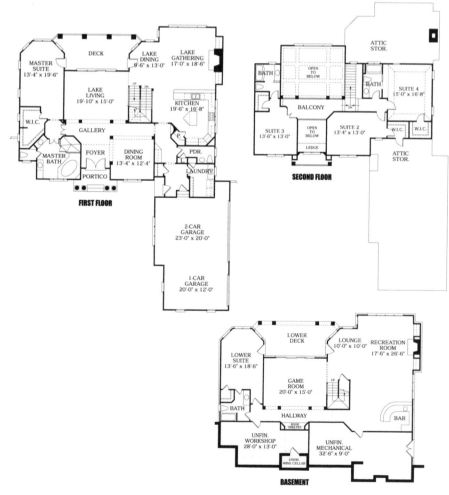

plan #

HPT9600396

STYLE: ITALIANATE

FIRST FLOOR: 2,538 SQ. FT.

SECOND FLOOR: 1,171 SQ. FT.

TOTAL: 3,709 SQ. FT.

BEDROOMS: 4

BATHROOMS: 3½

WIDTH: 67' - 7"

DEPTH: 85' - 1"

FOUNDATION: BASEMENT

SEARCH ONLINE @ EPLANS.COM

This impressive Mediterranean design is dazzled in Italianate style. A front portico offers a warm welcome into the main level. The master suite is located to the left and includes rear-deck access, a double walk-in closet, and pampering master bath. The island kitchen serves the formal and casual dining areas with ease. The casual gathering area is warmed by a fireplace. Three additional family suites reside upstairs, along with two baths and a balcony overlooking the two-story living room. The basement level adds a whole new layer of luxury, offering an additional suite, game room, recreation room, lounge area, wet bar, and unfinished workshop and mechanical space for future use.

ORDER BLUEPRINTS 24 HOURS, 7 DAYS A WEEK, AT 1-800-521-6797

plan #

HPT9600397

STYLE: TRADITIONAL

FIRST FLOOR: 2,603 SQ. FT.

SECOND FLOOR: 1,020 SQ. FT.

TOTAL: 3,623 SQ. FT.

BEDROOMS: 4

BATHROOMS: 4½

WIDTH: 76' - 8"

DEPTH: 68' - 0"

SEARCH ONLINE @ EPLANS.COM

Perhaps the most notable characteristic of this traditional house is its masterful use of space. The glorious great room, open dining room, and handsome den serve as the heart of the home. A cozy hearth room with a fireplace rounds out the kitchen and breakfast area. The master bedroom opens up to a private sitting room with a fireplace. Three family bedrooms occupy the second floor, each one with a private bath. Other special features include a four-car garage, a corner whirlpool tub in the master bath, a walk-in pantry and snack bar in the kitchen, and transom windows in the dining room.

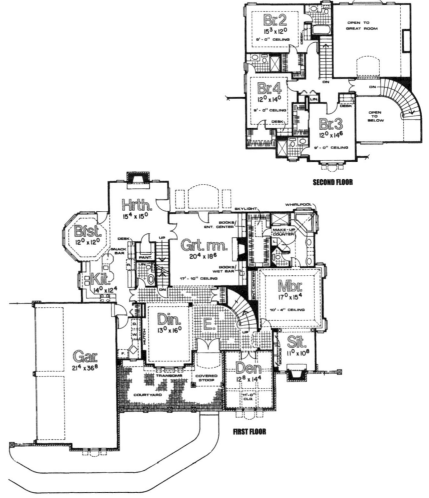

© Stephen Fuller, Inc.

SECOND FLOOR

FIRST FLOOR

plan #

HPT9600398

STYLE: NEO-ECLECTIC

FIRST FLOOR: 3,108 SQ. FT.

SECOND FLOOR: 512 SQ. FT.

TOTAL: 3,620 SQ. FT.

BEDROOMS: 3

BATHROOMS: 2½

WIDTH: 65' - 0"

DEPTH: 81' - 0"

FOUNDATION: WALKOUT

BASEMENT

SEARCH ONLINE @ EPLANS.COM

A sweet, traditional neighborhood home with eclectic touches, this spacious plan is sure to please. The formal spaces, including the bayed living room, are located near the entry, defined by arches. The gourmet kitchen serves the dining room through a butler's pantry, and opens to a bright breakfast nook. The vaulted great room features a fireplace for those chilly nights, and a sunroom for warm, lazy days. Twin bedrooms toward the front of the plan share a full bath; the master suite is tucked to the rear with a tray ceiling and a sumptuous bath. Bonus space is limited only by your imagination.

ORDER BLUEPRINTS 24 HOURS, 7 DAYS A WEEK, AT 1-800-521-6797

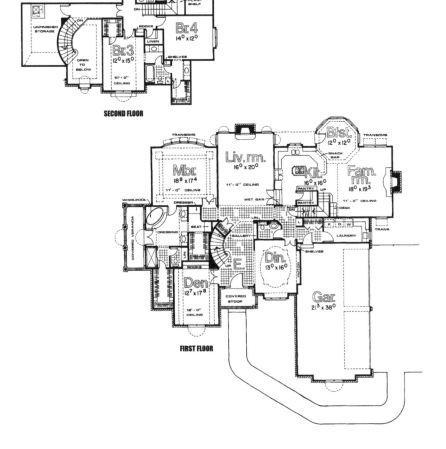

SECOND FLOOR

FIRST FLOOR

plan #
HPT9600399

STYLE: TRANSITIONAL

FIRST FLOOR: 2,789 SQ. FT.

SECOND FLOOR: 1,038 SQ. FT.

TOTAL: 3,827 SQ. FT.

BEDROOMS: 4

BATHROOMS: 3½

WIDTH: 78' - 0"

DEPTH: 73' - 8"

SEARCH ONLINE @ EPLANS.COM

The sophisticated lines and brick details of this house are stunning enhancements. The entry surveys a dramatic curved staircase. French doors open to the den, where a tiered ceiling and a bookcase wall provide a lofty ambiance. Large gatherings are easily accommodated in the dining room. The living room enjoys an 11-foot ceiling and a fireplace flanked by transom windows. For more casual living, the family room includes a raised-hearth fireplace and a built-in desk. The gourmet kitchen provides two pantries, an island cooktop, a wrapping counter, a snack bar, and private stairs to the second level. Four bedrooms include a pampering master suite on the first floor and three family bedrooms upstairs.

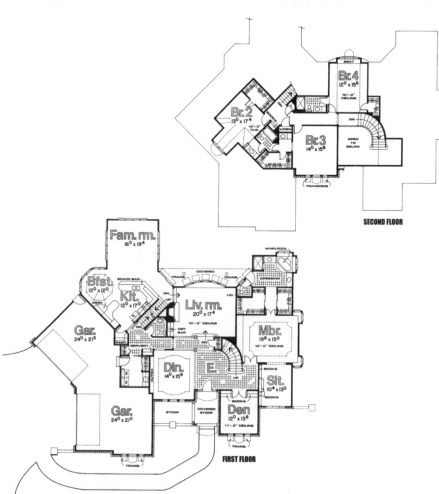

SECOND FLOOR

FIRST FLOOR

plan
HPT9600400

STYLE: TRADITIONAL
FIRST FLOOR: 2,813 SQ. FT.
SECOND FLOOR: 1,091 SQ. FT.
TOTAL: 3,904 SQ. FT.
BEDROOMS: 4
BATHROOMS: 3½
WIDTH: 85' - 5"
DEPTH: 74' - 8"

SEARCH ONLINE @ EPLANS.COM

Keystone lintels and an arched transom over the entry spell classic design for this four-bedroom home. The tiled foyer offers entry to any room you choose, whether it's the secluded den with its built-in bookshelves, the formal dining room, the formal living room with its fireplace, or the spacious rear family room and kitchen area with a sunny breakfast nook. The first-floor master suite features a sitting room with bookshelves, two walk-in closets, and a private bath with a corner whirlpool tub. Upstairs, two family bedrooms share a bath and enjoy separate vanities. A third family bedroom features its own full bath and a built-in window seat in a box-bay window.

ORDER BLUEPRINTS 24 HOURS, 7 DAYS A WEEK, AT 1-800-521-6797

plan #
HPT9600401

STYLE: NEO-ECLECTIC

FIRST FLOOR: 2,588 SQ. FT.

SECOND FLOOR: 1,375 SQ. FT.

TOTAL: 3,963 SQ. FT.

BONUS SPACE: 460 SQ. FT.

BEDROOMS: 4

BATHROOMS: 3½

WIDTH: 91' - 4"

DEPTH: 51' - 10"

FOUNDATION: CRAWLSPACE

SEARCH ONLINE @ EPLANS.COM

Though there are two entrances to this fine home, the one on the right is where friends and family should enter to truly absorb the grandeur of this design. The foyer is flanked by a bayed formal dining room and a bayed formal living room. Directly ahead is the lake gathering room, a spacious area with a welcoming fireplace, and access to the rear veranda. The L-shaped kitchen, complete with an island, includes plenty of space and convenient features like a wet bar, walk-in pantry, and built-in shelves. Located on the first floor for privacy, the master suite is complete with a huge dressing closet, access to the veranda, and a lavish bath.

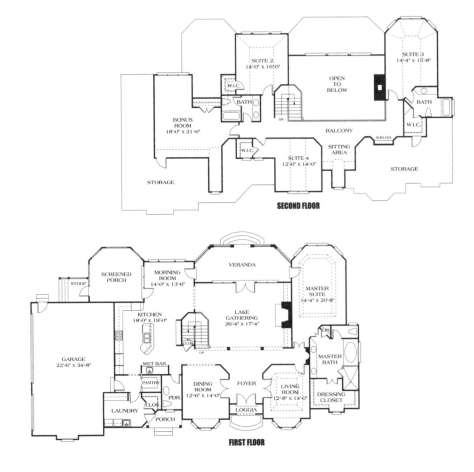

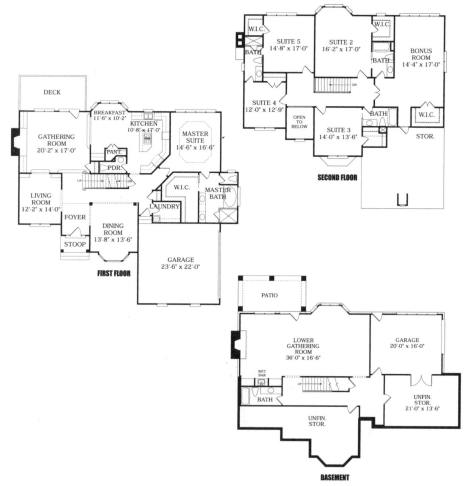

plan #

HPT9600402

STYLE: TRADITIONAL
FIRST FLOOR: 2,022 SQ. FT.
SECOND FLOOR: 1,556 SQ. FT.
TOTAL: 3,578 SQ. FT.
BONUS SPACE: 273 SQ. FT.
BEDROOMS: 5
BATHROOMS: 4½
WIDTH: 62' - 2"
DEPTH: 54' - 10"
FOUNDATION: BASEMENT

SEARCH ONLINE @ EPLANS.COM

The solidity of brick brings a feeling of timeless tradition to this five-bedroom home. Inside, the two-story foyer is flanked by the formal living room and the formal bayed dining room. A sunken gathering room features a warming fireplace and direct access to the rear deck. The breakfast room and nearby island kitchen help form a delightful open gathering space when joined with the gathering room. The lavish master bedroom suite, on the first floor, is sure to please with a large walk-in closet, a private master bath, and a detailed ceiling. Upstairs, four suites share three bathrooms as well as direct access to a spacious bonus room.

ORDER BLUEPRINTS 24 HOURS, 7 DAYS A WEEK, AT 1-800-521-6797

plan #

HPT9600403

STYLE: TRANSITIONAL

SQUARE FOOTAGE: 3,818

BEDROOMS: 4

BATHROOMS: 3½

WIDTH: 107' - 4"

DEPTH: 68' - 7"

FOUNDATION: SLAB

SEARCH ONLINE @ EPLANS.COM

This sprawling transitional facade incorporates brick quoins and a cast-stone arched entry to create a design of undeniable style and stature. The living room, with an eight-foot-wide fireplace, full-wall windows and a 14-foot ceiling, connects to the family room, which features yet another fireplace and an open wet bar. A study with a 14-foot ceiling and a bay window faces the front. The large kitchen is placed between the breakfast area and the formal dining room. A grand master suite includes His and Hers baths, each with walk-in closets. Right next door, Bedroom 2 is perfect for a nursery. Bedrooms 3 and 4 on the right of the home are separated from the master suite and share a full bath.

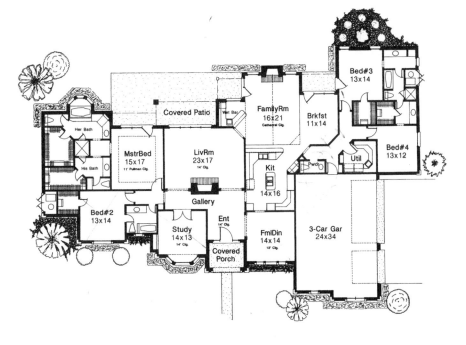

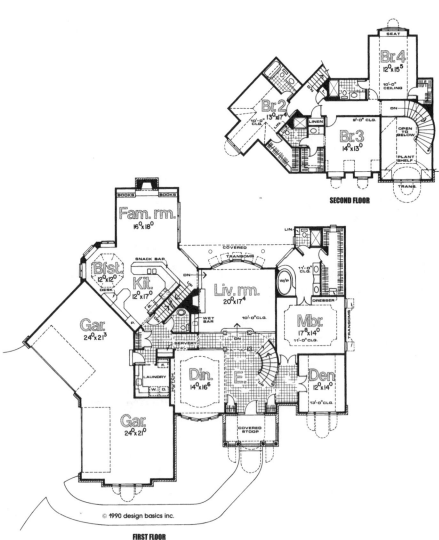

SECOND FLOOR

FIRST FLOOR

© 1990 design basics inc.

plan #
HPT9600404

STYLE: TRANSITIONAL
FIRST FLOOR: 2,617 SQ. FT.
SECOND FLOOR: 1,072 SQ. FT.
TOTAL: 3,689 SQ. FT.
BEDROOMS: 4
BATHROOMS: 4½
WIDTH: 83' - 5"
DEPTH: 73' - 4"

SEARCH ONLINE @ EPLANS.COM

A spectacular volume entry with a curving staircase opens through columns to the formal areas of this home. The sunken living room contains a fireplace, a wet bar, and a bowed window; the front-facing dining room offers a built-in hutch. The family room, with bookcases surrounding a fireplace, is open to a bayed breakfast nook, and both are easily served from the nearby kitchen. Placed away from the living area of the home, the den provides a quiet retreat. The master suite on the first floor contains an elegant bath and a huge walk-in closet. Second-floor bedrooms also include walk-in closets and private baths.

ORDER BLUEPRINTS 24 HOURS, 7 DAYS A WEEK, AT 1-800-521-6797

plan
HPT9600405

STYLE: TRANSITIONAL

FIRST FLOOR: 2,751 SQ. FT.

SECOND FLOOR: 1,185 SQ. FT.

TOTAL: 3,936 SQ. FT.

BEDROOMS: 4

BATHROOMS: 3½

WIDTH: 79' - 0"

DEPTH: 66' - 4"

FOUNDATION: SLAB, BASEMENT

SEARCH ONLINE @ EPLANS.COM

A grand brick facade, this home boasts muntin windows, multilevel rooflines, cut-brick jack arches, and a beautifully arched entry. A cathedral-ceilinged living room, complete with fireplace, and a family dining room flank the 20-foot-high entry. Relax in the family room, mix a drink from the wet bar, and look out through multiple windows to the covered veranda. A luxurious master suite includes a windowed sitting area looking over the rear view, private patio, full bath boasting a 10-foot ceiling, and a spacious walk-in closet On the second level, the three high-ceilinged bedrooms share two full baths and a study area with a built-in desk.

SECOND FLOOR

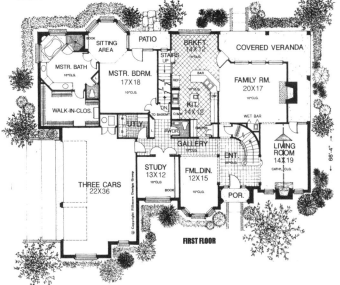

FIRST FLOOR

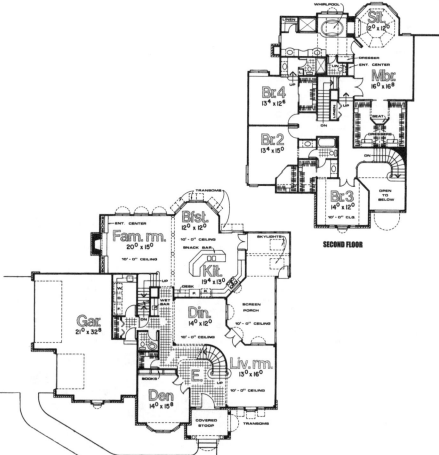

FIRST FLOOR

SECOND FLOOR

plan
HPT9600406

STYLE: NEO-ECLECTIC
FIRST FLOOR: 1,923 SQ. FT.
SECOND FLOOR: 1,852 SQ. FT.
TOTAL: 3,775 SQ. FT.
BEDROOMS: 4
BATHROOMS: 3½
WIDTH: 70' - 0"
DEPTH: 60' - 0"

SEARCH ONLINE @ EPLANS.COM

Breathtaking details and bright windows highlight this luxurious two-story home. Just off the spectacular entry is an impressive private den. The curved hall between the living and dining rooms offers many formal entertaining options. In the family room, three arched windows, a built-in entertainment centers and a fireplace flanked by bookcases enhance daily comfort. After ascending the front staircase and overlooking the dramatic entry, four large bedrooms are presented. Three secondary bedrooms include generous closet space and private access to a bath. A sumptuous master suite awaits the homeowners with its built-in entertainment center and His and Hers walk-in closets.

ORDER BLUEPRINTS 24 HOURS, 7 DAYS A WEEK, AT 1-800-521-6797

plan # HPT9600407

STYLE: NEO-ECLECTIC
FIRST FLOOR: 2,126 SQ. FT.
SECOND FLOOR: 1,680 SQ. FT.
TOTAL: 3,806 SQ. FT.
BEDROOMS: 4
BATHROOMS: 4½
WIDTH: 67' - 4"
DEPTH: 66' - 0"

SEARCH ONLINE @ EPLANS.COM

A striking facade imparts an "Old World" image with repetitive peaks, elegant windows, and a covered stoop framed by stately columns. The formal dining room with unique ceiling detail opens to a sunken living room. The living room then leads to the den, which offers a formal setting with French doors, a spider-beamed ceiling, and a built-in bookcase. A fully equipped kitchen holds a large walk-in pantry and rounded breakfast area, which is open to the hearth room. All the bedrooms enjoy special ceiling details, walk-in closets, and private baths. The master suite features a fireplace and a luxurious bath with a glass-block shower and a two-person whirlpool surrounded by windows.

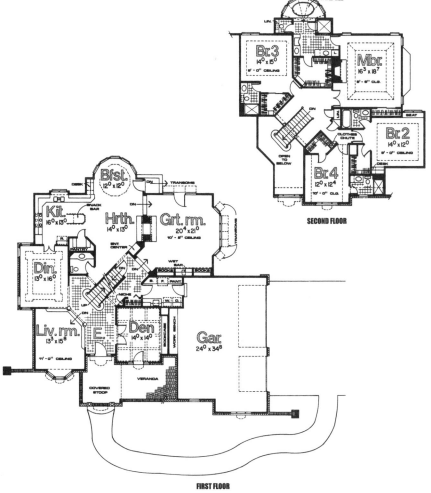

SECOND FLOOR

FIRST FLOOR

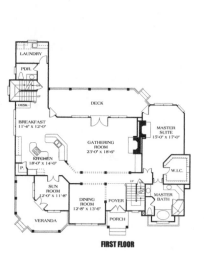

FIRST FLOOR

SECOND FLOOR

BASEMENT

plan#

HPT9600408

STYLE: NEO-ECLECTIC
FIRST FLOOR: 2,425 SQ. FT.
SECOND FLOOR: 1,398 SQ. FT.
TOTAL: 3,823 SQ. FT.
BONUS SPACE: 176 SQ. FT.
BEDROOMS: 4
BATHROOMS: 3½
WIDTH: 64' - 10"
DEPTH: 66' - 4"
FOUNDATION: BASEMENT

SEARCH ONLINE @ EPLANS.COM

Stone accents lend European flavor to this enchanting, modern home. A bonus space upstairs and future space in the basement allow endless opportunities for expansion and redesign. The first floor begins with a two-story foyer that opens up to a formal dining room on the left and an expansive gathering room ahead. Adorned by columns, a fireplace, and French doors, the gathering room will be the heart of the home. An open kitchen features "boomerang" counters, one a cooktop island and the other a double-sink serving bar. The sunroom opens through French doors to the veranda. On the far right, tucked away for privacy, the master suite is a dream come true. A romantic fireplace, deck access, and a lavish bath with a garden tub are the ultimate in luxury. The upper level can be accessed by two staircases and includes three suites and future space.

plan#

HPT9600409

STYLE: TRANSITIONAL

FIRST FLOOR: 2,496 SQ. FT.

SECOND FLOOR: 1,090 SQ. FT.

TOTAL: 3,586 SQ. FT.

BONUS SPACE: 265 SQ. FT.

BEDROOMS: 4

BATHROOMS: 3½

WIDTH: 76' - 0"

DEPTH: 60' - 0"

FOUNDATION: SLAB, BASEMENT

SEARCH ONLINE @ EPLANS.COM

Soaring stone and brick gables combine to grace the exterior of this French Country home, enhancing its European appeal. Inside, the two-story entry opens to a columned dining room on the right, through double doors to a study on the left, and straight ahead—an elegant, curving staircase and a gracious living room. The uniquely designed master suite contains a large walk-in closet and a luxurious master bath filled with amenities. An open floor plan brings the casual living areas together, connecting the island kitchen, octagonal breakfast room and family room. Passage to the rear covered patio is supplied by the breakfast room as well as the family room. The second floor offers three family bedrooms—one with its own bath—and a full bath with separate dressing areas.

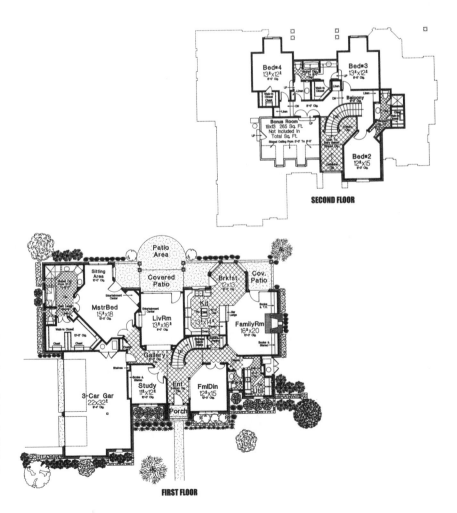

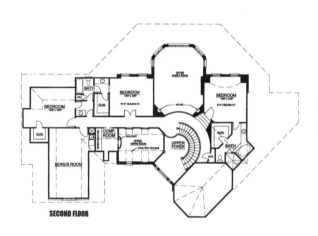

SECOND FLOOR

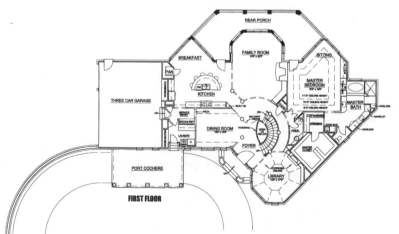

FIRST FLOOR

ptan#
HPT9600410

STYLE: FRENCH-ECLECTIC
FIRST FLOOR: 2,612 SQ. FT.
SECOND FLOOR: 1,300 SQ. FT.
TOTAL: 3,912 SQ. FT.
BONUS SPACE: 330 SQ. FT.
BEDROOMS: 4
BATHROOMS: 3½
WIDTH: 95' - 6"
DEPTH: 64' - 0"
FOUNDATION: BASEMENT

SEARCH ONLINE @ EPLANS.COM

Lovely stucco columns and a copper standing-seam roof highlight this stone-and-brick facade. An elegant New World interior starts with a sensational winding staircase, a carved handrail, and honey-hued hardwood floor. An open two-story formal dining room enjoys front-property views and leads to the gourmet kitchen through the butler's pantry, announced by an archway. Beyond the foyer, tall windows brighten the two-story family room and bring in a sense of the outdoors; a fireplace makes the space cozy and warm. The center food-prep island counter overlooks a breakfast niche that offers wide views through walls of windows and access to the rear porch.

ORDER BLUEPRINTS 24 HOURS, 7 DAYS A WEEK, AT 1-800-521-6797

plan #
HPT9600411

STYLE: NEO-ECLECTIC
FIRST FLOOR: 2,654 SQ. FT.
SECOND FLOOR: 1,013 SQ. FT.
TOTAL: 3,667 SQ. FT.
BEDROOMS: 4
BATHROOMS: 3½
WIDTH: 75' - 4"
DEPTH: 74' - 2"
FOUNDATION: CRAWLSPACE, SLAB, BASEMENT

SEARCH ONLINE @ EPLANS.COM

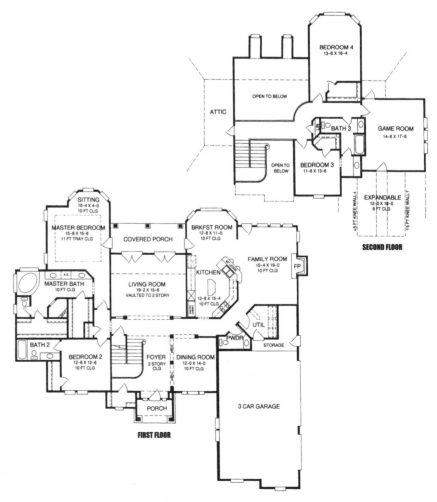

European accents shape the exterior of this striking family home. Inside, the foyer is open to the dining room on the right and the living room straight ahead. Here, two sets of double doors open to the rear covered porch. Casual areas of the home include a family room warmed by a fireplace and an island kitchen opening to a bayed breakfast room. The first-floor master retreat is a luxurious perk, which offers a bayed sitting area, a whirlpool bath, and large His and Hers walk-in closets. Bedroom 2—with its close proximity to the master suite—is perfect for a nursery or home office. Upstairs, Bedrooms 3 and 4 boast walk-in closets and share a bath. Future space is available just off the game room.

plan
HPT9600412

STYLE: FRENCH REVIVAL
SQUARE FOOTAGE: 3,942
BEDROOMS: 4
BATHROOMS: 3½
WIDTH: 97' - 0"
DEPTH: 82' - 0"
FOUNDATION: SLAB, BASEMENT

SEARCH ONLINE @ EPLANS.COM

This modern-day castle places luxurious living and comfortable spaces all on one level for a truly magnificent place to call home. Elegant flooring follows from the entry to the gallery creating a nice definition for the surrounding family room, dining room, and hearth-warmed great room. The kitchen is wide and open, accommodating multiple chefs, great for entertaining. The breakfast bay sheds light on the kitchen as well, for a cheery atmosphere throughout. Three family bedrooms are situated to the left, one of which enjoys a private bath. A library/study is conveniently located near the opulent master suite. Here, a sitting bay, lavish bath, and room-size walk-in closet will surely pamper. A four-car garage completes this grand plan.

ORDER BLUEPRINTS 24 HOURS, 7 DAYS A WEEK, AT 1-800-521-6797

plan #
HPT9600413

STYLE: FRENCH ECLECTIC
FIRST FLOOR: 2,844 SQ. FT.
SECOND FLOOR: 1,140 SQ. FT.
TOTAL: 3,984 SQ. FT.
BEDROOMS: 4
BATHROOMS: 3½
WIDTH: 79' - 0"
DEPTH: 70' - 7"
FOUNDATION: CRAWLSPACE,
SLAB, BASEMENT

SEARCH ONLINE @ EPLANS.COM

Wonderful rooflines and a stone facade lend storybook elegance to this beautiful French estate. With detailed windows and entries and decorative finial pinnacles, this home is reminiscent of 19th-Century Chateauesque architecture with a hint of Tudor charm. A natural-stone foyer leads to the living room on the right—complete with cathedral ceiling, wet bar, and extended-hearth fireplace—and the family room straight ahead, featuring a stone fireplace and access to the covered veranda. The island kitchen easily services the ample breakfast area for casual meals and the formal dining room with vaulted ceiling, perfect for entertaining. The first-floor master suite indulges with an enormous walk-in closet, step-up tub, and private covered patio. Up the dramatic staircase, children and guests will delight in three large bedrooms, a study, and two full baths. An optional recreation room would make an excellent game or exercise room.

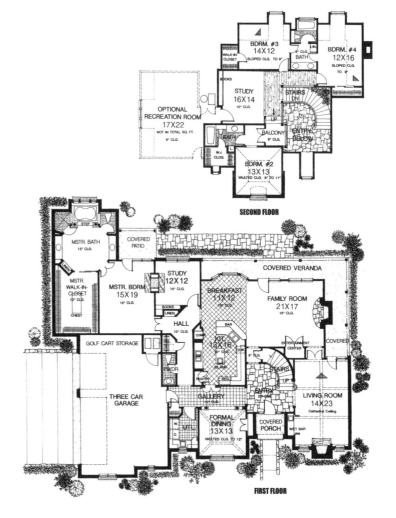

SECOND FLOOR

FIRST FLOOR

plan
HPT9600414

STYLE: FRENCH ECLECTIC
FIRST FLOOR: 3,030 SQ. FT.
SECOND FLOOR: 848 SQ. FT.
TOTAL: 3,878 SQ. FT.
BONUS SPACE: 320 SQ. FT.
BEDROOMS: 4
BATHROOMS: 4½
WIDTH: 88' - 0"
DEPTH: 72' - 1"
FOUNDATION: SLAB

SEARCH ONLINE @ EPLANS.COM

This dazzling and majestic European design features a stucco-and-stone facade, French shutters, and castle-like rooflines. The entry is flanked by a study with a fireplace and a formal dining room. A formal living room with a fireplace is just across the gallery. The master wing is brightened by a bayed sitting area and features a private bath that extends impressive closet space. The island kitchen overlooks the breakfast and great rooms. A guest suite is located on the first floor for privacy, and two additional family bedrooms reside upstairs, along with a future playroom.

ORDER BLUEPRINTS 24 HOURS, 7 DAYS A WEEK, AT 1-800-521-6797

plan #
HPT9600415

STYLE: FRENCH REVIVAL
SQUARE FOOTAGE: 3,549
BONUS SPACE: 426 SQ. FT.
BEDROOMS: 4
BATHROOMS: 3½
WIDTH: 85' - 0"
DEPTH: 85' - 4"
FOUNDATION: BASEMENT

SEARCH ONLINE @ EPLANS.COM

With brick and stone and multiple rooflines, this luxurious European cottage is sure to be the envy of the neighborhood. A formal dining room and study flank the entry. The great room is warmed by a massive hearth flanked by built-ins. The master suite is located to the left of the plan and includes a sitting bay, private bath, and huge walk-in closet. Three additional bedrooms are located on the right side of the plan.

plan #

HPT9600416

STYLE: FRENCH REVIVAL
SQUARE FOOTAGE: 3,510
BEDROOMS: 4
BATHROOMS: 3½
WIDTH: 91' - 0"
DEPTH: 72' - 10"
FOUNDATION: SLAB

SEARCH ONLINE @ EPLANS.COM

The French Revival style is reflected in this spacious one-story design. The tiled entry and gallery introduce the formal dining room, the great room with a warm fireplace, and a quiet study with built-ins and a bay window. The kitchen opens up to the breakfast bay. Two family bedrooms just beyond the kitchen share a compartmented bath, and both enjoy walk-in closets. The master bedroom is split from the family bedrooms for privacy and features a sitting bay that looks out to the covered patio. A spacious walk-in closet and super-luxurious bath provide the master suite with supreme comfort.

ORDER BLUEPRINTS 24 HOURS, 7 DAYS A WEEK, AT 1-800-521-6797

ptan #

HPT9600417

STYLE: FRENCH ECLECTIC

FIRST FLOOR: 2,700 SQ. FT.

SECOND FLOOR: 990 SQ. FT.

TOTAL: 3,690 SQ. FT.

BONUS SPACE: 365 SQ. FT.

BEDROOMS: 4

BATHROOMS: 3½

WIDTH: 76' - 0"

DEPTH: 74' - 1"

FOUNDATION: SLAB, BASEMENT, CRAWLSPACE

SEARCH ONLINE @ EPLANS.COM

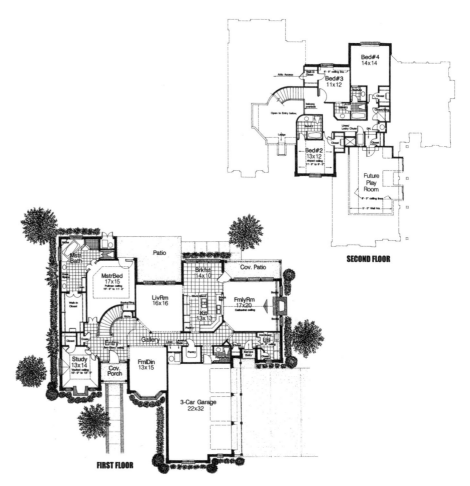

This European manor looks as if it was nestled in the French countryside. The combination of brick, stone, and rough cedar, and multiple chimneys add to the charm of the facade. The gracious two-story entry leads to all areas of the home. A beautiful curving staircase leads to an upper balcony overlooking the entry. The second floor consists of three bedrooms, each with connecting baths and walk-in closets. Space for a future playroom is located above the garage. Downstairs, the family area with a cathedral ceiling is open to the large kitchen and breakfast area. A large pantry is located near the kitchen. The cozy study has its own marble fireplace and a vaulted ceiling.

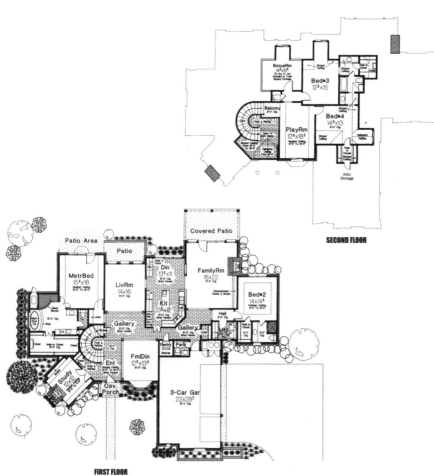

SECOND FLOOR

FIRST FLOOR

plan#
HPT9600418

STYLE: FRENCH ECLECTIC
FIRST FLOOR: 2,985 SQ. FT.
SECOND FLOOR: 938 SQ. FT.
TOTAL: 3,923 SQ. FT.
BEDROOMS: 4
BATHROOMS: 3½
WIDTH: 86' - 0"
DEPTH: 68' - 6"
FOUNDATION: SLAB, BASEMENT

SEARCH ONLINE @ EPLANS.COM

This French Country design, decorated with brick and stone, begins with a cedar-beamed entry. Fireplaces enhance the study and the family room, and the living room and family room both open to patios. The island kitchen works well with both the formal bayed dining room as well as the casual dining area to the back of the home. A secluded bedroom with a private bath can serve as a guest suite. The first-floor master suite is designed to pamper, with a huge walk-in closet, a lavish bath, and private access to the backyard. Upstairs, find two family bedrooms, a playroom, and bonus space.

© The Sater Design Collection, Inc.

plan
HPT9600419

STYLE: NEO-ECLECTIC
FIRST FLOOR: 2,815 SQ. FT.
SECOND FLOOR: 1,130 SQ. FT.
TOTAL: 3,945 SQ. FT.
BEDROOMS: 4
BATHROOMS: 3½
WIDTH: 85' - 0"
DEPTH: 76' - 8"
FOUNDATION: SLAB, BASEMENT

SEARCH ONLINE @ EPLANS.COM

Stone, stucco, beautiful windows, and a tile roof all combine to give this home plenty of classy curb appeal. An elegant entry leads to the grand foyer, which introduces the formal living room. Here, a bowed wall of windows shows off the rear veranda, and a two-sided fireplace warms cool evenings. A cozy study shares the fireplace and offers access to the rear veranda. Providing privacy as well as pampering, the first-floor master suite is complete with two walk-in closets, a deluxe bath, a stepped ceiling, and private access out-doors. For casual times, the leisure room features a fireplace, built-ins, a coffered ceiling, and out-door access. Upstairs, Bedrooms 2 and 3 share a bath; the guest suite has a private bath.

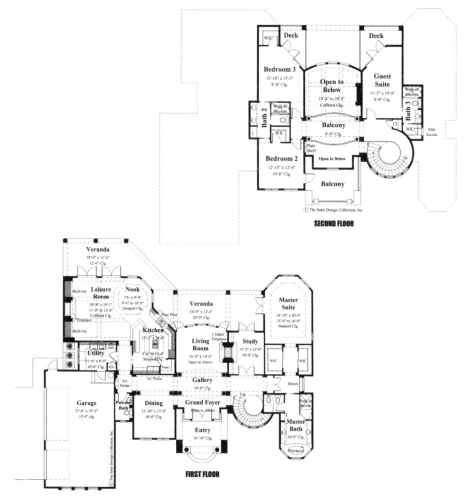

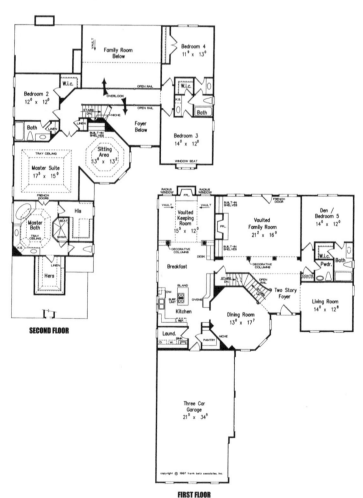

SECOND FLOOR

FIRST FLOOR

plan
HPT9600420

STYLE: NEO-ECLECTIC
FIRST FLOOR: 2,060 SQ. FT.
SECOND FLOOR: 1,817 SQ. FT.
TOTAL: 3,877 SQ. FT.
BEDROOMS: 5
BATHROOMS: 4½
WIDTH: 54' - 0"
DEPTH: 78' - 4"
FOUNDATION: CRAWLSPACE,
BASEMENT, SLAB

SEARCH ONLINE @ EPLANS.COM

Mesmerizing details make this luxurious home a distinct sensation. Stucco and stone, opulent arches and French shutters romanticize the exterior of its blissful perfection. Inside, a radiant staircase cascades into the two-story foyer. The eye-catching stone turret encloses the dining room. The formal living room is illuminated by two enormous arched windows. A wall of windows in the family room offers a breathtaking view of the backyard. The island kitchen adjoins the breakfast area and a walk-in pantry. A three-car garage completes the ground level. Upstairs, the master wing is almost doubled by its private sitting area. Double doors open into the master bath with a corner whirlpool tub. Enormous His and Hers walk-in closets are efficiently designed.

ORDER BLUEPRINTS 24 HOURS, 7 DAYS A WEEK, AT 1-800-521-6797

plan #
HPT9600421

STYLE: MEDITERRANEAN
FIRST FLOOR: 2,384 SQ. FT.
SECOND FLOOR: 1,234 SQ. FT.
TOTAL: 3,618 SQ. FT.
BONUS SPACE: 344 SQ. FT.
BEDROOMS: 5
BATHROOMS: 4½
WIDTH: 64' - 6"
DEPTH: 57' - 10"
FOUNDATION: CRAWLSPACE,
BASEMENT, SLAB

SEARCH ONLINE @ EPLANS.COM

Stucco and stone, French shutters, a turret-style bay, and lovely arches create a magical timeless style. A formal arch romanticizes the front entry, which opens to a two-story foyer. A bayed living room resides to the right, and a formal dining room is set to the left. Straight ahead, the vaulted two-story family room is warmed by an enchanting fireplace. The island kitchen is set between the breakfast and dining rooms. The master suite is enhanced by a tray ceiling and offers a lavish master bath with a whirlpool tub. Upstairs, Bedroom 2 offers another private bath and a walk-in closet. Bedrooms 3 and 4 each provide their own walk-in closets and share a full bath between them. The bonus room is perfect for a future home office or playroom.

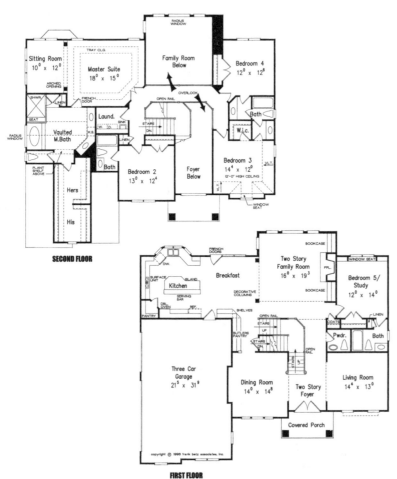

SECOND FLOOR

FIRST FLOOR

plan #
HPT9600422

STYLE: TRANSITIONAL
FIRST FLOOR: 1,786 SQ. FT.
SECOND FLOOR: 1,739 SQ. FT.
TOTAL: 3,525 SQ. FT.
BEDROOMS: 5
BATHROOMS: 4½
WIDTH: 59' - 0"
DEPTH: 53' - 0"
FOUNDATION: CRAWLSPACE,
BASEMENT, SLAB

SEARCH ONLINE @ EPLANS.COM

European details bring charm and a touch of joie de vivre to this traditional home. Casual living space includes a two-story family room with a centered fireplace. A sizable kitchen, with an island serving bar and a French door to the rear property, leads to the formal dining room through a convenient butler's pantry. The second floor includes a generous master suite with a sitting room defined by decorative columns and five lovely windows. Bedroom 2 has a private bath, and two additional bedrooms share a hall bath with compartmented lavatories.

ORDER BLUEPRINTS 24 HOURS, 7 DAYS A WEEK, AT 1-800-521-6797

plan# HPT9600423

STYLE: TRANSITIONAL

FIRST FLOOR: 2,506 SQ. FT.

SECOND FLOOR: 1,415 SQ. FT.

TOTAL: 3,921 SQ. FT.

BEDROOMS: 4

BATHROOMS: 3½

WIDTH: 80' - 5"

DEPTH: 50' - 4"

FOUNDATION: SLAB, BASEMENT

SEARCH ONLINE @ EPLANS.COM

A stately two-story home with a gracious, manorly exterior features a large, arched entryway as its focal point. Excellent brick detailing and brick quoins help make this exterior one of a kind. The large, two-story family area is adjacent to the living room with its cathedral ceiling and formal fireplace—a convenient arrangement for entertaining large groups, or just a cozy evening at home. A wrapping patio area allows for dining outdoors. The large kitchen is centrally located, with a second stairway leading to the second floor. The master suite features a volume ceiling and a sitting area overlooking the rear yard. The huge master bath includes two walk-in closets. The upper balcony overlooks the family area and the entryway.

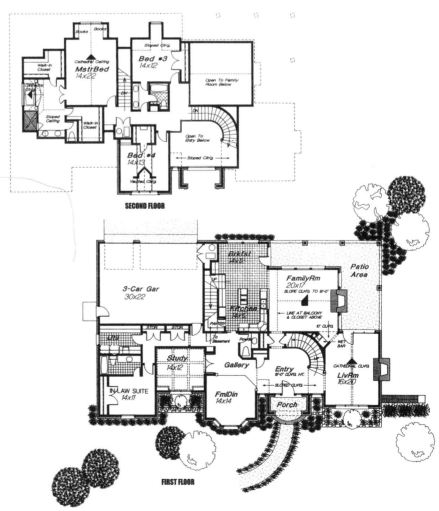

SECOND FLOOR

FIRST FLOOR

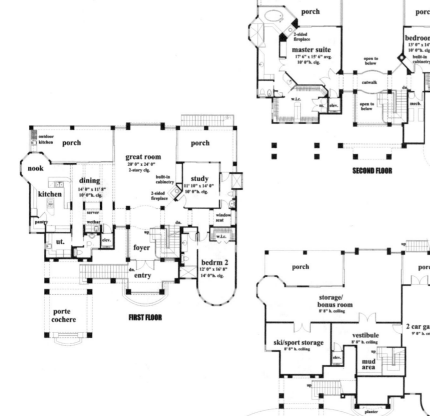

plan #

HPT9600424

STYLE: CRAFTSMAN
FIRST FLOOR: 2,391 SQ. FT.
SECOND FLOOR: 1,539 SQ. FT.
TOTAL: 3,930 SQ. FT.
BEDROOMS: 3
BATHROOMS: 3½
WIDTH: 71' - 0"
DEPTH: 69' - 0"
FOUNDATION: BASEMENT

SEARCH ONLINE @ EPLANS.COM

Climate is a key component of any mountain retreat, and outdoor living is an integral part of its design. This superior cabin features open and covered porches. A mix of matchstick details and rugged stone set off this lodge-house facade, concealing a well-defined interior. Windows line the breakfast bay and brighten the kitchen, which features a center cooktop island. A door leads out to a covered porch with a summer kitchen. The upper level features a secluded master suite with a spacious bath beginning with a double walk-in closet and ending with a garden view of the porch. A two-sided fireplace extends warmth to the whirlpool spa-style tub.

© 1998 Donald A. Gardner Architects, Inc.

plan
HPT9600425

STYLE: EUROPEAN COTTAGE
MAIN LEVEL: 2,297 SQ. FT.
LOWER LEVEL: 1,212 SQ. FT.
TOTAL: 3,509 SQ. FT.
BEDROOMS: 5
BATHROOMS: 5½
WIDTH: 70' - 10"
DEPTH: 69' - 0"

SEARCH ONLINE @ EPLANS.COM

A variety of exterior materials and interesting windows combine with an unusual floor plan to make this an exceptional home. It is designed for a sloping lot, with full living quarters on the main level, but with two extra bedrooms and a family room added to the lower level. A covered porch showcases a wonderful dining-room window and an attractive front door. The living room, enhanced by a fireplace, adjoins the dining room for easy entertaining. The island kitchen and a bayed breakfast room are to the left. Three bedrooms on this level include one that could serve as a study and one as a master suite with dual vanities, a garden tub, and a walk-in closet. A deck on this floor covers the patio off the lower-level family room, which has its own fireplace.

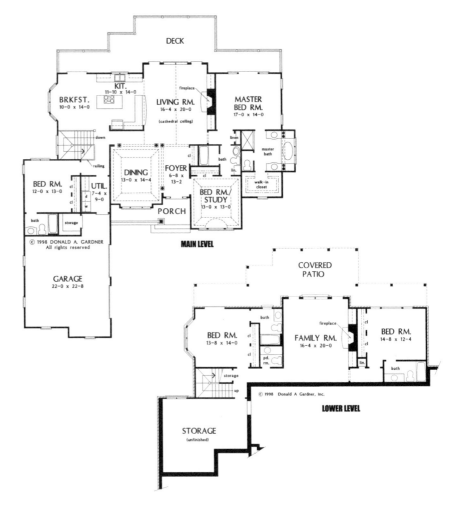

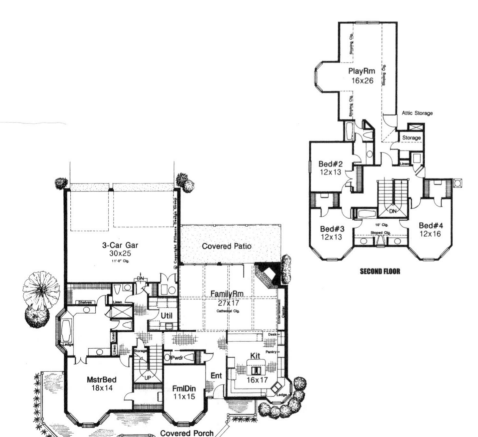

FIRST FLOOR

3-Car Gar 30x25
Covered Patio
FamilyRm 27x17 Cathedral Clg.
Util
MstrBed 18x14
Pwdr
UP
Kit 16x17
Ent
FmlDin 11x15
Covered Porch

SECOND FLOOR

PlayRm 16x26
Attic Storage
Storage
Bed#2 12x13
Bed#3 12x13
DN
Bed#4 12x16

plan#
HPT9600426

STYLE: FOLK VICTORIAN
FIRST FLOOR: 2,103 SQ. FT.
SECOND FLOOR: 1,460 SQ. FT.
TOTAL: 3,563 SQ. FT.
BEDROOMS: 4
BATHROOMS: 3½
WIDTH: 61' - 7"
DEPTH: 61' - 6"
FOUNDATION: SLAB

SEARCH ONLINE @ EPLANS.COM

This home boasts a beautiful front facade with Victorian detailing—including decorative pinnacles—and a sweeping covered porch. The family room has a cathedral ceiling, corner fireplace, entertainment center, and access to a rear covered patio. Both the family dining room and the master suite are enhanced with bay windows. The circular kitchen is packed full with amenities, including an island, knickknack ledge, pantry, and built-in desk. Upstairs are three bedrooms and two full baths. Bedrooms 3 and 4 have bay windows and share a full bath that includes twin vanities. Also on this floor is a playroom and attic storage.

plan⊕#
HPT9600427

STYLE: VICTORIAN

FIRST FLOOR: 1,538 SQ. FT.

SECOND FLOOR: 1,526 SQ. FT.

THIRD FLOOR: 658 SQ. FT.

TOTAL: 3,722 SQ. FT.

BEDROOMS: 5

BATHROOMS: 3½

WIDTH: 67' - 0"

DEPTH: 66' - 0"

FOUNDATION: BASEMENT

SEARCH ONLINE @ EPLANS.COM

This charming Victorian home is reminiscent of a time when letter writing was an art and the scent of lavender hung lightly in the air. However, the floor plan moves quickly into the present with a contemporary flair. A veranda wraps around the living room, providing entrance from each side. The hub of the first floor is a kitchen that serves the dining room, the family room, and the living room with equal ease. Located on the second floor are two family bedrooms, a full bath, and an opulent master suite. Amenities in this suite include a fireplace, a bay-windowed sitting room, a pampering master bath, and a private sundeck. The third floor holds two bedrooms—one a possible study—and a full bath.

SECOND FLOOR

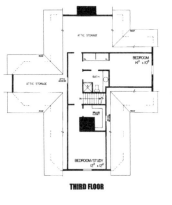

THIRD FLOOR

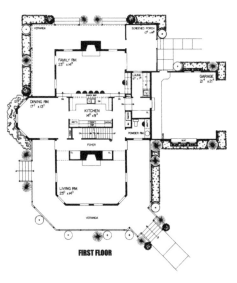

FIRST FLOOR

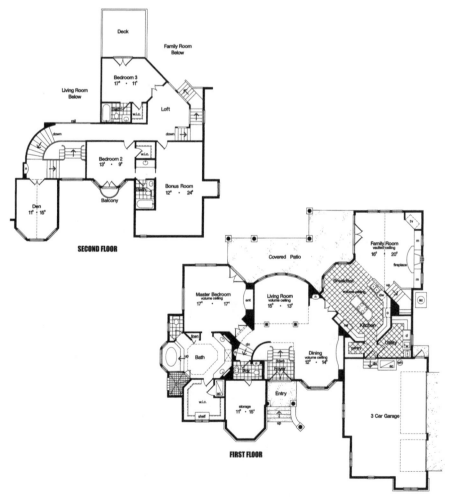

SECOND FLOOR

FIRST FLOOR

plan #

HPT9600428

STYLE: NEO-ECLECTIC
FIRST FLOOR: 2,285 SQ. FT.
SECOND FLOOR: 1,395 SQ. FT.
TOTAL: 3,680 SQ. FT.
BONUS SPACE: 300 SQ. FT.
BEDROOMS: 3
BATHROOMS: 3½
WIDTH: 73' - 8"
DEPTH: 76' - 2"
FOUNDATION: SLAB

SEARCH ONLINE @ EPLANS.COM

Now here is a one-of-a-kind house plan. Step down from the raised foyer into the grand gallery where columns define the living room. This central living area boasts an enormous bow window with a fantastic view to the covered patio. The formal dining room is to the right and the lavish master suite sits on the left. The family gourmet will find an expansive kitchen beyond a pair of French doors on the right. The secluded family room completes this first level. An enormous den is found on the first landing above, to the left of the foyer. Two bedroom suites and a loft occupy the second floor.

plan
HPT9600429

STYLE: NEO-ECLECTIC

FIRST FLOOR: 2,553 SQ. FT.

SECOND FLOOR: 1,370 SQ. FT.

TOTAL: 3,923 SQ. FT.

BONUS SPACE: 280 SQ. FT.

BEDROOMS: 3

BATHROOMS: 2½ + ½

WIDTH: 74' - 0"

DEPTH: 99' - 4"

FOUNDATION: SLAB

SEARCH ONLINE @ EPLANS.COM

The excitement of this chateau begins with its European-style elevation. The raised foyer welcomes guests into formal living and dining rooms, both with creative ceiling treatments. A popular home office is conveniently positioned near the master suite. The master bedroom features a tray ceiling and a sitting area. The master bath contains His and Hers vanities and walk-in closets. The family room combines with a nook and island kitchen for casual living space. Second-floor space includes two generous bedrooms with a shared bath, an activity room, a home theater with a minibar and future bonus space--great for another bedroom or study.

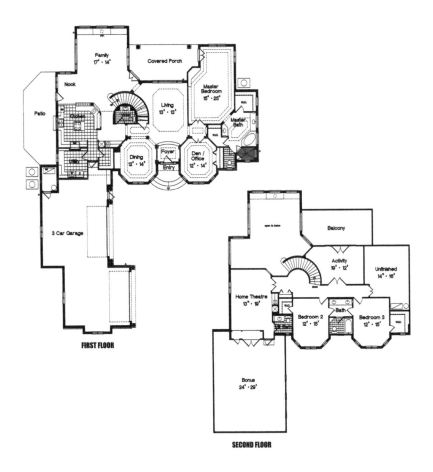

FIRST FLOOR

SECOND FLOOR

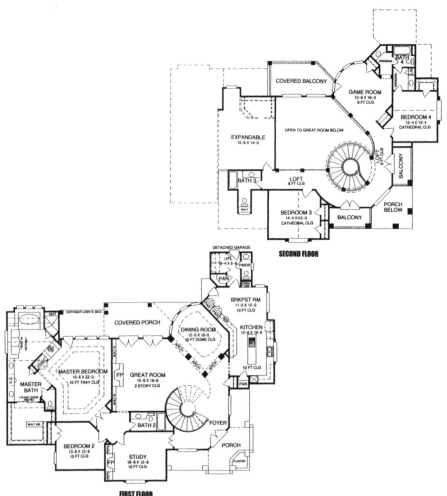

SECOND FLOOR

FIRST FLOOR

plan #

HPT9600430

STYLE: NEO-ECLECTIC
FIRST FLOOR: 2,772 SQ. FT.
SECOND FLOOR: 933 SQ. FT.
TOTAL: 3,705 SQ. FT.
BEDROOMS: 4
BATHROOMS: 4½
WIDTH: 74' - 8"
DEPTH: 61' - 10"
FOUNDATION: CRAWLSPACE, SLAB

SEARCH ONLINE @ EPLANS.COM

A truly grand entry—absolutely stunning on a corner lot—sets the eclectic, yet elegant tone of this four-bedroom home. The foyer opens to a dramatic circular stair, then on to the two-story great room that's framed by a second-story balcony. An elegant dining room is set to the side, distinguished by a span of arches. The gourmet kitchen features wrapping counters, a cooktop island, and a breakfast room. A front study and a secondary bedroom are nice accompaniments to the expansive master suite. A through-fireplace, a spa-style bath, and a huge walk-in closet highlight this area. Upstairs, a loft opens to two balconies overlooking the porch and leads to two family bedrooms and a game room.

plan #
HPT9600431

STYLE: PLANTATION

FIRST FLOOR: 2,578 SQ. FT.

SECOND FLOOR: 1,277 SQ. FT.

TOTAL: 3,855 SQ. FT.

BEDROOMS: 4

BATHROOMS: 4

WIDTH: 53' - 6"

DEPTH: 97' - 0"

FOUNDATION: PIER

SEARCH ONLINE @ EPLANS.COM

This charming Charleston design is full of surprises! Perfect for a narrow footprint, the raised foundation is ideal for a waterfront location. An entry porch introduces a winding staircase. To the right is a living room/library that functions as a formal entertaining space. A large hearth and two sets of French doors to the covered porch enhance the great room. The master suite is positioned for privacy and includes great amenities that work to relax the homeowners. Upstairs, three family bedrooms, two full baths, an open media room, and a future game room create a fantastic casual family space.

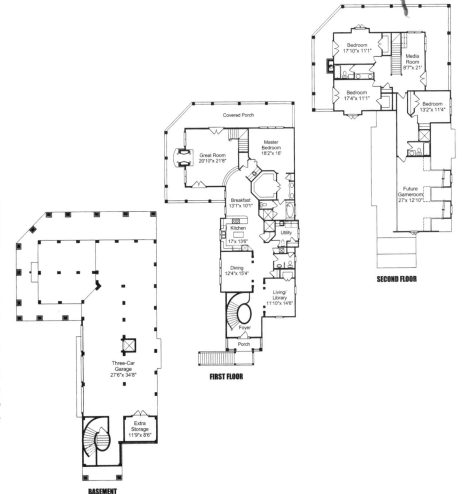

© Stephen Fuller, Inc.

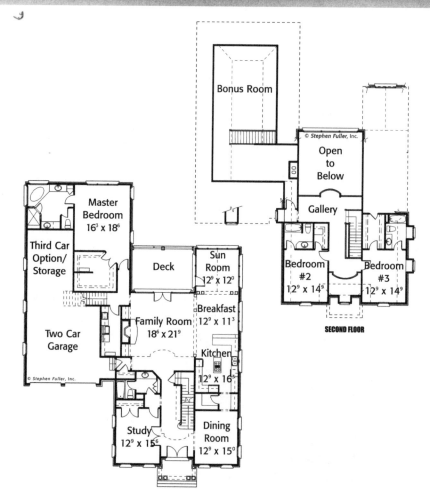

Bonus Room

Open to Below

© Stephen Fuller, Inc.

Gallery

Bedroom #2
12⁹ x 14⁵

Bedroom #3
12⁹ x 14⁹

SECOND FLOOR

Master Bedroom
16³ x 18⁶

Third Car Option/ Storage

Deck

Sun Room
12⁹ x 12⁰

Family Room
18⁶ x 21⁹

Breakfast
12⁹ x 11³

Two Car Garage

Kitchen
12⁹ x 16⁵

© Stephen Fuller, Inc.

Study
12⁹ x 15⁶

Dining Room
12⁹ x 15⁰

FIRST FLOOR

plan #
HPT9600432

STYLE: GEORGIAN
FIRST FLOOR: 2,719 SQ. FT.
SECOND FLOOR: 929 SQ. FT.
TOTAL: 3,648 SQ. FT.
BONUS SPACE: 530 SQ. FT.
BEDROOMS: 3
BATHROOMS: 4
WIDTH: 62' - 8"
DEPTH: 83' - 0"
FOUNDATION: WALKOUT BASEMENT

SEARCH ONLINE @ EPLANS.COM

A beautiful brick Georgian from one of our top designers, this three-bedroom plan is a pleasure to call home. The two-story foyer and family room have balcony overlooks from above, adding architectural interest. To the left of the foyer, the study opens with French doors; to the right, the dining room features butler's pantry access to the country kitchen, complete with a cooktop island. The breakfast nook opens to a vaulted sunroom. The master suite enjoys peace and quiet, along with an enormous walk-in closet and sumptuous bath with a corner tub. Two upstairs bedrooms, each with private baths and walk-in closets, share a bonus room.

© Stephen Fuller, Inc.

plan
HPT9600433

STYLE: GEORGIAN

FIRST FLOOR: 1,981 SQ. FT.

SECOND FLOOR: 1,935 SQ. FT.

TOTAL: 3,916 SQ. FT.

BEDROOMS: 5

BATHROOMS: 4

WIDTH: 65' - 0"

DEPTH: 64' - 10"

FOUNDATION: WALKOUT BASEMENT

SEARCH ONLINE @ EPLANS.COM

Take one look at this Early American Colonial home and you'll fall in love with its beauty, functionality, and luxuries. From the covered front porch, continue to the great room, where a fireplace and a bay window with wonderful rear-property views await. The kitchen will delight, with a wraparound counter that provides plenty of workspace for easy meal preparation. Up the grand staircase, the master suite revels in a private deck and pampering spa bath. Three additional bedrooms complete this level. Don't miss the first-floor guest room with an adjacent full bath.

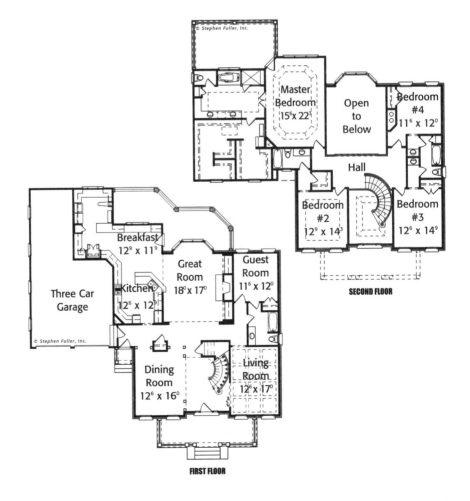

© Stephen Fuller, Inc.

Master Bedroom 15⁶ x 22⁵

Open to Below

Bedroom #4 11⁶ x 12⁰

Hall

Bedroom #2 12⁹ x 14³

Bedroom #3 12⁶ x 14⁹

SECOND FLOOR

Breakfast 12⁹ x 11⁹

Great Room 18⁰ x 17⁰

Guest Room 11⁶ x 12⁰

Three Car Garage

Kitchen 12⁶ x 12⁰

© Stephen Fuller, Inc.

Dining Room 12⁶ x 16⁰

Living Room 12⁶ x 17⁰

FIRST FLOOR

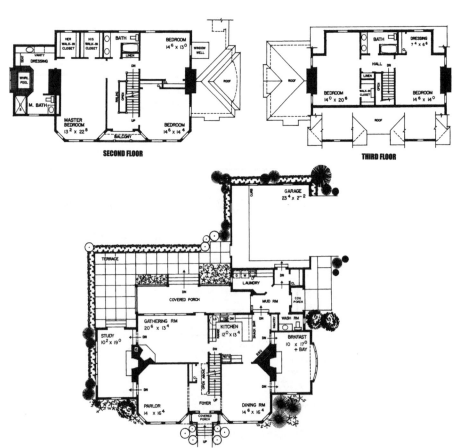

SECOND FLOOR

THIRD FLOOR

FIRST FLOOR

plan#
HPT9600434

STYLE: FOLK VICTORIAN
FIRST FLOOR: 1,683 SQ. FT.
SECOND FLOOR: 1,388 SQ. FT.
THIRD FLOOR: 808 SQ. FT.
TOTAL: 3,879 SQ. FT.
BEDROOMS: 5
BATHROOMS: 3½
WIDTH: 64' - 0"
DEPTH: 67' - 0"
FOUNDATION: BASEMENT

SEARCH ONLINE @ EPLANS.COM

This beautiful Folk Victorian has all the properties of others in its class. Living areas include a formal Victorian parlor, a private study, and large gathering room. The formal dining room has its more casual counterpart in a bay-windowed breakfast room. Both are near the well-appointed kitchen. Five bedrooms serve family and guest needs handily; three are on the second floor and two more on the third floor. The master suite includes a bath with whirlpool tub, separate shower, and two sinks. For outdoor entertaining there is a covered rear porch leading to a terrace. The two-car garage is arranged to the rear of the home and attaches to the main house at a service entrance near the laundry and mudroom.

plan
HPT9600435

STYLE: COLONIAL REVIVAL

FIRST FLOOR: 2,327 SQ. FT.

SECOND FLOOR: 1,431 SQ. FT.

TOTAL: 3,758 SQ. FT.

BONUS SPACE: 473 SQ. FT.

BEDROOMS: 5

BATHROOMS: 3½

WIDTH: 78' - 10"

DEPTH: 58' - 2"

FOUNDATION: CRAWLSPACE, BASEMENT

SEARCH ONLINE @ EPLANS.COM

This Early American classic was built with attention to the needs of an active family. The formal entrance allows guests to come and go in splendor, while the family can kick off their shoes in the mudroom. The step-saving kitchen is accented by an island for dinner preparations or school projects, and a pantry with tons of space. In the master suite, homeowners can relax in the whirlpool tub and revel in the ample walk-in closet. Second-floor family bedrooms provide privacy, walk-in closets, and two shared baths, both with dual vanities.

SECOND FLOOR

FIRST FLOOR

plan
HPT9600436

STYLE: COLONIAL REVIVAL
FIRST FLOOR: 2,416 SQ. FT.
SECOND FLOOR: 1,535 SQ. FT.
TOTAL: 3,951 SQ. FT.
BONUS SPACE: 552 SQ. FT.
BEDROOMS: 5
BATHROOMS: 3½
WIDTH: 79' - 2"
DEPTH: 63' - 6"
FOUNDATION: CRAWLSPACE,
BASEMENT

SEARCH ONLINE @ EPLANS.COM

A curved front porch, graceful symmetry in the details, and the sturdiness of brick all combine to enhance this beautiful two-story home. Inside, the two-story foyer introduces the formal rooms—the living room to the right and the dining room to the left—and presents the elegant stairwell. The L-shaped kitchen provides a walk-in pantry, an island with a sink, a butler's pantry, and an adjacent breakfast area. Perfect for casual gatherings, the family room features a fireplace and backyard access. Located on the first floor for privacy, the master suite offers a large walk-in closet and a lavish bath. Upstairs, four bedrooms— each with a walk-in closet—share two full baths and access to the future recreation room over the garage.

ORDER BLUEPRINTS 24 HOURS, 7 DAYS A WEEK, AT 1-800-521-6797

plan #
HPT9600437

STYLE: COLONIAL REVIVAL
FIRST FLOOR: 1,656 SQ. FT.
SECOND FLOOR: 1,440 SQ. FT.
THIRD FLOOR: 715 SQ. FT.
TOTAL: 3,811 SQ. FT.
BEDROOMS: 4
BATHROOMS: 3½
WIDTH: 72' - 0"
DEPTH: 36' - 0"
FOUNDATION: BASEMENT

SEARCH ONLINE @ EPLANS.COM

This home recalls the home built by George Read II in New Castle, Delaware, around 1791. Its Georgian roots are evident in its symmetry and the Palladian window, keystone lintels, and parapeted chimneys. Notice, however, the roundhead dormer windows, roof balustrades, and arched front-door transom, which reflect the Federal styling that was popular at the end of the 18th Century. Three massive chimneys support six fireplaces, including one in each first-floor room and two in the master suite! The country kitchen also boasts an island cooktop, a built-in desk, a pantry, and sliding glass doors to the terrace. The second floor contains two family bedrooms, in addition to the luxurious master suite, and the top floor adds a fourth bedroom and a hobby/studio area. The garage includes an L-shaped curb for a work table and storage.

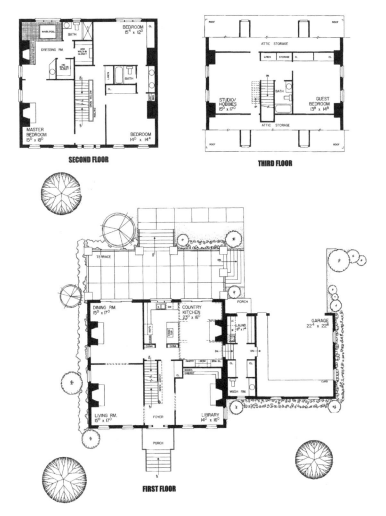

SECOND FLOOR

THIRD FLOOR

FIRST FLOOR

SECOND FLOOR

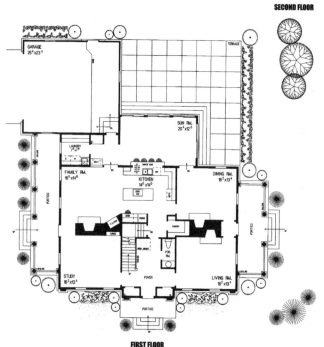

FIRST FLOOR

plan #
HPT9600438

STYLE: FEDERAL
FIRST FLOOR: 1,972 SQ. FT.
SECOND FLOOR: 1,533 SQ. FT.
TOTAL: 3,505 SQ. FT.
BEDROOMS: 3
BATHROOMS: 2½
WIDTH: 66' - 4"
DEPTH: 66' - 4"
FOUNDATION: BASEMENT

SEARCH ONLINE @ EPLANS.COM

This home recalls the Longfellow House in Cambridge, Massachusetts, residence of the poet for 45 years. Featuring a hipped roof with a widow's walk, it was built in 1759 by Major John Vassall, an ardent Tory who was driven out of the house in 1774. It served for a while as George Washington's command center. Longfellow's residency began in 1837, when he came to Harvard to teach English. Elegant two-story pilasters frame the front entrance and are repeated at the corners. Two porches retain the symmetry and add outdoor living space. On the first floor are the formal living and dining rooms, each with a fireplace. A front study connects to the family room, which offers built-ins and another fireplace. Upstairs are three bedrooms, including a wonderful master suite with a sitting room and a deluxe private bath.

ORDER BLUEPRINTS 24 HOURS, 7 DAYS A WEEK, AT 1-800-521-6797

plan #

HPT9600439

TYLE: GREEK REVIVAL

FIRST FLOOR: 1,877 SQ. FT.

SECOND FLOOR: 1,877 SQ. FT.

TOTAL: 3,754 SQ. FT.

BEDROOMS: 4

BATHROOMS: 3½

WIDTH: 65' - 0"

DEPTH: 53' - 0"

FOUNDATION: BASEMENT

SEARCH ONLINE @ EPLANS.COM

The gracious hospitality and the genteel, easy lifestyle of the South are personified in this elegant Southern Colonial home. Contributing to the exterior's stucco warmth are shutters, a cupola, and square columns surrounding the home. Inside, the warmth continues with six fireplaces throughout the home: in the formal dining room, living room, family room—and on the second floor—family bedroom, romantic master bedroom, and master bath. The second floor contains two family bedrooms—each with its own bath—and a lavish master bedroom with a balcony and a pampering bath. A study/bedroom with a balcony completes the upstairs. Plans for a detached garage with an enclosed lap pool are included with the blueprints.

SECOND FLOOR

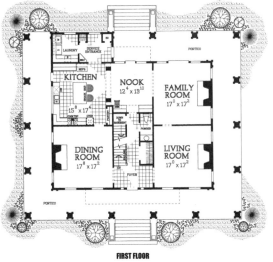

FIRST FLOOR

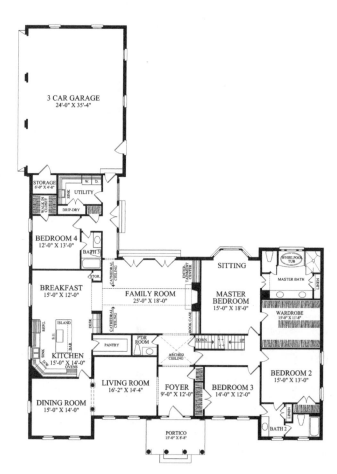

plan #

HPT9600440

STYLE: GEORGIAN
SQUARE FOOTAGE: 3,600
BEDROOMS: 4
BATHROOMS: 3½
WIDTH: 76' - 2"
DEPTH: 100' - 10"
FOUNDATION: CRAWLSPACE,
BASEMENT

SEARCH ONLINE @ EPLANS.COM

Graceful columns combine with stunning symmetry on this fine four-bedroom home. Inside, the foyer opens to the formal living room on the left and then leads back to the spacious family room. Here, a fireplace waits to warm cool fall evenings and built-ins accommodate your book collection. The efficient island kitchen offers plenty of counter and cabinet space, easily serving both the formal dining room and the sunny breakfast area. A separate bedroom resides back by the garage and features a walk-in closet. Two more family bedrooms are at the front right side of the home and share a full bath. The lavish master suite is complete with a huge walk-in closet, a bayed sitting area, and a sumptuous bath.

ORDER BLUEPRINTS 24 HOURS, 7 DAYS A WEEK, AT 1-800-521-6797

plan # HPT9600441

STYLE: GEORGIAN
FIRST FLOOR: 2,814 SQ. FT.
SECOND FLOOR: 979 SQ. FT.
TOTAL: 3,793 SQ. FT.
BEDROOMS: 4
BATHROOMS: 3½
WIDTH: 98' - 0"
DEPTH: 45' - 10"
FOUNDATION: SLAB, BASEMENT

SEARCH ONLINE @ EPLANS.COM

A covered, columned porch and symmetrically placed windows welcome you to this elegant brick home. The formal living room offers built-in bookshelves and one of two fireplaces, the other being found in the spacious family room. A gallery running between these rooms leads to the sumptuous master suite, which includes a sitting area, a private covered patio, and a bath with two walk-in closets, dual vanities, a large shower, and a garden tub. The step-saving kitchen features a work island and a snack bar. The breakfast and family rooms offer doors to the large covered veranda. Upstairs you'll find three bedrooms and attic storage space. The three-car garage even has room for a golf cart.

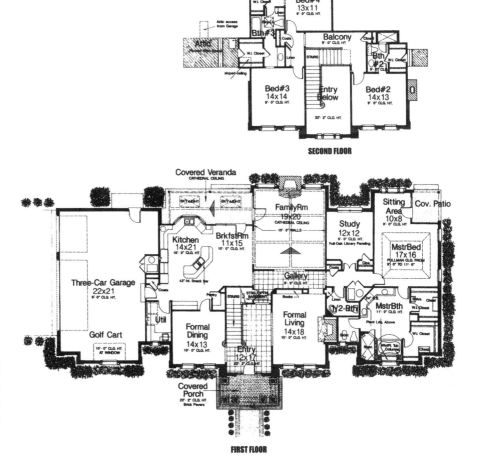

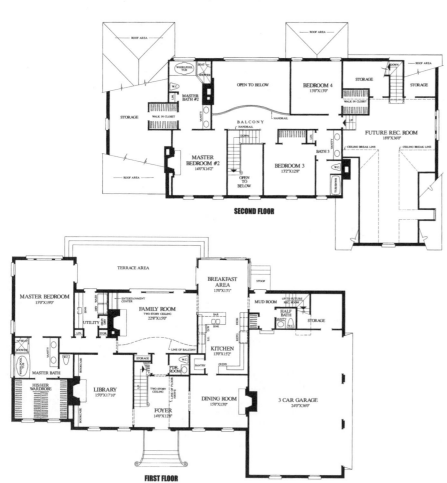

SECOND FLOOR

FIRST FLOOR

plan #
HPT9600442

STYLE: GEORGIAN
FIRST FLOOR: 2,492 SQ. FT.
SECOND FLOOR: 1,313 SQ. FT.
TOTAL: 3,805 SQ. FT.
BONUS SPACE: 687 SQ. FT.
BEDROOMS: 4
BATHROOMS: 3½ + ½
WIDTH: 85' - 10"
DEPTH: 54' - 6"
FOUNDATION: CRAWLSPACE,
BASEMENT

SEARCH ONLINE @ EPLANS.COM

Although the exterior of this Georgian home is entirely classical, the interior boasts an up-to-date floor plan that's a perfect fit for today's lifestyles. The large central family room, conveniently near the kitchen and breakfast area, includes a fireplace and access to the rear terrace; fireplaces also grace the formal dining room and library. The master suite, also with terrace access, features a spacious walk-in closet and a bath with a whirlpool tub. Upstairs, a second master suite—great for guests—joins two family bedrooms. Nearby, a large open area can serve as a recreation room.

ORDER BLUEPRINTS 24 HOURS, 7 DAYS A WEEK, AT 1-800-521-6797

plan #

HPT9600443

STYLE: COLONIAL REVIVAL

FIRST FLOOR: 1,895 SQ. FT.

SECOND FLOOR: 1,661 SQ. FT.

TOTAL: 3,556 SQ. FT.

BEDROOMS: 4

BATHROOMS: 3½

WIDTH: 86' - 10"

DEPTH: 39' - 1"

FOUNDATION: BASEMENT

SEARCH ONLINE @ EPLANS.COM

A two-story pillared entrance portico and tall multipane windows, flanking the double front doors, accentuate the facade of this Southern Colonial design. This brick home is stately and classic in its exterior appeal. The three-car garage opens to the side so it does not disturb the street view. Formal living and dining rooms are at each end of the foyer. The living room is complemented by a music room or an optional bedroom with a full bath nearby. The formal dining room and the informal breakfast room are easily served by the kitchen. The spacious family room features a built-in wet bar. The second floor contains two family bedrooms and the luxurious master suite with a private bath.

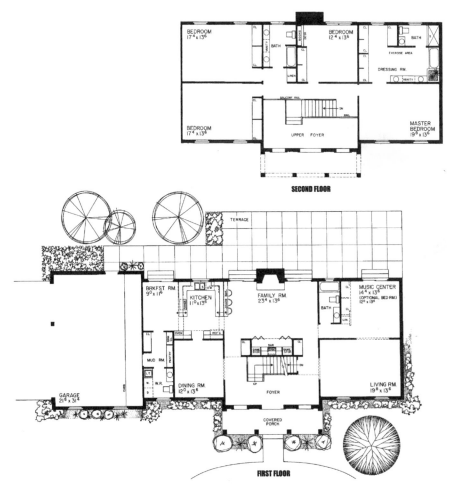

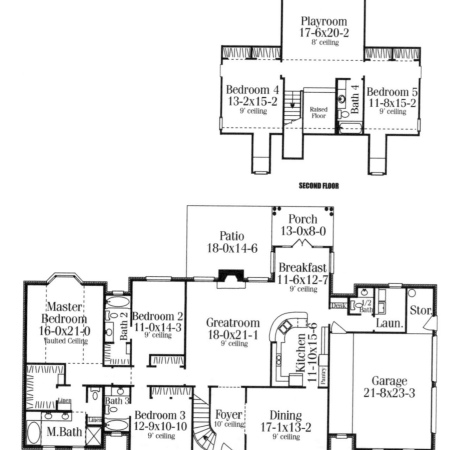

Playroom
17-6x20-2
8' ceiling

Bedroom 4
13-2x15-2
9' ceiling

Raised Floor

Bath 4

Bedroom 5
11-8x15-2
9' ceiling

SECOND FLOOR

Porch
13-0x8-0

Patio
18-0x14-6

Breakfast
11-6x12-7
9' ceiling

Master Bedroom
16-0x21-0
Vaulted Ceiling

Bath 2

Bedroom 2
11-0x14-3
9' ceiling

Greatroom
18-0x21-1
9' ceiling

Kitchen
11-10x15-6

Desk

1/2 Bath

Laun.

Stor.

Garage
21-8x23-3

Bath 3

Linen

Linen

M.Bath

Bedroom 3
12-9x10-10
9' ceiling

Foyer
10' ceiling

Dining
17-1x13-2
9' ceiling

Pantry

©Larry James Designs

Porch
43-0x7-0

FIRST FLOOR

plan #
HPT9600444

STYLE: COLONIAL REVIVAL
FIRST FLOOR: 2,497 SQ. FT.
SECOND FLOOR: 1,028 SQ. FT.
TOTAL: 3,525 SQ. FT.
BEDROOMS: 5
BATHROOMS: 4½
WIDTH: 87' - 0"
DEPTH: 57' - 5"
FOUNDATION: BASEMENT,
CRAWLSPACE, SLAB

SEARCH ONLINE @ EPLANS.COM

Perfect symmetry is pleasing in this Southern country cottage. Accent arches and two false chimneys add architectural interest outside; inside, a curving staircase and delicate touches lend charm and sophistication. The central great room will surely be a gathering place, with a fireplace framed by windows and easy access to the rest of the living areas. Two generous bedrooms, each with private baths, precede the master suite. The vaulted master bedroom has a bayed window, enormous walk-in closet and pampering bath. Upstairs, two bedrooms and a playroom are flexible to meet your family's needs.

plan #

HPT9600445

STYLE: COLONIAL REVIVAL

FIRST FLOOR: 2,380 SQ. FT.

SECOND FLOOR: 1,295 SQ. FT.

TOTAL: 3,675 SQ. FT.

BEDROOMS: 4

BATHROOMS: 3½

WIDTH: 77' - 4"

DEPTH: 58' - 4"

FOUNDATION: WALKOUT BASEMENT

SEARCH ONLINE @ EPLANS.COM

Finely crafted porches—front, side, and rear—make this home a classic in traditional Southern living. Past the large French doors, the impressive foyer is flanked by the formal living and dining rooms. Beyond the stair is a vaulted great room with an expanse of windows, a fireplace, and built-in bookcases. From here, the breakfast room and kitchen are easily accessible and open to a private side porch. The master suite provides a large bath, two spacious closets, and a fireplace. The second floor contains three bedrooms with private bath access and a playroom.

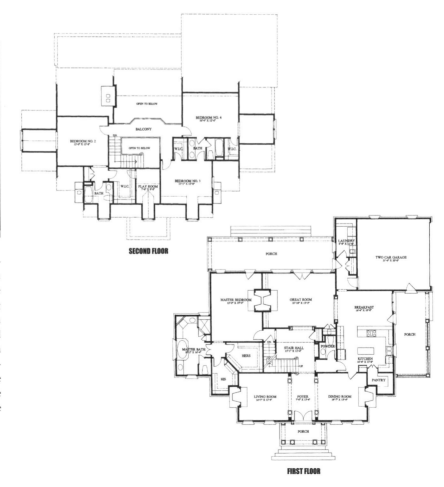

© Stephen Fuller, Inc.

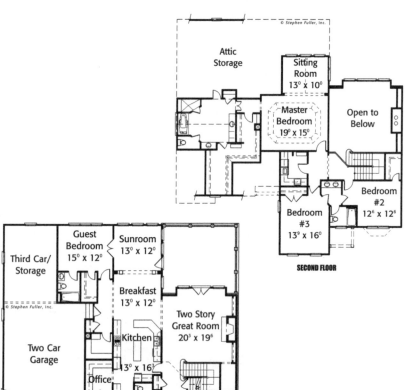

Attic Storage

Sitting Room
13⁰ x 10⁰

Master Bedroom
19⁰ x 15⁰

Open to Below

Bedroom #2
12⁶ x 12⁶

Bedroom #3
13⁹ x 16⁰

© Stephen Fuller, Inc.

SECOND FLOOR

Guest Bedroom
15⁰ x 12⁰

Sunroom
13⁰ x 12⁰

Third Car/Storage

Breakfast
13⁰ x 12⁰

Two Story Great Room
20³ x 19⁶

Kitchen
13⁰ x 16⁵

© Stephen Fuller, Inc.

Two Car Garage

Office

Dining Room
13⁰ x 15⁰

Study
13³ x 12⁰

FIRST FLOOR

plan
HPT9600446

STYLE: COLONIAL REVIVAL
FIRST FLOOR: 2,194 SQ. FT.
SECOND FLOOR: 1,695 SQ. FT.
TOTAL: 3,889 SQ. FT.
BEDROOMS: 4
BATHROOMS: 3½
WIDTH: 64' - 4"
DEPTH: 63' - 0"
FOUNDATION: WALKOUT BASEMENT

SEARCH ONLINE @ EPLANS.COM

This classic Northeastern Colonial home is a dream to own, with shingle and stone outside, and a comfortable family plan inside. In the two-story great room, a fireplace warms, and French doors invite outdoor living. To the left of the island kitchen, the office accesses a private porch. The aptly named sunroom is accessed from the breakfast nook, or through French doors from the guest room, complete with a private bath. Upstairs, the deluxe master suite includes a sitting area, vaulted bath, and Z-shaped walk-in closet. Two additional bedrooms share a full bath.

ORDER BLUEPRINTS 24 HOURS, 7 DAYS A WEEK, AT 1-800-521-6797

© Stephen Fuller, Inc.

plan#
HPT9600447

STYLE: COLONIAL REVIVAL

FIRST FLOOR: 2,175 SQ. FT.

SECOND FLOOR: 1,647 SQ. FT.

TOTAL: 3,822 SQ. FT.

BEDROOMS: 4

BATHROOMS: 3½

WIDTH: 64' - 4"

DEPTH: 63' - 0"

FOUNDATION: WALKOUT BASEMENT

SEARCH ONLINE @ EPLANS.COM

Step into comfort in this beautiful brick Southern Colonial. Enter to find a plan designed with you in mind. The dining room and study allow plenty of natural light at the front of the home. Continue to the great room, offering an extended-hearth fireplace and French doors to the rear patio. The guest suite is tucked away with a private bath and French-door access to the sunroom. Upstairs, the master bedroom will surround you in luxury, with a sitting room bathed in light, a vaulted bath with a spa tub, and a Z-shaped walk-in closet. Two additional bedrooms share a full bath.

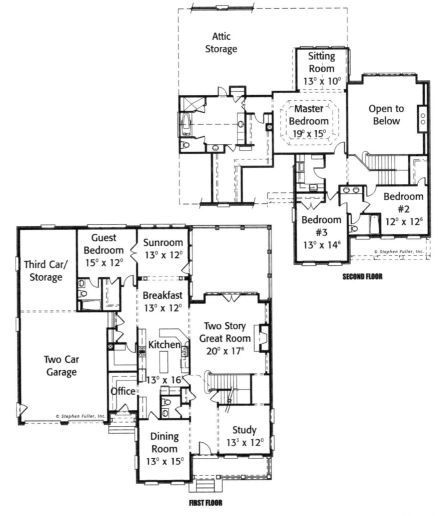

SECOND FLOOR

FIRST FLOOR

DESIGNS FROM 3,500 TO 3,999 SQ. FT.

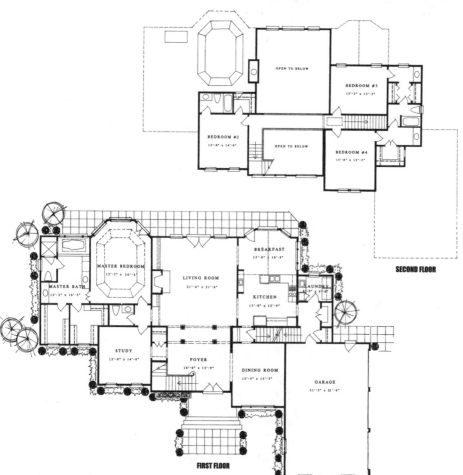

FIRST FLOOR

SECOND FLOOR

HPT9600448

STYLE: FRENCH ECLECTIC
FIRST FLOOR: 2,461 SQ. FT.
SECOND FLOOR: 1,114 SQ. FT.
TOTAL: 3,575 SQ. FT.
BEDROOMS: 4
BATHROOMS: 3½
WIDTH: 84' - 4"
DEPTH: 63' - 0"
FOUNDATION: WALKOUT
BASEMENT

SEARCH ONLINE @ EPLANS.COM

A myriad of glass and ornamental stucco detailing complements the asymmetrical facade of this two-story home. Inside, the striking, two-story foyer provides a dramatic entrance. To the right is the formal dining room. An efficient L-shaped kitchen and bayed breakfast nook are conveniently located near the dining area. The living room, with its welcoming fireplace, opens through double doors to the rear terrace. The private master suite provides access to the rear terrace and adjacent study. The master bath is sure to please with its relaxing garden tub, separate shower, grand His and Hers walk-in closets, and a compartmented toilet. The second floor contains three large bedrooms, one with a private bath; the others share a bath.

384   ULTIMATE HOME PLAN REFERENCE   ORDER BLUEPRINTS 24 HOURS, 7 DAYS A WEEK, AT 1-800-521-6797

plan
HPT9600449

STYLE: NEO-ECLECTIC

FIRST FLOOR: 2,049 SQ. FT.

SECOND FLOOR: 1,468 SQ. FT.

TOTAL: 3,517 SQ. FT.

BEDROOMS: 4

BATHROOMS: 4½

WIDTH: 57' - 0"

DEPTH: 44' - 0"

FOUNDATION: CRAWLSPACE

SEARCH ONLINE @ EPLANS.COM

This charming country manor offers bright, open living areas for a comfortable family home. The foyer opens to formal rooms on either side—the living room on the left and elegant dining room on the right. The kitchen is expertly positioned with a handy island that overlooks a light-filled breakfast nook. The family room is equipped with a fireplace and access to the rear covered porch. The master suite reigns supreme on this level, delighting with dual walk-in closets and a pampering spa bath. The upper level accommodates three generous bedroom suites and a large recreation room. A two-car garage with a side entrance makes this plan perfect for a corner lot.

PHOTO COURTESY OF LIVING CONCEPTS HOME PLANNING

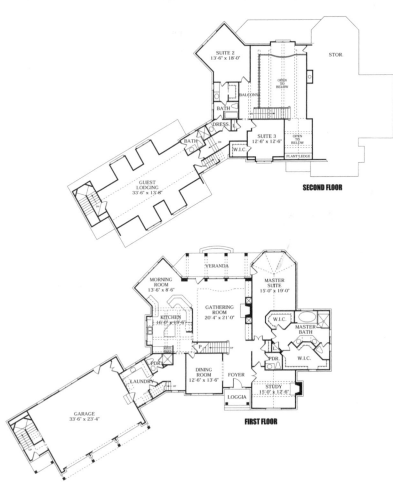

SUITE 2
13'-6" x 18'-0"

STOR.

OPEN TO BELOW

BALCONY

BATH

DRESS

SUITE 3
12'-6" x 12'-6"

OPEN TO BELOW

BATH

W.I.C.

PLANT'LEDGE

GUEST LODGING
33'-6" x 13'-8"

SECOND FLOOR

VERANDA

MORNING ROOM
13'-6" x 8'-6"

MASTER SUITE
15'-0" x 19'-0"

KITCHEN
16'-0" x 19'-6"

GATHERING ROOM
20'-4" x 21'-0"

W.I.C.

MASTER BATH

P

PDR.

W.I.C.

DINING ROOM
12'-6" x 13'-6"

FOYER

LAUNDRY

STUDY
15'-0" x 12'-6"

GARAGE
33'-6" x 23'-4"

LOGGIA

FIRST FLOOR

plan
HPT9600450

STYLE: COUNTRY
FIRST FLOOR: 2,660 SQ. FT.
SECOND FLOOR: 914 SQ. FT.
TOTAL: 3,574 SQ. FT.
BEDROOMS: 3
BATHROOMS: 4½
WIDTH: 114' - 8"
DEPTH: 75' - 10"
FOUNDATION: CRAWLSPACE

SEARCH ONLINE @ EPLANS.COM

Gently curved arches and dormers contrast with the straight lines of gables and wooden columns on this French-style stone exterior. Small-paned windows are enhanced by shutters; tall chimneys and a cupola add height. Inside, a spacious gathering room with an impressive fireplace opens to a cheery morning room. The kitchen is a delight, with a beam ceiling, triangular work island, walk-in pantry, and angular counter with a snack bar. The nearby laundry room includes a sink, a work area, and plenty of room for storage. The first-floor master suite boasts a bay-windowed sitting nook, a deluxe bath, and a handy study.

plan
HPT9600451

STYLE: COUNTRY

FIRST FLOOR: 2,782 SQ. FT.

SECOND FLOOR: 1,027 SQ. FT.

TOTAL: 3,809 SQ. FT.

BEDROOMS: 4

BATHROOMS: 4½

WIDTH: 78' - 2"

DEPTH: 74' - 6"

FOUNDATION: BASEMENT

SEARCH ONLINE @ EPLANS.COM

Filled with specialty rooms and abundant amenities, this countryside house is the perfect dream home. Double doors open into an angled foyer, flanked by a music room and a formal great room warmed by a fireplace. The music room leads to the master wing of the home, which includes a spacious bath with a dressing area and double walk-in closet. The great room is the heart of the home—its central position allows access to the island kitchen, formal dining room, and library. Stairs behind the kitchen lead upstairs to a balcony, accessing three family bedrooms. The lower level features a billiard room, hobby room, media room, and future possibilities.

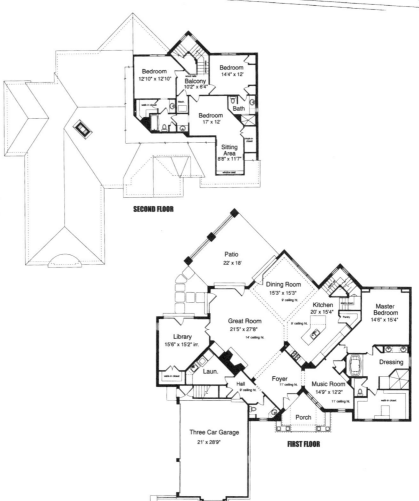

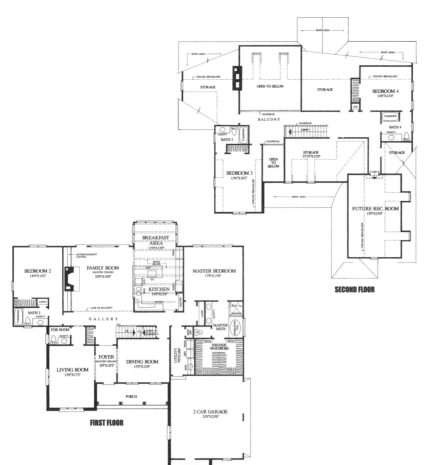

SECOND FLOOR

FIRST FLOOR

plan
HPT9600452

STYLE: COLONIAL REVIVAL
FIRST FLOOR: 2,568 SQ. FT.
SECOND FLOOR: 981 SQ. FT.
TOTAL: 3,549 SQ. FT.
BEDROOMS: 4
BATHROOMS: 4½
WIDTH: 66' - 8"
DEPTH: 71' - 0"
FOUNDATION: BASEMENT

SEARCH ONLINE @ EPLANS.COM

A smattering of architectual styles blend effort-lessly to create this delightful two-story home. The foyer is flanked by the formal dining room and the living room. To the rear, the island kitchen and breakfast area enjoy a beamed ceiling bringing a bit of the rustic exterior inside. The family room offers a cozy space for informal gatherings with its warming fireplace. The master suite sits on the far right; Bedroom 2, on the far left, would double easily as a guest room giving adequate privacy. Two additional bedrooms, each with private baths, reside on the second floor as does space for a future rec room.

ORDER BLUEPRINTS 24 HOURS, 7 DAYS A WEEK, AT 1-800-521-6797

THIS HOME, AS SHOWN IN THE PHOTOGRAPH, MAY DIFFER FROM THE ACTUAL BLUEPRINTS. FOR MORE DETAILED INFORMATION, PLEASE CHECK THE FLOOR PLANS CAREFULLY.

plan # HPT9600453

STYLE: MEDITERRANEAN
MAIN LEVEL: 2,391 SQ. FT.
UPPER LEVEL: 922 SQ. FT.
LOWER LEVEL: 1,964 SQ. FT.
TOTAL: 5,277 SQ. FT.
BONUS SPACE: 400 SQ. FT.
BEDROOMS: 4
BATHROOMS: 4½
WIDTH: 63' - 10"
DEPTH: 85' - 6"
FOUNDATION: BASEMENT

SEARCH ONLINE @ EPLANS.COM

Here's an upscale multilevel plan with expansive rear views. The first floor provides an open living and dining area, defined by decorative columns and enhanced by natural light from tall windows. A breakfast area with a lovely triple window opens to a sunroom, which allows light to pour into the gourmet kitchen. The master wing features a tray ceiling in the bedroom, two walk-in closets, and an elegant private vestibule leading to a lavish bath. Upstairs, a reading loft overlooks the great room and leads to a sleeping area with two suites. A recreation room, exercise room, office, guest suite, and additional storage are available in the finished basement.

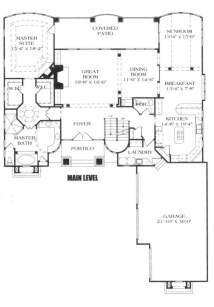

MAIN LEVEL

UPPER LEVEL

REAR EXTERIOR

LOWER LEVEL

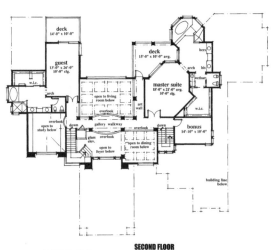

SECOND FLOOR

FIRST FLOOR

plan #
HPT9600454

STYLE: SPANISH COLONIAL REVIVAL
FIRST FLOOR: 3,667 SQ. FT.
SECOND FLOOR: 1,862 SQ. FT.
TOTAL: 5,529 SQ. FT.
BONUS SPACE: 140 SQ. FT.
BEDROOMS: 4
BATHROOMS: 5½
WIDTH: 102' - 0"
DEPTH: 87' - 0"
FOUNDATION: SLAB

SEARCH ONLINE @ EPLANS.COM

Sweeping heights lend a grand stroke to many of the rooms in this estate: the study, the grand foyer, the dining room, and the living room. The living and dining room ceilings are coffered. Upstairs, the master suite enjoys a full list of appointments, including an exercise (or bonus) room, a tub tower with a vaulted cove-lit ceiling, and a private deck. Also on this floor is a guest bedroom with an observation deck (or make this a spectacular study to complement the master suite). Other special details include: a pass-through outdoor bar, an outdoor kitchen, a work-shop area, two verandas, and a glass elevator.

ptan
HPT9600455

STYLE: SW CONTEMPORARY
FIRST FLOOR: 3,770 SQ. FT.
SECOND FLOOR: 634 SQ. FT.
TOTAL: 4,404 SQ. FT.
BEDROOMS: 4
BATHROOMS: 3½
WIDTH: 87' - 0"
DEPTH: 97' - 6"
FOUNDATION: SLAB

SEARCH ONLINE @ EPLANS.COM

This fresh and innovative design creates unbeatable ambiance. The breakfast nook and family room both open to a patio—a perfect arrangement for informal entertaining. The dining room is sure to please with elegant pillars separating it from the sunken living room. A media room delights both with its shape and by being convenient to the nearby kitchen or great for snack runs. A private garden surrounds the master bath and its spa tub and enormous walk-in closet. The master bedroom is enchanting with a fireplace and access to the outdoors. Additional family bedrooms come in a variety of different shapes and sizes; Bedroom 4 reigns over the second floor and features its own full bath.

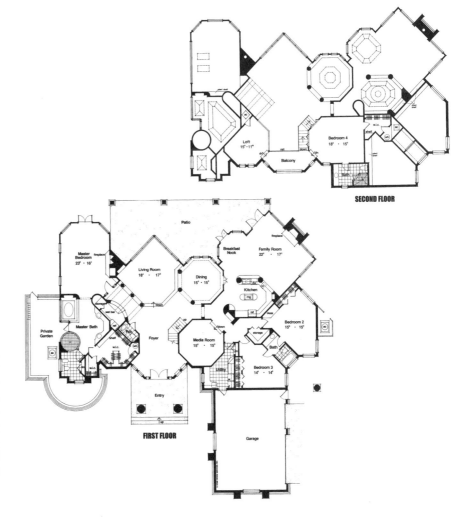

OPTIONAL LAYOUT

plan
HPT9600456

STYLE: MEDITERRANEAN
SQUARE FOOTAGE: 4,222
BONUS SPACE: 590 SQ. FT.
BEDROOMS: 4
BATHROOMS: 5
WIDTH: 83' - 10"
DEPTH: 112' - 0"
FOUNDATION: SLAB

SEARCH ONLINE @ EPLANS.COM

The striking facade of this magnificent estate is just the beginning of the excitement you will encounter inside. The foyer passes the formal dining room on the way to the columned gallery. The formal living room opens to the rear patio and has easy access to a wet bar. The contemporary kitchen has a work island and all the amenities for gourmet preparation. The family room will be a favorite for casual entertainment. The family sleeping wing begins with an octagonal vestibule and has three bedrooms with private baths. The master wing features a private garden and an opulent bath.

   ORDER BLUEPRINTS 24 HOURS, 7 DAYS A WEEK, AT 1-800-521-6797

ptan#
HPT9600457

STYLE: MEDITERRANEAN

MAIN LEVEL: 2,262 SQ. FT.

LOWER LEVEL: 1,822 SQ. FT.

TOTAL: 4,084 SQ. FT.

BEDROOMS: 4

BATHROOMS: 3½

WIDTH: 109' - 11"

DEPTH: 46' - 0"

FOUNDATION: BASEMENT

SEARCH ONLINE @ EPLANS.COM

This exquisite home is definitely Mediterranean, with its corner quoins, lintels, and tall entry. This home features a dining room, a massive family room with a fireplace, a gourmet kitchen with a breakfast area, and a laundry room. Finishing the first floor is a lavish master suite, which enjoys a vast walk-in closet, a sitting area, and a pampering private bath. The finished basement features three suites, two full baths, a pool room, and a recreation room/theater along with two storage rooms.

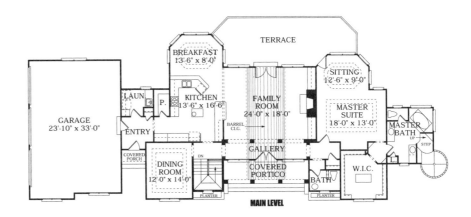

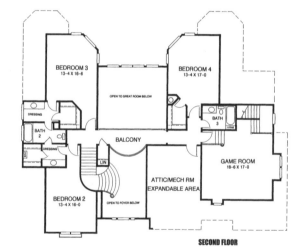

SECOND FLOOR

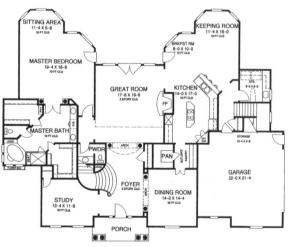

FIRST FLOOR

plan #
HPT9600458

STYLE: TRANSITIONAL
FIRST FLOOR: 2,639 SQ. FT.
SECOND FLOOR: 1,625 SQ. FT.
TOTAL: 4,264 SQ. FT.
BEDROOMS: 4
BATHROOMS: 3½
WIDTH: 73' - 8"
DEPTH: 58' - 6"
FOUNDATION: SLAB,
CRAWLSPACE, BASEMENT

SEARCH ONLINE @ EPLANS.COM

This home offers both luxury and practicality. A study and dining room flank the foyer, and the great room offers a warming fireplace and double French-door access to the rear yard. A butler's pantry acts as a helpful buffer between the kitchen and the columned dining room. Double bays at the rear of the home form the keeping room and the breakfast room on one side and the master bedroom on the other. Three family bedrooms and two baths grace the second floor. A game room is perfect for casual family time.

ORDER BLUEPRINTS 24 HOURS, 7 DAYS A WEEK, AT 1-800-521-6797

plan
HPT9600459

STYLE: MEDITERRANEAN

FIRST FLOOR: 3,264 SQ. FT.

SECOND FLOOR: 1,671 SQ. FT.

TOTAL: 4,935 SQ. FT.

BEDROOMS: 4

BATHROOMS: 3½

WIDTH: 96' - 10"

DEPTH: 65' - 1"

FOUNDATION: SLAB, CRAWLSPACE

SEARCH ONLINE @ EPLANS.COM

A very efficient plan that minimizes the use of enclosed hallways creates a very open feeling of space and orderliness. As you enter the foyer you have a clear view through the spacious living room to the covered patio beyond. The formal dining area is to the right and the master wing is to the left. The master bedroom boasts a sitting area, access to the patio, His and Hers walk-in closets, dual vanities, a walk-in shower, and a compartmented toilet. A large island kitchen overlooks the nook and family room, which has a built-in media/fireplace wall. Three additional bedrooms and two full baths complete the plan.

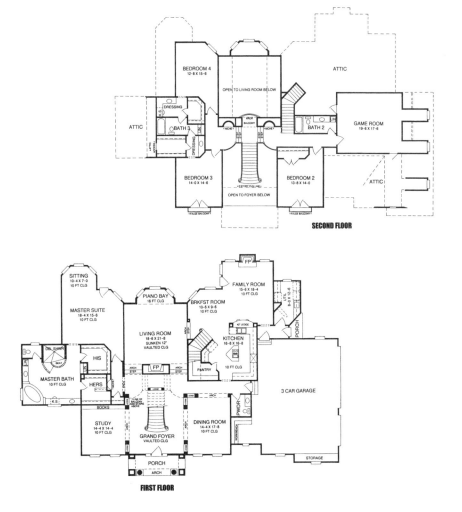

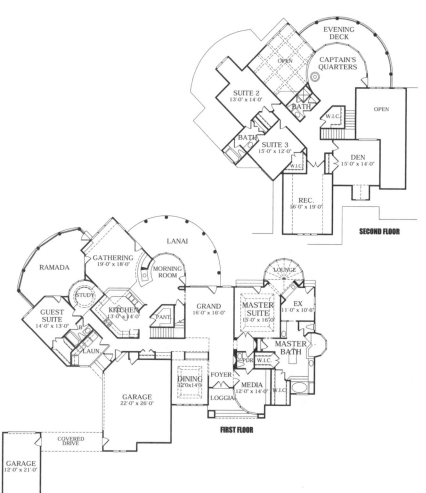

SECOND FLOOR

FIRST FLOOR

plan #
HPT9600460

STYLE: MEDITERRANEAN
FIRST FLOOR: 3,329 SQ. FT.
SECOND FLOOR: 1,485 SQ. FT.
TOTAL: 4,814 SQ. FT.
BEDROOMS: 4
BATHROOMS: 4½
WIDTH: 106' - 6"
DEPTH: 89' - 10"
FOUNDATION: CRAWLSPACE

SEARCH ONLINE @ EPLANS.COM

A curved wall of windows leads to the entrance of this fine home. The lavish master suite features two walk-in closets, a deluxe bath with a separate tub and shower and two vanities, a separate lounge, and an exercise room. On the other end of the home, find the highly efficient kitchen, a spacious gathering room, a round morning room and study, and a quiet guest suite. The second level is equally deluxe with two suites, a recreation room, a quiet den, and a large open area called the captain's quarters that opens to an evening deck.

FOR MORE DETAILED INFORMATION, PLEASE CHECK THE FLOOR PLANS CAREFULLY.

plan (#)
HPT9600461

STYLE: ITALIANATE
FIRST FLOOR: 3,734 SQ. FT.
SECOND FLOOR: 418 SQ. FT.
TOTAL: 4,152 SQ. FT.
BEDROOMS: 3
BATHROOMS: 4½
WIDTH: 82' - 0"
DEPTH: 107' - 0"
FOUNDATION: SLAB

SEARCH ONLINE @ EPLANS.COM

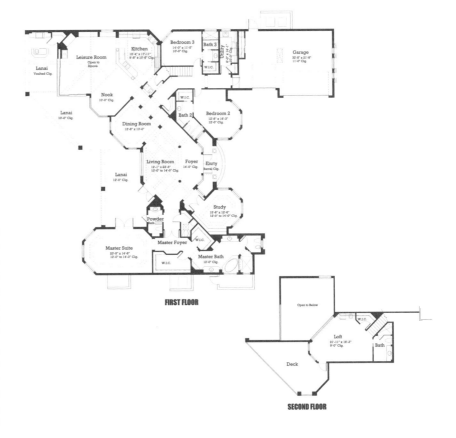

FIRST FLOOR

SECOND FLOOR

Softly angled turrets add sweet drama to this dreamy Mediterranean manor, as a rambling interior plays function to everyday life. Beautiful interior columns in the foyer offer a fine introduction to open spacious rooms. A secluded master suite features a beautiful bay window, a coffered ceiling, and French doors to the lanai. Across the master foyer, the private bath satisfies the homeowners' needs by offering a whirlpool tub, separate shower, private vanities and two walk-in closets. Bedroom 2 includes a sitting bay, a walk-in closet, and a private bath. Upstairs, a spacious loft offers room for computers and books. A wet bar, walk-in closet, and full bath with a shower provide the possibility of converting this area to a bedroom suite.

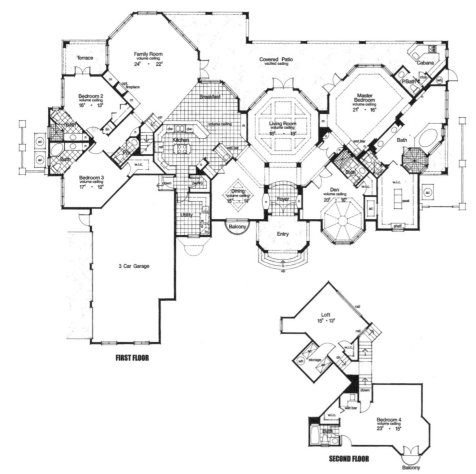

FIRST FLOOR

SECOND FLOOR

plan
HPT9600462

STYLE: MEDITERRANEAN

FIRST FLOOR: 3,739 SQ. FT.

SECOND FLOOR: 778 SQ. FT.

TOTAL: 4,517 SQ. FT.

BEDROOMS: 4

BATHROOMS: 5½ + ½

WIDTH: 105' - 0"

DEPTH: 84' - 0"

FOUNDATION: SLAB

SEARCH ONLINE @ EPLANS.COM

This estate embraces the style of an elegant region of Southern France. Double doors open to a formal columned foyer and give views of the octagonal living room beyond. To the left is the formal dining room that connects to the kitchen via a butler's pantry. To the right is an unusual den with octagonal reading space. The master wing is immense. It features a wet bar, private garden, and exercise area. Two secondary bedrooms have private baths; Bedroom 2 has a private terrace. An additional bedroom with a private bath resides on the second floor, making it a perfect student's retreat. Also on the second floor is a game loft and storage area.

plan
HPT9600463

STYLE: NEO-ECLECTIC

FIRST FLOOR: 2,899 SQ. FT.

SECOND FLOOR: 1,472 SQ. FT.

TOTAL: 4,371 SQ. FT.

BEDROOMS: 4

BATHROOMS: 3½

WIDTH: 69' - 4"

DEPTH: 76' - 8"

FOUNDATION: SLAB

SEARCH ONLINE @ EPLANS.COM

Finished with French Country adornments, this estate home is comfortable in just about any setting. Main living areas are sunk down just a bit from the entry foyer, providing them with soaring ceilings and sweeping views. The family room features a focal fireplace. A columned entry gains access to the master suite where separate sitting and sleeping areas are defined by a three-sided fireplace. There are three bedrooms upstairs; one has a private bath. The sunken media room on this level includes storage space. Look for the decks on the second level.

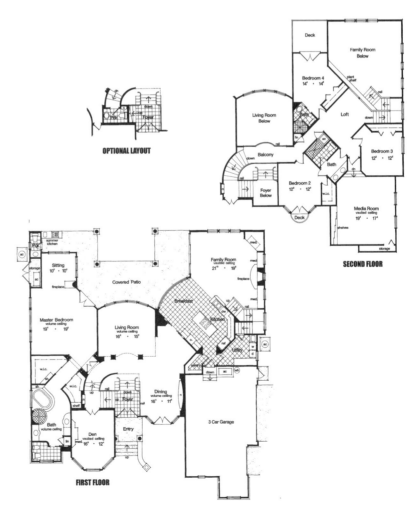

OPTIONAL LAYOUT

SECOND FLOOR

FIRST FLOOR

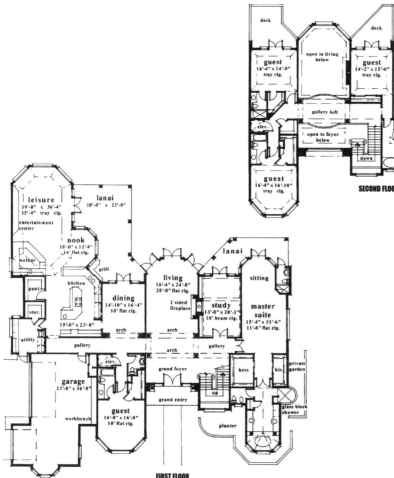

SECOND FLOOR

FIRST FLOOR

plan(#)
# HPT9600464

STYLE: MEDITERRANEAN
FIRST FLOOR: 4,760 SQ. FT.
SECOND FLOOR: 1,552 SQ. FT.
TOTAL: 6,312 SQ. FT.
BEDROOMS: 5
BATHROOMS: 6½
WIDTH: 98' - 0"
DEPTH: 103' - 8"
FOUNDATION: SLAB

SEARCH ONLINE @ EPLANS.COM

This home features a spectacular blend of arch-top windows, French doors, and balusters. An impressive informal leisure room has a 16-foot tray ceiling, an entertainment center, and a grand ale bar. The large gourmet kitchen is well appointed and easily serves the nook and formal dining room. The master suite has a large bedroom and a bayed sitting area. His and Hers vanities and walk-in closets and a curved glass-block shower are highlights in the bath. The staircase leads to the deluxe secondary guest suites, two of which have observation decks to the rear and each with their own full baths.

ORDER BLUEPRINTS 24 HOURS, 7 DAYS A WEEK, AT 1-800-521-6797

HOLZHAUER INC. 95

plan
HPT9600465

STYLE: MEDITERRANEAN

FIRST FLOOR: 3,546 SQ. FT.

SECOND FLOOR: 1,213 SQ. FT.

TOTAL: 4,759 SQ. FT.

BEDROOMS: 4

BATHROOMS: 3½

WIDTH: 96' - 0"

DEPTH: 83' - 0"

FOUNDATION: BASEMENT

SEARCH ONLINE @ EPLANS.COM

This grand home offers an elegant, welcoming residence with a Mediterranean flair. Beyond the grand foyer, the spacious living room provides views of the rear grounds and opens to the veranda and rear yard through three pairs of French doors. An arched galley hall leads past the formal dining room to the family areas. Here, an ample gourmet kitchen easily serves the nook and the leisure room. The master wing includes a study or home office. Upstairs, each of three secondary bedrooms features a walk-in closet, and two bedrooms offer private balconies.

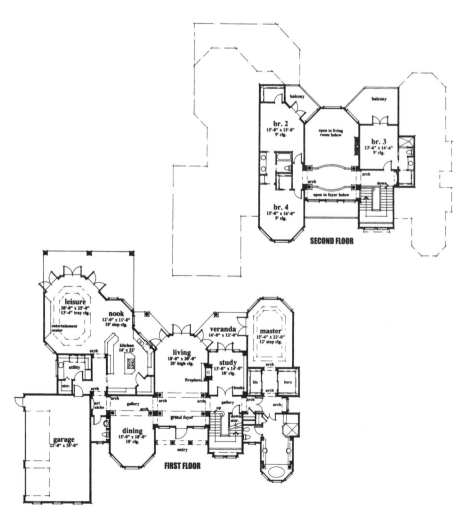

HOLZHAUER INC. 95

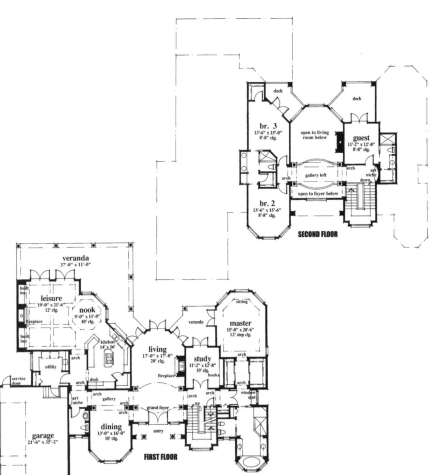

SECOND FLOOR

deck

br. 3
13'-6" x 15'-6"
8'-8" clg.

open to living room below

deck

guest
11'-2" x 12'-8"
8'-8" clg.

gallery loft

br. 2
13'-6" x 15'-6"
8'-8" clg.

open to foyer below

FIRST FLOOR

veranda
37'-0" x 11'-0"

leisure
19'-0" x 21'-6"
12' clg.

nook
9'-0" x 11'-0"
10' clg.

sitting

veranda

master
15'-8" x 20'-6"
12' step clg.

kitchen
14' x 16'

living
17'-0" x 17'-0"
20' clg.

study
11'-2" x 12'-8"
10' clg.

utility

service door

art niche

gallery

desk

fireplace

books

window seat

garage
21'-6" x 35'-2"

dining
13'-0" x 16'-0"
10' clg.

grand foyer

entry

up

plan
HPT9600466

STYLE: MEDITERRANEAN
FIRST FLOOR: 3,027 SQ. FT.
SECOND FLOOR: 1,079 SQ. FT.
TOTAL: 4,106 SQ. FT.
BEDROOMS: 4
BATHROOMS: 3½
WIDTH: 87' - 4"
DEPTH: 80' - 4"
FOUNDATION: BASEMENT

SEARCH ONLINE @ EPLANS.COM

The inside of this design is just as majestic as the outside. The grand foyer opens to a two-story living room with a fireplace and magnificent views. Dining in the bayed formal dining room will be a memorable experience. A well-designed kitchen is near a sunny nook and a leisure room with a fireplace and outdoor access. The master wing includes a separate study and an elegant private bath. The second level features a guest suite with its own bath and deck, two family bedrooms (Bedroom 3 also has its own deck), and a gallery loft with views to the living room below.

ORDER BLUEPRINTS 24 HOURS, 7 DAYS A WEEK, AT 1-800-521-6797

© The Sater Design Collection, Inc.

plan #
HPT9600467

STYLE: MEDITERRANEAN

FIRST FLOOR: 2,850 SQ. FT.

SECOND FLOOR: 1,155 SQ. FT.

TOTAL: 4,005 SQ. FT.

BONUS SPACE: 371 SQ. FT.

BEDROOMS: 4

BATHROOMS: 4½

WIDTH: 71' - 6"

DEPTH: 83' - 0"

FOUNDATION: SLAB

SEARCH ONLINE @ EPLANS.COM

Stone, stucco, and soaring rooflines combine to give this elegant Mediterranean design a stunning exterior. The interior is packed with luxurious amenities, from the wall of glass in the living room to the whirlpool tub in the master bath. A dining room and study serve as formal areas, and a leisure room with a fireplace offers a relaxing retreat. The first-floor master suite boasts a private bayed sitting area. Upstairs, all three bedrooms include private baths; Bedroom 2 and the guest suite also provide walk-in closets.

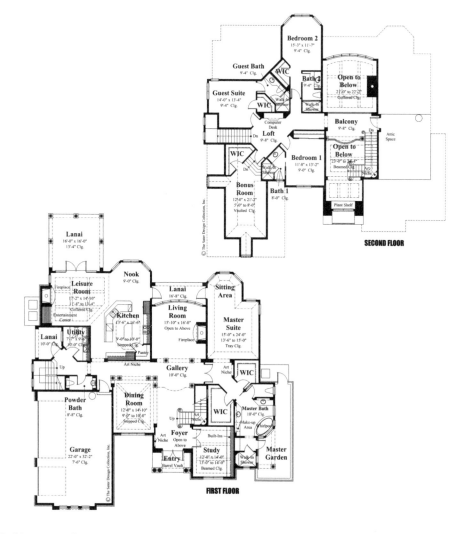

HOLZHAUER INC.

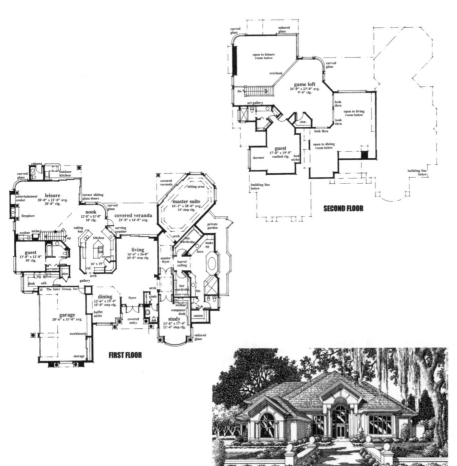

FIRST FLOOR

SECOND FLOOR

ALTERNATE EXTERIOR

plan
HPT9600468

STYLE: MEDITERRANEAN
FIRST FLOOR: 4,138 SQ. FT.
SECOND FLOOR: 1,269 SQ. FT.
TOTAL: 5,407 SQ. FT.
BEDROOMS: 3
BATHROOMS: 3½ + ½
WIDTH: 90' - 0"
DEPTH: 85' - 0"
FOUNDATION: SLAB

SEARCH ONLINE @ EPLANS.COM

Most of the living in this grand home takes place on the first floor. This allows two-story ceilings in the living room and the leisure room. The master suite occupies its own wing of the home and features a private study, a marvelous bath, and a bedroom with a step ceiling. Two guest suites are perfect for family and friends. The upstairs suite is completely private. Features that may already be on your wish list include a private master suite garden, abundant built-ins, a three-car garage, impressive storage, and covered outdoor spaces. The leisure room features corner sliding glass doors and a wet bar. Two different exteriors are available for this home, please specify when ordering.

© The Sater Design Collection, Inc.

plan#

HPT9600469

STYLE: SPANISH COLONIAL
FIRST FLOOR: 3,025 SQ. FT.
SECOND FLOOR: 1,639 SQ. FT.
TOTAL: 4,664 SQ. FT.
BONUS SPACE: 294 SQ. FT.
BEDROOMS: 4
BATHROOMS: 4½
WIDTH: 70' - 0"
DEPTH: 100' - 0"
FOUNDATION: SLAB

SEARCH ONLINE @ EPLANS.COM

A Spanish Colonial masterpiece, this family-oriented design is ideal for entertaining. Double doors reveal a foyer, with a columned dining room to the right and a spiral staircase enclosed in a turret to the left. Ahead, the great room opens above to a soaring coffered ceiling. Here, a bowed window wall and a two-sided fireplace (shared with the study) make an elegant impression. The country-style kitchen is a host's dream, with an adjacent wet bar, preparation island, and space for a six-burner cooktop. Near the leisure room, a bayed nook could serve as a breakfast or reading area. The master suite is a pampering sanctuary, with no rooms directly above and personal touches you will surely appreciate. Upstairs, two bedrooms, one with a window seat, and a guest suite with a balcony, all enjoy private baths and walk-in closets.

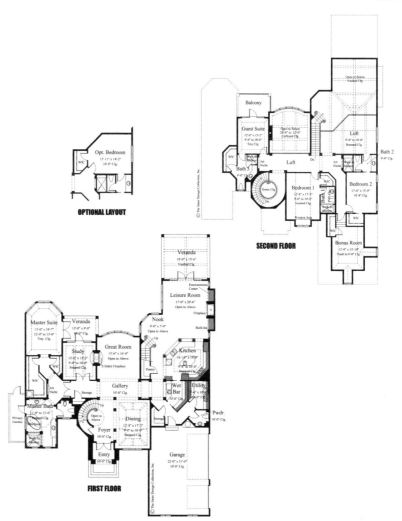

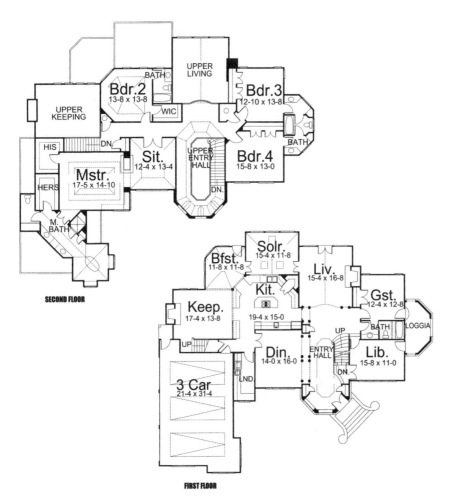

SECOND FLOOR

- BATH
- UPPER LIVING
- Bdr.2 13-8 x 13-8
- WIC
- Bdr.3 12-10 x 13-8
- UPPER KEEPING
- BATH
- HIS
- DN
- Sit. 12-4 x 13-4
- UPPER ENTRY HALL
- Bdr.4 15-8 x 13-0
- HERS
- Mstr. 17-5 x 14-10
- DN
- M. BATH

FIRST FLOOR

- Solr. 15-4 x 11-8
- Bfst. 11-8 x 11-8
- Liv. 15-4 x 16-8
- Kit. 19-4 x 15-0
- Gst. 12-4 x 12-8
- Keep. 17-4 x 13-8
- BATH
- LOGGIA
- UP
- UP
- Din. 14-0 x 16-0
- ENTRY HALL
- Lib. 15-8 x 11-0
- 3 Car 21-4 x 31-4
- LND.
- DN

ptan# HPT9600470

STYLE: FRENCH REVIVAL
FIRST FLOOR: 2,559 SQ. FT.
SECOND FLOOR: 2,140 SQ. FT.
TOTAL: 4,699 SQ. FT.
BEDROOMS: 5
BATHROOMS: 4
WIDTH: 80' - 0"
DEPTH: 67' - 0"
FOUNDATION: BASEMENT

SEARCH ONLINE @ EPLANS.COM

Accommodate your life's diverse pattern of formal occasions and casual times with this spacious home. The exterior of this estate presents a palatial bearing; the interior is both comfortable and elegant. Formal areas are graced with amenities to make entertaining easy. Casual areas are kept intimate, but no less large. The solarium serves both with skylights and terrace access. Guests will appreciate a private guest room and a bath with loggia access on the first floor. Family bedrooms and the master suite are upstairs. Note the gracious ceiling treatments in the master bedroom, its sitting room, and Bedroom 2.

plan#
HPT9600471

STYLE: FRENCH REVIVAL

FIRST FLOOR: 2,267 SQ. FT.

SECOND FLOOR: 2,209 SQ. FT.

TOTAL: 4,476 SQ. FT.

BEDROOMS: 4

BATHROOMS: 3½

WIDTH: 67' - 2"

DEPTH: 64' - 10"

FOUNDATION: CRAWLSPACE

SEARCH ONLINE @ EPLANS.COM

Keystone arches, a wonderful turret, vertical shutters, and decorative stickwork over the entry add to the charm of this fine home. A formal dining room at the front of the plan is complemented by the breakfast bay at the rear. An angled snack bar/counter separates the island kitchen from the gathering room. An adjoining recreation room offers a wet bar and a second flight of stairs to the sleeping quarters. Bay windows brighten the master suite and Suite 2, both with private baths. Two more bedrooms share a full bath that includes a dressing area and twin vanities. The laundry room is on this level for convenience.

SECOND FLOOR

FIRST FLOOR

REAR EXTERIOR

SECOND FLOOR

FIRST FLOOR

plan
HPT9600472

STYLE: FRENCH REVIVAL
FIRST FLOOR: 5,152 SQ. FT.
SECOND FLOOR: 726 SQ. FT.
TOTAL: 5,878 SQ. FT.
BEDROOMS: 4
BATHROOMS: 5½
WIDTH: 146' - 7"
DEPTH: 106' - 7"
FOUNDATION: SLAB

SEARCH ONLINE @ EPLANS.COM

Luxury abounds in this graceful manor. The formal living and dining rooms bid greeting as you enter and the impressive great room awaits more casual times with its cathedral ceiling and raised-hearth fireplace. A gallery hall leads to the kitchen and the family sleeping wing on the right and to the study, guest suite, and master suite on the left. The large island kitchen offers a sunny breakfast nook. The master suite includes a bayed sitting area, a dual fireplace shared with the study, and a luxurious bath. Each additional bedroom features its own bath and sitting area. Upstairs is a massive recreation room with a sunlit studio area and a bridge leading to an attic over the garage.

plan
HPT9600473

STYLE: FRENCH REVIVAL
FIRST FLOOR: 3,058 SQ. FT.
SECOND FLOOR: 2,076 SQ. FT.
TOTAL: 5,134 SQ. FT.
BEDROOMS: 4
BATHROOMS: 4½
WIDTH: 79' - 6"
DEPTH: 73' - 10"
FOUNDATION: SLAB,
BASEMENT, CRAWLSPACE

SEARCH ONLINE @ EPLANS.COM

This sweeping European facade, featuring a majestic turret-style bay, will easily be a standout in the neighborhood and a family favorite. The foyer opens to a spacious formal receiving area. Double doors from the living room open to the rear porch for outdoor activities. The master wing features a sitting area, a luxurious master bath, and two walk-in closets. The spacious island kitchen works with the bayed breakfast room for more intimate meals. The family room offers a warm and relaxing fireplace. A private, raised study, three-car garage, and utility room complete the first floor. Upstairs, three additional family bedrooms share the second floor with a music loft, hobby room, and game room.

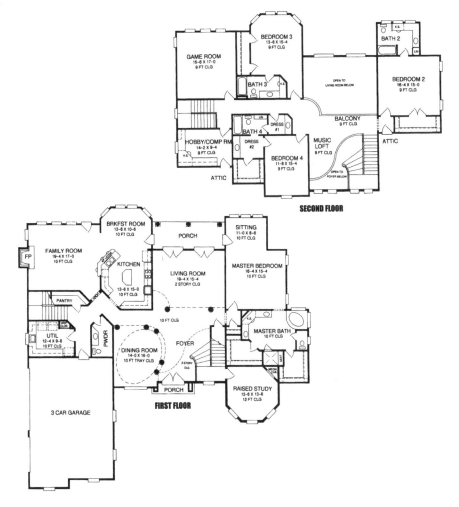

© 1999 Donald A. Gardner, Inc.

SECOND FLOOR

FIRST FLOOR

plan#
HPT9600474

STYLE: FRENCH ECLECTIC
FIRST FLOOR: 3,520 SQ. FT.
SECOND FLOOR: 1,638 SQ. FT.
TOTAL: 5,158 SQ. FT.
BONUS SPACE: 411 SQ. FT.
BEDROOMS: 5
BATHROOMS: 4½
WIDTH: 96' - 6"
DEPTH: 58' - 8"

SEARCH ONLINE @ EPLANS.COM

This custom-designed estate home elegantly combines stone and stucco, arched windows, and stunning exterior details under its formidable hipped roof. The two-story foyer is impressive with its grand staircase, tray ceiling, and overlooking balcony. Equally remarkable is the generous living room with a fireplace and a coffered two-story ceiling. The kitchen, breakfast bay, and family room with a fireplace are all open to one another for a comfortable, casual atmosphere. The first-floor master suite indulges with numerous closets, a dressing room, and a fabulous bath. Upstairs, four more bedrooms are topped by tray ceilings, three have walk-in closets and two have private baths. The three-car garage boasts additional storage and a bonus room above.

ORDER BLUEPRINTS 24 HOURS, 7 DAYS A WEEK, AT 1-800-521-6797

plan
HPT9600475

STYLE: FRENCH REVIVAL
FIRST FLOOR: 3,703 SQ. FT.
SECOND FLOOR: 1,427 SQ. FT.
TOTAL: 5,130 SQ. FT.
BONUS SPACE: 1,399 SQ. FT.
BEDROOMS: 4
BATHROOMS: 3½ + ½
WIDTH: 125' - 2"
DEPTH: 58' - 10"
FOUNDATION: WALKOUT BASEMENT

SEARCH ONLINE @ EPLANS.COM

This magnificent estate is detailed with exterior charm: a porte cochere connecting the detached garage to the house, a covered terrace, and oval windows. The first floor consists of a lavish master suite, a cozy library with a fireplace, a grand room/solarium combination, and an elegant formal dining room with another fireplace. Three bedrooms dominate the second floor—each features a walk-in closet. For the kids, there is a play-room, and, up another flight of stairs, is a room for future expansion into a deluxe studio with a fireplace. Over the three-car garage, there is space for a future mother-in-law or maid's suite.

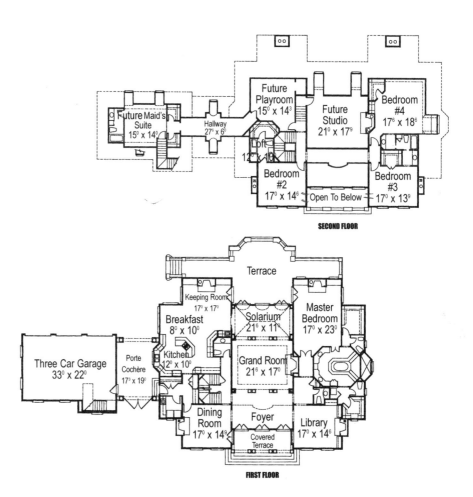

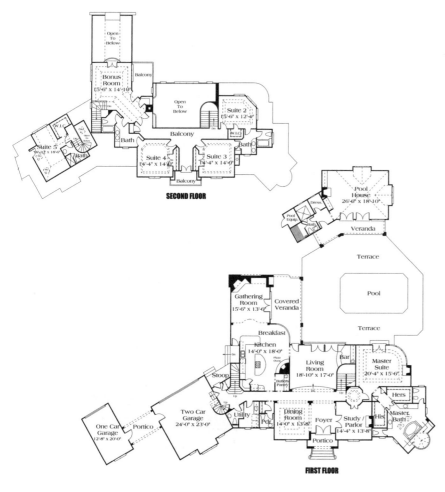

SECOND FLOOR

FIRST FLOOR

ptan#
HPT9600476

STYLE: FRENCH REVIVAL
FIRST FLOOR: 3,307 SQ. FT.
SECOND FLOOR: 1,642 SQ. FT.
TOTAL: 4,949 SQ. FT.
BONUS SPACE: 373 SQ. FT.
BEDROOMS: 5
BATHROOMS: 4½ + ½
WIDTH: 143' - 3"
DEPTH: 71' - 2"
FOUNDATION: CRAWLSPACE

SEARCH ONLINE @ EPLANS.COM

You'll be amazed at what this French Country estate has to offer. A study/parlor and a formal dining room announce a grand foyer. Ahead, the living room offers a wet bar and French doors to the rear property. The kitchen is dazzling, with an enormous pantry, oversized cooktop island... even a pizza oven! The gathering room has a corner fireplace and accesses the covered veranda. To the far right, the master suite is a delicious retreat from the world. A bowed window lets in light and a romantic fireplace makes chilly nights cozy. The luxurious bath is awe-inspiring, with a Roman tub and separate compartmented toilet areas—one with a bidet. Upstairs, three family bedrooms share a generous bonus room. A separate pool house is available, which includes a fireplace, full bath, and dressing area.

    ORDER BLUEPRINTS 24 HOURS, 7 DAYS A WEEK, AT 1-800-521-6797

plan
HPT9600477

STYLE: CLASSIC REVIVAL
FIRST FLOOR: 2,959 SQ. FT.
SECOND FLOOR: 1,326 SQ. FT.
TOTAL: 4,285 SQ. FT.
BONUS SPACE: 999 SQ. FT.
BEDROOMS: 4
BATHROOMS: 4½
WIDTH: 90' - 0"
DEPTH: 58' - 8"
FOUNDATION: WALKOUT BASEMENT

SEARCH ONLINE @ EPLANS.COM

The impressive two-story facade with a raised front pediment gives this home a stately image. Inside, the two-story foyer opens to an adjacent study and dining room. An open rail from the gallery above looks down on the foyer and living room below to give a very open appeal to the formal area of the home. The master suite, with rich appointments and access to the study, provides the perfect retreat. The kitchen is situated in a casual arrangement with the breakfast area and keeping room. Upstairs, three large bedrooms and an optional guest suite, maid's quarters, or bonus room meet the needs of a growing family.

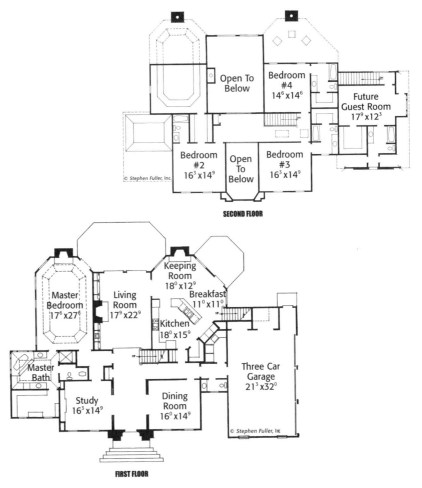

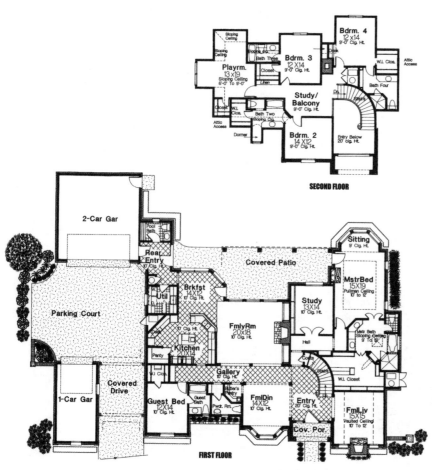

SECOND FLOOR

FIRST FLOOR

plan #
HPT9600478

STYLE: TUDOR REVIVAL
FIRST FLOOR: 3,248 SQ. FT.
SECOND FLOOR: 1,426 SQ. FT.
TOTAL: 4,674 SQ. FT.
BEDROOMS: 5
BATHROOMS: 5½ + ½
WIDTH: 99' - 10"
DEPTH: 74' - 10"
FOUNDATION: BASEMENT

SEARCH ONLINE @ EPLANS.COM

Multiple rooflines; a stone, brick, and siding facade; and an absolutely grand entrance combine to give this home the look of luxury. A striking family room showcases a beautiful fireplace framed with built-ins. The nearby breakfast room streams with light and accesses the rear patio. The kitchen features an island workstation, walk-in pantry, and plenty of counter space. A guest suite is available on the first floor, perfect for when family members visit. The first-floor master suite enjoys easy access to a large study, bayed sitting room, and luxurious bath. Private baths are also included for each of the upstairs bedrooms.

HPT9600479

STYLE: FRENCH REVIVAL
FIRST FLOOR: 3,420 SQ. FT.
SECOND FLOOR: 2,076 SQ. FT.
TOTAL: 5,496 SQ. FT.
BONUS SPACE: 721 SQ. FT.
BEDROOMS: 4
BATHROOMS: 5½ + ½
WIDTH: 85' - 6"
DEPTH: 102' - 6"
FOUNDATION: CRAWLSPACE

SEARCH ONLINE @ EPLANS.COM

Classic French elements along with style and balance give this home great curb appeal. The foyer leads to the gallery and on to the grand room, complete with its bank of windows, a fireplace, and built-ins. Two more fireplaces can be found in the family room and the study, off the foyer. A secondary staircase leads from the kitchen/breakfast area to the recreational room on the second level. A pool room and office are tucked over the garage, and three bedroom suites and four full baths complete this floor. The master suite is located on the first level, allowing for privacy.

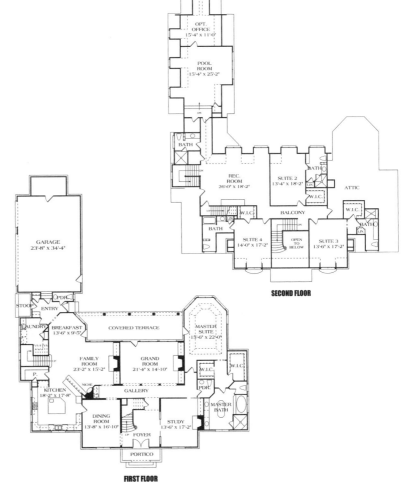

SECOND FLOOR

FIRST FLOOR

SECOND FLOOR

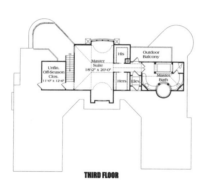

THIRD FLOOR

FIRST FLOOR

BASEMENT

plan #
HPT9600480

STYLE: FRENCH REVIVAL
FIRST FLOOR: 2,971 SQ. FT.
SECOND FLOOR: 2,199 SQ. FT.
THIRD FLOOR: 1,040 SQ. FT.
TOTAL: 6,210 SQ. FT.
BEDROOMS: 5
BATHROOMS: 4½
WIDTH: 84' - 4"
DEPTH: 64' - 11"
FOUNDATION: BASEMENT

SEARCH ONLINE @ EPLANS.COM

Symmetry and stucco present true elegance on the facade of this five-bedroom home, and the elegance continues inside over four separate levels. Note the formal and informal gathering areas on the main level: the music room, the lake living room, the formal dining room, and the uniquely shaped breakfast room. The second level contains three large bedroom suites—one with its own bath—a spacious girl's room for play time, and an entrance room to the third-floor master suite. Lavish is the only way to describe this suite. Complete with His and Hers walk-in closets, a private balcony, an off-season closet, and a sumptuous bath, this suite is designed to pamper the homeowner. In the basement is yet more room for casual get-togethers. Note the large sitting room as well as the hobby/crafts room. And tying it all together, an elevator offers stops at each floor.

plan
HPT9600481

STYLE: FRENCH REVIVAL

FIRST FLOOR: 3,568 SQ. FT.

SECOND FLOOR: 1,667 SQ. FT.

TOTAL: 5,235 SQ. FT.

BEDROOMS: 4

BATHROOMS: 3½

WIDTH: 86' - 8"

DEPTH: 79' - 0"

FOUNDATION: WALKOUT BASEMENT

SEARCH ONLINE @ EPLANS.COM

The ornamental stucco detailing on this home creates an Old World charm. The two-story foyer with a sweeping curved stair opens to the large formal dining room and study. The two-story great room overlooks the rear patio. A large kitchen with an island workstation opens to an octagonal-shaped breakfast room and the family room. The master suite, offering convenient access to the study, is complete with a fireplace, two walk-in closets, and a bath with twin vanities and a separate shower and tub. A staircase located off the family room provides additional access to the three second-floor bedrooms that each offer walk-in closets and plenty of storage.

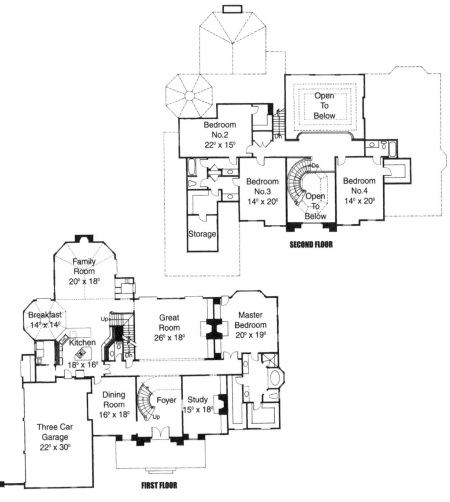

COPYRIGHT LARRY E. BELK

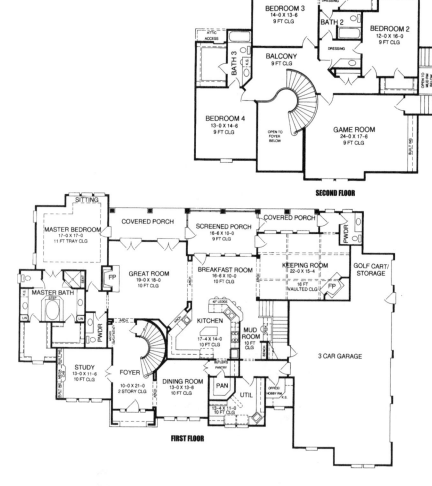

SECOND FLOOR

FIRST FLOOR

plan
HPT9600482

STYLE: ENGLISH REVIVAL
FIRST FLOOR: 3,033 SQ. FT.
SECOND FLOOR: 1,545 SQ. FT.
TOTAL: 4,578 SQ. FT.
BEDROOMS: 4
BATHROOMS: 3½ + ½
WIDTH: 91' - 6"
DEPTH: 63' - 8"
FOUNDATION: CRAWLSPACE,
SLAB, BASEMENT

SEARCH ONLINE @ EPLANS.COM

This majestic storybook cottage, from the magical setting of rural Europe, provides the perfect home for any large family with a wealth of modern comforts within. A graceful staircase cascades from the two-story foyer. To the left, a sophisticated study offers a wall of built-ins. To the right, a formal dining room is easily served from the island kitchen. The breakfast room accesses the rear screened porch. Fireplaces warm the great room and keeping room. Two sets of double doors open from the great room to the rear covered porch. The master bedroom features private porch access, a sitting area, lavish bath, and two walk-in closets. Upstairs, three additional family bedrooms offer walk-in closet space galore! The game room is great entertainment for both family and friends. A three-car garage with golf-cart storage completes the plan.

ORDER BLUEPRINTS 24 HOURS, 7 DAYS A WEEK, AT 1-800-521-6797

plan#
HPT9600483

STYLE: FRENCH REVIVAL
FIRST FLOOR: 2,608 SQ. FT.
SECOND FLOOR: 1,432 SQ. FT.
TOTAL: 4,040 SQ. FT.
BEDROOMS: 4
BATHROOMS: 3½
WIDTH: 89' - 10"
DEPTH: 63' - 8"
FOUNDATION: CRAWLSPACE, SLAB

SEARCH ONLINE @ EPLANS.COM

A distinctively French flair is the hallmark of this European design. Inside, the two-story foyer provides views to the huge great room beyond. A well-placed study off the foyer provides space for a home office. The kitchen, breakfast room, and sunroom are adjacent to lend a spacious feel. The great room is visible from this area through decorative arches. The master suite includes a roomy sitting area and a lovely bath with a centerpiece whirlpool tub flanked by half-columns. Upstairs, Bedrooms 2 and 3 share a bath that includes separate dressing areas.

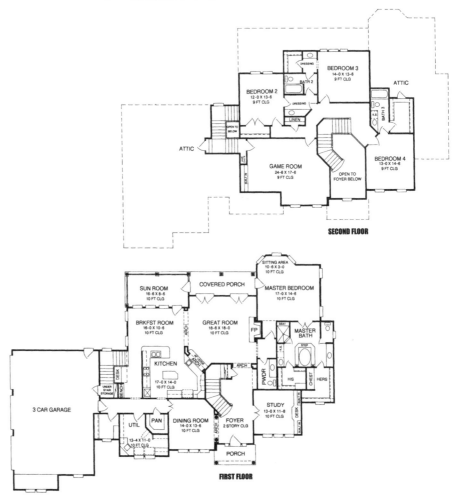

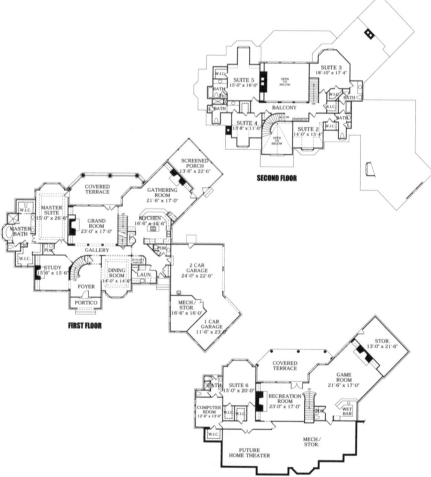

SECOND FLOOR

SUITE 5 15'-0" x 16'-0"
OPEN TO BELOW
SUITE 3 18'-10" x 17'-4"
BATH
W.I.C.
BALCONY
BATH
SUITE 4 13'-8" x 11'-0"
OPEN TO BELOW
SUITE 2 14'-0" x 15'-4"
W.I.C.
BATH

FIRST FLOOR

SCREENED PORCH 13'-6" x 22'-6"
COVERED TERRACE
GATHERING ROOM 21'-6" x 17'-0"
MASTER SUITE 15'-0" x 26'-6"
W.I.C.
GRAND ROOM 23'-0" x 17'-0"
KITCHEN 16'-6" x 16'-6"
MASTER BATH
GALLERY
PDR
STUDY 15'-6" x 15'-6"
DINING ROOM 14'-0" x 14'-6"
LAUN.
2 CAR GARAGE 24'-0" x 22'-6"
W.I.C.
FOYER
PORTICO
MECH./STOR. 16'-6" x 16'-0"
1 CAR GARAGE 11'-6" x 23'-0"

BASEMENT

STOR. 13'-0" x 21'-6"
COVERED TERRACE
GAME ROOM 21'-6" x 17'-0"
BATH
SUITE 6 15'-0" x 20'-0"
RECREATION ROOM 23'-0" x 17'-0"
COMPUTER ROOM 12'-6" x 13'-0"
W.I.C.
W.I.C.
WET BAR
W.I.C.
FUTURE HOME THEATER
MECH./STOR.

plan
HPT9600484

STYLE: FRENCH COUNTRY
FIRST FLOOR: 3,309 SQ. FT.
SECOND FLOOR: 1,694 SQ. FT.
TOTAL: 5,003 SQ. FT.
BEDROOMS: 5
BATHROOMS: 4½ + 2 HALF-BATHS
WIDTH: 112' - 9"
DEPTH: 97' - 0"
FOUNDATION: BASEMENT

SEARCH ONLINE @ EPLANS.COM

Three levels of luxury highlight the livability of this French Country manor. A formal portico welcomes you inside to a foyer that introduces a beautiful curved staircase. To the left, the study features a fireplace with flanking built-ins. To the right, the formal dining room is easily served from the island kitchen. The grand room presents a massive hearth and accesses the rear terrace. The gathering room and nook are also warmed by a fireplace and access a rear screened porch. The first-floor master suite provides a private bath and two walk-in closets. Upstairs, a balcony overlooks the grand room below. Four additional family bedrooms reside on this level. The basement level is reserved for pure entertainment and includes a recreation room, game room complete with a wet bar, a sitting room, future home theater, guest suite, and computer room.

ORDER BLUEPRINTS 24 HOURS, 7 DAYS A WEEK, AT 1-800-521-6797

plan
HPT9600485

STYLE: TUDOR REVIVAL
FIRST FLOOR: 3,767 SQ. FT.
SECOND FLOOR: 2,602 SQ. FT.
TOTAL: 6,369 SQ. FT.
BONUS SPACE: 677 SQ. FT.
BEDROOMS: 5
BATHROOMS: 6½
WIDTH: 131' - 0"
DEPTH: 99' - 11"
FOUNDATION: CRAWLSPACE

SEARCH ONLINE @ EPLANS.COM

Shake-covered dormers and stone accents high-light this brick country home. Tall chimneys support three fireplaces—in the gathering room, the grand room, and the study. Distinctive features include built-ins flanking the fireplaces, a large work island and walk-in pantry in the kitchen, and a laundry room with plenty of counter space for sorting and folding. The master suite offers private access to the terrace, two huge walk-in closets, and His and Hers baths sharing only the tub and shower area. Three flights of stairs lead upstairs to four family bedroom suites with private baths, a home theater, and bonus space over one of the two-car garages.

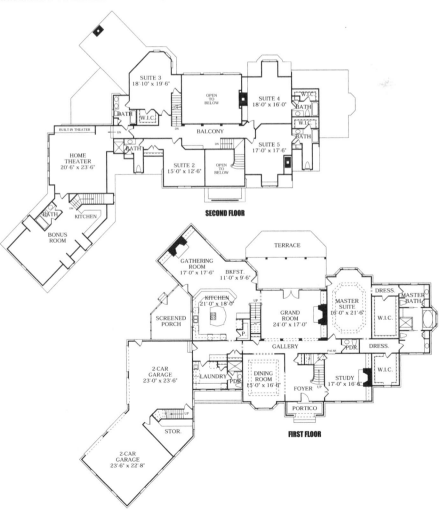

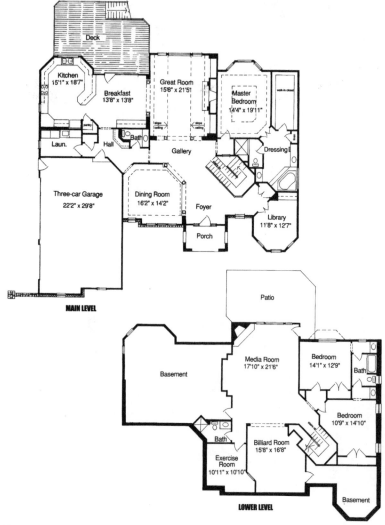

MAIN LEVEL

LOWER LEVEL

plan #
HPT9600486

STYLE: NEO-ECLECTIC
MAIN LEVEL: 2,582 SQ. FT.
LOWER LEVEL: 1,746 SQ. FT.
TOTAL: 4,328 SQ. FT.
BEDROOMS: 3
BATHROOMS: 3½
WIDTH: 70' - 8"
DEPTH: 64' - 0"
FOUNDATION: BASEMENT

SEARCH ONLINE @ EPLANS.COM

Stone accents provide warmth and character to the exterior of this home. An arched entry leads to the interior, where elegant window styles and dramatic ceiling treatments create an impressive showplace. The gourmet kitchen and breakfast room offer a spacious area for chores and family gatherings, and provide a striking view through the great room to the fireplace. An extravagant master suite and a library with built-in shelves round out the main level. On the lower level, two additional bedrooms, a media room, a billiards room, and an exercise room complete the home.

ORDER BLUEPRINTS 24 HOURS, 7 DAYS A WEEK, AT 1-800-521-6797

Bill McFadden

plan
HPT9600487

STYLE: TUDOR REVIVAL
FIRST FLOOR: 3,560 SQ. FT.
SECOND FLOOR: 1,783 SQ. FT.
TOTAL: 5,343 SQ. FT.
BEDROOMS: 4
BATHROOMS: 3½
WIDTH: 121' - 2"
DEPTH: 104' - 4"
FOUNDATION: CRAWLSPACE

SEARCH ONLINE @ EPLANS.COM

Multipane windows and a natural stone facade com-plement this Tudor Revival estate. A two-story foyer leads to a central grand room. A formal dining room to the front offers a fireplace. To the left, a cozy study with a second fireplace features built-in cab-inetry. The sleeping quarters offer luxurious ameni-ties. The master bath includes a whirlpool tub in a bumped-out bay, twin lavatories, and two walk-in closets. Upstairs, three suites, each with a walk-in closet and one with its own bath, share a balcony hall. A home theater beckons family and friends toward the back of the second floor. An apartment over the garage will house visiting or live-in rela-tives or may be used as a maid's quarters.

REAR EXTERIOR

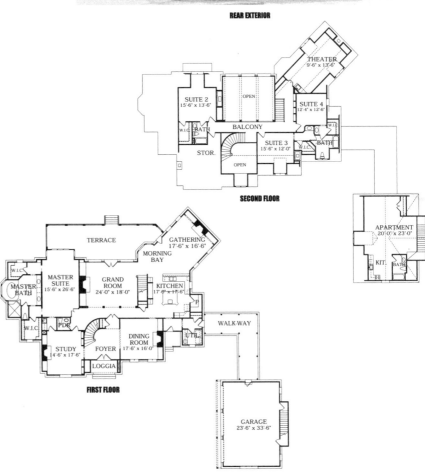

SECOND FLOOR

FIRST FLOOR

plan #
HPT9600488

STYLE: TUDOR
FIRST FLOOR: 3,170 SQ. FT.
SECOND FLOOR: 1,384 SQ. FT.
TOTAL: 4,554 SQ. FT.
BEDROOMS: 4
BATHROOMS: 4½
WIDTH: 99' - 0"
DEPTH: 64' - 1"
FOUNDATION: SLAB

SEARCH ONLINE @ EPLANS.COM

This French cottage design offers a charming array of exterior materials and a floor plan full of modern amenities. Inside, the foyer is flanked by the formal dining room and study. The master wing consists of a bedroom with a bayed sitting area, a pampering master bath, and two huge walk-in closets. A gallery hall leads to the formal living room with a fireplace. The kitchen, breakfast nook, and family room assemble the casual area of the home. Upstairs, three family bedrooms each offer their own private bath. The recreation room down the hall is perfect for a large family.

plan
HPT9600489

STYLE: TUDOR REVIVAL

SQUARE FOOTAGE: 4,825

BEDROOMS: 4

BATHROOMS: 4½

WIDTH: 155' - 6"

DEPTH: 60' - 4"

FOUNDATION: SLAB

SEARCH ONLINE @ EPLANS.COM

In this English Country design, a series of hipped roofs covers an impressive brick facade accented by fine wood detailing. Formal living and dining rooms flank the foyer, and the nearby media room is designed for home theater and surround sound. Fireplaces warm the living room and the family room, which also boasts a cathedral ceiling. The kitchen offers plenty of work space, a bright breakfast nook, and access to two covered patios. Convenient to all areas of the house, the barrel-vaulted study has a wall of windows and French doors that can be closed for private meetings or quiet relaxing. All four bedrooms have private baths and walk-in closets. The master suite has the added luxury of a glass-enclosed sitting area.

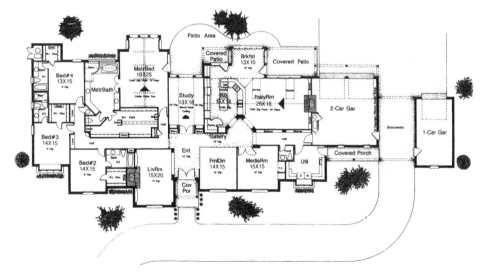

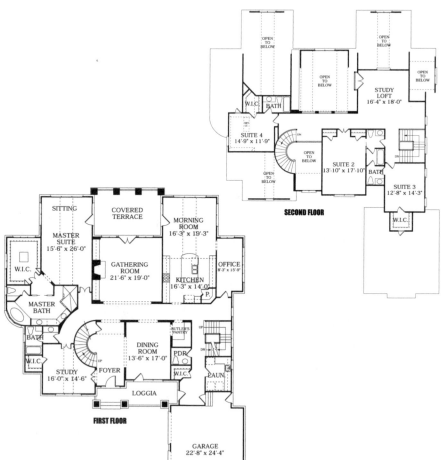

SECOND FLOOR

SUITE 4
14'-9" x 11'-9"

STUDY LOFT
16'-4" x 18'-0"

SUITE 2
13'-10" x 17'-10"

SUITE 3
12'-8" x 14'-3"

FIRST FLOOR

SITTING

COVERED TERRACE

MORNING ROOM
16'-3" x 19'-3"

MASTER SUITE
15'-6" x 26'-0"

GATHERING ROOM
21'-6" x 19'-0"

KITCHEN
16'-3" x 14'-0"

OFFICE
8'-3" x 15'-9"

MASTER BATH

DINING ROOM
13'-6" x 17'-0"

BUTLER'S PANTRY

STUDY
16'-0" x 14'-6"

FOYER

PDR

LAUN

LOGGIA

GARAGE
22'-8" x 24'-4"

plan #
HPT9600490

STYLE: CRAFTSMAN
FIRST FLOOR: 3,562 SQ. FT.
SECOND FLOOR: 1,594 SQ. FT.
TOTAL: 5,156 SQ. FT.
BEDROOMS: 4
BATHROOMS: 4½
WIDTH: 74' - 6"
DEPTH: 92' - 0"
FOUNDATION: BASEMENT

SEARCH ONLINE @ EPLANS.COM

Exquisite Craftsman character is the hallmark of this incredible design. A front loggia welcomes you inside to a foyer where the curved staircase is flanked by a dining room and a study. The gathering room is warmed by a fireplace flanked by built-ins. The master suite is enhanced with a spacious sitting area, pampering whirlpool bath, and large walk-in closet. The gourmet kitchen extends into a morning nook that accesses the rear covered terrace. Three additional suites are located upstairs, along with a spacious study loft. Don't miss the impressive basement level, which includes a recreation room served by a bar, an entertainment room with a fireplace, and access to the covered terrace, an exercise room, and a handy workshop area.

ORDER BLUEPRINTS 24 HOURS, 7 DAYS A WEEK, AT 1-800-521-6797

© 1996 Donald A. Gardner Architects, Inc.

HPT9600491

STYLE: TRADITIONAL
SQUARE FOOTAGE: 4,523
BEDROOMS: 4
BATHROOMS: 4½
WIDTH: 114' - 4"
DEPTH: 82' - 3"

SEARCH ONLINE @ EPLANS.COM

Large and rambling, this four-bedroom home is sure to please every member of the family. The homeowner will especially appreciate the master bedroom suite. Here, luxuries such as His and Hers bathrooms, two walk-in closets, and a tray ceiling await to pamper. For gatherings, the spacious great room lives up to its name, with a fireplace, built-ins, a tray ceiling, and access to the rear porch. The kitchen features an island cooktop/snack bar, a walk-in pantry and an adjacent bayed breakfast room. A sunroom is also nearby. Note the storage in the three-car garage.

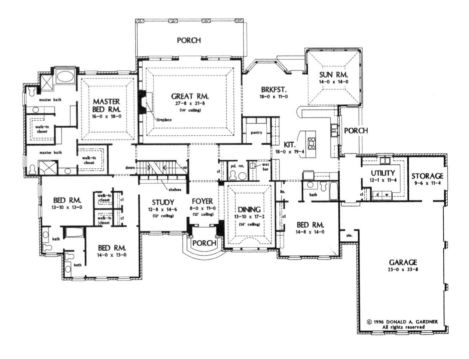

© 1996 DONALD A. GARDNER
All rights reserved

© 2001 Donald A. Gardner, Inc.

plan #
HPT9600492

STYLE: STICK VICTORIAN
MAIN LEVEL: 3,040 SQ. FT.
LOWER LEVEL: 1,736 SQ. FT.
TOTAL: 4,776 SQ. FT.
BEDROOMS: 5
BATHROOMS: 4½
WIDTH: 106' - 5"
DEPTH: 104' - 2"

SEARCH ONLINE @ EPLANS.COM

Looking a bit like a mountain resort, this fine Rustic style home is sure to be the envy of your neighborhood. Entering through the elegant front door, one finds an open staircase to the right and a spacious great room directly ahead. Here, a fireplace and a wall of windows give a cozy welcome. A lavish master suite begins with a sitting room complete with a fireplace and continues to a private porch, large walk-in closet, and sumptuous bedroom area. The gourmet kitchen adjoins a sunny dining room that offers access to a screened porch.

ORDER BLUEPRINTS 24 HOURS, 7 DAYS A WEEK, AT 1-800-521-6797

plan #
HPT9600493

STYLE: CRAFTSMAN
MAIN LEVEL: 2,932 SQ. FT.
LOWER LEVEL: 1,556 SQ. FT.
TOTAL: 4,488 SQ. FT.
BEDROOMS: 3
BATHROOMS: 3½ + ½
WIDTH: 114' - 0"
DEPTH: 82' - 11"
FOUNDATION: BASEMENT

SEARCH ONLINE @ EPLANS.COM

The interior of this home boasts high ceilings, a wealth of windows, and interestingly shaped rooms. A covered portico leads into a roomy foyer, which is flanked by an office/study, accessible through French doors. Just beyond the foyer, a huge, vaulted family room highlights columns decorating the entrance and positioned throughout the room. The island kitchen nestles close to the beautiful dining room, which features rear property views through the bay window and a nearby door to the terrace. The main level master suite enjoys two walk-in closets and a lavish bath, as well as access to a covered terrace. The lower level is home to the remaining bedrooms, including Suites 2 and 3, an abundance of storage, a recreation room, and a large mechanical/storage room.

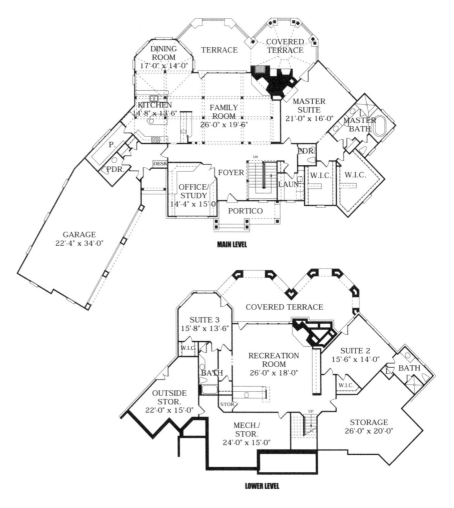

SECOND FLOOR

FIRST FLOOR

plan #
HPT9600494

STYLE: FEDERAL
FIRST FLOOR: 2,482 SQ. FT.
SECOND FLOOR: 1,722 SQ. FT.
TOTAL: 4,204 SQ. FT.
BEDROOMS: 5
BATHROOMS: 3½
WIDTH: 95' - 0"
DEPTH: 51' - 0"
FOUNDATION: BASEMENT

SEARCH ONLINE @ EPLANS.COM

This early American recreation is representative of the stately Federal styles of Colonial times. A beautifully curved stairway spirals into the foyer. To the left, double doors open to a family room. To the right, another set of double doors opens to a formal dining room. Straight ahead, the living room is brightened by a wall of windows overlooking the rear porch and is warmed by a cozy family fireplace. An island kitchen with a breakfast bar and a nook are located nearby. The garage conveniently connects directly to the kitchen. The first-floor master suite features rear-porch access, a private bath and an enormous walk-in closet. Upstairs, four additional family bedrooms share two hall baths.

plan⊕
HPT9600495

STYLE: FARMHOUSE

FIRST FLOOR: 3,120 SQ. FT.

SECOND FLOOR: 1,083 SQ. FT.

TOTAL: 4,203 SQ. FT.

BEDROOMS: 4

BATHROOMS: 4½

WIDTH: 118' - 1"

DEPTH: 52' - 2"

FOUNDATION: CRAWLSPACE, SLAB

SEARCH ONLINE @ EPLANS.COM

The blending of natural materials and a nostalgic farmhouse look give this home its unique character. Inside, a sophisticated floor plan includes all the amenities demanded by today's upscale family. Three large covered porches—one on the front and two on the rear—provide outdoor entertaining areas. The kitchen features a built-in stone fireplace visible from the breakfast and sun rooms. The master suite includes a large sitting area and a luxurious bath. Upstairs, two additional bedrooms and a large sitting room will please family and guests.

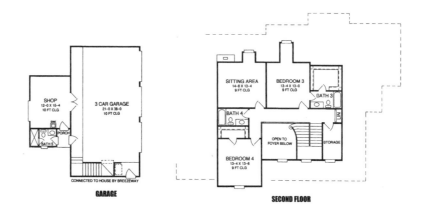

GARAGE

SECOND FLOOR

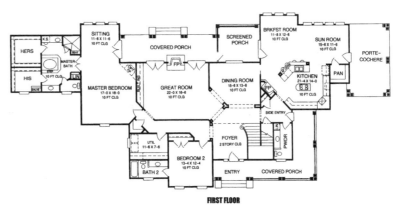

FIRST FLOOR

SECOND FLOOR

FIRST FLOOR

plan#
HPT9600496

STYLE: GEORGIAN
FIRST FLOOR: 2,603 SQ. FT.
SECOND FLOOR: 1,660 SQ. FT.
TOTAL: 4,263 SQ. FT.
BONUS SPACE: 434 SQ. FT.
BEDROOMS: 5
BATHROOMS: 5½ + ½
WIDTH: 98' - 0"
DEPTH: 56' - 8"
FOUNDATION: CRAWLSPACE,
BASEMENT

SEARCH ONLINE @ EPLANS.COM

This fine example of the Georgian style of architecture offers a wonderful facade with Southern charm. The foyer is flanked by the formal dining room and the living room. The efficient kitchen is situated between the sunny breakfast nook and the dining room. The family room opens to the backyard. The master suite enjoys an opulent bath and large walk-in closet. The second floor presents three bedrooms and two baths.

plan
HPT9600497

STYLE: COLONIAL REVIVAL
FIRST FLOOR: 2,938 SQ. FT.
SECOND FLOOR: 1,273 SQ. FT.
TOTAL: 4,211 SQ. FT.
BEDROOMS: 4
BATHROOMS: 3½ + ½
WIDTH: 101' - 10"
DEPTH: 74' - 2"
FOUNDATION: BASEMENT

SEARCH ONLINE @ EPLANS.COM

A pedimented entry, dormer window, and covered porch accent the facade of this staunch New England home. Inside, a sunken living room to the right of the foyer includes a fireplace. To the left, the study/library offers the option of built-in cabinets and adjoins the family room, which features a raised-hearth fireplace and access to a side porch. The island kitchen serves a morning room and a formal dining room. A tray ceiling augments the master suite, which offers a private terrace and a bath with a soothing whirlpool tub. Upstairs, two bedrooms with private dressing areas share a full bath; a third bedroom has its own bath.

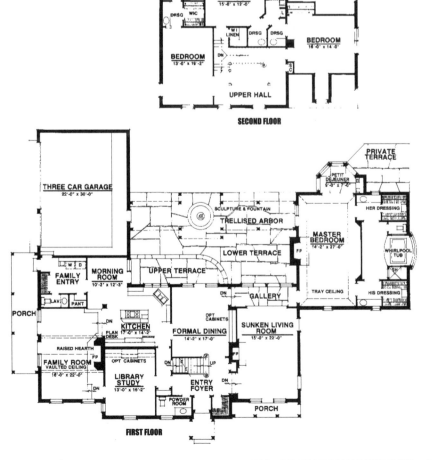

COURTESY OF LIVING CONCEPTS HOME PLANNING

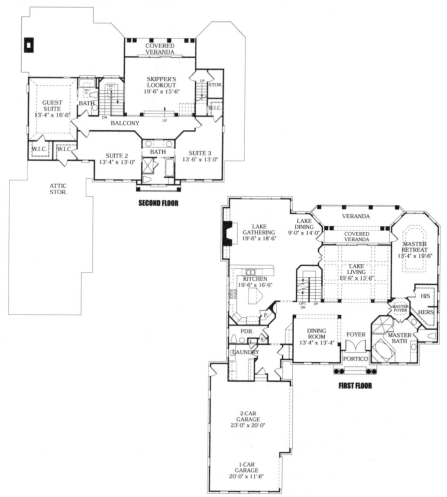

SECOND FLOOR

- COVERED VERANDA
- SKIPPER'S LOOKOUT 19'-6" x 15'-6"
- STOR.
- GUEST SUITE 13'-4" x 16'-6"
- BATH
- W.I.C.
- BALCONY
- W.I.C.
- W.I.C.
- SUITE 2 13'-4" x 13'-0"
- BATH
- SUITE 3 13'-6" x 13'-0"
- ATTIC STOR.

FIRST FLOOR

- VERANDA
- LAKE DINING 9'-0" x 14'-0"
- COVERED VERANDA
- MASTER RETREAT 13'-4" x 19'-6"
- LAKE GATHERING 19'-6" x 18'-6"
- LAKE LIVING 19'-6" x 15'-6"
- KITCHEN 19'-6" x 16'-6"
- HIS
- HERS
- MASTER FOYER
- P.
- PDR.
- DINING ROOM 13'-4" x 13'-4"
- FOYER
- MASTER BATH
- LAUNDRY
- PORTICO
- 2-CAR GARAGE 23'-0" x 20'-0"
- 1-CAR GARAGE 20'-0" x 11'-6"

plan #

HPT9600498

STYLE: NEO-ECLECTIC
FIRST FLOOR: 2,538 SQ. FT.
SECOND FLOOR: 1,581 SQ. FT.
TOTAL: 4,119 SQ. FT.
BEDROOMS: 4
BATHROOMS: 3½
WIDTH: 67' - 7"
DEPTH: 84' - 5"
FOUNDATION: BASEMENT

SEARCH ONLINE @ EPLANS.COM

Double columns flank the grand portico of this fine two-story home. Inside, the foyer presents a formal living room. This room welcomes all with a beam ceiling and a wall of windows to the rear veranda. The C-shaped kitchen offers a work-surface island, a walk-in pantry, and easy access to the spacious gathering room. Located on the first floor for privacy, the master suite is lavish with its luxuries. Upstairs, two family suites—each with a walk-in closet—share a full bath, and the large guest suite features another walk-in closet as well as a private bath.

ORDER BLUEPRINTS 24 HOURS, 7 DAYS A WEEK, AT 1-800-521-6797

COPYRIGHT 1993 LARRY E. BELK

plan#
HPT9600499

STYLE: COLONIAL REVIVAL

FIRST FLOOR: 3,722 SQ. FT.

SECOND FLOOR: 1,859 SQ. FT.

TOTAL: 5,581 SQ. FT.

BEDROOMS: 5

BATHROOMS: 4½

WIDTH: 127' - 10"

DEPTH: 83' - 9"

FOUNDATION: SLAB

SEARCH ONLINE @ EPLANS.COM

A richly detailed entrance sets the elegant tone of this luxurious design. Rising gracefully from the two-story foyer, the staircase is a fine prelude to the great room beyond, where a fantastic span of windows on the back wall overlooks the rear grounds. The dining room is located off the entry and has a lovely coffered ceiling. The kitchen, breakfast room, and sunroom are conveniently grouped for casual entertaining. The elaborate master suite enjoys a coffered ceiling, private sitting room, and spa-style bath. The second level consists of four bedrooms with private baths and a large game room featuring a rear stair.

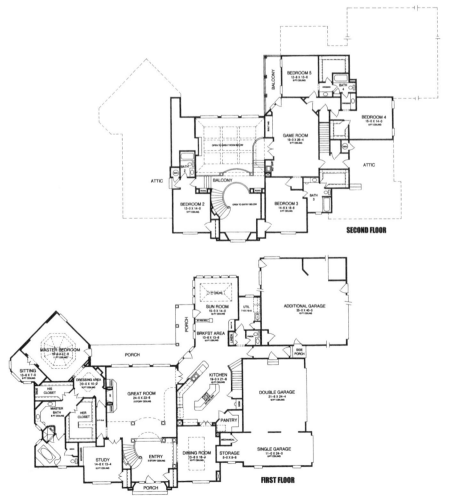

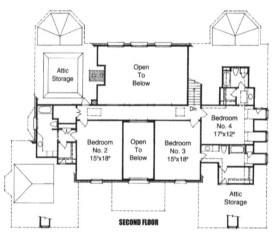

SECOND FLOOR

FIRST FLOOR

plan
HPT9600500

STYLE: GREEK REVIVAL
FIRST FLOOR: 3,509 SQ. FT.
SECOND FLOOR: 1,564 SQ. FT.
TOTAL: 5,073 SQ. FT.
BEDROOMS: 4
BATHROOMS: 4½ + ½
WIDTH: 86' - 6"
DEPTH: 67' - 3"
FOUNDATION: WALKOUT
BASEMENT

SEARCH ONLINE @ EPLANS.COM

Classic symmetry sets off this graceful exterior, with two sets of double columns framed by tall windows and topped with a detailed pediment. Just off the foyer, the study and dining room present an elegant impression. The gourmet kitchen offers a food-preparation island and a lovely breakfast bay. The central gallery hall connects casual living areas with the master wing. A delightful dressing area with a split vanity and a bay window indulges the lavish master bath. The master bedroom features a bumped-out glass sitting area, a tray ceiling, and a romantic fireplace. Upstairs, three bedroom suites are pampered with private baths.

plan#

HPT9600501

STYLE: GEORGIAN

FIRST FLOOR: 2,988 SQ. FT.

SECOND FLOOR: 1,216 SQ. FT.

TOTAL: 4,204 SQ. FT.

BONUS SPACE: 485 SQ. FT.

BEDROOMS: 4

BATHROOMS: 4½ + ½

WIDTH: 83' - 0"

DEPTH: 70' - 4"

FOUNDATION: CRAWLSPACE, BASEMENT

SEARCH ONLINE @ EPLANS.COM

Palladian windows, fluted pilasters, and a pedimented entry give this home a distinctly Colonial flavor. Inside, the two-story foyer is flanked by the formal dining and living rooms. The spacious, two-story family room features a fireplace, built-ins, and backyard access. A large country kitchen provides a work island, walk-in pantry, planning desk, and breakfast area. The lavish master suite offers a tremendous amount of closet space, as well as a pampering bath. A nearby study could also serve as a nursery. Upstairs, three bedrooms, each with a private bath, have access to the future recreation room over the garage.

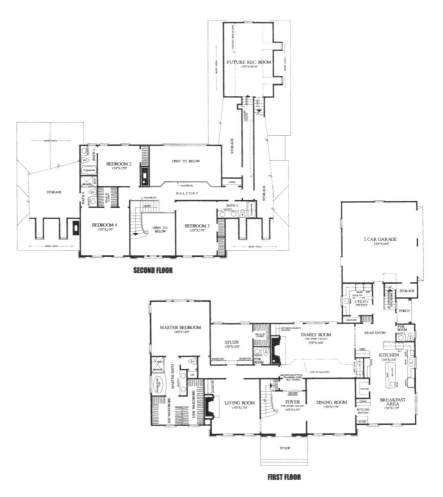

SECOND FLOOR

FIRST FLOOR

OPTIONAL BONUS ROOM BATH & CLOS. NOT INCLUDED IN TOTAL SQ. FT.

SLOPED CLG. 5.5 TO 9'

BDRM.#2 12X16

RECREATION ROOM 18X21

HALL

GALLERY

BDRM.#4 15X12

STAIRS

ENTRY BELOW

BDRM.#3 15X13

STORAGE

SECOND FLOOR

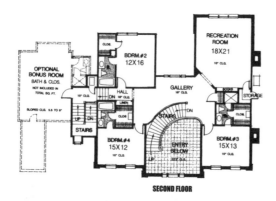

COVERED PATIO

FAMILY ROOM 17X22

COVERED PATIO

SITTING AREA 10x13

STUDY 12X14

MSTR. BDRM. 15X19

KIT 12X22

BRKFT. 11X20

FOUR CAR GARAGE

GALLERY

WALK-IN CLOSET

MSTR. BATH

FORMAL DINING 15X13

STAIRS

ENTRY

FORMAL LIVING 15X19

WALK-IN CLOSET

PORCH

FIRST FLOOR

plan
HPT9600502

STYLE: GEORGIAN
FIRST FLOOR: 3,599 SQ. FT.
SECOND FLOOR: 1,621 SQ. FT.
TOTAL: 5,220 SQ. FT.
BONUS SPACE: 356 SQ. FT.
BEDROOMS: 4
BATHROOMS: 5½
WIDTH: 108' - 10"
DEPTH: 53' - 10"
FOUNDATION: SLAB, BASEMENT

SEARCH ONLINE @ EPLANS.COM

A grand facade detailed with brick corner quoins, stucco flourishes, arched windows, and an elegant entrance presents this home. A spacious foyer is accented by curving stairs and flanked by a formal living room and a formal dining room. For cozy times, a through-fireplace is located between a large family room and a quiet study. The master bedroom is designed to pamper, with two walk-in closets, a two-sided fireplace, a bayed sitting area and a lavish private bath. Upstairs, three secondary bedrooms each have a private bath and a walk-in closet. Also on this level is a spacious recreation room, perfect for a game room or children's playroom.

plan
HPT9600503

STYLE: NEO-ECLECTIC

FIRST FLOOR: 3,170 SQ. FT.

SECOND FLOOR: 1,515 SQ. FT.

TOTAL: 4,685 SQ. FT.

BEDROOMS: 4

BATHROOMS: 3½

WIDTH: 76' - 0"

DEPTH: 75' - 8"

FOUNDATION: SLAB

SEARCH ONLINE @ EPLANS.COM

This modern Colonial home exhibits bold style and striking good looks. Historic details inside and out set the tone for a carefully designed plan with today's family in mind. Formal rooms at the front of the home welcome guests; to the rear, the family room basks in the sunlight of wide, tall windows. The well-planned kitchen is equipped with an island and walk-in pantry, and extends into a breakfast bay that is surrounded with natural light. The master wing includes a bayed sunroom and lavish bath with a corner whirlpool tub. Three generous bedrooms, a craft room, and a future game room inhabit the second floor.

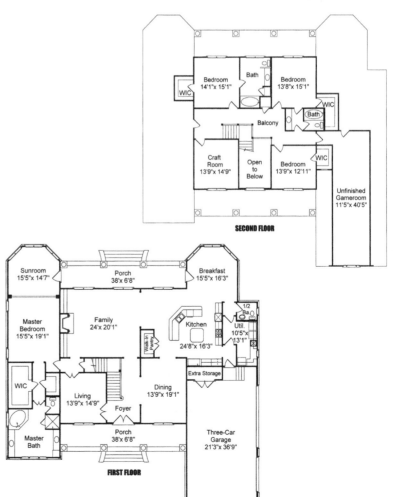

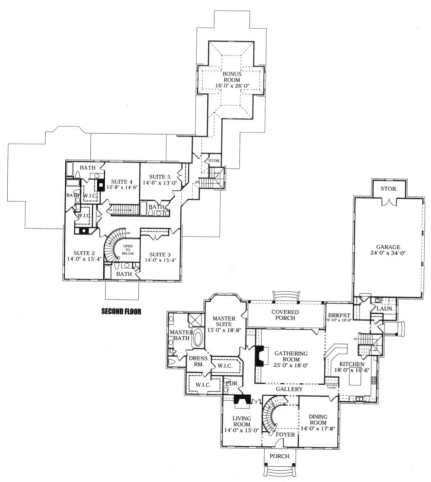

SECOND FLOOR

BONUS ROOM 16'-0" x 26'-0"

STOR.

BATH

SUITE 4 12'-8" x 14'-6"

SUITE 5 14'-6" x 13'-0"

BATH W.I.C.

BATH

W.I.C.

OPEN TO BELOW

SUITE 2 14'-0" x 15'-4"

SUITE 3 14'-0" x 15'-4"

BATH

STOR.

GARAGE 24'-0" x 34'-0"

FIRST FLOOR

MASTER SUITE 15'-0" x 18'-8"

COVERED PORCH

BRKFST 9'-10" x 10'-0"

LAUN.

MASTER BATH

GATHERING ROOM 25'-0" x 18'-0"

DRESS. RM.

W.I.C.

KITCHEN 18'-0" x 19'-6"

BUTLER'S PANTRY

W.I.C.

PDR.

GALLERY

LIVING ROOM 14'-0" x 15'-0"

DINING ROOM 14'-0" x 17'-8"

FOYER

PORCH

plan #
HPT9600504

STYLE: GEORGIAN
FIRST FLOOR: 3,120 SQ. FT.
SECOND FLOOR: 2,079 SQ. FT.
TOTAL: 5,199 SQ. FT.
BONUS SPACE: 587 SQ. FT.
BEDROOMS: 5
BATHROOMS: 5½
WIDTH: 92' - 11"
DEPTH: 99' - 10"
FOUNDATION: CRAWLSPACE

SEARCH ONLINE @ EPLANS.COM

This exquisite Williamsburg design is given a stately presence by its elegant brick exterior and a beautiful abundance of windows. Inside, the foyer introduces a curved staircase gracefully spiraling to the second floor. The formal living and dining rooms are found at the front of the home. Across the gallery, the spacious gathering room features a fireplace and overlooks the rear covered porch. To the right, the island kitchen connects to the breakfast room. A laundry room extends into the garage. The master wing features a luxurious bath, dressing room, and two walk-in closets. Four additional family bedrooms reside upstairs. A bonus room above the garage is great for a private home office.

plan#
HPT9600505

STYLE: NEO-CLASSICAL REVIVAL

FIRST FLOOR: 3,615 SQ. FT.

SECOND FLOOR: 1,066 SQ. FT.

TOTAL: 4,681 SQ. FT.

BONUS SPACE: 979 SQ. FT.

BEDROOMS: 4

BATHROOMS: 4½

WIDTH: 90' - 0"

DEPTH: 63' - 0"

FOUNDATION: BASEMENT

SEARCH ONLINE @ EPLANS.COM

A sweeping central staircase is just one of the impressive features of this lovely estate home. Four fireplaces—in the library, family room, grand room, and master-suite sitting room—add a warm glow to the interior; the master suite, grand room, and family room all open to outdoor terrace space. There's plenty of room for family and guests—a guest suite sits to the front of the plan, joining the master suite and two more family bedrooms. Upstairs, a large bonus area—possibly a mother-in-law suite—offers a petite kitchen and walk-in closet; a full bath is nearby.

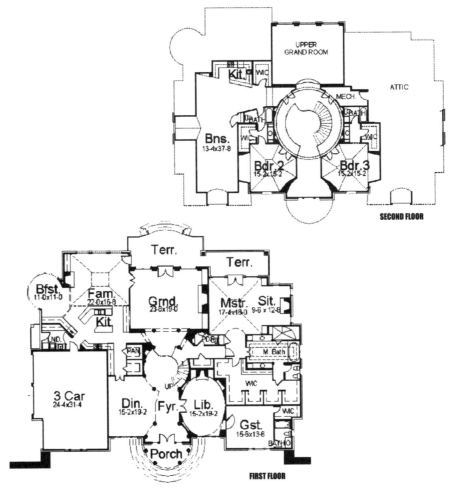

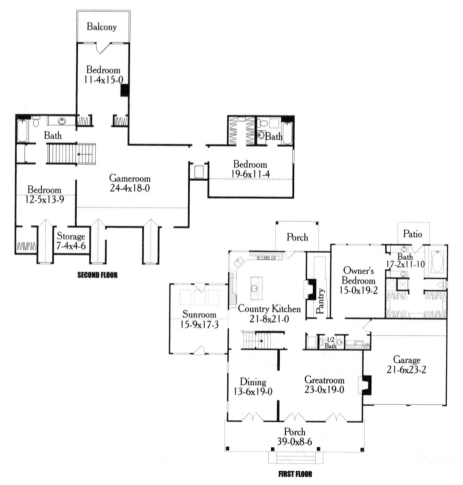

plan #

HPT9600506

STYLE: COLONIAL REVIVAL
FIRST FLOOR: 2,588 SQ. FT.
SECOND FLOOR: 1,578 SQ. FT.
TOTAL: 4,166 SQ. FT.
BEDROOMS: 4
BATHROOMS: 3½
WIDTH: 78' - 6"
DEPTH: 56' - 6"
FOUNDATION: SLAB,
CRAWLSPACE, BASEMENT

SEARCH ONLINE @ EPLANS.COM

This Colonial Revival home offers a Cape Cod exterior with a covered front porch. Symmetry abounds with three dormers above three pairs of French doors with fanlights. The addition of a sunroom on the left washes the interior with sunlight. The front-facing great room adjoins the formal dining room, which has easy access to the country kitchen where a fireplace adds atmosphere and an oversized pantry adds plenty of storage. The master suite is tucked away behind the garage for privacy with a full bath and enormous walk-in closet. The second floor holds three bedrooms, two full baths, and a spacious game room.

ORDER BLUEPRINTS 24 HOURS, 7 DAYS A WEEK, AT 1-800-521-6797

plan
HPT9600507

STYLE: COLONIAL REVIVAL

FIRST FLOOR: 3,170 SQ. FT.

SECOND FLOOR: 1,914 SQ. FT.

TOTAL: 5,084 SQ. FT.

BONUS SPACE: 445 SQ. FT.

BEDROOMS: 4

BATHROOMS: 3½

WIDTH: 100' - 10"

DEPTH: 65' - 5"

FOUNDATION: CRAWLSPACE

SEARCH ONLINE @ EPLANS.COM

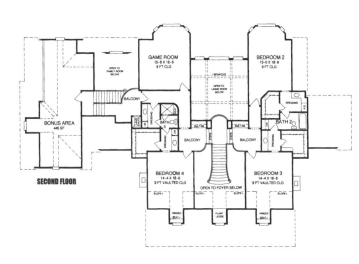

This elegantly appointed home is a beauty inside and out. A centerpiece stair rises gracefully from the two-story grand foyer. The kitchen, breakfast room, and family room provide open space for the gathering of family and friends. The beam-ceilinged study and the dining room flank the grand foyer and each includes a fireplace. The master bedroom features a cozy sitting area and a luxury master bath with His and Hers vanities and walk-in closets. Three large bedrooms and a game room complete the second floor. A large expand-able area is available at the top of the rear stair.

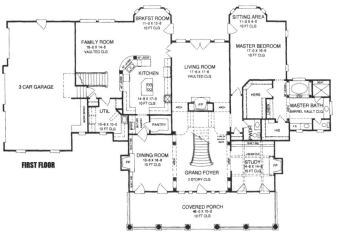

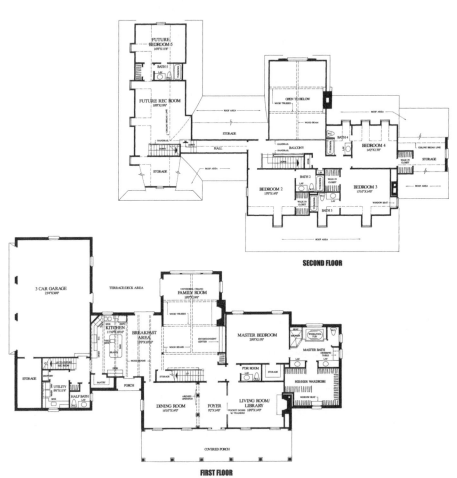

SECOND FLOOR

FIRST FLOOR

plan #
HPT9600508

STYLE: DUTCH COLONIAL
FIRST FLOOR: 3,016 SQ. FT.
SECOND FLOOR: 1,283 SQ. FT.
TOTAL: 4,299 SQ. FT.
BONUS SPACE: 757 SQ. FT.
BEDROOMS: 4
BATHROOMS: 4½ + ½
WIDTH: 105' - 0"
DEPTH: 69' - 0"
FOUNDATION: CRAWLSPACE

SEARCH ONLINE @ EPLANS.COM

With 10-foot wood-beam ceilings on the first floor and nine-foot ceilings upstairs, this Dutch Colonial offers plenty of aesthetic appeal. Enter the foyer to a dining room with an arched entrance on the left, and to the right, a living room/library with transom pocket doors and a fireplace. The kitchen is full of modern amenities, including an island with a vegetable sink and a snack bar. The master wing provides peace and quiet—and a few surprises! Details like a window seat, whirlpool tub, and storage space make it a welcome retreat. Upstairs, three bedroom suites, each with private baths, offer room for family and guests. Future space is available for expansion.

ORDER BLUEPRINTS 24 HOURS, 7 DAYS A WEEK, AT 1-800-521-6797

plan # HPT9600509

STYLE: SOUTHERN COLONIAL
FIRST FLOOR: 2,998 SQ. FT.
SECOND FLOOR: 1,556 SQ. FT.
TOTAL: 4,554 SQ. FT.
BONUS SPACE: 741 SQ. FT.
BEDROOMS: 4
BATHROOMS: 4½
WIDTH: 75' - 6"
DEPTH: 91' - 2"
FOUNDATION: CRAWLSPACE

SEARCH ONLINE @ EPLANS.COM

The paired double-end chimneys, reminiscent of the Georgian style of architecture, set this design apart from the rest. The covered entry opens to the columned foyer with the dining room on the left and the living room on the right, each enjoying the warmth and charm of a fireplace. Beyond the grand staircase, the family room delights with a third fireplace and a window wall that opens to the terrace. The expansive kitchen and breakfast area sit on the far left; the master suite is secluded on the the right with its pampering private bath. The second floor holds three additional bedrooms (including a second master bedroom,) three full baths, a computer room, and the future rec room.

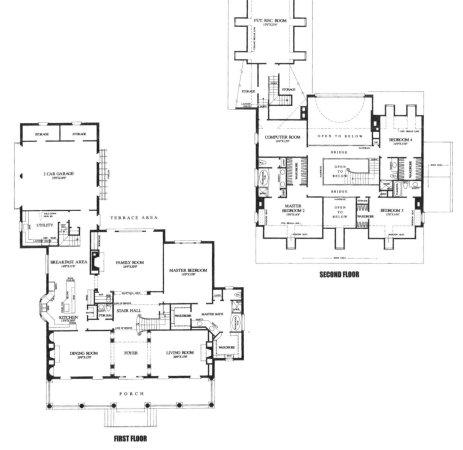

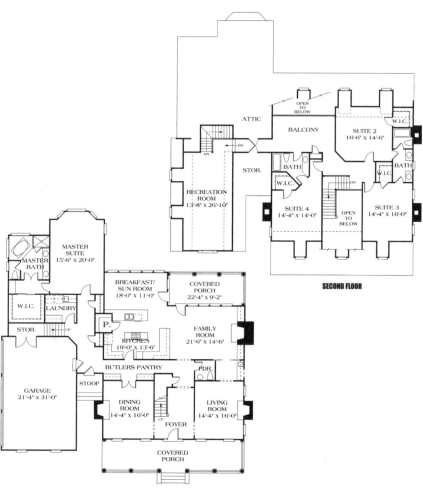

SECOND FLOOR

FIRST FLOOR

plan #
HPT9600510

STYLE: COLONIAL REVIVAL
FIRST FLOOR: 2,647 SQ. FT.
SECOND FLOOR: 1,372 SQ. FT.
TOTAL: 4,019 SQ. FT.
BONUS SPACE: 453 SQ. FT.
BEDROOMS: 4
BATHROOMS: 3½
WIDTH: 72' - 10"
DEPTH: 71' - 8"
FOUNDATION: CRAWLSPACE

SEARCH ONLINE @ EPLANS.COM

Pedimented dormers rise above a gabled roof and a welcoming front porch on this four-bedroom home. The foyer leads to the living and dining rooms, both warmed by fireplaces. A third fireplace, surrounded by built-in shelves, adorns the family room. Light flows into the breakfast room and family room through ribbons of windows. Gourmet cooks will enjoy the kitchen with its cooktop island, walk-in pantry, and acres of counter space. Note the butler's pantry that connects the kitchen and formal dining room. A separate wing houses the master suite and its private bath. Three bedroom suites featuring walk-in closets, two full baths, and a recreation room complete the second floor.

plan
HPT9600511

STYLE: COLONIAL REVIVAL

SQUARE FOOTAGE: 4,038

BEDROOMS: 4

BATHROOMS: 4½

WIDTH: 98' - 0"

DEPTH: 90' - 0"

FOUNDATION: BASEMENT, CRAWLSPACE, SLAB

SEARCH ONLINE @ EPLANS.COM

Reminiscent of the old Newport mansions, this luxury house has volume ceilings, a glamorous master suite with a hearth-warmed sitting area, a glassed-in sunroom, a home office, three porches with a deck, and a gourmet kitchen with a pantry. Graceful French doors are used for all the entrances and in the formal living and dining rooms. The magnificent kitchen boasts a large pantry. A centrally positioned family room is graced with a large fireplace and is accessed by the rear porch, living room and dining room.

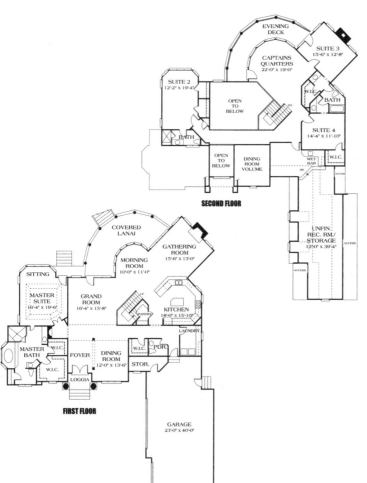

plan #

HPT9600512

STYLE: TRANSITIONAL

FIRST FLOOR: 2,547 SQ. FT.

SECOND FLOOR: 1,637 SQ. FT.

TOTAL: 4,184 SQ. FT.

BONUS SPACE: 802 SQ. FT.

BEDROOMS: 4

BATHROOMS: 3½

WIDTH: 74' - 0"

DEPTH: 95' - 6"

FOUNDATION: CRAWLSPACE

SEARCH ONLINE @ EPLANS.COM

Double columns flank a raised loggia that leads to a beautiful two-story foyer. Flanking this elegance to the right is a formal dining room. Straight ahead, under a balcony and defined by yet more pillars, is the spacious grand room. A bow-windowed morning room and a gathering room feature a full view of the rear lanai and beyond. The master bedroom suite is lavish with its amenities, which include a bayed sitting area, direct access to the rear terrace, a walk-in closet, and a sumptuous bath.

plan # HPT9600513

STYLE: COLONIAL REVIVAL

FIRST FLOOR: 3,414 SQ. FT.

SECOND FLOOR: 1,238 SQ. FT.

TOTAL: 4,652 SQ. FT.

BEDROOMS: 4

BATHROOMS: 3½

WIDTH: 90' - 6"

DEPTH: 78' - 9"

FOUNDATION: BASEMENT

SEARCH ONLINE @ EPLANS.COM

Country meets traditional in this splendid design. A covered front porch offers a place to enjoy the sunrise or place a porch swing. With the formal areas flanking the foyer, an open flow is established between the column-accented dining room and the library with its distinguished beam ceiling. The two-story great room features a wall of windows looking out to the rear grounds. On the left, the gourmet kitchen serves up casual and formal meals to the breakfast and hearth rooms with the dining room just steps away. The master bedroom enjoys a sitting area with an array of view-catching windows, a spacious dressing area, and an accommodating walk-in closet. Three family bedrooms—one with a private bath—complete the second level.

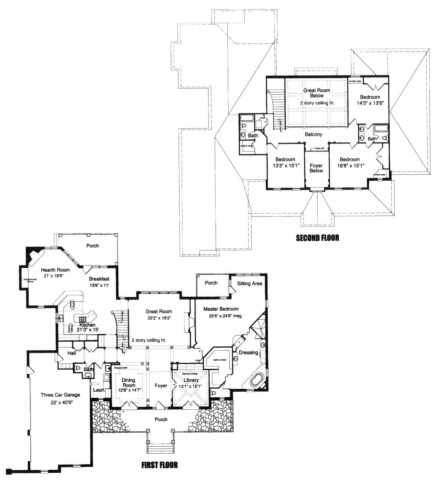

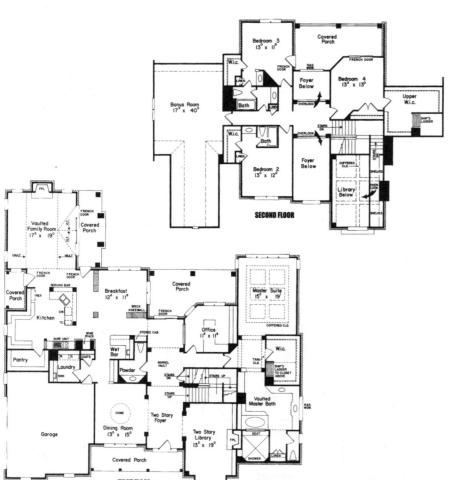

plan

HPT9600514

STYLE: TRADITIONAL
FIRST FLOOR: 3,218 SQ. FT.
SECOND FLOOR: 1,240 SQ. FT.
TOTAL: 4,458 SQ. FT.
BONUS SPACE: 656 SQ. FT.
BEDROOMS: 4
BATHROOMS: 3½
WIDTH: 76' - 0"
DEPTH: 73' - 10"
FOUNDATION: BASEMENT

SEARCH ONLINE @ EPLANS.COM

This design features a breathtaking facade with an upper rear balcony, four covered porches, and an inconspicuous side garage. The foyer is flanked by the dining room and the two-story library, which includes a fireplace and built-in bookcases. The elegant master bath provides dual vanities, a bright radius window, and a separate leaded-glass shower. A unique double-decker walk-in closet provides plenty of storage. Nearby, a home office offers stunning views of the backyard. Upstairs, two family bedrooms share a compartmented bath and a covered porch; a third offers a private bath. A bonus room is included for future expansion.

ORDER BLUEPRINTS 24 HOURS, 7 DAYS A WEEK, AT 1-800-521-6797

HELPFUL BOOKS FROM HOME PLANNERS · 1-800-322-6797

or visit our online bookstore at eplans.com

1 BIGGEST & BEST

1001 of our Best-Selling Plans in One Volume. 1,074 to 7,275 square feet. 704 pgs. $12.95 IK1

2 ONE-STORY

450 designs for all lifestyles. 810 to 5,400 square feet. 448 pgs. $9.95 OS2

3 MORE ONE-STORY

475 Superb One-Level Plans from 800 to 5,000 square feet. 448 pgs. $9.95 MO2

4 TWO-STORY

450 Best-Selling Designs for 1½ and 2-stories. 448 pgs. $9.95 TS2

5 VACATION
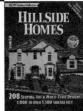
430 designs for Recreation, Retirement, and Leisure. 448 pgs. $9.95 VS3

6 HILLSIDE

208 designs for Split-Levels, Bi-Levels, Multi-Levels, and Walkouts. 224 pgs. $9.95 HH

7 FARMHOUSE

300 fresh designs from Classic to Modern. 320 pgs. $10.95 FCP

8 COUNTRY HOUSES

208 unique home plans that combine Traditional Style and Modern Livability. 224 pgs. $9.95 CN

9 BUDGET-SMART

200 Efficient Plans from 7 Top Designers, that you can really afford to build! 224 pgs. $8.95 BS

10 BARRIER-FREE

Over 1,700 products and 51 plans for Accessible Living. 128 pgs. $15.95 UH

11 ENCYCLOPEDIA

500 exceptional plans for all styles and budgets— The Best Book of its Kind! 528 pgs. $9.95 ENC3

12 SUN COUNTRY

175 Designs from Coastal Cottages to Stunning Southwesterns. 192 pgs. $9.95 SUN

13 AFFORDABLE

300 modest plans for savvy homebuyers. 256 pgs. $9.95 AH2

14 VICTORIAN

210 striking Victorian and Farmhouse designs from today's top designers. 224 pgs. $15.95 VDH2

15 ESTATE

Dream big! Eighteen designers showcase their biggest and best plans. 224 pgs. $16.95 EDH3

16 LUXURY

170 lavish designs, over 50% brand-new plans added to a most elegant collection. 192 pgs. $12.95 LD3

17 WILLIAM E. POOLE

100 classic house plans from William E. Poole. 224 pgs. $17.95 WP2

18 HUGE SELECTION

650 home plans— from Cottages to Mansions 464 pgs. $8.95 650

19 SOUTHWEST

120 designs in Santa Fe, Spanish, and Contemporary Styles. 192 pgs. $14.95 SI

20 COUNTRY CLASSICS

130 Best-Selling Home Plans from Donald A. Gardner. 192 pgs. $17.95 DAG2

21 COTTAGES

245 Delightful retreats from 825 to 3,500 square feet. 256 pgs. $10.95 COOL

22 CONTEMPORARY

The most complete and imaginative collection of contemporary designs available. 256 pgs. $10.95 CM2

23 FRENCH COUNTRY

Live every day in the French countryside using these plans, landscapes and interiors. 192 pgs. $14.95 PN

24 SOUTHWESTERN

138 designs that capture the spirit of the Southwest. 144 pgs. $10.95 SW

25 SHINGLE-STYLE

155 home plans from Classic Colonials to Breezy Bungalows. 192 pgs. $12.95 SNG

26 NEIGHBORHOOD

170 designs with the feel of main street America. 192 pgs. $12.95 TND

27 CRAFTSMAN

170 Home plans in the Craftsman and Bungalow style. 192 pgs. $12.95 CC

28 GRAND VISTAS
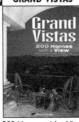
200 Homes with a View. 224 pgs. $10.95 GV

29 MULTI-FAMILY

115 Duplex, Multiplex & Townhome Designs. 128 pgs. $17.95 MFH

30 WATERFRONT

200 designs perfect for your Waterside Wonderland. 208 pgs. $10.95 WF

That's why we've expanded our library of do-it-yourself titles to help you along.

31 NATURAL LIGHT

223 Sunny home plans for all regions.
240 pgs. $8.95 NA

32 NOSTALGIA

100 Time-Honored designs updated with today's features.
224 pgs. $14.95 NOS

33 DREAM HOMES

50 luxury home plans. Over 300 illustrations.
256 pgs. $19.95 SOD2

34 NARROW-LOT
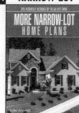
245 versatile designs up to 50 feet wide.
256 pgs. $9.95 NL2

35 SMALL HOUSES

Innovative plans for sensible lifestyles.
224 pgs. $8.95 SM2

36 OUTDOOR

74 easy-to-build designs, lets you create and build your own backyard oasis.
128 pgs. $9.95 YG2

37 GARAGES
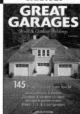
145 exciting projects from 64 to 1,900 square feet.
160 pgs. $9.95 GG2

38 PLANNER

A Planner for Building or Remodeling your Home.
318 pgs. $17.95 SCDH

39 HOME BUILDING

Everything you need to know to work with contractors and subcontractors.
212 pgs. $14.95 HBP

40 RURAL BUILDING
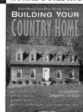
Everything you need to know to build your home in the country.
232 pgs. $14.95 BYC

41 VACATION HOMES

Your complete guide to building your vacation home.
224 pgs. $14.95 BYV

42 DECKS

A brand new collection of 120 beautiful and practical decks.
144 pgs. $9.95 DP2

43 GARDENS & MORE

225 gardens, landscapes, decks and more to enhance every home.
320 pgs. $19.95 GLP

44 EASY-CARE

41 special landscapes designed for beauty and low maintenance.
160 pgs. $14.95 ECL

45 BACKYARDS

40 designs focused solely on creating your own specially themed backyard oasis.
160 pgs. $14.95 BYL

46 BEDS & BORDERS
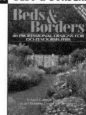
40 Professional designs for do-it-yourselfers
160 pgs. $14.95 BB

YES! PLEASE SEND ME THE BOOKS I'VE INDICATED:

B O O K   O R D E R   F O R M

To order your books, just check the box of the book numbered below and complete the coupon. We will process your order and ship it from our office within two business days. Send coupon and check (in U.S. funds).

❏ 1:IKI...........$12.95	❏ 17:WP2...........$17.95	❏ 33:SOD2...........$19.95
❏ 2:OS2...........$9.95	❏ 18:650...........$8.95	❏ 34:NL2...........$9.95
❏ 3:MO2...........$9.95	❏ 19:SI...........$14.95	❏ 35:SM2...........$8.95
❏ 4:TS2...........$9.95	❏ 20:DAG2...........$17.95	❏ 36:YG2...........$9.95
❏ 5:VS3...........$9.95	❏ 21:COOL...........$10.95	❏ 37:GG2...........$9.95
❏ 6:HH...........$9.95	❏ 22:CM2...........$10.95	❏ 38:SCDH...........$17.95
❏ 7:FCP...........$10.95	❏ 23:PN...........$14.95	❏ 39:HBP...........$14.95
❏ 8:CN...........$9.95	❏ 24:SW...........$10.95	❏ 40:BYC...........$14.95
❏ 9:BS...........$8.95	❏ 25:SNG...........$12.95	❏ 41:BYV...........$14.95
❏ 10:UH...........$15.95	❏ 26:TND...........$12.95	❏ 42:DP2...........$9.95
❏ 11:ENC3...........$9.95	❏ 27:CC...........$12.95	❏ 43:GLP...........$19.95
❏ 12:SUN...........$9.95	❏ 28:GV...........$10.95	❏ 44:ECL...........$14.95
❏ 13:AH2...........$9.95	❏ 29:MFH...........$17.95	❏ 45:BYL...........$14.95
❏ 14:VDH2...........$15.95	❏ 30:WF...........$10.95	❏ 46:BB...........$14.95
❏ 15:EDH3...........$16.95	❏ 31:NA...........$8.95	
❏ 16:LD3...........$12.95	❏ 32:NOS...........$14.95	

Books Subtotal .... $ _____
ADD Postage and Handling (allow 4–6 weeks for delivery) ...... $ _4.00_
Sales Tax: (AZ & MI residents, add state and local sales tax.) .... $ _____
YOUR TOTAL (Subtotal, Postage/Handling, Tax) .... $ _____

YOUR ADDRESS (PLEASE PRINT)

Name _____
Street _____
City _____ State _____ Zip _____
Phone (_____) _____ — _____

YOUR PAYMENT

TeleCheck® Checks By Phone℠ available
Check one: ❏ Check ❏ Visa ❏ MasterCard ❏ American Express
Required credit card information:

Credit Card Number_____
Expiration Date (Month/Year) / _____
Signature Required _____

Canadian Customers Order Toll Free 1-877-223-6389

Home Planners, LLC
3275 W. Ina Road, Suite 220, Dept. BK, Tucson, AZ 85741

HPT96

eplans.com

THE GATEWAY
TO YOUR NEW HOME

Looking for more plans? Got questions?
Try our one-stop home plans resource—eplans.com.

We'll help you streamline the plan selection process, so your dreams can become reality faster than you ever imagined. From choosing your home plan and ideal location to finding an experienced contractor, eplans.com will guide you every step of the way.

Mix and match! Explore! At eplans.com you can combine all your top criteria to find your perfect match. Search for your ideal home plan by any or all of the following:
> Number of bedrooms or baths,
> Total square feet,
> House style,
> Designer, and
> Cost.

With over 10,000 plans, the options are endless. Colonial, ranch, country, and Victorian are just a few of the house styles offered. Keep in mind your essential lifestyle features—whether to include a porch, fireplace, bonus room, or main-floor laundry room. And the garage—how many cars must it accommodate, if any? By filling out the preference page on eplans.com, we'll help you narrow your search.

At eplans.com we'll make the building process a snap to understand. At the click of a button you'll find a complete building guide. And our eplans task planner will create a construction calendar just for you. Here you'll find links to tips and other valuable information to help you every step of the way—from choosing a site to moving day.

For your added convenience, our home plans experts are available for live, one-on-one chats at eplans.com. Building a home may seem like a complicated project, but it doesn't have to be—particularly if you'll let us help you from start to finish.

COPYRIGHT DOS & DON'TS

Blueprints for residential construction (or working drawings, as they are often called in the industry) are copyrighted intellectual property, protected under the terms of United States Copyright Law and, therefore, cannot be copied legally for use in building. However, we've made it easy for you to get what you need to build your home, without violating copyright law. Following are some guidelines to help you obtain the right number of copies for your chosen blueprint design.

COPYRIGHT DO

■ Do purchase enough copies of the blueprints to satisfy building requirements. As a rule for a home or project plan, you will need a set for yourself, two or three for your builder and subcontractors, two for the local building department, and one to three for your mortgage lender. You may want to check with your local building department or your builder to see how many they need before you purchase. You may need to buy eight to 10 sets; note that some areas of the country require purchase of vellums (also called reproducibles) instead of blueprints. Vellums can be written on and changed more easily than blueprints. Also, remember, plans are only good for one-time construction.

■ Do consider reverse blueprints if you want to flop the plan. Lettering and numbering will appear backward, but the reversed sets will help you and your builder better visualize the design.

■ Do take advantage of multiple-set discounts at the time you place your order. Usually, purchasing additional sets after you receive your initial order is not as cost-effective.

■ Do take advantage of vellums. Though they are a little more expensive, they can be changed, copied, and used for one-time construction of a home. You will receive a copyright release letter with your vellums that will allow you to have them copied.

■ Do talk with one of our professional service representatives before placing your order. They can give you great advice about what packages are available for your chosen design and what will work best for your particular situation.

COPYRIGHT DON'T

■ Don't think you should purchase only one set of blueprints for a building project. One is fine if you want to study the plan closely, but will not be enough for actual building.

■ Don't expect your builder or a copy center to make copies of standard blueprints. They cannot legally—most copy centers are aware of this.

■ Don't purchase standard blueprints if you know you'll want to make changes to the plans; vellums are a better value.

■ Don't use blueprints or vellums more than one time. Additional fees apply if you want to build more than one time from a set of drawings. ■

HANLEY WOOD HOMEPLANNERS ADVANTAGE
SELECTION!
CONVENIENCE!
SERVICE!

hanley▲wood
HomePlanners
ORDERING IS EASY

GETTY IMAGES

HANLEY WOOD HOMEPLANNERS HAS EVERYTHING YOU NEED TO BUILD THE home of your dreams, and with more than 50 years of experience in the industry, we make it as easy as possible for you to reach those goals. Just follow the steps on these pages and you'll receive a high-quality, ready-to-build set of home blueprints, plus everything else you need to make your home-building effort a success.

WHERE TO BEGIN?
1. CHOOSE YOUR PLAN

■ Browsing magazines, books, and eplans.com can be an exciting and rewarding part of the home-building process. As you search, make a list of the things you want in your dream home—everything from number of bedrooms and baths to details like fireplaces or a home office.

■ Take the time to consider your lot and your neighborhood, and how the home you choose will fit with both. And think about the future—how might your needs change if you plan to live in this house for five, 10, or 20 years?

■ With thousands of plans available, chances are that you'll have no trouble discovering your dream home. If you find something that's almost perfect, our Customization Program can help make it exactly what you want.

■ Most important, be sure to enjoy the process of picking out your new home!

WHAT YOU'LL GET WITH YOUR ORDER

Each designer's blueprint set is unique, but they all provide everything you'll need to build your home. Here are some standard elements you can expect to find in your plans:

1. FRONT PERSPECTIVE
This artist's sketch of the exterior of the house gives you an idea of how the house will look when built and landscaped.

2. FOUNDATION PLANS
This sheet shows the foundation layout including support walls, excavated and unexcavated areas, if any, and foundation notes. If your plan features slab construction rather than a basement, the plan shows footings and details for a monolithic slab. This page, or another in the set, may include a sample plot plan for locating your house on a building site.

3. DETAILED FLOOR PLANS
These plans show the layout of each floor of the house. Rooms and interior spaces are carefully dimensioned and keys are given for cross-section details provided later in the plans. The positions of electrical outlets and switches are shown.

4. HOUSE CROSS-SECTIONS
Large-scale views show sections or cutaways of the foundation, interior walls, exterior walls, floors, stairways, and roof details. Additional cross-sections may show important changes in floor, ceiling, or roof heights, or the relationship of one level to another. Extremely valuable during construction, these sections show exactly how the various parts of the house fit together.

5. INTERIOR ELEVATIONS
These elevations, or drawings, show the design and placement of kitchen and bathroom cabinets, laundry areas, fireplaces, bookcases, and other built-ins. Little extras, such as mantelpiece and wainscoting drawings, plus molding sections, provide details that give your home that custom touch.

6. EXTERIOR ELEVATIONS
Every blueprint set comes with drawings of the front exterior, and may include the rear and sides of your house as well. These drawings give necessary notes on exterior materials and finishes. Particular attention is given to cornice detail, brick, and stone accents or other finish items that make your home unique.

hanley ▲ wood
HomePlanners
ORDERING IS EASY

HANLEY WOOD HOMEPLANNERS ADVANTAGE
ORDER 24 HOURS!
1-800-521-6797

GETTING DOWN TO BUSINESS
2. PRICE YOUR PLAN

BLUEPRINT PRICE SCHEDULE

PRICE TIERS	1-SET STUDY PACKAGE	4-SET BUILDING PACKAGE	8-SET BUILDING PACKAGE	1-SET REPRODUCIBLE*
P1	$20	$50	$90	$140
P2	$40	$70	$110	$160
P3	$70	$100	$140	$190
P4	$100	$130	$170	$220
P5	$140	$170	$210	$270
P6	$180	$210	$250	$310
A1	$440	$490	$540	$660
A2	$480	$530	$580	$720
A3	$530	$590	$650	$800
A4	$575	$645	$705	$870
C1	$625	$695	$755	$935
C2	$670	$740	$800	$1000
C3	$715	$790	$855	$1075
C4	$765	$840	$905	$1150
L1	$870	$965	$1050	$1300
L2	$945	$1040	$1125	$1420
L3	$1050	$1150	$1240	$1575
L4	$1155	$1260	$1355	$1735
SQ1				.35/SQ. FT.

PRICES SUBJECT TO CHANGE

* REQUIRES A FAX NUMBER

plan ⑂
READY TO ORDER

Once you've found your plan, get your plan number and turn to the following pages to find its price tier. Use the corresponding code and the Blueprint Price Schedule above to determine your price for a variety of blueprint packages.

Keep in mind that you'll need multiple sets to fulfill building requirements, and only reproducible sets may be altered or duplicated.

To the right you'll find prices for additional and reverse blueprint sets. Also note in the following pages whether your home has a corresponding Deck or Landscape Plan, and whether you can order our Quote One® cost-to-build information or a Materials List for your plan.

IT'S EASY TO ORDER
JUST VISIT
EPLANS.COM OR CALL
TOLL-FREE
1-800-521-6797

PRICE SCHEDULE FOR ADDITIONAL OPTIONS

OPTIONS FOR PLANS IN TIERS P1-P6	COSTS
ADDITIONAL IDENTICAL BLUEPRINTS FOR "P1-P6" PLANS	$10 PER SET
REVERSE BLUEPRINTS (MIRROR IMAGE) FOR "P1-P6" PLANS	$10 FEE PER ORDER
1 SET OF DECK CONSTRUCTION DETAILS	$14.95 EACH
DECK CONSTRUCTION PACKAGE (INCLUDES 1 SET OF "P1-P6" PLANS, PLUS 1 SET STANDARD DECK CONSTRUCTION DETAILS)	ADD $10 TO BUILDING PACKAGE PRICE

OPTIONS FOR PLANS IN TIERS A1-SQ1	COSTS
ADDITIONAL IDENTICAL BLUEPRINTS IN SAME ORDER FOR "A1-L4" PLANS	$50 PER SET
REVERSE BLUEPRINTS (MIRROR IMAGE) WITH 4- OR 8-SET ORDER FOR "A1-L4" PLANS	$50 FEE PER ORDER
SPECIFICATION OUTLINES	$10 EACH
MATERIALS LISTS	$70 EACH

IMPORTANT EXTRAS	COSTS
ELECTRICAL, PLUMBING, CONSTRUCTION, AND MECHANICAL DETAIL SETS	$14.95 EACH; ANY TWO $22.95; ANY THREE $29.95; ALL FOUR $39.95
HOME FURNITURE PLANNER	$15.95 EACH
REAR ELEVATION	$10 EACH
QUOTE ONE® SUMMARY COST REPORT	$29.95
QUOTE ONE® DETAILED COST ESTIMATE (FOR MORE DETAILS ABOUT QUOTE ONE®, SEE STEP 3.)	$60

IMPORTANT NOTE
■ THE 1-SET STUDY PACKAGE IS MARKED "NOT FOR CONSTRUCTION."

Source Key
HPT96

PLAN #	PRICE TIER	PAGE	MATERIALS LIST	QUOTE ONE®	DECK	DECK PRICE	LANDSCAPE	LANDSCAPE PRICE	REGIONS
HPT9600001	SQ1	5							
HPT9600002	SQ1	6	Y						
HPT9600003	SQ1	7							
HPT9600004	C2	8							
HPT9600005	C1	9							
HPT9600006	C1	10							
HPT9600007	C3	11							
HPT9600008	L1	12							
HPT9600009	L1	13							
HPT9600010	C2	14							
HPT9600011	C4	15							
HPT9600012	C4	16	Y						
HPT9600013	C1	17	Y						
HPT9600014	A3	18	Y						
HPT9600015	A3	19	Y						
HPT9600016	C1	20							
HPT9600017	A3	21	Y						
HPT9600018	A4	22	Y	Y					
HPT9600019	SQ1	23							
HPT9600020	A3	24	Y						
HPT9600021	A2	25							
HPT9600022	A4	26	Y						
HPT9600023	L2	27							
HPT9600024	C2	28							
HPT9600025	A4	29							
HPT9600026	A2	30							
HPT9600027	A3	31							
HPT9600028	A4	32							
HPT9600029	A2	33	Y						
HPT9600030	A3	34	Y						
HPT9600031	A2	35	Y						
HPT9600032	A2	35	Y						
HPT9600033	A2	36	Y						
HPT9600034	A1	36	Y						
HPT9600035	A2	37	Y						
HPT9600036	A1	37	Y						
HPT9600037	A3	38	Y						
HPT9600038	A2	39	Y						
HPT9600039	A2	39	Y						
HPT9600040	A3	40	Y						
HPT9600041	A2	40	Y						
HPT9600042	A2	41	Y						
HPT9600043	A3	41	Y	Y	ODA016	P2			
HPT9600044	A3	42	Y						
HPT9600045	A2	42							
HPT9600046	A4	43							
HPT9600047	A1	43							
HPT9600048	A3	44							
HPT9600049	A4	45							
HPT9600050	A4	45							
HPT9600051	A2	46	Y		ODA006	P2	OLA021	P3	123568
HPT9600052	A2	47	Y						
HPT9600053	A2	47							
HPT9600054	A3	48							
HPT9600055	A2	48	Y						
HPT9600056	A4	49							
HPT9600057	A4	49							
HPT9600058	A3	50	Y						
HPT9600059	A3	51	Y						
HPT9600060	A3	51	Y						
HPT9600061	A3	52	Y						
HPT9600062	A3	52	Y						
HPT9600063	A3	53	Y						
HPT9600064	A3	53	Y						
HPT9600065	A4	54							
HPT9600066	A2	55	Y						
HPT9600067	A2	55	Y						
HPT9600068	A1	56	Y						
HPT9600069	A2	56	Y						
HPT9600070	A2	57							
HPT9600071	A2	58							
HPT9600072	A3	59	Y						
HPT9600073	A3	59	Y						
HPT9600074	A2	60	Y						
HPT9600075	A4	60							
HPT9600076	A4	61							
HPT9600077	A1	62	Y						
HPT9600078	A1	62	Y						
HPT9600079	A1	63	Y						
HPT9600080	A4	63							
HPT9600081	A2	64							
HPT9600082	A2	64							
HPT9600083	A1	65	Y						
HPT9600084	A3	65	Y						
HPT9600085	A2	66	Y						
HPT9600086	A2	66							
HPT9600087	A4	67	Y						
HPT9600088	C1	68							
HPT9600089	C1	69							
HPT9600090	A4	70	Y						
HPT9600091	A3	71							
HPT9600092	A3	72							
HPT9600093	A3	72	Y						
HPT9600094	A4	73	Y						
HPT9600095	A4	73	Y	Y					
HPT9600096	A3	74							
HPT9600097	A3	74							
HPT9600098	A4	75							
HPT9600099	A3	75	Y						
HPT9600100	A4	76	Y						
HPT9600101	A3	76							
HPT9600102	A3	77	Y						
HPT9600103	A3	78	Y						
HPT9600104	A4	78	Y						
HPT9600105	A3	79	Y						
HPT9600106	A4	79	Y						
HPT9600107	C2	80							
HPT9600108	A4	80							
HPT9600109	C1	81							
HPT9600110	A4	81	Y						
HPT9600111	A4	82	Y						
HPT9600112	A4	82	Y						
HPT9600113	A4	83	Y						
HPT9600114	A4	83	Y						
HPT9600115	A3	84							
HPT9600116	A4	85	Y						
HPT9600117	C1	85							
HPT9600118	A3	86							
HPT9600119	A4	86	Y						
HPT9600120	A4	87	Y						
HPT9600121	A4	87	Y						
HPT9600122	A3	88							
HPT9600123	A3	88							
HPT9600124	A3	89							
HPT9600125	A4	90	Y						
HPT9600126	A4	90	Y						
HPT9600127	A4	91	Y						
HPT9600128	A3	91							
HPT9600129	A4	92			ODA013	P2	OLA001	P3	123568
HPT9600130	C1	92							
HPT9600131	A4	93	Y						
HPT9600132	A3	93	Y						

PLAN #	PRICE TIER	PAGE	MATERIALS LIST	QUOTE ONE®	DECK	DECK PRICE	LANDSCAPE	LANDSCAPE PRICE	REGIONS
HPT9600133	A3	94	Y						
HPT9600134	A3	95	Y						
HPT9600135	A3	96	Y						
HPT9600136	A3	96	Y						
HPT9600137	C1	97							
HPT9600138	A4	97	Y						
HPT9600139	C1	98							
HPT9600140	C1	98							
HPT9600141	C1	99							
HPT9600142	A4	99	Y						
HPT9600143	A3	100							
HPT9600144	C1	100							
HPT9600145	C1	101	Y						
HPT9600146	C1	102	Y						
HPT9600147	C1	103	Y						
HPT9600148	C1	104	Y						
HPT9600149	A4	105							
HPT9600150	A4	106							
HPT9600151	C2	106							
HPT9600152	A4	107	Y						
HPT9600153	C1	107	Y						
HPT9600154	C2	108	Y						
HPT9600155	C1	108	Y						
HPT9600156	SQ1	109							
HPT9600157	C2	109	Y	Y					
HPT9600158	C1	110	Y						
HPT9600159	C1	110							
HPT9600160	A4	111							
HPT9600161	A4	111							
HPT9600162	A4	112	Y						
HPT9600163	C2	113	Y	Y					
HPT9600164	C2	114							
HPT9600165	C2	115							
HPT9600166	C2	116							
HPT9600167	SQ1	117							
HPT9600168	A4	118	Y						
HPT9600169	C1	119	Y	Y			OLA025	P3	123568
HPT9600170	C2	120	Y	Y					
HPT9600171	C2	121							
HPT9600172	C1	122	Y						
HPT9600173	A4	123	Y						
HPT9600174	C2	124							
HPT9600175	C1	125	Y						
HPT9600176	C1	126							
HPT9600177	C2	127							
HPT9600178	C1	128	Y						
HPT9600179	C1	129	Y						
HPT9600180	C2	130							
HPT9600181	A4	131	Y				OLA004	P3	123568
HPT9600182	C2	132							
HPT9600183	C1	133							
HPT9600184	A4	134	Y						
HPT9600185	C1	134	Y						
HPT9600186	C2	135	Y						
HPT9600187	A4	136							
HPT9600188	A4	137							
HPT9600189	C1	138							
HPT9600190	A4	139							
HPT9600191	C1	140	Y		ODA012	P3	OLA010	P3	1234568
HPT9600192	C1	141	Y						
HPT9600193	C2	142							
HPT9600194	C1	143	Y						
HPT9600195	C1	144	Y						
HPT9600196	C1	144	Y						
HPT9600197	C1	145	Y						
HPT9600198	C1	146	Y						
HPT9600199	C1	146	Y						
HPT9600200	C1	147	Y						
HPT9600201	C1	148	Y						
HPT9600202	C2	148							
HPT9600203	C1	149	Y	Y					
HPT9600204	A4	149	Y						
HPT9600205	A4	150							
HPT9600206	C1	150							
HPT9600207	SQ1	151	Y						
HPT9600208	A4	151							
HPT9600209	C2	152							
HPT9600210	C2	152							
HPT9600211	C2	153							
HPT9600212	C2	153							
HPT9600213	C2	154							
HPT9600214	A4	154	Y						
HPT9600215	A4	155	Y	Y	ODA012	P3	OLA016	P4	1234568
HPT9600216	A4	155	Y						
HPT9600217	C1	156	Y						
HPT9600218	C1	156	Y						
HPT9600219	C2	157	Y	Y					
HPT9600220	A4	157	Y						
HPT9600221	C1	158	Y	Y	ODA006	P2	OLA021	P3	123568
HPT9600222	C2	159	Y	Y			OLA039	P3	347
HPT9600223	C1	160	Y						
HPT9600224	C1	161	Y						
HPT9600225	C1	162	Y						
HPT9600226	C2	163	Y						
HPT9600227	C1	164	Y						
HPT9600228	C2	165	Y	Y					
HPT9600229	C2	166	Y	Y	ODA012	P3	OLA024	P4	123568
HPT9600230	C1	167	Y						
HPT9600231	C2	168	Y	Y					
HPT9600232	C2	169	Y						
HPT9600233	C2	170	Y						
HPT9600234	C2	171	Y						
HPT9600235	C2	172	Y						
HPT9600236	C2	173	Y						
HPT9600237	C4	174							
HPT9600238	SQ1	175							
HPT9600239	C3	176							
HPT9600240	SQ1	177	Y	Y					
HPT9600241	C3	178							
HPT9600242	C3	179							
HPT9600243	C3	180							
HPT9600244	C3	181							
HPT9600245	C2	182	Y						
HPT9600246	C3	183	Y	Y			OLA014	P4	12345678
HPT9600247	C2	184	Y						
HPT9600248	C3	185	Y						
HPT9600249	C1	186	Y						
HPT9600250	C1	187	Y						
HPT9600251	C3	188							
HPT9600252	SQ1	189	Y	Y					
HPT9600253	C3	190							
HPT9600254	SQ1	191							
HPT9600255	C3	192							
HPT9600256	SQ1	193							
HPT9600257	C3	194							
HPT9600258	C3	195							
HPT9600259	C3	196	Y						
HPT9600260	C2	197	Y						
HPT9600261	C3	198	Y	Y					
HPT9600262	C3	199							
HPT9600263	C4	200					OLA004	P3	123568
HPT9600264	C2	201	Y	Y			OLA007	P4	1234568

PLAN #	PRICE TIER	PAGE	MATERIALS LIST	QUOTE ONE®	DECK	DECK PRICE	LANDSCAPE	LANDSCAPE PRICE	REGIONS
HPT9600265	SQI	202	Y						
HPT9600266	C2	203	Y						
HPT9600267	C2	204	Y						
HPT9600268	CI	205							
HPT9600269	SQI	206							
HPT9600270	C2	207					OLA004	P3	123568
HPT9600271	C2	208	Y				OLA015	P4	123568
HPT9600272	CI	209							
HPT9600273	CI	210	Y				OLA040	P4	123467
HPT9600274	SQI	211	Y	Y					
HPT9600275	C2	212	Y						
HPT9600276	A4	213	Y						
HPT9600277	CI	214							
HPT9600278	C2	215							
HPT9600279	C2	216	Y						
HPT9600280	C2	217							
HPT9600281	C2	218							
HPT9600282	C2	219							
HPT9600283	CI	220	Y	Y	ODA011	P2	OLA018	P3	12345678
HPT9600284	CI	221	Y						
HPT9600285	CI	222							
HPT9600286	CI	223							
HPT9600287	SQI	224	Y						
HPT9600288	C2	225	Y	Y	ODA011	P2	OLA025	P3	123568
HPT9600289	C2	226	Y						
HPT9600290	C2	227	Y						
HPT9600291	C2	228	Y						
HPT9600292	C2	229	Y						
HPT9600293	C2	230							
HPT9600294	C2	231	Y						
HPT9600295	C3	232							
HPT9600296	C2	233	Y						
HPT9600297	C3	234							
HPT9600298	C3	235							
HPT9600299	C3	236							
HPT9600300	C3	236							
HPT9600301	C3	237	Y	Y			OLA038	P3	7
HPT9600302	C2	238	Y	Y			OLA038	P3	7
HPT9600303	C3	239	Y	Y			OLA037	P4	347
HPT9600304	C3	240							
HPT9600305	C3	241	Y	Y			OLA036	P4	12356
HPT9600306	C3	242	Y	Y			OLA038	P3	7
HPT9600307	SQI	243	Y	Y			OLA001	P3	123568
HPT9600308	SQI	244							
HPT9600309	C2	245							
HPT9600310	C3	246							
HPT9600311	C3	247							
HPT9600312	C3	248							
HPT9600313	C4	249	Y						
HPT9600314	C2	250							
HPT9600315	C4	251	Y						
HPT9600316	C2	252							
HPT9600317	A4	253	Y						
HPT9600318	C4	254							
HPT9600319	C2	255							
HPT9600320	C3	256	Y	Y			OLA008	P4	1234568
HPT9600321	C2	257							
HPT9600322	C2	258							
HPT9600323	C2	259	Y						
HPT9600324	C4	260							
HPT9600325	C4	261							
HPT9600326	SQI	262	Y				OLA001	P3	123568
HPT9600327	C2	263	Y						
HPT9600328	C2	264	Y						
HPT9600329	C2	265	Y	Y			OLA008	P4	1234568
HPT9600330	SQI	266							

PLAN #	PRICE TIER	PAGE	MATERIALS LIST	QUOTE ONE®	DECK	DECK PRICE	LANDSCAPE	LANDSCAPE PRICE	REGIONS
HPT9600331	SQI	267							
HPT9600332	C4	268							
HPT9600333	C2	269							
HPT9600334	C2	270	Y						
HPT9600335	SQI	271	Y	Y					
HPT9600336	C3	272	Y						
HPT9600337	C3	273	Y						
HPT9600338	CI	274							
HPT9600339	SQI	275							
HPT9600340	C3	276	Y	Y			OLA024	P4	123568
HPT9600341	SQI	277	Y						
HPT9600342	SQI	278	Y	Y					
HPT9600343	C4	279							
HPT9600344	C4	280							
HPT9600345	CI	281							
HPT9600346	C4	282							
HPT9600347	C2	283	Y						
HPT9600348	C3	284							
HPT9600349	C4	285							
HPT9600350	SQI	286							
HPT9600351	SQI	287	Y						
HPT9600352	C4	288							
HPT9600353	C3	289							
HPT9600354	SQI	290	Y	Y					
HPT9600355	SQI	291	Y						
HPT9600356	SQI	292							
HPT9600357	SQI	293	Y	Y					
HPT9600358	SQI	294	Y						
HPT9600359	C3	295							
HPT9600360	C2	296							
HPT9600361	C2	297	Y						
HPT9600362	C2	298	Y	Y	ODA007	P3	OLA018	P3	12345678
HPT9600363	C4	299							
HPT9600364	C3	300	Y						
HPT9600365	C2	301							
HPT9600366	C4	302							
HPT9600367	C4	303							
HPT9600368	C3	304	Y						
HPT9600369	C3	305							
HPT9600370	SQI	306	Y						
HPT9600371	SQI	307	Y						
HPT9600372	C3	308	Y						
HPT9600373	C3	309							
HPT9600374	C3	310	Y						
HPT9600375	C2	311	Y						
HPT9600376	C4	312							
HPT9600377	C4	313	Y	Y					
HPT9600378	SQI	314	Y	Y					
HPT9600379	LI	315							
HPT9600380	SQI	316	Y		ODA011	P2	OLA012	P3	12345678
HPT9600381	C3	317							
HPT9600382	SQI	318							
HPT9600383	C4	319	Y						
HPT9600384	L2	320							
HPT9600385	SQI	321							
HPT9600386	LI	322							
HPT9600387	SQI	323							
HPT9600388	LI	324							
HPT9600389	C3	325							
HPT9600390	C3	326							
HPT9600391	SQI	327	Y				OLA001	P3	123568
HPT9600392	C3	328	Y						
HPT9600393	C3	329	Y				OLA001	P3	123568
HPT9600394	C4	330							
HPT9600395	LI	331							
HPT9600396	SQI	332							

PLAN #	PRICE TIER	PAGE	MATERIALS LIST	QUOTE ONE®	DECK	DECK PRICE	LANDSCAPE	LANDSCAPE PRICE	REGIONS
HPT9600397	SQI	333	Y	Y					
HPT9600398	C3	334							
HPT9600399	SQI	335	Y						
HPT9600400	SQI	336	Y						
HPT9600401	C3	337							
HPT9600402	LI	338							
HPT9600403	SQI	339							
HPT9600404	SQI	340	Y						
HPT9600405	SQI	341							
HPT9600406	C4	342	Y						
HPT9600407	C3	343	Y						
HPT9600408	SQI	344							
HPT9600409	SQI	345							
HPT9600410	SQI	346							
HPT9600411	SQI	347							
HPT9600412	C4	348							
HPT9600413	C4	349							
HPT9600414	SQI	350							
HPT9600415	C3	351							
HPT9600416	C2	352							
HPT9600417	SQI	353							
HPT9600418	C3	354							
HPT9600419	LI	355							
HPT9600420	SQI	356							
HPT9600421	LI	357							
HPT9600422	SQI	358							
HPT9600423	SQI	359							
HPT9600424	L2	360							
HPT9600425	SQI	361	Y						
HPT9600426	C3	362							
HPT9600427	C3	363	Y	Y			OLA024	P4	123568
HPT9600428	SQI	364							
HPT9600429	SQI	365							
HPT9600430	C4	366							
HPT9600431	LI	367							
HPT9600432	C3	368							
HPT9600433	C3	369							
HPT9600434	LI	370	Y	Y	ODA012	P3	OLA017	P3	123568
HPT9600435	LI	371							
HPT9600436	L2	372							
HPT9600437	C3	373	Y						
HPT9600438	C3	374	Y	Y			OLA016	P4	1234568
HPT9600439	LI	375	Y	Y	ODA011	P2	OLA003	P3	123568
HPT9600440	LI	376							
HPT9600441	SQI	377	Y						
HPT9600442	LI	378							
HPT9600443	LI	379	Y						
HPT9600444	C3	380							
HPT9600445	SQI	381	Y	Y					
HPT9600446	C3	382							
HPT9600447	C3	383							
HPT9600448	LI	384							
HPT9600449	C3	385							
HPT9600450	C3	386	Y						
HPT9600451	SQI	387							
HPT9600452	LI	388							
HPT9600453	SQI	389	Y						
HPT9600454	L3	390							
HPT9600455	SQI	391							
HPT9600456	SQI	392	Y						
HPT9600457	L2	393							
HPT9600458	LI	394					OLA008	P4	1234568
HPT9600459	SQI	395							
HPT9600460	SQI	396	Y						
HPT9600461	SQI	397							
HPT9600462	SQI	398							

PLAN #	PRICE TIER	PAGE	MATERIALS LIST	QUOTE ONE®	DECK	DECK PRICE	LANDSCAPE	LANDSCAPE PRICE	REGIONS
HPT9600463	SQI	399							
HPT9600464	SQI	400	Y	Y			OLA008	P4	1234568
HPT9600465	SQI	401	Y						
HPT9600466	SQI	402	Y						
HPT9600467	SQI	403							
HPT9600468	SQI	404							
HPT9600469	SQI	405							
HPT9600470	SQI	406							
HPT9600471	L2	407							
HPT9600472	SQI	408							
HPT9600473	LI	409							
HPT9600474	L2	410	Y						
HPT9600475	SQI	411	Y						
HPT9600476	SQI	412	Y						
HPT9600477	SQI	413							
HPT9600478	SQI	414							
HPT9600479	SQI	415							
HPT9600480	SQI	416							
HPT9600481	SQI	417							
HPT9600482	C4	418							
HPT9600483	C4	419							
HPT9600484	L3	420							
HPT9600485	SQI	421							
HPT9600486	C4	422							
HPT9600487	SQI	423	Y						
HPT9600488	C4	424							
HPT9600489	LI	425							
HPT9600490	SQ3	426							
HPT9600491	SQI	427	Y						
HPT9600492	SQI	428	Y						
HPT9600493	L2	429							
HPT9600494	C4	430	Y						
HPT9600495	LI	431							
HPT9600496	L2	432							
HPT9600497	C4	433							
HPT9600498	C4	434							
HPT9600499	SQI	435					OLA017	P3	123568
HPT9600500	L3	436							
HPT9600501	L2	437							
HPT9600502	SQI	438							
HPT9600503	SQI	439							
HPT9600504	L3	440							
HPT9600505	SQI	441							
HPT9600506	C3	442	Y						
HPT9600507	LI	443							
HPT9600508	L2	444							
HPT9600509	L2	445							
HPT9600510	SQI	446							
HPT9600511	C4	447	Y						
HPT9600512	L2	448	Y						
HPT9600513	SQI	449	Y						
HPT9600514	SQI	450							

ORDER ONLINE AT EPLANS.COM

WE OFFER A VARIETY OF USEFUL TOOLS THAT CAN HELP YOU THROUGH EVERY STEP OF THE home-building process. From our Materials List to our Customization Program, these items let you put our experience to work for you to ensure that you get exactly what you want out of your dream house.

MATERIALS LIST

For many of the designs in our portfolio, we offer a customized list of materials that helps you plan and estimate the cost of your new home. The Materials List outlines the quantity, type, and size of materials needed to build your house (with the exception of mechanical system items). Included are framing lumber, windows and doors, kitchen and bath cabinetry, rough and finished hardware, and much more. This handy list helps you or your builder cost out materials and serves as a reference sheet when you're compiling bids.

SPECIFICATION OUTLINE

This valuable 16-page document can play an important role in the construction of your house. Fill it in with your builder, and you'll have a step-by-step chronicle of 166 stages or items crucial to the building process. It provides a comprehensive review of the construction process and helps you choose materials.

QUOTE ONE®

The Quote One® system, which helps estimate the cost of building select designs in your zip code, is available in two parts: the Summary Cost Report and the Material Cost Report.

The Summary Cost Report, the first element in the package, breaks down the cost of your home into various categories based on building materials, labor, and installation, and includes three grades of construction: Budget, Standard, and Custom. Make even more informed decisions about your project with the second element of our package, the Material Cost Report. The material and installation cost is shown for each of more than 1,000 line items provided in the standard-grade Materials List, which is included with this tool. Additional space is included for estimates from contractors and subcontractors, such as for mechanical materials, which are not included in our packages.

If you are interested in a plan that does not indicate the availability of Quote One®, please call and ask our sales representatives, who can verify the status for you.

CUSTOMIZATION PROGRAM

If the plan you love needs something changed to make it perfect, our customization experts will ensure that you get nothing less than your dream home. Purchase a reproducible set of plans for the home you choose, and we'll send you our easy-to-use customization request form via e-mail or fax. For just $50, our customization experts will provide an estimate for your requested revisions, and once it's approved, that charge will be applied to your changes. You'll receive either five sets or a reproducible master of your modified design and any other options you select.

BUILDING BASICS

If you want to know more about building techniques—and deal more confidently with your subcontractors—we offer four useful detail sheets. These sheets provide non-plan-specific general information, but are excellent tools that will add to your understanding of Plumbing Details, Electrical Details, Construction Details, and Mechanical Details. These fact-filled sheets will help answer many of your building questions, and help you learn what questions to ask your builder and subcontractors.

GETTY IMAGES

HANLEY WOOD
HOMEPLANNERS
ADVANTAGE

ORDER 24 HOURS!
1-800-521-6797

HANDS-ON HOME FURNITURE PLANNER

Effectively plan the space in your home using our Hands-On Home Furniture Planner. It's fun and easy—no more moving heavy pieces of furniture to see how the room will go together. The kit includes reusable peel-and-stick furniture templates that fit on a 12"x18" laminated layout board—enough space to lay out every room in your house.

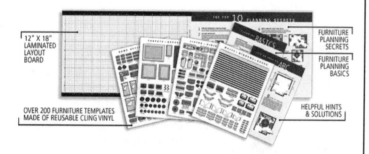

12" X 18" LAMINATED LAYOUT BOARD

OVER 200 FURNITURE TEMPLATES MADE OF REUSABLE CLING VINYL

THE TOP 10 PLANNING SECRETS

BASICS

ABC

FURNITURE PLANNING SECRETS

FURNITURE PLANNING BASICS

HELPFUL HINTS & SOLUTIONS

DECK BLUEPRINT PACKAGE

Many of the homes in this book can be enhanced with a professionally designed Home Planners Deck Plan. Those plans marked with a **D** have a corresponding deck plan, sold separately, which includes a Deck Plan Frontal Sheet, Deck Framing and Floor Plans, Deck Elevations, and a Deck Materials List. A Standard Deck Details Package, also available, provides all the how-to information necessary for building any deck. Get both the Deck Plan and the Standard Deck Details Package for one low price in our Complete Deck Building Package.

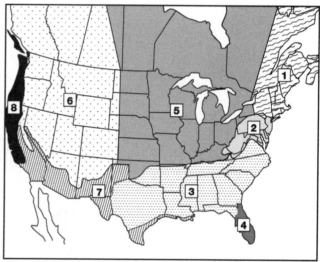

LANDSCAPE BLUEPRINT PACKAGE

Homes marked with an **L** in this book have a front-yard Landscape Plan that is complementary in design to the house plan. These comprehensive Landscape Blueprint Packages include a Frontal Sheet, Plan View, Regionalized Plant & Materials List, a sheet on Planting and Maintaining Your Landscape, Zone Maps, and a Plant Size and Description Guide. Each set of blueprints is a full 18" x 24" with clear, complete instructions in easy-to-read type.

Our Landscape Plans are available with a Plant & Materials List adapted by horticultural experts to eight regions of the country. Please specify from the following regions when ordering your plan:

Region 1: Northeast
Region 2: Mid-Atlantic
Region 3: Deep South
Region 4: Florida & Gulf Coast
Region 5: Midwest
Region 6: Rocky Mountains
Region 7: Southern California & Desert Southwest
Region 8: Northern California & Pacific Northwest